Theft by Finding

Theft by Finding

Diaries (1977–2002)

David Sedaris

Little, Brown and Company

New York Boston London

Little, Brown and Company
Hachette Book Group
1290 Avenue of the Americas, New York, NY 10104
littlebrown.com

First Edition: May 2017

Little, Brown and Company is a division of Hachette Book Group, Inc. The Little, Brown name and logo are trademarks of Hachette Book Group, Inc.

The publisher is not responsible for websites (or their content) that are not owned by the publisher.

The Hachette Speakers Bureau provides a wide range of authors for speaking events. To find out more, go to hachettespeakersbureau.com or call (866) 376-6591.

ISBN 978-0-316-15472-7 (hc) / 978-0-316-55246-2 (large print) / 978-0-316-55665-1 (signed edition) / 978-0-316-50820-9 (international)
LCCN 2016959026

10 9 8 7 6 5 4 3 2 1

LSC-H

Book design by Marie Mundaca

Printed in the United States of America

For Dawn "Friendship Flower" Erickson

Author's Note

Occasionally in this book I have changed people's names or slightly altered their physical descriptions. In some cases I've changed a name because the person in the preceding entry was also a Jim or a Mary, and I wanted to avoid confusion. (How is it that I have so many Steves in my life and only one Thelma?)

I've rewritten things when they were unclear or, as was more often the case in the early years, when the writing was clunky and uninviting.

Theft by Finding

Introduction

Not long after deciding to release a book of diary entries, I came upon a five-pound note. I'd been picking up trash alongside a country road in West Sussex, and there it was between a potato-chip bag and a half-full beer can that had drowned slugs in it. Given the exchange rate, the bill amounted to around $8.15, which, as my mother would have said, "Ain't nothing." A few days later I met with my friend Pam in London. The subject of windfalls came up, and when I mentioned the money she asked if I'd spent it.

"Well, of course," I said.

"In the U.K., if you discover something of value and keep it, that's *theft by finding*," she told me. "You're supposed to investigate whether it was lost or stolen, though in this case— five pounds—of course you're fine."

Theft by Finding. It was, I thought, the perfect title for this book. When it comes to subject matter, all diarists are different. I was never one to write about my feelings, in part because they weren't that interesting (even to me) but mainly because they were so likely to change. Other people's feelings, though, that was a different story. Got a bone to pick with your stepmother or the manager of the place where you worked until yesterday? Please, let's talk!

If nothing else, a diary teaches you what you're interested in. Perhaps at the beginning you restrict yourself to issues of social injustice or all the unfortunate people trapped beneath the rubble in Turkey or Italy or wherever the last great earthquake hit. You keep the diary you feel you should be keeping, the one that, if discovered by your mother or college roommate, would leave them thinking, *If only I was as civic-minded/bighearted/philosophical as Edward!*

After a year, you realize it takes time to rail against injustice, time you might better spend questioning fondue or describing those ferrets you couldn't afford. Unless, of course, social injustice is your thing, in which case—knock yourself out. The point is to find out who you are and to be true to that person. Because so often you can't. *Won't people turn away if they know the real me?* you wonder. *The me that hates my own child, that put my perfectly healthy dog to sleep? The me who thinks, deep down, that maybe* The Wire *was overrated?*

What I prefer recording at the end—or, more recently, at the start—of my day are remarkable events I have observed (fistfights, accidents, a shopper arriving with a full cart of groceries in the express lane), bits of overheard conversation, and startling things people have told me. These people could be friends but just as easily barbers, strangers on a plane, or cashiers. A number of their stories turned out to be urban legends: the neighbor of a relative whose dead cat was stolen from the trunk of a car, etc. I hope I've weeded those out. Then there are the jokes I've heard at parties and book signings over the years. They were obviously written by someone—all jokes are—but the authors are hardly ever credited in the retelling.

Another thing I noticed while going through my forty years of diaries is that many of the dates are wrong. For instance,

---

* I do not think *The Wire* was overrated.

there might be three October 1, 1982s. This was most likely because I didn't know what day it was. Time tends to melt and run together when you don't have a job. In that prelaptop era, you had to consult a newspaper or calendar to find out if it was Wednesday the eighth or Thursday the ninth. This involved getting up, so more often than not, I'd just stay put and guess. Quite often I'd even get the month wrong.

It might look like my average diary entry amounts to no more than seven sentences, but in fact I spend an inordinate amount of time writing about my day—around forty-five minutes, usually. If nothing big happened, I'll reflect on a newspaper article or a report I heard on the radio. I'm not big on weather writing but have no policy against it. Thus when life gets really dull, I'll just look out the window and describe the color of the sky. That will lead to something else, most often: a bird being mean to another bird or the noise a plane makes.

Starting around 1979 I began numbering my entries. It's a habit I still maintain.

December 28, 2016

One. It's only December and already...

Two. Dad called on my birthday. "I'm trying to visualize where you're living," he said. "Are there a lot of power lines out where you are?"

Three. Hugh stormed out of the kitchen yesterday, leaving me, Candy, Amy, and Ingrid, who was in the middle of a story about her mother.

Four. I ran into Michael at the Waitrose...

Five. Carrie Fisher died yesterday...

Six. Hugh just came in and told me...

This is what cavemen did before paragraphs were invented, and I'm not sure why I don't just indent or hit the space bar twice. Another old-fashioned practice I maintain is carrying a notebook, a small one I keep in my shirt pocket and never leave the house without. In it I register all the little things that strike me, not in great detail but just quickly. The following morning I'll review what I jotted down and look for the most meaningful moment in the previous day, the one in which I felt truly present. It could have been seeing an old friend, or just as likely it could have been watching a stranger eat a sandwich with his eyes closed. (That happened recently, and was riveting.)

Every so often, I'll record something that might entertain or enlighten someone, and those are the bits I set aside. I thought I'd eventually put them in a book of diary entries, but when the printout reached a height of eight inches, I decided that maybe two volumes—the second of which will cover the years 2003 to 2017—would make more sense. It's worth mentioning that this is *my* edit. Of the roughly eight million words handwritten or typed into my diary since September 5, 1977, I'm including only a small fraction. An entirely different book from the same source material could make me appear nothing but evil, selfish, generous, or even, dare I say, sensitive. On any given day I am all these things and more: stupid, cheerful, misanthropic, cruel, narrow-minded, open, petty—the list goes on and on.

A different edit, no doubt a more precise one, would have involved handing my diary over to someone else, but that is something I can't imagine doing, unless, perhaps, that person is a journalist. (They never get beyond the third page, which they usually call "the middle," as in "I'd hoped to finish this before our interview but am only in the middle!")

That said, I don't really expect anyone to read this from start to finish. It seems more like the sort of thing you might dip in and out of, like someone else's yearbook or a collection of jokes.

Introduction

It wasn't easy revisiting what are now 156 volumes of my diary. I broke the job up—a month or two per day—but after reading about me, I'd have to spend the rest of the day *being* me. I don't know that I've ever done anything quite so exhausting. Hugh would be in the next room and hear me shout things like "Will you *just shut up!*" and "Who cares about the goddamn pocket square!"

"Who are you talking to?" he'd ask.

"Me in 2001," I'd answer.

By then I could see the light at the end of the tunnel. The early years, 1977 to 1983, were the bleakest. I was writing my diaries by hand back then. The letters were small and, fueled by meth, a typical entry would go on for pages—solid walls of words, and every last one of them complete bullshit. I've included very little of that time in this book. It's like listening to a crazy person. The gist is all you need, really.

The diary lightened up when I moved to Chicago, partly because I was in a big city but mainly because I felt so much better about myself. I'd finally done what I'd talked about doing for so many years: I'd left the town I grew up in. I'd gone back to college and actually graduated. There was all the more reason to feel good when, in the fall of 1990, I moved to New York. I was only writing at night back then, either smashed or getting there. You'd think I'd have addressed my drinking, at least in the privacy of my diary, but it's rarely mentioned. To type that word—*alcoholic*—would have made it real, so I never recounted the talking-tos I got from Hugh and certain helpful people in my family.

Similarly, it took me a while in the 1970s to write the word *gay.* "Oh, please," I said out loud to my twenty-year-old self while reading my earliest diaries. "Who do you think you're kidding?"

This project made evident all the phases I've gone through

over the years, and how intensely. Oh, the ink that was spilled over finding the correct phone number of someone who'd obviously—and for good reason—given me a fake one, over losing weight, over my French homework. Later I'd throw myself into catching flies and feeding them to spiders, and all this leads me to wonder, *What's next?* Judging from my past it could be anything: collecting hair, crossbreeding rodents in my basement—who knows?

I was also struck while rereading my diaries by the number of people I knew in 1980 whom I'm still close with now. It's so hard to predict which friends will last and which will fade away. Quite often I'd move and lose half the contacts in my address book, people I thought would be with me forever. It's not that we outgrew one another. They just couldn't be bothered to put a stamp on a letter. Or I couldn't. Of course it's easier now with email.

It was interesting to read back through a diary and come upon someone who would wind up being very important, who would drop out of nowhere and change the direction of my life: Hugh, Jim McManus, Meryl Vladimer, Geoff Kloske, Ira Glass, Andy Ward. I'd have thought the initial meetings would be momentous, that I'd recognize salvation when it presented itself—"There you are!"—but more often than not, each of them was just someone I shook hands with, then sat down later at my desk thinking, *What was that person's name again?* Hugh was different. Him I remembered. With the others, though, it's sort of heartening. You never know whose hand you're going to shake.

Then there were those who died: my mother, my sister Tiffany, Don Congdon, the lovely David Rakoff. I'd reread the entries that featured these people and curse myself for not including more. Why did I not transcribe their every word? And shouldn't I get cracking so that when friends and family members die in the future I'll have something greater and more comforting to reflect upon? That's the thing with a diary, though. In order to record your life, you sort of need to live it. Not at your desk, but beyond it. Out in the world where it's so beautiful and complex and painful that sometimes you just need to sit down and write about it.

1977

September 5, 1977
Sacramento, California
Ronnie and I got a ride from Lonnie and Tammy, who are on their way to Mount Shasta. The state fair is in town, and Sherri Lewis is performing. We slept out in the open next to the American River.

September 8, 1977
Mount Hood, Oregon
Sidetracked en route to Yakima. We met a couple named Pops and Jeannie who will pick us up at six tomorrow morning and take us to an orchard. Pops, who calls himself a "fruit tramp," guessed Ronnie and I might make $300 between the two of us before the season is over.

We're sleeping tonight on a golf course. I feel the way I always feel before starting a new job—nervous.

September 11, 1977
Odell, Oregon
I wonder how long three minutes is? My soft-boiled eggs are on the woodstove, tumbling in their little pan. It's Sunday, our day off. Raining. Ronnie and I are living in a wood cabin with a soft brass bed, a fridge, four chairs, a table, and lots of logs. Sometimes a cat comes in and I feed him (her?) hot dogs. My socks are drying, the floor needs sweeping, and the couple in

the trailer next door are eating. This morning I saw the wife trudging to the outhouse in her bathrobe.

We're working for a man named Norm. His friends call him Peewee. It's cold enough outside to see my breath. Acorns are falling on the roof.

October 20, 1977
Vancouver, British Columbia
After a hotel for $8.50 a night, Ronnie and I found an apartment that's $30 a week for the both of us. I worry about money, but when it's gone, it's gone. I smoked my first cigarette. It's embarrassing, but you do get a buzz off it. I did, anyway, on Davie Street.

October 25, 1977
Vancouver
I now own a black jacket and a pair of brown heavy wool trousers that come up past my navel and button at the ankle. Canadian Army pants? When it comes to clothes, all anyone has to say is "That looks good," and I'll buy it. So I was walking down the street in my new uniform, very happy, when a guy looked me over and said to his friend, "Who's the faggot?"

Then I was just an idiot with stupid clothes on. Ronnie and I leave tomorrow. I'll be glad to go.

The dryers in Canada cost 10 cents for fifteen minutes.

October 26, 1977
Everett, Washington
At the Beehive Café one egg is 25 cents. It's $2 for an egg at Denny's.

Yesterday we were picked up by two fishermen, Ed and Reilly. Then we got a ride with Mark, who let us sleep in his trailer. At six this morning, he bounded into the living room naked and said, "Let's go!"

He had just returned from his high school reunion. He was in the band.

October 27, 1977
Blaine, Oregon
Some asshole stopped last night and pointed at Ronnie, saying, "I'll take the girl."

October 29, 1977
Portland, Oregon
Ronnie and I are at the Broadway Hotel, a cheap and depressing place. Scary. There is a real poor and a funky poor. This is the real kind. The lobby is full of dying old people, cripples, and a girl who ate hamburger after hamburger, pouring ketchup on every bite. Toilets are down the hall. Our carpet has vomit on it. We have a torn-up kitchen chair and a nasty bed. The second floor smells like doughnuts, but ours smells like puke and piss. Our fellow guests, winos and the down-on-their-luck, are the ones our parents always warned us about.

November 6, 1977
San Francisco, California
I called home and talked to Mom. It was so nice to hear her voice, I didn't want to hang up. She said Paul was hurt that I hadn't written to him, but I just did a few days ago.

November 9, 1977
Bakersfield, California
We finally made it to Bakersfield. The countryside here is flat and scrubby. A guy named Doug gave us a nice long ride and told us about his cousin who got stabbed.

Last night under the stars in a pasture in our sleeping bags, I poured my guts out and said things I was afraid to admit even to myself. And you know, it felt good and not as hopeless as I thought. All that had been inside for so long.

November 11, 1977
Kingman, Arizona
Last night we crawled into the dry, sandy riverbed next to the Texaco station across the road from the Liberty Bell Lounge and slept. It is warm, and we are waiting for Al, the Apache guy who rescued us from the Hoover Dam. Ronnie and I were there for hours. At one point a patrolman stopped and told us we were in a bad place to get a ride. Duh.

It got dark. Camping meant climbing sharp rocks to more sharp rocks. By the Coke machine at the Mead Lake lookout point, we ate a can of kidney beans. I can't recall the brand. No change, so no Coke. Then Al and Phil stopped. Their car was packed, but Al said he couldn't bear to see anyone stranded like that. They spent the night at the B&R Motel but promised to fetch us this morning and carry us on to Phoenix.

Someone said a few days ago, "Whatever you do, don't get stuck in Kingman," but Phil says, "Don't believe everything you hear or fifty percent of what you see."

November 12, 1977
Tucson, Arizona
There are a lot of older hitchhikers in Tucson. At the urinal I met Jimmy Buck. He offered us a ride to Texas—six hundred miles—if we'd help him unload a truckful of grapes. We did and are on our way.

November 16, 1977
Temple, Texas
Civilization means not waiting five hours for a ride. Round Rock is civilized, Austin is too, but I'm not sure about Temple.

Right after I wrote that, a Scientologist in a Rambler drove up, a mural painter from Dallas. A good guy. Ronnie left her guitar in his car. So long, guitar. The Scientologist played tapes. We smoked pot. In Austin we were picked up by an alcoholic. He's been arrested for drunk driving four times. "SOL," he said. "Shit out of luck." He said he wasn't drunk now but would definitely be arrested if they gave him a Breathalyzer.

November 21, 1977
West Virginia?
Ronnie and I went our separate ways in Cullowhee. She's heading to Raleigh, and I'm underneath an interstate bridge waiting for the rain to calm down. Several of the drivers that stopped today took off laughing just as I reached their cars looking grateful and relieved. There are a lot of dead birds down here. I feel itchy.

November 23, 1977
Kent, Ohio
I got here yesterday afternoon. Then Todd and I each took three hits of sugar cube acid. Too much. It was a real bad trip, like torture, enough to turn someone into a Christian. I've been up for two days.

Coming here by myself from Cullowhee, I had my first bad ride—a thirty-five-year-old with flag decals on the windshield of his pickup truck. Ray T., his name was. He picked me up in Knoxville and said he'd take me forty miles. First he spent three hours playing pool and drinking beer. I waited outside in a rocking chair and smoked a joint. I should have left, but the highway was deserted. No cars, and I was twenty miles from the interstate.

After Ray T. left the bar, he was weaving and slurring his words. I figured I'd get out once we hit a busy road because you really don't want to be in a car with a drunk. His conversation was hard to follow, and he stopped every mile or so to pee or light a cigarette. When he saw two girls hitchhiking, he picked them up and gave them a ride to their door. Then he had a cheeseburger. It started to rain. When we hit the interstate, I said, "You can just let me out here."

He said no, he couldn't let me hitchhike in this weather. He said I had to spend the night with him. He was drunk and yelling, "Ray T. always gets what he wants, and this is what I want."

I asked him again to let me out, and he said no. Then he started asking me questions. "When was the last time you jacked off? Sometimes does it get hard just thinking about it?" He told me to move close to him, and when I said no he grabbed me and yanked me over and stuck his hand down my pants. I was afraid. It was late, raining, and he was speeding and drunk. If I'd hit him or tried to get away, we could have had an accident. I was scared and humiliated. When he pulled off onto a smaller road, I opened the door and jumped out. He stopped and I grabbed my wet knapsack from the back and ran.

It was cold, and I heard him come after me. Then he got back in his truck, and when I saw it heading in my direction, I hid. After he drove off, I turned and ran onto the interstate and waved my arms. In a few minutes three assholes stopped and took me to Cincinnati. They were from Illinois and threw cans out the window. One of them said that niggers should still be slaves. I thought, *Oh, boy. What a day.*

December 1, 1977
West Virginia

I'm in a seafood place drinking coffee. I need to get to Raleigh, but so far rides are sparse. I have a joint and $3. I remember being appalled when David Larson hitchhiked to North Carolina with $1 in his pocket, and now here I am. I started the day with a ceramic pig but abandoned it after it got to be a drag to carry.

December 15, 1977
Chapel Hill, North Carolina

I found a job today, just like I told myself I would. Three dollars an hour washing dishes at the Carolina Coffee Shop.

1978

January 13, 1978
Chapel Hill
1. I'm cold.
2. I'm bored.
3. I spilled a full glass of ginger ale on the floor and have nothing to clean it up with.
4. I went to the grocery store and spent $5.37 on total crap.
5. I made beans and franks on my hot plate and it was just a mushy mess.
6. I want to be in school.
7. My radio is suffering from me falling asleep on it.

February 23, 1978
Chapel Hill
I am totally frustrated and can't relieve it. Nothing to go back to, and nothing to look forward to.

?, 1978
Raleigh, North Carolina
Last night Dad caught me off guard by asking me to leave and not come back. We can't begin to reason with each other. I said awful things, and he said he wanted to smother me. I cried and am glad. Gretchen says the three best times to smoke a cigarette are:

1. after food
2. after sex
3. after crying

I hadn't cried since I started smoking, and she was right—it was a good cigarette. Then Gretchen cried. She always comes to my defense. What would I do without her? And Mom cried, and Lisa. Everyone cried but Dad. Now he says that Thursday night he wants to talk to me. I'm guessing the topic will be self-respect.

April 19, 1978
Chapel Hill
Uh Uh Uh Uh Uh Uh Uh Uh Uh Uh Uh Uh Uh Uh Uh Uh
Uh Uh Uh Uh Uh Uh Uh Uh Uh Uh Uh Uh Uh Uh Uh Uh Uh
Uh Uh Uh Uh Uh Uh Uh Uh Uh Uh Uh Uh Uh Uh Uh Uh Uh
Uh Uh Uh Uh Uh Uh Uh Uh Uh Uh Uh Uh Uh Uh Uh Uh Uh
Uh Uh Uh Uh Uh Uh Uh Uh Uh Uh Uh Uh Uh Uh Uh Uh Uh
Uh Uh Uh Uh Uh Uh Uh Uh Uh Uh Uh Uh Uh Uh Uh Uh Uh
Uh Uh Uh Uh Uh Uh Uh Uh Uh Uh Uh Uh Uh Uh Uh Uh Uh
Uh Uh Uh Uh Uh Uh Uh Uh Uh Uh Uh Uh Uh Uh Uh Uh Uh
Uh Uh Uh Uh Uh Uh Uh Uh Uh Uh Uh Uh Uh Uh Uh Uh Uh
Uh Uh Uh Uh Uh Uh Uh Uh Uh Uh Uh Uh Uh Uh Uh Uh Uh
Uh Uh Uh Uh Uh Uh Uh Uh Uh Uh Uh Uh Uh Uh Uh Uh Uh
Uh Uh Uh Uh Uh Uh Uh Uh Uh Uh Uh Uh Uh Uh Uh Uh Uh
Uh Uh Uh Uh Uh Uh Uh Uh Uh Uh Uh Uh Uh Uh Uh Uh Uh

June 14, 1978
Atlantic Beach, North Carolina
Overheard:
"I always thought I was close to God, but climbing those mountains, I mean, it just brought me closer."

"If welfare can buy these niggers a Continental, it can buy some poor white kid a horse."

June 23, 1978
Chapel Hill
I have $211 and it doesn't make any sense.

September 6, 1978
Odell
I'm back in Odell finally. In the trailer instead of the cabin. Promoted? Norm begins many of his sentences with the words "A guy oughtta..." He told me that the cherry crop was good and that his dog, Ringo, died. I have five days until apple picking starts.

September 10, 1978
Odell
I scrubbed my trailer floors with Janitor in a Drum and listened to the radio—country music mainly. Talked to Rodrigo, who uses *camebackir* as a verb meaning "to come back." *Nosotros combackamos.* "We come back."

September 13, 1978
Odell
Picking started. Apple Betty, the cat I let in, is eating a tea bag and I'm too tired to stop her.

September 18, 1978
Odell
Norm came by, very drunk. We both smoke menthols. He likes to explain things about farming. He says, "Why, heck, Dave..." "Why, heck, Dave, you should come here in the summer and hike and camp."

He has confidence in my picking, though I drop a lot and sometimes break branches. Breaking branches is called *trashing*. *Skirting* is picking the low-hanging fruit on someone else's tree. This is what Norm calls an Okie tactic.

September 22, 1978
Odell

We began the Bosc pears today, just me and Jesus. Norm dismissed all the others, all Mexicans. They liked to have a good time at night, using their car headlights as lamps and always with the radio on. They were late this morning, so that was it—fired.

Tonight I went to the grocery store. I ran up a bill of $6.50 with only $1 to pay for it.

September 26, 1978
Odell

While picking today I thought about capital punishment, Alaska, Eudora Welty, and blindness.

If you talk to people, you can have whatever you want.

No matter where you go, you cannot escape the Bee Gees, either on a radio or on a jukebox.

I once considered suing Farrah Fawcett for invasion of privacy. Hardly a day passed when I didn't see her on a magazine cover, an ad, a poster. She was destroying my life, but now she's OK.

Ronnie was the first person I met who didn't live at home. That year in Cullowhee we went to see *The Day of the Locust,* my favorite movie. The man at the box office gave us a discount, saying, "I can't charge full price for something without a plot!"

September 28, 1978
Odell

In 1951 Norm worked at the sawmill and a guy named Barney Bailey gave him the nickname Peewee, which is what everyone here calls him. Barney Bailey has a wife he calls Buffalo Grass. Buffalo Grass Bailey. After filling the final pear bin, Norm, Jesus, and I drank beer. I made $211.24 this season. Back in Raleigh I have $150 in savings. That's a total of $361.24.

I am optimistic that things will fall into place, and one day I'll be sitting in New York City with correct bus fare in my pocket.

September 29, 1978
Odell

I hitched to the employment office in Hood River and talked to a woman named Sylvia. She is sending me to a fruit-packing plant—$3.41 an hour to sort the bad apples from the good. She said, "And, my, it's tedious." I would work from four to twelve at night.

October 1, 1978
Newport, Oregon

Leaving Hood River, I was picked up hitchhiking by a man named John who wants me to work for him cutting and polishing jade and taking things to the crafts market in Portland. I can also clean his pool, help finish his sailboat, and install solar panels on his house. He said at one point or another:

1. "You haven't lived until you've sailed."
2. "I had a bubble put on top."
3. "The day will come for you to marry."
4. "I have wooden legs."

He's invited me to his workshop on Tuesday morning.

October 2, 1978
Odell

Yesterday was one of those miserable days for hitchhiking. It took almost thirteen hours to get back from Ted's place in Newport, most of it walking. My first ride was with a Catholic priest. He was in robes and had a rifle in the backseat. Later I found $14.50 worth of unwrapped gay-sex magazines in the woods when I hiked off the road to pee. What are the chances? I think the guys posing were all in jail at one time or another. They're all skinny with acne and it's pretty clear they aren't enjoying themselves.

October 3, 1978
Odell

I went to John's and saw his studio. He explained what all his tools do and then he suggested that he could pay me in Christmas gifts. If he has a pool, two cars, two Streamline trailers, and a home with two fireplaces in it, he can pay me in real money. I don't think his wife likes me too much. Christians are strange people.

I went to the packinghouse at four. The presize machine is broken, so now I won't start until Thursday.

October 4, 1978
Odell

John wants me to go to church with his family this weekend.

He tells me that my life is empty, but it isn't quite because I bought some pot today.

October 5, 1978
Odell

Halfway through my first shift at the packing plant, I realized I had never imagined anything could be so boring. I remove leaves from pears and discard them into a wet, ever-growing pile. All of us in rubber gloves, our eyes dead. In the break room, the women talk about canning their backyard fruit.

October 12, 1978
Odell

I am now a Teamster, Local 607. I had no choice. I asked the women on the belt what it means exactly, but no one really understands it. Membership is $25; dues are $12.50 a month. There's free medical and dental but only after three years, by which point you'd be insane.

October 16, 1978
Odell

After I paid my membership and first month's dues, Duckwall–Pooley cut its night-packing crew. Workers with seniority were given the sixteen jobs in presize, so until at least the middle of November, I'm laid off and will have to live on John's $2 an hour.

On the way home after getting the news, I came across a very drunk Mexican guy whose car was in a ditch. It was Jesus's brother, and because I didn't know what else to do, I brought him back to my trailer. We were up until four, me talking my high school Spanish. Now it's seven. I'm at Scotty's Café and he's asleep in my bed.

With the layoff, I'm worried about money. Two people at the plant told me about a possible job picking mushrooms underground with a miner's hat on. I'm not so sure about John. On Sunday he took me to his church. There was a lot of swaying back and forth, a lot of crying and praising His name. Then I went to lunch at his house. They don't allow their kids to trick-or-treat. On the way home he told me how he lost his legs. Then he removed one and showed me the stump, which made me think of a denuded chicken wing.

October 17, 1978
Odell

Today my shoes are twice as heavy. They're also green. Everything is green from the chrome oxide I used to polish John's jade. The insides of my ears are green. So is my snot.

John has a fifteen-foot-long, five-foot-tall block of jade that was originally bought by General Perón in Argentina, who wanted a statue of his wife Eva carved from it. John says it cost $100,000. Minus, I guess, the $14 he paid me today to polish a few thin slices of it.

October 30, 1978
Odell

Sylvia from the employment office invited me to have dinner with her family. Everyone ate something different: her husband, meat loaf; her grandson, a pork chop; me, a hamburger; and her, cottage cheese. She played *Fiddler on the Roof* and danced around her kitchen. What a delight she is.

John's legs were aching at work, so he took them off and rolled around in a wheelchair. He was in the merchant marines. Meanwhile, I hear the plant is laying people back on.

October 31, 1978
Odell

I gave a guy at the plant my address, and last night he came by. Tom has a rose tattooed on his shoulder and two hearts on his forearm. We went to the trailer where he lives with his mother, and maybe one day I'll get into what happened there. Right now I want to take a bus to Kent. I want to be with my friends, not going to church with John or staring down a dildo collection at Tom's. It's up to me. In a week I could be in Ohio, or I could still be here.

November 9, 1978
Odell

Tom came by, mad. He said, "I thought we were friends." Then he said that friends have sex, and it doesn't matter whether I want to or not. I should just do it because *he* wants to. Before he left he told me that I'll never find anyone to love.

To hell with him. I'm saving myself for marriage.

I seem to grow more confused every day. Sometimes I think I was better off in Chapel Hill or Kent, just getting high and hanging out.

Also it's so cold here, too cold to do anything but sit in front of the space heater. Right now I'm wearing long underwear, a flannel shirt, a pajama shirt, a sweater, a jacket, a coat, and a hat. Inside.

Later:

I plugged in a second space heater. It worked for two minutes before the circuit blew. Then it was back to the cold, only with no lights. I tried to cry, but nothing came out, so I coughed instead.

This morning Norm fixed the circuit and I began to winterize my trailer with a new sense of urgency.

November 30, 1978
Odell
John hung a sign in the workshop that reads JESUS IS LORD HERE. The good news is that I start back at Duckwall–Pooley on Monday. Two weeks later I'll be on a bus headed home.

December 5, 1978
Odell
I don't pull leaves off apples and pears anymore. Now I'm in bin repair. My hands are bloody ribbons. I lug, staple, and nail the 150-pound crates the fruit arrives in. When there's nothing to do, I don't have to pretend there's something to do. It's humiliating to have to look busy.

Mexicans have been great for rides lately, especially young ones. It's so hard to put things into focus right now. Maybe in a few years I can make sense of this fall in Oregon. These are just notes. By then, though, this time will be touched by sentiment.

December 16, 1978
Odell
I've returned all my library books and given the orchard cat a big Christmas can of dog food. My last ride home from work was with a Bridge of the Gods toll collector. He looked like a Punch-and-Judy puppet and said that in the summertime, the job pays off because young women wear "scanties" and you're never too old to take a peek. John wanted me to carry a package to Cheyenne but changed his mind. So that's it. My next bed will be in Raleigh.

1979

January 1, 1979
Raleigh

On New Year's Eve, Ronnie's friend Avi and I wrote on the street with Valium. Later we went to his friend Julia's. She has a cardinal in her freezer. I saw it.

January 18, 1979
Raleigh

I have been working at the Empire (my new name for Mom and Dad's rental properties). Today Mom helped, and she and I talked about prayer in school. She is an agnostic. *The Phil Donahue Show* has gotten her thinking. Today she said, "The Bible's view of women stinks."

January 19, 1979
Raleigh

Amy babysits and scours the houses for dirty magazines, which she then brings home. She really is divine for her age (seventeen). Today while I shoveled the driveway, she asked what I thought the filthiest word was. I said *cunt*. In her opinion, it's *fuckwad*. She said it sends chills down her spine. The other day we went to see *Midnight Express*. She was really loud during the torture scenes and kept squirming in her seat, saying, "Shit, oh, shit."

January 20, 1979
Raleigh

I met and went home with Eduardo, a twenty-eight-year-old Costa Rican now living in Raleigh. It's fun to see where people live. Eduardo has quite a few black-light posters. I never thought I'd do this—go home with strangers—but it's OK with the right stranger.

January 24, 1979
Raleigh

For the umpteenth time I'm swearing off drugs. Lily and I took acid and then rubbed MDA into our gums. It was great in her apartment, then we went to a dinner party for a while. Then we went to see *Pink Flamingos*. Then back to her place, where I prayed until I fell asleep. Lesson: Never be where you don't want to be on acid.

January 29, 1979
Raleigh

Today I worked at the Empire on Gloria Penny's sewer line. Her backyard was covered with lumps of shit and green toilet paper.

In current events, a sixteen-year-old in San Diego opened fire on an elementary school playground with an M16 and 250 rounds of ammunition. The pope is in Mexico.

March 1, 1979
Raleigh

I'm depressed because I withdrew $75 from my savings account. It's the same passbook I've had since 1966, and I'm only on the third page!

March 8, 1979
New York, New York
All over downtown I'm seeing posters reading:

Doctors' Warning:
Deadly Disease.
Leprosy Disease.
Stay Away from
the Women Tramps.
Men Caught
Leprosy
and Tuberculosis
from the
Women Tramps.
You Will Endanger
Your Family with
Deadly Disease.
Stay Away from
the Women Tramps
or You Will Be in a Bad Ward
and Suffer Terrible the Rest of Your Life
with Tuberculosis and Leprosy.

March 11, 1979
Raleigh
On our way home from New York, Lily and I stopped in Baltimore, where we went to Edith's Shopping Bag and got Edie Massey's autograph. She was in *Pink Flamingos* and *Female Trouble* and will be in *Polyester,* which isn't out yet. I bought a magazine, Lily got a button, and when we told Edie she looked good, she pulled off her nice hair and screeched, "It's a wig."

Every man on the street was old and dirty and looked like he was on his way to an adult bookstore.

March 28, 1979
Raleigh
I found a job. Today I'll work, really work, for the first time since December. I've been hired as a waiter at a little restaurant next to the Arthur Murray Dance Studio called the Breakfast House, so I'm up at five. The last time I was up at five was because I hadn't gone to bed yet.

March 29, 1979
Raleigh
Everyone at the job is very nice. Especially Mary, the cook. I made $13 in tips, mostly in dimes and quarters.

There was an accident yesterday at the Three Mile Island nuclear plant, so a lot of people talked about it.

April 16, 1979
Raleigh
Dad on friendship: "Sure, some people are nice. Real nice. Nice like carpets so you can walk all over them."

May 3, 1979
Raleigh
I am in trouble with Lisa's landlady, Cleo. Last night D. came to visit with a friend. They were loud on the stairs. Cleo was woken up by the noise and called me, saying, "Now, listen, Andrew. We can't have this."

"I'm sorry," I said. "It won't—"

"We just can't have it."

I hope I haven't gotten Lisa evicted. She's at Bob's every night, but still, it's her apartment. All the tenants here are old and everything bothers them. They make me think of Mrs. Covington, who comes into the Breakfast House every day. She complains if I don't fill her coffee cup to the top, and then when I do, she complains that it's too full.

So I'm in trouble and need to find an apartment by next Friday.

May 7, 1979
Raleigh

Ronnie and I spent the day apartment hunting. My best option is in the house next door to the IHOP, with a fireplace, a finished-off sunporch I could use as a bedroom, a living room, and a small kitchen. The bathtub is almost miniature.

We talked to a landlord with an apartment on Ashe Ave. He said he would rent to me if:

1. I am not an atheist
2. I do not "carouse"
3. I do not smoke marijuana
4. I do not have parties (a $50-per-person fee is charged for every "jerk" I invite)
5. I do not have black friends
6. my friends don't belong to any "hate groups like the NAACP that call us white people *honkies*"
7. I don't get pregnant (he evicts unmarried pregnant women)

He said all of this seriously, and afterward Ronnie gave me a pair of pants.

May 12, 1979
Raleigh

Yesterday was move-in day into the apartment next to the IHOP. The place is bigger than I remembered. It feels nice and empty, and after getting settled, I took some LSD—not enough to see God, and not enough to think too much.

May 17, 1979
Raleigh

Gas in four states is now selling for over $1 a gallon. I'd love to work in a service station just so I could hear people complain. Apartment life is good. I'm using my ironing board as a kitchen table.

May 21, 1979
Raleigh

Nell Styron is the hostess of the Upstairs Restaurant, and today was the first time I'd seen her without a bow in her hair. Ronnie and I ate there this afternoon. We had taken some acid, so we had borscht for the pretty color. I'm so afraid lately that she'll get hurt or killed. What would I do without her?

May 24, 1979
Raleigh

Something cruel:

Yesterday I caught a wasp and put him in a jar in the living room. Later I threw in a dead bee, and the wasp chewed it up. Last night I poured Canada Dry and Comet into the jar. The wasp rolled over on his back, kicked up his legs, and died in a matter of minutes. I felt really bad about it. Lots of people kill wasps, but I made it suffer. He was large, though, so I figured it was either him or me.

I really try to refrain from marijuana until at least ten thirty at night, but when it's put in front of me, I forget how miserable it makes me feel. I get nauseated and don't move around as much. At night, though, I take a bath and listen to the radio. At night, it's great.

June 1, 1979
Raleigh
Conversation at work:

> Me: Are you Italian?
> Italian guy: Just do your job and minda you own business.

June 3, 1979
Raleigh
Conversation I overheard at the IHOP:

> Woman: Excuse me, may I join you for a moment?
> Billy (who is blind and doesn't wear dark glasses): Yes, ma'am.
> Woman: You can't see me. I'm just an old woman with a favor to ask.
> Billy: Yes?
> Woman: I'd like to pay for your meal. I'm from Durham.
> Billy: Have you lived in Durham all your life?
> Woman: Yes, my husband died unexpectedly. Here's a ten-dollar bill.
> Billy: I've been blind since I was born.
> Woman: Trust in the Lord, He's all we've got now.
> Billy: Yes, all we've got.
> Woman: Yes.
> Billy: Yes.
> Woman: Did you ask how old I am?
> Billy: No.

Woman: Well, God bless you.
Billy: Yes, you too.

June 6, 1979
Raleigh
A joke Jane at work told me:

> Man to a woman he'd just screwed: If I'd known you
> were a virgin, I'd have taken more time.
> Woman: If I'd known you had more time, I would have
> taken my panty hose off.

June 13, 1979
Raleigh
I was walking home when someone in a passing car leaned
out the window and spat right in the center of my face.

I am reading *The World According to Garp.*

June 14, 1979
Raleigh
On the bus yesterday morning, I ran into D., who has a
Mohawk and goes to court tomorrow on two counts of
drunk-and-disorderly conduct, one count of trespassing, and
one count of urinating on a woman's leg. She'd promised to
sleep with him if he bought her beers, so he did. Then she ran
off with her friends, so he caught up and peed on her skirt.

June 21, 1979
Raleigh
This morning I found $6 in the parking lot of the Arthur
Murray Dance Studio. In the ninth grade I found $1, but since

then it's just been change. Jane called in sick at the restaurant today, so I worked alone and made $25, part of which I spent immediately on a dime bag and part of which I spent later on paint.

June 29, 1979
Raleigh

Miss Woodard was my teacher in the third grade. She was Paul's and Amy's as well. On June 7 she retired and the school proclaimed her a champ. One day when I had her, a kid wet his pants during geography, and she told the class that Steve was just excited about learning. Even in 1964 I thought that was funny.

July 1, 1979
Raleigh

It's been a couple of days since I've written. Friday night I took some LSD and arranged five yellow Kodak boxes in the front yard. It was good acid. It made me notice color a lot, and I could read and not get depressed. Saturday I took some crystal and spent all night doing rubbings of envelopes. Now I'll be off for three days.

I found out that Jack and Mary, the night managers at work, secretly refer to me as "the space cadet." God, that makes me mad.

July 6, 1979
Raleigh

Yesterday afternoon three black women beckoned me to their car and told me that my fly was down. I thanked them because nobody ever tells you things like that.

July 7, 1979
Raleigh

Last night, after taking a bath and ironing, I went to the Capital Corral (gay bar) and met L., who was older than me—thirty-five, maybe. We talked about the normal things you talk about and then came back here. He didn't say anything about my artwork but suggested right away that we sit on the bed in our underwear. But L. wasn't wearing underwear. Instead he had on diapers and rubber pants.

I was not braced.

L.'s favorite phrase was "a real turn-on."

Diapers were "a real turn-on," as was being peed on and being five. "Daddy," he said, "if I was your little boy, how would you dress me? Would my little rubber pants be tight?"

I was a nervous wreck. L. was disappointed that I wouldn't play along, and I think it was pretty clear I just wanted him to crawl home. I went into the kitchen for a long time, and when I came back to the bedroom, he was asleep.

September 1, 1979
Raleigh

My favorite way to take crystal: I sit backward on the toilet with the seat down, facing the wall, the green jade box I made in Oregon on the tank lid. I always cut the speed on the Patti Smith *Radio Ethiopia* album. I use a razor, then snort it with a straw, and when I'm through I stand outside the bathroom and think of how nice my jade box is.

September 17, 1979
Ithaca, New York

This is the third autumn in a row I've gone off to pick apples. Avi and I left Raleigh on Tuesday in his Volvo and drove through Virginia, then to his parents' house in Pittsburgh.

We arrived in Ithaca yesterday. Last night we saw the movie *Manhattan* on campus and slept in a graveyard beneath a headstone that read BOYS.

Along the way we picked up a hitchhiker, a guy from Queens going to Buffalo. Now Avi can't find his traveler's checks, so we're going to fill out a police report.

September 24, 1979
Knowlesville, New York
Avi and I found rooms at this hotel in Knowlesville. It's run by a man named Brad who has nine children by two marriages. Here are his three rules:

1. No enjoyment of showers on Friday and Saturday nights. This doesn't mean they can't be *taken,* but they have to be short. The bar features country-and-western music on weekends, and if we use all the hot water, there won't be enough for "the broads in the ladies' rooms." "Hey," he said, "put yourself in my shoes."
2. "It's all right if youse brings a cunt up to your rooms for the night, but, hey, two nights, three nights, and you got to pay for it. Put yourself in my shoes."
3. Pay in advance.

We hit a dog last night while trying to find the hotel. Avi swears it was a terrier, but to me it looked like a poodle. We knocked on seven doors searching for its owner, most of them trailer doors with loud TVs inside. "No, it's not ours," people would say. "We got a retriever." "We got a collie." "The lady down the road has dogs. Maybe a hundred. Maybe fifty. At night they bark, a din so great you need earplugs. But us, we're used to it. G'night, boys."

We follow our noses to the house, which smells like dog

38

shit. "How many do you have?" Avi asks the woman, who answers, "Enough."

She says the poodle or terrier we hit wasn't hers. Then we drive back and find that the dog is no longer there by the side of the road. It's run off. So we give up.

October 1, 1979
Knowlesville

Avi and I went to Rochester for the weekend and had a car accident—my first. I was disappointed: no blood. I would have enjoyed just a trickle. First the stick shift came off in Avi's hand, so we spent the day at George's brother's house. George is a picker and his brother is a mechanic. All I did was sit in a folding chair and drink grape juice. It was all right. Then later, while Avi was driving, the hood opened up. He couldn't see where we were going, and when we struck a telephone pole, my head hit the windshield and broke it. No blood, though. None at all.

October 14, 1979
Knowlesville

There was a major fight at the hotel late last night between the owner, Brad, and his daughter Ginger, who is eighteen:

Brad: Where are my goddamn pants?
Ginger: In the dryer.
Brad: No, they're not. Somebody took my goddamn pants.
Ginger: It wasn't me.
Brad: Was too. (*The sound of someone being slapped.*) Bitch.
Ginger: Go ahead, tie me up and gag me like you did to Mom.

Brad: (*More slaps.*) Bitch, whore.

Ginger: (*Sobs.*) I hate you. I hate this goddamn place
and I'm sick and tired of being called a whore.

Brad: Who called you a whore?

Ginger: Three people. I'm getting out of here. I'll go live
on the streets. You think I'm such a whore, then I'll
go live like one.

Brad: (*More slaps.*) I hate you.

Ginger: I hate *you.*

Brad: You don't care.

Ginger: I don't care. I'll go to Albion or Medina.

(*Exit Brad. Enter Stepmother.*)

Stepmother: Just because everybody calls you a whore
doesn't mean you have to act like one.

Ginger: I'm sick of it. I don't want to wait tables for
him no more. Everybody calls me a whore just because I got big tits.

Stepmother: Who called you one?

Ginger: Sugar. Sugar did. Sugar's got an ass-whupping
coming.

(*More sobs.*)

Last week, under Avi's window, a man from the hotel
bar hit a woman for dancing with another man. When we
mentioned it to Brad, he said that if she was dancing with
someone else, she deserved to be beaten.

October 19, 1979
Knowlesville

Today we began picking Golden Delicious, the most fragile. I
was on the end row, beside the avenue of poplars, and while
working I thought of my sister Amy. At lunch Avi and I took
thirty-five apples and sent them in a box to the gang back in

Raleigh. Each one we wrapped in something different: a sock, a glove, a Xerox of an apple. They were McIntoshes, Macouns, Goldens, and Northern Spies, each then tied in string with a name tag on it.

This was payday. So far I have $400 in savings.

October 26, 1979
Knowlesville
It must have snowed twelve times today, though never for more than three minutes at a stretch. That didn't stop us from picking, though.

In the morning over coffee, Doreen, our waitress, who last month told us that at the age of six she was raped by her father, announced that she once worked at a carnival gaming booth and is now a lesbian living in a trailer with her girlfriend, Rocky.

I said I was gay too, and she seemed happy and pointed out other gay customers. "That woman over there, dressed like a man? She's a dyke who drives a truck and is named Peewee."

Doreen has Rocky's face decoupaged to her key chain and told me that the two of them were married last year at a gay church in Florida.

October 28, 1979
Knowlesville
Jean and George, two pickers I overheard this morning:

Jean: You're picking too slow, George. If you hurry up
    we can get out of here.
George: You're the slow one.
Jean: My breakfast hasn't affected me yet.
George: Honey, your breakfast is in my pants.

November 6, 1979
Knowlesville
Picking ended. I feel like camp is over. In the barn, a party. A long table was set up, and I liked watching everyone but me get plastered. Lots of silly speeches. It's interesting to work with people for almost six weeks but never see them all together.

December 8, 1979
Raleigh
I started work back at the Breakfast House today and learned that my gas-company credit rating has slipped to a B. Was ill all day yesterday. When the meth catches up to you, you find yourself paying for it. When on a spree, I'm convinced I can smoke three packs of cigarettes, not eat, and run all over town with no consequences.

1980

January 1, 1980
Raleigh

I gave away all my meth yesterday. It's either give it up or become an addict and lose all my hair and teeth. I never sleep or eat anymore. I never leave my apartment.

January 26, 1980
Raleigh

I've been a mature twenty-three-year-old adult for one month. Last night I lay in bed from three o'clock until four thirty, starting to panic. Some meth this morning, some now. I think I'll give the rest away, because after several days and nights it starts to get hairy. I got a lot done, though—made ten valentines, started on a shroud, took some egg crates and attached them to a broiler pan and a great photo of a chicken from the *Washington Post*. It all came together, all this stuff in my closet.

I've started peeing in my kitchen, into empty jars, then replacing the lids and putting them on the shelf. I'm considering saving a month's worth.

February 7, 1980
Raleigh

Last night up 'til five a.m. Finished four more crates. Took far too much speed in the course of the day and spent today coming down, down, down. Slept until noon, took a bath without bothering to rinse the thick layer of Comet from the bottom of the tub. Went back to bed until four. Then another bath and up to begin my day. Bought baby bottles, toothpaste, aspirin.

February 26, 1980
Raleigh
Both the crates I entered into a biennial at the NC Museum were accepted. Both. Not one, but two. There were fourteen hundred entries, and only forty-five were chosen.

March 8, 1980
Raleigh
Tiffany was on TV last night. It was a show about Élan and other places similar to the one she's been exiled to. In her snippet she was standing in a boxing ring with a bar across her eyes. I've been writing to her since she left, but she just sent a letter and told me to stop.

I'm going to start saving dirty napkins at work.

March 9, 1980
Raleigh
Last night I took my first quaalude, and, boy, did it wreck me. I was totally useless—not quite like being drunk, but close. None of the queasiness, just really relaxed. Relaxed to the point of idiocy. Coming home, walking up my stairs, I fell. Then I fell twice in my apartment and decided I was better off on the ground, crawled to my alarm clock, set it, and crawled to bed.

March 18, 1980
Raleigh
I have just taken amphetamines stolen from a drugstore.

They're given to hyperactive children to make them even more hyperactive so they'll get tired and pass out, giving their parents a rest.

Last night I went stark raving mad. I had a list of calls to make and used the same two dimes for five hours before coming to the conclusion that all three friends were together having a wonderful time and talking about me. I paced, made messes, finally cooked pork chops, and tried to read magazines.

April 8, 1980
Raleigh

I'm on this pure meth I got from W.'s friend Liz. It's moist and foul-tasting, super-severe, and I haven't figured out the right dose yet. Allyn from downstairs tried it too. Then she and I threw a party that was fine until two drunk guys wandered over from the IHOP and crawled into bed with Dee Dee's nine-year-old daughter, who was asleep in the other room.

April 11, 1980
Raleigh

I've got $12, no job, and unpaid rent. I'm depressed, I'm broke, and soon I'll be out of drugs. I feel so sleazy and cheap. Still, I have two sculptures in the art museum.

April 25, 1980
Raleigh

I began work, sort of, at Irregardless's lunch place downtown. It's two and a half hours a day. People order at the counter, and my job is to carry their trays to their tables when their food is ready. The hard part is figuring out what to say. I eventually settled on "Here you go." It felt good to have somewhere I had to be, to have someone expecting me.

April 29, 1980
Raleigh

I worked at the Empire today, clearing someone's backyard of kudzu. Dad drove me home afterward. "I'm a fifty-eight-year-old man with the mind of a twenty-one-year-old," he said in the car.

An hour later I was smoking opium with Allyn from downstairs. We didn't feel much, so we put on a Ravi Shankar album and plugged in some colored lights, hoping that might help, but it didn't.

May 6, 1980
Raleigh

Ronnie's new roommate, K., eats only raw vegetables. It's to keep her in shape for all the drugs she takes. We talked last night and she said it was just a matter of time before grocery stores start selling human meat. She really believes this.

July 7, 1980
Raleigh

I was accepted into the SECCA (Southeastern Center for Contemporary Art) show. My name will be published in the catalog, so once again I'll get to see it in print. Now I'd like to get into the phone book.

July 30, 1980
Raleigh

I've been raging for three days, so I was grateful when H. gave me half a quaalude, which I'll down as soon as we reach the reception for the SECCA show. This is probably a mistake.

August 7, 1980
Raleigh

I haven't written in a week. Hence the news in brief:

I packed everything into my crates and carried them downstairs. Allyn and I lived together for a few days. Then she moved to Pittsburgh. Gretchen moved into my old place.

Julia is gone, moved to New York.

The night of the SECCA reception, it must have been a hundred degrees. It was good to see my photos again. The quaalude wasn't such a bad idea after all.

Tulip, the dog Ronnie was looking after, killed the next-door neighbor's Chihuahua. Ronnie is wrecked, Tulip oblivious.

On August 2 I went to the beach for five days with the family. We stayed in a condo with air-conditioning and now I have a tan.

In Pittsburgh Allyn will go to school. Lately I think of going back to college, maybe the Art Institute of Chicago. Just being together enough to apply would be an accomplishment. Talking to Lyn, I realize I'm still young.

October 1, 1980
Raleigh

Gretchen and her friend Carl found a fetal puppy this morning on a sidewalk at NC State. Now it's upstairs in her freezer and she's named it Pokey.

* * *

Some crank called the house and told Mom he wanted to eat her pussy—his words, not mine. "Isn't that sick?" she told me. "I'm a fifty-year-old woman."

Actually, I think she's fifty-one.

October 9, 1980
Raleigh

If by Monday at five I haven't given the phone company $79, they'll cut off my service and make my life miserable until they get their money. I was better off when I lived upstairs and used the pay phone at the IHOP, except of course that people couldn't call me.

October 10, 1980
Raleigh

I dropped my telephone again. Now it never rings and I have to guess if someone is trying to contact me.

October 19, 1980
Raleigh

Randall, the gay alcoholic in the house next door, boldly peeps through my windows. "Boy, you sure rock in that chair a lot," he said last week, his face pressed against my screen.

This time I was lying on my bed with Katherine's cats. I'm watching them while she's out of town. I can be very mushy, and he watched me kissing them and saying that all the other cats in the neighborhood were jealous of their beauty. Then I heard, "David. David. It's me, Randall. Listen, I'm running low on money and wonder if I can maybe borrow thirty-five cents for cigarettes."

He has to be forty years old, at least.

December 20, 1980
Raleigh

A girl who lived down the street from us when we were growing up got married. Dad reminds me that not only is Andrea a college graduate, but her husband is too, and that they both made good grades. After the reception, tipsy, Mom and Dad stopped by for coffee. It was the first time they visited together.

1981

January 6, 1981
Raleigh

Ronnie and I worked last night on the performance piece we're calling *HUD* (for Housing and Urban Detectives). I've borrowed Paul's typewriter for two weeks and given notice at Irregardless. My last day is Friday, January 16. The performance is Saturday. Meanwhile, I've applied for a job as a teacher's aide at the Tammy Lynn home for the retarded.

February 1, 1981
Raleigh

We went to Lance's for dinner last night and I learned that he keeps a dead rattlesnake in his freezer. He found it on the highway somewhere. The snake's not messy dead, just missing some guts, and even frozen solid it still looks alive. Margaret wants to photograph it in my freshly painted apartment, but I'm afraid to even remove it from the bag. Were my dad to see it, he'd drop dead of a heart attack—wham, no questions asked. Half the people I know have dead animals in their freezers: reptiles, birds, mammals. Is that normal?

February 17, 1981
Raleigh

Mom took me to the IHOP for lunch and told me not to worry about the $20 I owe her. It's her birthday.

February 20, 1981
Raleigh

I went tonight to the Winn-Dixie on Person Street, across from the Krispy Kreme. It's a low-income neighborhood, right on the line separating the white and black areas of town. I was walking from the parking lot to the front door when I saw a man enter. He was tall and black, clearly drunk, and behind him were two girls, laughing and pointing. The man was pushing an empty cart, and just inside the door, one of his feet caught on the carpet. He fell to his knees, and a moment later the cart he'd been putting all his weight on fell over as well. With nothing to support him, he crashed face-first onto the floor. I was maybe twenty feet away but didn't rush forward to help him. No one did. I was looking for magazines, so I decided at the last minute to try the Fast Fare across the street instead. When they didn't have what I wanted, I returned to the Winn-Dixie, where the man was still lying on the floor. It made me uncomfortable, so I decided to skip the magazines and just go to Krispy Kreme instead.

February 25, 1981
Raleigh

Jean Harris was convicted of second-degree murder. I kind of liked her.

February 26, 1981
Raleigh

Mom dropped by this morning with at least $60 worth of groceries: pork chops, chicken, hamburger meat, salami, cheese, cereal, eggs, oil, pancake mix, broccoli, canned tomatoes, corn, beans, pasta, bread, syrup, oatmeal. I feel guilty and grateful.

Later I went to the design school and saw Komar and Melamid, the Soviet dissident artists, who are funny. They showed a photo of a human skull placed atop a horse skeleton and claimed it was a Minotaur. Then they showed three bones glued together and said it was a triangladon. I sold them my soul for $1.

March 17, 1981
Raleigh
I went to pick up my pieces that were rejected by the Wake County show. "Oh, yes," the woman said when I gave her my name, "you're the one with the little cardboard boxes."

"Yes, that's me." I'd wanted to get in just to trouble people like her.

I'm making corn bread for dinner again. Last night I had an omelet with old rice in it.

April 5, 1981
Raleigh
Wednesday's performance went very well—sixty-four people. I was convinced there would only be eight. Everyone was very warm afterward, complimentary. On Friday I felt divorced from the action. Can't tell whether or not the audience noticed. There were sixty-nine of them that night. Large party afterward, lots of people, half of them strangers. I had four Scotches and passed out before making a major spectacle of myself.

April 6, 1981
Raleigh
Quickly approaching rock bottom as far as money is concerned. I haven't paid the rent yet. Tonight I bought a box of

pancake mix, a dozen eggs, and a pint of milk. I have $5 to my name, and even that is owed.

April 7, 1981
Raleigh

"Base metals. There is no gold." I took my fraternity pin, the one I found last year, to two pawnshops, thinking I could use the money to settle my phone bill. They want $65 right this minute. Every time I go to pay in person, they have me dial 2. That puts me in touch with a professional scolder who tells me I wouldn't be in this fix if I had paid my bills when they were due. I tried today to put down $5, and the woman laughed in my face and gave me until Friday.

On returning home, I called Joe, who might have some work for me. Then I called Lou Stark and agreed to paint her living room in exchange for $20 and some food. I'm getting $159 back from the IRS, so in a pinch I could ask Mom to front it for me.

April 8, 1981
Raleigh

I worked for Joe today, cleaning windows in a passive solar house owned by a marriage counselor and his wife, a home-ec teacher. He has work for me tomorrow as well. On the ride home with S., I smoked a joint. It was too early for me, but I couldn't say no. So there I was, high at three o'clock in the afternoon. Later I rode my bike downtown, feeling refreshed. Bought some tempera paint and some milk.

A phone call:

Woman: Hello, David?
Me: Yes.

Woman: This is Sandra.

Me: Do I know you?

Woman: Yes, you know me.

Me: From where?

Woman: Oh, come on, you slept here last night.

Me: You must have the wrong David. This is David Sedaris.

Woman: I know. You slept here last night and left your jockstrap.

Me: I don't even own a jockstrap.

Woman: You sound like some kind of faggot to me.

(She hangs up, which is unfair, as I didn't get a chance to respond.)

April 12, 1981
Raleigh

Friday night we went to dinner at the Villa Capri. Mom got lost on the way there. She took two or three incorrect turns and wound up jumping the median when she realized we were in the wrong lane and a car was heading directly toward us. Her excuse was that she hadn't had a drink yet.

April 16, 1981
Raleigh

I modeled for Susan's drawing class this afternoon and had an eerie feeling that everyone was staring at me. Half an hour of thirty-second poses, then an hour and a half of five-minute poses. The class was told to emphasize my head, face, and shoulders. I brought a bag of tricks and disguises. I picked my nose, sucked my thumb, sulked, wore a cylinder on my head, prayed, really pulled out all the stops. I'd never model naked, but with clothes on it's all right.

April 17, 1981
Raleigh

Today I dug a ditch and later it rained, so I finished painting Lou Stark's living room. She paid me $20, bean-burger mix, and four turkey legs. One of them I took upstairs to Gretchen's cat, Neil, who had been asleep on a blanket and wheezed with delight.

April 21, 1981
Raleigh

I thought I was back to eating pancakes. They're nothing to look forward to, but a box of the instant mix (just add water) is only $1.05 at Big Star. I'd just stirred up a batch when Mom came by with some groceries. I accepted them reluctantly— "Aw, what are you *doing?*"—but am so grateful. In the bag was a chicken, a brick of frozen flounder, orange juice, a can of peaches, a loaf of bread, and a can of pinto beans. The only way to assuage my guilt is to make a super-beautiful papier-mâché rabbit for next Sunday. I started one a few days ago, and as of now it looks more like a dog than a Greek Easter bunny.

July 3, 1981
Raleigh

There is a new cancer that strikes only homosexual men. I heard about it on the radio tonight.

July 13, 1981
Raleigh

Joe interviewed a carpenter named T.W. for a job and asked at the end, "Now, do you have any questions for *me?*"

"Yeah," T.W. said. "Did you get any pussy last night?"

July 14, 1981
Raleigh
I've had it with construction work. Today I:

> stepped on three nails
> was stung by a bee
> fell off a flatbed truck
> lost control of a wheelbarrow and drove it into a tree
>   with everyone watching

The day started when I went with Joe to the labor pool and picked up a man named Luther, who is black and has five kids. He can push a full wheelbarrow up a ramp with no problem. He can carry sixteen two-by-fours at one time. "I got five kids, so I can do anything," he kept saying. His only question—and he asked it all day—was "What's *he* doing here?" Meaning me.

Luther laughed hardest when I fell off the truck. When I returned from the van after looking for staples, he said I'd been gone so long he figured I'd walked into town. That got a great response. In total, he told on me three times.

To top it all off, after coming home and cleaning up, I went next door to the IHOP and was ignored by all the waitresses, who are mad at me for some reason.

July 17, 1981
Raleigh
T.W. the carpenter looks like Hansel from the fairy tale. Not Hansel grown-up, but just Hansel bigger. He has a Dutch Boy haircut and went to Vietnam in 1968. "You ever seen an anteater?" he asks.

"No."

"What about your uncle?"

T.W. is married to Candy, and they have two daughters, Raelyn and Lacey. They're not allowed to date until they're sixteen. That's the rule, and the older one has been complaining about it. "She's hot as a nigger bride," T.W. says. For lunch today he had a Little Debbie cake, a Mello Yello, and a can of Beanee Weenees.

July 20, 1981
Raleigh
Today I applied insulating jackets to Rob's water heaters. He's the owner of the house we're working on, and sometimes he can be obnoxious. "Well, that's a Jew for you," Bobby, one of the carpenters, said.

To make him uncomfortable, I told him that I was Jewish. Bobby then explained that there are two kinds of Jews. "There are Jews and then there are *Jews,*" he said.

Bobby's wife was in a trailer fire. There are eleven kids in his family. I questioned his constant use of the word *nigger,* and afterward he and T.W. used it nonstop just to annoy me.

August 2, 1981
Raleigh
Ronnie is incensed over the royal wedding. "Did you know that silkworms spun the fabric for her dress?"

"Silkworms spin everyone's silk," I told her. "That's where silk comes from."

Somewhere she heard that four hundred bears were killed and turned into hats. We went to the movies, and all I thought the entire time was *Where on earth does she get her information from?*

August 12, 1981
Raleigh
Today T.W. and I worked alone, nailing siding onto the Pratts' house. I made mistakes, and he was patient until I took a measurement and marked the tape instead of the board. He asked then if I thought I'd ever amount to anything. His tone suggested that if I *did* think I'd amount to anything, I was fooling myself.

T.W. comments on every woman he sees, with no exceptions. We ate lunch together at the Golden Skillet. A waitress was bending over to clear a table, and he smacked his lips and commented loudly on what he'd rather be eating.

Spook girls have good legs, he says. "There's a pretty little spook girl works over to the nigger store. I'd like to take her home to my wife and say, 'Here you go. Treat her like a sister.' Get me some pigger nussy, some soul hole."

"Monkey and the baboon playing in the grass. Monkey sticks his fingers up the baboon's ass."

"It was easier to get pussy back when girls didn't have no cars and had to depend on men for rides."

"Slippery as a puppy's peter."

"Get me a granny raisin cake. It's got a pitcher of an old granny on the cover with her hair all up in a bun. If they don't got none, buy me a male Hershey bar—you know, the kind with the nuts."

To a fifteen-year-old girl he called out, "C'mere so I can smell of it."

At the end of the day he decided that I'm too shy with women.

August 13, 1981
Raleigh
Today T.W. asked, "Did you get any cootie last night?" At the

sight of one girl, he said, "She could make a bulldog break her chain." When a young woman passed on a bike, he yelled after her, "Don't you know it's illegal to peddle pussy in this town?"

August 14, 1981
Raleigh
Today I helped T.W., mainly fetching tools. He says my problem is that I had me some college and that all those students at Kent State should have been lined up and shot. T.W. is a member of the Johnston County KKK. At lunchtime he said he was so hungry he could eat a horse dick fried in tar. We went to the Big Star to buy lunch. It's my grocery store, the one I shop at, and I withered when he started barking at women like a puppy.

T.W.'s best hunting dog just died. He has her kidneys and her spleen in a jar in the front seat of his truck. After work he planned to take them to the vet.

August 27, 1981
Emerald Isle, North Carolina
Dad wants to buy a beach house and name it Apedia, after Yia Yia's hometown in Greece. He does this every year—gets us all cranked up about a cottage. The real estate agent told him at the start of our vacation that the age of the private beach house is over, that times are changing, and that he might want to consider a condo instead. One of the ones we're staying in is for sale, so Mom sits up late, drinking wine and thinking of how she might rearrange the interior. If we buy a place, we'll need to rent it out at least ten weeks a year. That means furnishing it with stuff we won't cry over when it gets broken or damaged or stolen.

Dad says, "A guy needs a place where he can gaze into the

ocean and sort things out." It costs more to have a condo on the end, with a view of the water, but he says hell, you might as well go all out.

Today I got a pair of beach sneakers called Gold Seal Sea Dogs.

August 30, 1981
Raleigh

On our last night at the beach, at around three a.m., we started throwing sopping-wet washcloths at each other. The sound of one smacking against someone's face, or their back, was the funniest thing ever. Tiffany was great company this week. Every night we got high on the beach and made up coastal limericks. This morning Dad had us wait in the hot car while he returned the keys to Carteret County Realty and talked to someone about financing the condo he swears we're buying. He was in there for twenty minutes. The condo is $110,000. I can't believe we're falling for this again.

September 17, 1981
Raleigh

I've had it with Briggs Hardware. Again today when they asked what I was looking for, I was at a loss to tell them. "Something wooden," I've said in the past. "Something shiny."

I don't want a tool to do something with; I'm just looking for something to draw. In the toy department, I asked to look at one of their jack-in-the-boxes. The saleswoman got snippy when I didn't want to buy it, and when I reached for my knapsack and said I could explain, she said, "I don't want to see none of your old mess."

I turned to leave and saw all the employees standing at the front counter talking about me. They think they're hot stuff because the store was pictured in *National Geographic*.

From there I went to Monroe Tire & Service. No luck, and as I was leaving, a man came in with a horribly burned face.

September 26, 1981
Raleigh
While I was walking down Hillsborough Street after visiting Lyn last night, a carload of drunk guys pulled alongside me and shouted threats. "Fucking faggot!" they yelled. "We'll kick your ass." They were really into it, acting as if I'd done something to them personally, or to their mothers. At one point I was pretty sure they were going to get out of the car and start something. I wondered then if it would be too undignified to take off and run into the Hilton. As it was, I ignored them until they drove off. "Faggot." It seems to be written all over my face lately.

October 1, 1981
Raleigh
Tomorrow I return to work at Mrs. Winters's house. Last spring her porch was painted, and I'm to scrape up the drips. She'll likely stand over me while I do it, monitor me the way she did when I removed her storm windows. She'll play radio station WPJL (We Proclaim Jesus Lord) and pick, pick, pick.

She and her husband cleaned Trailways buses for forty years, and because they're black, I imagine they've heard every insult in the book.

Tonight at the IHOP I sat next to four NC State students. One of them was planning to break up with his girlfriend because she'd spoken to another guy. Another was short on money, and his friends offered to cover his bill if he'd drink the entire pitcher of raspberry syrup. I was willing to add another 50 cents if he could do it without throwing up.

I'm going through another talk-radio phase. Last night I listened to *Open Line,* where the guest was Hap Hansen, the channel 28 weatherman, who explained how he lost forty pounds. Most of the calls were from friends of his.

October 6, 1981
Raleigh
I've paid my rent and my phone bill, leaving me with 43 cents. In the late afternoon I went with Mom and Dad, who are thinking of buying a rental unit on Clark Avenue, a duplex— this instead of the beach house that was all just talk. The current tenants weren't home, and while I was walking through the place, almost snooping but not quite, I came across a kitten taking a nap in a red NC State beanbag chair.

Last night on *Open Line,* the guests were from the Anti-Defamation League. Klan members and jerks called, saying they'd drive the Jew carpetbaggers out of the South and back to where they came from. I am into *Open Line.*

October 7, 1981
Raleigh
Lisa and I have started taking Greek classes at the church. Our teacher is Jimmy Nixon, and there are nine students. Six of them are children, and I can't figure out what they're doing there. Most of them sound excellent to me, though, really, what do I know? Class is two hours long. During the fifteen-minute break that comes in the middle, Lisa and I ran out front to smoke. There is one full-blooded American in the class, a woman who's taking it to satisfy her husband.

October 9, 1981
Raleigh
I had a cheeseburger for breakfast and then plastered Daisy Leach's hallway. On her refrigerator is posted a recipe for "Granny's Bible Cake." Ingredients include John chapters 12 through 18, Matthew chapter 3, and a pinch of Leviticus. Miss Leach is planning to paint her kitchen yellow, like her neighbor Mrs. McGillis did.

I mentioned this to Mrs. McGillis, who said, "Monkey see, monkey do."

October 12, 1981
Raleigh
I've started the now-empty Jernigan apartment. Someone in their family left a note on the bathroom door reading, GENTLEMEN: BE LIKE DAD, NOT LIKE SIS. LIFT THE LID BEFORE YOU PISS.

They left behind a Day-Glo poster of astrological sex positions, which made me think of the apartment a few doors down and of a picture Gretchen and I found while emptying everything out. It was a crude drawing of a man screwing a woman from behind, and on the bottom was written ROLL OVER, MY DEER.

There are always treasures left behind at the Empire apartments.

October 19, 1981
Raleigh
There are no grocery stores directly en route from Mom and Dad's rental units on Colleton. You pass a couple of 7-Eleven–type places, but nowhere that has actual food. If I ride a half mile out of my way, I can stop at the Winn-Dixie on Person Street.

All the fruits and vegetables there are prepackaged, so you can't buy just one onion or lemon or sweet potato. It's all in plastic, so you can't even squeeze something to tell if it's ripe. Their stacks of canned specials are a joke. How are two small cans of tomatoes for $1 a bargain? The prices are crazy, which kills me, seeing as it's in one of the city's poorest neighborhoods. The cashiers are white and young, wearing Van Halen T-shirts under their uniform tops. I passed one of the girls on her break and she was sitting on the filthy floor next to the entrance. They don't even carry pints of milk at this Winn-Dixie—you have to buy a whole expensive gallon.

October 23, 1981
Raleigh
While I was riding my bike home from Colleton after painting last night, three black guys started throwing rocks and bottles at me. Again I was faced with a decision: *Do I give them the pleasure of speeding up, or do I just continue at a regular pace and pretend this isn't happening?* I'm guessing that if one of the bottles had hit me in the head, they'd just have laughed and run away while I crashed onto the street.

This morning a girl almost ran over Lou Stark at the crosswalk in front of Jimmy's Market. Lou was together enough to get the license plate. Then she called the girl's parents. She's from Mount Olive, apparently, and Lou got her into big trouble.

The three who threw rocks and bottles at me were on foot, so I couldn't get anyone in trouble.

October 25, 1981
Raleigh
Again last night I went to Lyn's and watched *The PTL* (Praise the Lord) *Club*. Jim Bakker, the cohost, is desperate for $50

million. He looks like a baby monkey. Not just a baby. Not just a monkey.

October 29, 1981
Raleigh

When Gretchen went off to RISD she left behind her cat, Neil, who was abandoned a few months earlier by Randall. After swearing she was not my responsibility, I let her in. Now every day I regret it. Neil breaks every pet rule in the book. If she were a person, she'd hang out at the Trailways station.

November 6, 1981
Raleigh

I worked for Joe, painting solar window boxes that look like coffins and will be installed later this week in low-income areas.

Neil is being punished for jumping onto the counter and eating my raw scrambled eggs. I'll probably untie her tomorrow.

November 10, 1981
Raleigh

We began installing the solar window boxes in Garner, where everyone has either ceramic animals or junked cars in their yard. The first woman whose house we went to lives with her husband and her father, who has cancer. She told us that with bursitis in both shoulders it's difficult to raise her windows, and of course Pa's no help, what with the cancer and all. When we arrived, she put two of her three dogs in the cellar. They commenced barking and she yelled, "Peanut and Pee Wee, y'all need to shut up!" Finally she opened the door a few inches, and when the dogs stuck their faces through, she kicked them into silence. One of them stole the slipper off her foot, and that made her even madder.

The woman said that $100 worth of heating oil now costs $175 and that she don't know what the hell Ronald Reagan is doing to us poor people. Did we know? she asked.

The last stop of the day was behind the Purina plant. I'd never been to that neighborhood. Every house we went to had TVs on.

The window boxes are easy to install. Tomorrow we'll do more. Today it was seasonably cold and the sky was white.

November 11, 1981
Raleigh

At all the rural houses we stopped at today, the men wore overalls. One gave Bobby a mess of collards for his wife. A mess of collards, he said, spells good sex.

A woman in Garner told us that she tries her best to serve the Lord but that these are hard times for Christians. Before we left she asked us to repair her screen door so she can look out at the landscape God has provided her.

November 21, 1981
Raleigh

A friend of Susan Toplikar's was hit by a cinder block thrown from a passing truck. He'd been walking along the side of the road, and the cinder block broke several ribs. After crawling onto the porch of a house, he banged on the door, but the people wouldn't answer until he passed out.

1982

January 4, 1982
Raleigh

I stopped opening my telephone bills months ago. Still they scream at me from the cabinet over the sink where I keep them. The last bill I paid was in late summer, and because the envelope that arrived today was light, I opened it. Light envelopes mean they've had it. The letter inside said that if I didn't pay them $65 by tomorrow, they would take my phone away.

I called to negotiate, and the woman scolded me. "Why on earth don't you pay monthly?"

"I don't know." I pleaded, and she gave me until Thursday the seventh. By then I'll have enough for the phone but nothing toward my already late rent.

I wondered why the rent and bill situation always has to be so desperate. Then I realized I *made* it desperate. I *am* desperate.

I saw an ad in the paper for a waiter at the Capital Club. I didn't apply because if they hired me, I'd have to miss *All Things Considered* every night. Plus I don't have the outfit to apply in, or the look.

When I lived in San Francisco I was just as desperate, so desperate I applied for a waiter job at a place called Henry Africa's. You had to be twenty-one to wait tables. I wasn't but lied and said I was. The guy in charge told me to come back

tomorrow with my birth certificate. He was dressed in a sa-
fari outfit.

January 8, 1982
Raleigh
I spent the day crawling underneath the Ewing house and trying to think of one good thing to say about it. For a while,
hunched over on my hands and knees, I used a rake to collect trash. Among my findings were two pornographic novels
without their covers. They were from the late 1950s and
pretty tame by today's standards. One of them had black-and-
white pictures of women in it. Mainly it showed their bosoms.
Under each picture was a short paragraph, the author trying
to be funny, most often. The models were on the big side.

I gave the books to Bobby and his best friend Dougie, who
is working with us this week. In the afternoon I walked into
the backyard and saw them drinking Mountain Dews and examining the pictures. "This one here's got pretty little titties,"
I heard Dougie say. He has red hair, an ex-wife, and a three-
year-old daughter.

Today I broke a rake, a shovel, and a hammer—every tool
that was placed in my hands. I saw a lot of centipedes under
the house. After I crawled through a pile of cat shit, I decided
to call it a day and go home.

January 10, 1982
Raleigh
Neil has left some fluid on the bed. It isn't urine. It doesn't
smell bad. It's just fluid.

January 11, 1982
Raleigh
Again this morning I found fluid on my birthday blanket. This

time I rubbed Neil's nose in it and put her out for a while. She makes a habit out of everything.

January 13, 1982
Raleigh

My phone has been disconnected, so I called Southern Bell. The woman I talked to said that it would stay cut off until I paid my bill.

"But I *did* pay it," I said. "Seventy-five dollars just last week."

They couldn't verify it, so I went through my trash and found my receipt inside a can of lima beans. It was covered with rust-colored juice. The woman at the phone company addressed me as "Mrs. Sedaris" until I couldn't stand it anymore and corrected her. That always happens. They think I'm a woman—a woman named David.

January 14, 1982
Raleigh

Lisa, Bob, and I drove on ice to see *Body Heat*. It was nice of them to invite me and to go out in this weather. The problem is that Lisa talks through everything, and loudly. It hardly ever has anything to do with the action taking place on-screen. Tonight, in the most suspenseful moment, just as William Hurt was about to open the booby-trapped door of the boathouse, Lisa touched my shoulder and leaned close. "Do you remember how to say the word *snowman* in Greek?" she asked. "I've forgotten since our last lesson and it's driving me crazy."

Afterward, she and Bob played a game of Space Invaders in the lobby. They weren't haunted by the movie the way I was, and by the time we reached the car, *Body Heat* was, for them, forgotten.

January 19, 1982
Raleigh
Again today I dug ditches in the cold rain. After work I met James at the Laundromat. He's black and a bit older than me, and these are a few of the things he said:

"I bet you're sixteen years old."
"I just like to be nice and meet new people."
"I love all kinds of music."
"I unwind in South Carolina."
"Why doesn't your wife do the laundry?"
"Aren't you a family man?"
"Don't you be lonely living here alone?"
"I've never met anyone like you."

I gave him my phone number because he wants to cook me dinner.

January 23, 1982
Raleigh
James called last night at one. He was looking for an Amoco station and asked if I wanted to come along for the ride. I was awake, so I said OK. He pulled up a while later in a blue car that had four doors and was new and clean. We drove for almost an hour to all the stations he knew were closed. Then, four blocks from my apartment, we went to one that was lit up.

It was two a.m., and when we opened the door to the inside where you pay, a camera flash went off. They do that because of theft. Afterward James talked about prison life. He's never been but was stopped once for speeding by a state trooper and said it was the most terrifying experience of his life.

The Hardee's on Edenton Street was open, so we went there and he bought a medium-size Pepsi. We drove to Apollo

Heights to look at his house, but we didn't go in. James lives with his brother but will soon move to Fox Ridge, a new apartment complex for middle-class black people. The rent will be three-fourths of his monthly salary.

When James's other brother was killed in Vietnam, the government sent someone to inform the family. That was in 1967. His mother worked in a school cafeteria. I asked a million questions, and he was good about answering them.

"Can I trust you?" he asked in the front seat of his car.

"I wouldn't if I were you," I told him.

He asked if we could be friends, and I said you shouldn't ask things like that. It sounds too third-grade. If you're meant to be friends with someone, you'll be friends. There's no need to talk about it.

James asked a lot of questions a person shouldn't ask. Back at the apartment, during sex, I thought about a lot of different things; my new trash can, for instance, with the pedal. I was a thousand miles away and wishing I'd never answered the phone.

February 1, 1982
Raleigh
Outside the A&P I saw a woman with thick, stiff legs pushing an empty cart through the parking lot. Her hair was in braids, and she turned to me, saying, "They forgot to give me my groceries, goddamn them." I followed her inside, but slowly. She walked like the Tin Man. I went to the A&P looking for a bargain, and when I didn't find one, I went to the Big Star. Chickens look bigger when they're wrapped tighter.

February 4, 1982
Raleigh
On the phone last night Gretchen told me that I'm rotting

away in a crummy house next to the IHOP. I got angry because it's true and changed the subject to next year's Christmas.

February 5, 1982
Raleigh

This morning I stepped on a nail. Afterward I had to literally pry it out of my foot. I mean, it was in all the way up to the board. Now my foot is swollen, and it hurts to walk across the room.

On the bright side, it's taken my mind off my inflamed penis. Maybe tomorrow I can cut off a few fingers to take attention away from my foot.

February 6, 1982
Raleigh

The Big Star is still holding their poultry-sale extravaganza: mixed fryer parts for 35 cents a pound. I told Dad about it, and he said it was a joke and that all the parts would be wings, backs, and necks.

He was almost right. They also threw in some hearts and livers.

I thought I'd never fall asleep last night. My foot was throbbing. The Rescue Mission gives crutches to people who are temporarily handicapped on the condition that you return them later, so I went with Margaret and got a pair. Then I tied them to my bike handles and rode to the library. Crutches are a real drag, but I like having people open doors for me.

February 9, 1982
Raleigh

My burning penis is not syphilis or gonorrhea but just some kind of bladder infection. That's the good news. The bad is that they've finally cut off my gas. I haven't paid the bill since May, yet still the total is only $30. Added to that is a $15 reconnection fee.

My grandfather Leonard was like that, like me. He would avoid bills and loan what money he had to friends. Mom grew up having her father wander home drunk and broke. I'm not drunk or generous, just broke.

February 10, 1982
Raleigh
After a four-day weekend I returned to work and was hit on the head by a brick. I was under a house, lying on my back and stapling insulation to the floor joists above me. The brick was loose and it landed on my eyebrow, taking a number of hairs and leaving a lump, which I sort of like because it makes me look tough.

In the afternoon I helped a guy named Pat carry furniture. It annoys me when someone assumes he's stronger than me and calls for a third set of hands to help. I am not a physically weak person, just uncoordinated. Pat is a real chatterbox. While moving stuff, I learned:

He has nine brothers and sisters.
He is from Wisconsin.
Once he had a rod stuck up his penis to search for scar
    tissue.
He got married in Rhode Island in 1973.
He went to Vietnam.
He refinished his own dresser.
He has a thirty-four-inch waist.
He once found a pie safe in a Carrboro mechanic's shop.
He subscribes to *Workshop* magazine.
He bought his stereo in 1969.

Meanwhile, Charles has been fired. His replacement is a guy named Tommy. Tommy is Dougie's cousin and frequently talks about "gnawing on some pussy."

That sounds pretty severe, to gnaw on it. Tommy's sister is a lesbian. She's straightforward about it, and when she brings her girlfriends home to meet the family, Tommy's father kisses them on the mouth, hoping, his son says, "to get the sweet taste of pussy on his lips."

With T.W. gone, there hasn't been much sex talk on the job site. That's changed now. I listen but never speak.

Driving home from Greek class, we passed a weaving drunk on the street. "That man lives in my apartment complex and once asked me to go with him to Charades Lounge for a drink," Lisa told me. She lit a cigarette. "I would have gone if I'd known for certain that he was going to pay."

February 11, 1982
Raleigh

Mrs. Ewing was at home this afternoon. She works as a maid for a car dealer and his insurance-selling wife. Her daughter-in-law chose the paint for the exterior of the house and luckily she likes it. "Now, I'm a lady and I like lady colors," she said. "I like me some pink and yellow." Mrs. Ewing begins stories with the line "You won't believe this, but one time . . . "

Her son was in Vietnam and has had several nervous breakdowns since returning home. "It's hard for him to find a job once they learn he's been in a nerve center," she said. Again today when it was time for her to leave, she said, "I'm gone." And she was.

February 12, 1982
Raleigh
Charlie Gaddy was at the IHOP, causing heads to turn. He is the anchorman on *Eyewitness News* and a local celebrity. At the restaurant, one woman after another stepped over to say hello. One asked which syrup he preferred, and he said, "In my opinion, the blueberry is best."

Tomorrow S. and I are going shopping in Chapel Hill. I want to find a good birthday gift for Mom and am willing to spend $20. She's been a very good mother this year, so I'm looking for a German-made windup mouse. That would be the perfect gift.

I worked today with a black man named Charles T. who backed into a Southern Bell van as we were leaving Capital City Truck Rental in our huge flatbed. Charles T. can't make out a word white people say. After he asked "What?" fifteen times, I started talking like him and he understood.

Charles T. plays cards in a one-story brick house behind the landfill. Last week he lost $400. We passed the Wakefield Apartments, and he pointed to a unit and told me that a few days ago, two brothers lost $9,000 gambling there. "The key to life is knowing when to stop," he said. Then noon came, and he stopped working and left. Off to play cards, I guess.

February 14, 1982
Raleigh
Last night Dad came to visit. He walked in without knocking and went straight to my bed and lay down on it. Then he closed his eyes and was out for quite a while. Again he'd waited until the last minute to buy Mom a Valentine's gift.

Before leaving, he looked around my living room and kitchen. Then he said, "Well, aren't *we* domestic."

After reaching the sidewalk he returned and asked if my apartment was always this warm. Then he left again and returned again to ask if the building heats with gas or oil.

When I was in high school, Dad would sometimes come into my room and lie on my bed. Sometimes he'd talk, but most often he was silent.

February 15, 1982
Raleigh

New word: *bourgeois,* meaning pussy. Tommy says he's glad he's married and can get all the bourgeois he needs and don't have to choke the chicken like single men do. He talks a lot about kicking his wife's ass. He'll kick her ass clean across the room if she doesn't have supper ready when he gets home. He'll kick her ass if she won't give him bourgeois when he needs it. Today he wore a T-shirt with ANIMAL written on it. The thing about Tommy is that he's more than a little ugly, especially compared to Bobby, who's compact and cute. Tommy and Dougie and Bobby talk about Misty and Debbie and Jackie. They treat me with a kind of detached, patronizing humor that probably should bother me but doesn't.

Last night I went crazy for marijuana. I was Jack Lemmon tearing up the greenhouse in *Days of Wine and Roses.* I looked for (and found) pot in the folds of album covers I had used to deseed long-ago ounces and quarters. I found some under the sofa cushions. Then I pulled out the couch and looked under the radiator. I turned the place inside out and got a little stoned but not much.

February 16, 1982
Raleigh

Tommy's wife cooked chicken and rice, so he didn't have to beat her ass last night. It was right there on the table when he got home. He uses the word *nigger* loudly and freely in that neighborhood, and it annoys me because we are guests there. What if Mrs. Ewing heard him? She'd be so hurt.

February 17, 1982
Raleigh

Yesterday morning I poured boiling water onto my left foot. I was making coffee and looking out the window at the guy in the next-door apartment, who was wearing a cowboy hat. Of course I stopped pouring once I'd burned myself. As the skin peeled off, I wondered when this string of bad luck might end.

February 19, 1982
Raleigh

Someone has drawn a swastika on the outer wall of Mrs. Ewing's back porch and written beneath it IMMORTALITY.

"Ain't that just about the silliest thing you've ever seen in your life?" she said when I pointed it out. "We ain't Nazis here, and you know that's a Nazi sign." She laughed. "We ain't Nazis and we ain't Communists neither."

After she left for work, I went looking for the door to her hot-water heater and found a magazine called *Players' Exchange*. It's for black swingers and is arranged by state. There were only two North Carolina swingers listed. One was a submissive lesbian who wrote that she was potty-trained and ready to travel.

I'm assuming the magazine belongs to Mrs. Ewing's son, the one who was in Vietnam and lives with her.

February 28, 1982
Raleigh
I went to the movies last night with Sally and Lyn's friend Mitch, who is gay and cute and wore a pink sweater. He lives in Atlanta. On his little finger was a ring with jewels in it. As the movie started, he emptied half his popcorn bucket into my lap, saying, "Here, David, have some."

It wasn't an accident, but I wasn't sure how hard to laugh. I don't know how to react to Mitch.

March 11, 1982
Raleigh
Mrs. Ewing has an unplugged freezer on her back porch. She opened the door of it yesterday, and after gagging at the horrible smell that came out of it, she saw a tail and screamed. I covered my face and discovered that the tail was attached to a squirrel, a rotting one in a paper bag.

Mrs. Ewing covered her mouth as well and told me that she's afraid of squirrels. When she sees them in her yard, she runs. "How did that thing get into my freezer?" she asked. "And in a bag!"

Her son Chester, who was in Vietnam and has nerve trouble, stepped out to complain about the odor and told his mother that he'd put the squirrel in the freezer, thinking she might want to cook it. Then he returned to his room and shut the door—didn't even help clean up the mess.

"I ain't never cooked a squirrel in my life," Mrs. Ewing said after he'd gone. "Wouldn't know how to, wouldn't want to."

We have painted her bedroom Pink Whisper with brown trim—her idea. The dining room is a shade called Zest.

March 15, 1982
Raleigh

I worked late and the Kerwins invited me to join them for dinner. I said that I couldn't because I had Greek class—a lie, but I don't know them well enough to eat with them. I should have said yes because I'm broke until Thursday and wound up having Cream of Wheat for dinner.

March 17, 1982
Raleigh

Dad called last night to ask if I wanted to go to Greece with him, Lisa, and Paul. He's paying for the plane tickets and hotels, so of course I said yes—how could I not? They're all going for two weeks, but I think I'll stay longer. I figure I'll need at least $600. I'll also need to make accommodations for Neil, who's mine now, completely.

March 25, 1982
Raleigh

Yesterday was Dougie's birthday, and he wore a cap with a Confederate flag on it to work. Here we are in a black neighborhood, already unwelcome. I don't get it. I'm surprised to learn that he's only twenty-two, not because he looks so young but because he has a three-year-old daughter who's in his ex-wife's custody. I'd been told he married a wealthy woman for her money, which is hard to believe because he's such an ugly guy.

To celebrate his birthday, Dougie went with Bobby and Tommy to a club called the Switch. They must have gotten really loaded, as the only one who came in today was Bobby, and he didn't show up until noon. There was a lump on his head, and he said that he got it when two bouncers took his watch and threw him out. He didn't seem angry about it, just resigned.

April 2, 1982
Raleigh
This morning a female sheriff walked through my front door without knocking. I went into the kitchen, and after I identified myself, she apologized. She was looking for apartment number 6. I was glad to point it out to her. I hope she takes those two and locks them up.

I received another ultimatum from the phone company. They demanded $60, so I went down this afternoon and gave them $30. While in line I saw Lloyd D. He was a tenant of Mom and Dad's who moved out, owing them $600 in back rent. I ran into him twice after he got his eviction notice. On both occasions he said, "How can your daddy do this? Doesn't he realize I'm his last white tenant?"

Lloyd is an alcoholic. He was drunk at the phone company office and very difficult to understand. He took forever at the window, talking about the weather and so on, and after he walked away, the cashier rolled her eyes.

April 9, 1982
Raleigh
Mom called the tenants in one of the Colleton Road units to tell them a repairman was coming to fix the water heater. The wife answered. Her voice is high and soft, and—like a lot of people, probably—Mom mistook her for a child. "Can I please speak to your daddy?" she asked.

"Uh-uh, Wendy," the wife said. "Sorry, babe." Then she hung up.

Mom told me this, and we laughed and laughed. Do the tenants know they're our dinner conversation? In our minds we all but own them.

April 10, 1982
Raleigh

Mom locked herself out of the house and had to crawl under the railing onto the sundeck. She's not an athletic person, not limber in any way, so it's such a startling image, her legs dangling in empty air.

Jokes I heard:

Q. What's better than roses on a piano?
A. Tulips (two lips) on an organ.

Q. Did you hear about the man with French asthma?
A. He could only catch his breath in snatches.

April 13, 1982
Raleigh

Tommy breaks into drugstores to steal Valium. This is how he supplements his income. He and Bobby and I drove over to the Fast Fare for snacks this afternoon. There I was with two guys without shirts who stopped on our way out to play six rounds of a video game called Frogger.

As I rode home from work, one of the handlebars came off my bike. So that's another thing to take care of.

April 15, 1982
Raleigh

Bobby brought his three-year-old son to work with him. An unsupervised child on a construction site. I seized up whenever he approached a Skilsaw, but Bobby had a good attitude. "Cover your ears, Brian!" he'd yell. Brian was eating caramels. They got all over his hands and, subsequently, his ears.

April 17, 1982
Raleigh

Yesterday, while riding home, Joe and I saw a topless woman run down Edenton Street. She seemed to have come from the church and had her arms crossed over her breasts. I'd guess she was in her late twenties, plump, and wearing cutoff jeans. A man was leaning against the church, watching her and laughing.

Later I went to the art auction at the design school. My piece went for $7. I tell myself that most of the thirty or so people there were students without much money, but still, $7! I was so embarrassed I left and came home. Then I took a nap and woke up depressed.

April 20, 1982
Raleigh

Bobby accidentally broke his wife's wrist during an argument. She visited us on the job site today and talked about it while drinking a Mountain Dew held in her good hand. Misty is small and pretty in the way that a country-and-western singer might be. She recently started an executive secretarial course at Hardbarger Business College. This is her first semester, and she's taking a spelling class. "Let me give you a little pop quiz," she said to Joe. "Spell *class-action lawsuit*."

I thought she'd hit him with something a little harder, like *arbitration*.

April 24, 1982
Raleigh

Tiffany left Raleigh and went back to Maine to work at the reform school she went to, Élan. I've missed her, so it was good to talk on the phone and hear about her new life. One of the delinquents she's assigned to kidnapped two children, drowned them, put their bodies in plastic bags, and left them on the curb for the garbagemen.

That's a bit more than delinquent, I think.

April 27, 1982
Raleigh

Bobby met his wife, Misty, at Skate Town, where we used to go as kids. Today after her spelling class, she came by the job site, and the three of us went to Hardee's for lunch. They ordered roast beef sandwiches and then entered a contest. First prize is an all-expenses-paid trip to the World's Fair, and while eating they speculated on who'd watch Brian if they won. Their best bet is Misty's sister in Charlotte, they decided, and after dropping him off, they could spend the night in Bobby's truck.

Then somehow we got onto the subject of shaving, which led to the shaving of legs. In Hardee's at lunchtime, the place half full with black people, Misty looked around and observed that most nigger ladies have hair on their legs. Bobby said gorillas don't shave neither. I flinched again and again, but they were oblivious and seemed almost innocent.

Susan Toplikar is going to New York for a year. Her place is bigger and cheaper than mine, so we talked and arranged for me to sublet it while she's away. The neighborhood, Oakwood, is more settled than where I am now. It's not all NC State students.

April 30, 1982
Raleigh

Joe and I were on the construction site when a man in a black car stopped to rage at us. "It ain't fair for white men to come into this neighborhood and get jobs working on our people's houses," he said—a reasonable charge. He asked how much the homes we'd built were renting for, and when we told him they were for sale, not rent, he called Joe an ugly name.

"What did you say?" Joe asked.

"I ain't afraid of you," the man said.

He drove away, and I thought of him all afternoon until a bee flew into my eye.

May 10, 1982
Raleigh

I have cooked a chicken that already smelled bad two days ago. In my heart I know it's spoiled, but I plan to eat it anyway because I'm hungry. For lunch I had a hamburger the size of a Susan B. Anthony dollar. All day long I installed doorknobs. It was all right.

May 20, 1982
Raleigh

Tiffany called to say she's coming home. She's miserable at Élan. For the last three days her job has been to observe a girl in isolation who carves ugly words into her arms with splinters. "I didn't come up here to be a prison matron," she said.

She thought of staying and finding work somewhere else but decided she can't live in a state with only one zip code.

May 26, 1982
Raleigh

This was our last night of Greek class. The Compos girls were out of hand, though, to be fair, they're just kids. I'll miss going there every week and studying with Lisa.

May 27, 1982
Raleigh

Tommy got into a fight at Shirley's Lounge, a biker bar. The management threw him out, so he jumped into his car and ran over the management. He already had a DUI and wasn't supposed to be driving but did anyway. An undercover cop followed him and shot out two of his car windows. When the officer got out of his Camaro, Tommy ran him over as well. Both victims are in the hospital, and he's in jail instead of at work.

June 1, 1982
Raleigh

I'm going through my annual college-anxiety phase. It happens every year at graduation time. I used to think I could teach myself anything I needed to know, but I'm not sure I believe that anymore. I'd like to be educated and mature.

June 6, 1982
Raleigh

At the Capital Corral I met a college freshman named Brant, who had his high school graduation tassel hanging from his rearview mirror. He told me that Heart is his favorite band, and during sex he kept telling me that he loved me and wanted to get married, presumably in the next five weeks before he returns to Norfolk for the summer.

June 18, 1982
Raleigh

I called the number Brant gave me, and it was made-up. Then I called all the dorms at Louisburg College and was told there is no Brant. Tricked again.

July 30, 1982
Raleigh
Just as I'm packing to move into Susan's and go to Greece, SECCA writes and invites me to have a solo show a year from now. This is huge for me. After getting the letter, I bought $15 worth of cat food.

August 6, 1982
Athens, Greece
Since Dad's arrival, all he's done is yell at people. He'll ask someone on the street for directions, then tell them they don't know what they're talking about. He speaks combat Greek, and the people he talks to speak it back. Still, it was good to see him and Lisa and Paul. Three days alone here wasn't such a great idea, especially in a room that's an oven. I brought my transistor radio. There's an OK jazz program, but everything else is Greek music.

There are a lot of blind people in Athens. A man got on the train tonight with what looked like mayonnaise in his eyes.

August 13, 1982
Heraklion, Crete
Dad bought us deck-class tickets—the cheapest—and while he and Lisa and Paul slept on benches, I stayed up and drank retsina with a stout Dutch girl. Her hair was short, like a boy's, and she looked hard into my eyes when she spoke.

Over the course of the evening, I learned the following:

1. Her brother died three years ago in an automobile accident, and she cried for two years straight.
2. Last year she had an affair with a woman.
3. An apartment in Amsterdam is expensive.
4. A Greek man lured her to his apartment recently and

tried to make love at her. That was how she said it: "Make love *at* me."

5. Germans are terrible people. She said this again and again—insisted on it. I have no reason to dislike them, so I just said "Huh" a lot.

On the bus from the port to Heraklion, I met Wally, an opera student at Columbia. We talked throughout the four-hour trip, and when I later introduced him to Dad, Wally addressed him as "sir." I wanted to sleep with him.

August 18, 1982
Athens

I go to a toy store and say, in Greek, "How much is the small dog?" I'm in a good mood, doing what I love—shopping. The woman is the rudest person I've met so far and says in flawless English that the dog winds up but is broken. Old and broken.

"That's all right," I say.

She then chides me for wanting a broken toy.

I leave and come back three times, and each time she's meaner. After she leaves I buy the dog from her assistant, who gives me a huge discount. What do I care that it's broken?

August 20, 1982
Athens/Patras

Dad, Paul, and Lisa left for Raleigh this morning. I walked them to Syntagma Square, where they caught a bus to the airport. Now I am one of the traveling youth. Single. I went to the post office and then returned to the hotel to pack and catch the bus to Patras. From there I'll go by ferry to Brindisi, and then on to Rome against Dad's better judgment.

"Italian men will get you drunk in order to rob you," he warned.

On my way out of the hotel, I heard a man on the phone at the front desk trying to change his flight. He said it was an emergency, that his mother died and he needs to get back to America as soon as possible. That can't be true, can it?

Later:

After our bus arrived in Patras, the driver made me help him pick up all the garbage people had left behind and throw it out the window. This town is the Greek Baltimore. I got a hotel room with four beds in it. That was fine until three other people showed up and claimed them. Roommates! And a shower is extra. Next door is a bumper-car pavilion. The thuds are fairly constant.

I went out tonight after dinner and had a beer at a gas station with a table in front of it. The owner had a live duck in her hands. When I went to pay, I saw her in the back room, wringing its neck and singing along to the radio. This place makes me feel stoned.

August 30, 1982
Athens

Back in Athens after Rome. The bus ride from Patras was dismal. I'd run out of books, so all I could do was stare out the window. After we arrived at the station, I met Rosa Rubio from Madrid. She speaks only Spanish, and after talking for a few hours, I brought her to my hotel. The room has three beds in it, so I offered her one and she was beside herself—hadn't seen a real mattress in weeks, she told me. I gave her my black-and-white-striped referee shirt because it never really looked good on me. I bought us dinner and drinks. She hadn't spoken to anyone in four days, and she was very patient with my Spanish. I enjoyed her company, and it was nice to treat someone, to be in a position to.

September 20, 1982
Raleigh
A joke I heard:

Q. Do you know how to bake toilet paper?
A. No, but I know how to brown it on one side.

October 11, 1982
Raleigh
I was riding my bike down Hillsborough Street when a carload of girls pulled up beside me. They yelled something I didn't understand, and then one of them hit me over the head with a broom and they all shrieked—funniest thing ever. I was going full speed, and had I wrecked, they'd certainly have driven off. From now on I'm going to carry a rock in my bike basket. When something like this happens, I'm ruined for days.

November 21, 1982
Raleigh
I ran into Brant last night, the college student I met last spring who said he loved me three times and then gave me a fake phone number. Since I last saw him, he's grown a sketchy mustache, which brings out his bad complexion and makes his chin look weak. "Remember me?" I asked. "Your name is Brant, your favorite band is Heart, you go to Louisburg College and have your graduation tassel hanging off your rearview mirror."

He looked at me for a second and said, "All I remember is that you're a Jew."

I didn't correct him because of the way he said it, the word

Jew spat out as if it were *leper*. Both of us walked away then, though I swear I did it first.

December 19, 1982
Raleigh

Tuesday is Lisa's birthday. She will be twenty-seven. I always told myself that when I'm that age, I'll make a drastic change. I'm not sure why twenty-seven; maybe because it's the age Avi and Katherine and Allyn were when I met them.

1983

January 25, 1983
Raleigh

Paul's birthday was four days ago, but we celebrated it last night. I gave him $6.50, which is a lot for a fifteen-year-old. Sort of.

Afterward I went home and called R., another person who's given me a wrong phone number. He said when we met that he'd like to have a wife and children—that he's actually had sex with a woman. "Did you have to force yourself?" I asked.

He said yes.

I have much more respect for drag queens than I do for all these full-grown men lying about who they really are. Plus R. never makes his bed, so, really, who needs him?

February 14, 1983
Raleigh

Blind Billy was at the IHOP tonight. He doesn't wear dark glasses, and his eyes are wild-looking. Sometimes he'll yell out, "I'd like some more iced tea, please!" or "I think I'm ready for dessert!" If he hears someone settle into a nearby booth, he's likely to start a conversation about sports, any kind will do as long as it involves a ball. Billy most often comes in alone, but tonight he was with another blind man who is new to both the IHOP and the YMCA, where Billy has lived for twelve years. The new guy plays blind baseball.

In the afternoons he connects his wrist with a shoestring to a sighted person's and jogs.

While eating, he asked Billy a number of questions. "Does anyone bother you in the shower at the Y? Is there hot water in the morning?" He asked about the discount blind people get on taxi service. "I'm told it applies from eight a.m. until six at night. Is that right? I've got friends I'd like to visit."

Billy said he didn't remember. He last took a cab six years ago.

The new guy talked about the library for the blind and some good books he'd listened to lately. He mentioned one and Billy said, "Did you listen to that Villanova game on Saturday night? Now that was something!" He's really loud. All he'd talk about was sports until the new guy mentioned an audiobook on World War II. Then Billy said, yelling, "Now those German people, they talk ugly! Sounds like everything they have to say is just pure meanness. I bet they can sure give somebody hell. Same with those Japanese."

February 18, 1983
Raleigh

Last night was Mom's birthday. Sometimes the group doesn't work, and people wander off after eating, but last night it was good, and everyone remained seated for hours afterward. At one point, out of nowhere, Mom told Lisa that she wasn't the first person on earth to do it in the backseat of a car. "You won't be the last either," she said.

February 24, 1983
Raleigh

A joke I heard:

Q. Why don't Haitians take baths?
A. They'd rather wash up onshore.

May 26, 1983
Raleigh

All day I worked for Dean and didn't notice until I got to the IHOP that my hands and forearms were smeared with walnut stain. It looked awful, like I'd been fisting someone. When the waitress came, I leaned forward and hid my arms under the table. On returning home, I noticed that my apartment smells like cat urine.

June 5, 1983
Raleigh

Last night on my way to the IHOP I was pulled over by a Pontiac with three high black guys in it. They said they were selling pot and asked if I was a cop.

"I sure am," I said, at which point three of the four car doors opened. Were they going to run or beat me up? I wondered.

I said I was only kidding—"Do I look like a cop to you?"—and the guy in the front passenger seat held up a small bag of pot he wanted $15 for.

Something felt wrong, so I said no. It's probably not a good idea to buy drugs in the middle of the street. If they'd taken my money and driven off, I really couldn't have complained to anyone.

June 26, 1983
Raleigh

I spent last night with Ferris, a UNC student who once shot and killed someone who was breaking into his house. He was fifteen at the time and said that the rifle blew a hole right through the burglar's chest. I don't know if he was telling the truth, but either way it was strange. Ferris was chunky, with a handsome face. This morning he called his mother—collect. She has two houses and is buying him a condominium in Chapel Hill. We had sex five times, and he stayed for coffee.

June 27, 1983
Raleigh
I went to the Winn-Dixie and was heading across the parking lot in the direction of home when four black people in a car beckoned me over. They were two young couples, one up front and the other in the back. "Hey," the girl in the front said, "you look like Al Pacino."

July 1, 1983
Raleigh
This is Friday. I worked hard all week and have paid my rent and bills. There is $60 left over, so I can't complain. After coming home, I listened to the radio and cleaned up a little. A woman on *All Things Considered* wrote a book of advice called *If You Want to Write* and mentioned the importance of keeping a diary. It was valuable, she said, because after a while you'd stop being forced and pretentious and become honest and unafraid of your thoughts.

All week Dean and I have been talking about school—a graduate program for him and undergrad for me. I wrote to the School of the Art Institute of Chicago and asked for a catalog. It's a small step, but at least it's something. I've only been to Chicago once. It was in 1978. I was taking a bus to Oregon and had just enough time during our stopover to run to the museum and buy postcards.

July 12, 1983
Raleigh
Susan comes back August 1, so I've started looking for a new apartment. The man I met with today, Mr. H., addressed me

as "sport" and showed me a dark, trashy place on Edenton Street. When I commented on how small it was, he suggested I erect a sheet of plywood in the hall and expand a little. "Or you can talk to the old gal across from you. She don't use her parlor much and might probably let you sit in there sometimes."

The woman he was referring to heard Mr. H.'s voice and stepped out to talk to him. She is small, less than five feet tall, an American Indian perhaps, and it seems she is going to court next week. "I'm just worried my previous felony might be held against me."

"You tell Curtis for me that if he testifies against you, I'll kick his mama out of here so fast it'll make her head spin," Mr. H. said. "'Cause I ain't putting up with no shit or no trash."

Shit was Mr. H.'s favorite word, and he used it fourteen times before I stopped counting. "Shit, you could just move the bed into the kitchen." "Shit, you got a fire escape. Sit out there, why don't you!" "Shit, get yourself some plywood and a couple of cinder blocks and you can fix that right up."

The apartment I looked at has a sign on the door reading WARNING, THE PERSON LIVING HERE HAS A GUN AND WILL USE IT.

I told Mr. H. I'm still looking at places, and he shook my hand, saying, "So long, Bo."

There are three vacancies in the Vance Apartments, also on Edenton Street. I noticed the empty windows and called the Realtor for an appointment. Only weird gay people, old ladies, and drunks live at the Vance. It's scandalous, and the one-bedrooms go for $220 a month. That means that with bills, etc., I'll have to put aside $60 a week, which is almost $10 a day.

August 3, 1983
Raleigh

It's taking me a while to adjust to the new apartment. I'm on a corner, so there's traffic noise and more pedestrians than I'm used to. Last night I was sanding one of the sculptures for my SECCA show. It was dark outside, and two black men yelled something up to me. I didn't want to get into anything, so I pretended I couldn't hear them. Five minutes later there was someone at my door. I opened it, and it was the two guys who had yelled. They thought I was painting the apartment and asked if it was for rent.

The two looked to be in their late thirties. I told them that the apartment was mine but that there were other vacancies. One of the men started to ask if he could look at my place. What stopped him, most likely, was how suspicious it sounded, but I said, "Sure, come on in." I was happy to have visitors, and after a tour I wrote down the name of the realty company, wondering as I did so whether or not they allowed blacks. They can't say they don't, of course, but in the short time I've been here I haven't noticed any black people coming or going. They're really not free to live where they want in this town.

August 13, 1983
Raleigh

This afternoon a woman knocked on my door and asked if there were any rooms to rent. She was missing her front teeth and had a duffel bag over her shoulder. I'm not sure why she chose my door to knock on. Why climb up to the second floor? Why not ask one of the people forever hanging out on the front stoop?

August 26, 1983
Emerald Isle

Paul and I went out swimming yesterday. The current was strong, and I realized after a few minutes that I could no longer touch the bottom. He was farther out than I was, and the harder we swam toward the shore, the farther away we seemed to get. "Try harder!" I yelled.

"Fuck you!" Paul yelled back.

Both of us started to panic after that. I thought of him drowning and of how much trouble I'd be in. I could almost picture it, heaped on top of the grief I'd be feeling. I grabbed him then, and we both gave it all we had and were eventually washed ashore. It was terrifying.

August 30, 1983
Raleigh

The woman next door seems to be moving out. Apparently there was a big fight while I was at the beach and the police were called. Bessie told me this. "Those two was having a free-for-all," she said, meaning, I guess, the woman and her boyfriend. She added that the woman had two dogs that would shit in the apartment. "Then she'd pick up the turds and toss them out the window," Bessie said.

September 22, 1983
Raleigh

Last night the neighbors had a huge fight. The woman, who it seems did *not* move out, is obese with red hair. She works at a pool hall and lives with a thin, trashy man who's around my age. They hold hands a lot on the street and use the phone at Watkins Grill because they don't have one of their own.

Their argument started at midnight. I was up working, so I put a glass against the wall. The woman was slurring and yelling about him running around with a hussy—such an old-fashioned word. Apparently he can't hold down a job and spends his days drinking, doing drugs, and watching TV. They haven't made love in three days. She won't let him because all he wants is to get his rocks off. "You want to climb on and climb off, but I'm a lovin' kind of woman."

He said she's nothing but a cocktease, and when she brought up the hussy again he called her a fat whore.

"Am not."

"Are too."

"Am not."

"Are too."

"Am not."

"Are too."

Then he said that at least he knows who his father is. "Your mother was just a whore like you."

"No, *your* mother was a whore."

"No, yours was."

"No, yours was."

She called him a sorry son of a bitch and then he threw her against the wall I had my glass against. When he then walked into the other room, she went berserk, shouting, "Hussy!" Doors were slammed, things broke. I'd have called the police if I'd had a phone, but it hasn't been connected yet.

Bessie told me this goes on all the time. They fight and then the police are called. A few weeks ago he was led away in handcuffs, but the next day he was back. I guess it's just their way.

October 3, 1983
Raleigh
At the mailbox this afternoon I met Faye, the heavy woman next door with the red hair. She asked if I had change for a

quarter, and while I went through my pockets she asked if I knew anyone who had a phone. She said she needed to call her daddy, so I let her in.

When Faye got no answer, she asked if she could try again later. Then she said that if I needed any furniture, just holler because she and her boyfriend, Vic, have a whole lot. A few minutes later she returned with a woman who's even bigger than she is. The friend had knocked on my door yesterday and asked if Johnny was here.

"I'm afraid I don't know any Johnny," I told her.

It turns out Faye has a cat as well, a Siamese named Tiki. She saw Neil when she was using the phone and asked if I'd be interested in having the two of them mate. On her way out, she told me that she has two beautiful daughters that Social Services has taken. She hasn't seen them since December 24, but if she and Vic are good, she can maybe get them back. "The woman in one oh three is a hussy," Faye said. "She's forty-one, but I'm just twenty-nine and had never been in jail in my life until last year." She asked if I'd make some puppets for her beautiful daughters and told me that while she was out the other day, Vic had the hussy right there in their bed. To get him back she also made love with someone in the exact same spot. Last Friday she cut Vic, and the police arrived while she still had the knife in her hand. "I threw it under the bed," she told me. "He beats me up sometimes. I have bruises, but don't you never call the police on us. We're not allowed to get into trouble."

October 4, 1983
Raleigh

Faye's friend came at seven thirty to use the phone. She's short and fat and has a tattoo on her left shoulder. Halter tops show it off, so she always wears one, regardless of the weather. The friend has buckteeth and wears a lot of jewelry. I was busy and didn't want her using my phone, but she said it was an emergency. I'm thinking I need to put a note on my door, though I'm not sure what it will say.

October 6, 1983
Raleigh

Since moving downtown I've been going to Jimmy's Market, which is four blocks from my apartment. I mainly shop for little things. I got cat food, beer, and a pack of cigarettes there late this afternoon and was walking my bike toward home when three men spread across the sidewalk and blocked my path. They were older, in their forties and fifties. Poorly dressed. "Hey, white boy," one of them said. "Give me a cigarette."

I had a freshly lit one in my hand and was proceeding around them when one of the men came from behind and grabbed my shoulder. Meanwhile, another guy planted himself in front of my bike. "Go any further and I'll beat the shit out of you." He said that he should take my grocery bag and smack me over the head with it. "What do you think of that?"

The man wore an army shirt and a stocking cap. His lower teeth were brown and worn down to nubs. He had my bike by the handlebars while his friends stood just behind me. There was no one ahead of me on the sidewalk. There was no traffic. "Goddamn it," the man said. "I tole you to give me a cigarette."

I said nothing, and he called me a sissy white boy—three times. He said he should knock my sissy teeth down my throat, that he would too.

I looked at him, expecting to get hit and wondering if I might actually lose a few teeth. Then I'd be one of those guys who lives in the Vance Apartments and is missing some teeth—I'd belong there. It never occurred to me that I'd win the fight. I haven't hit anyone since the third grade, while this guy looked to have been doing it all his life. Plus he had backup, which he kept looking at over my shoulders.

"I'm going to fuck up this bike," the man said. He tightened his grip on the handlebars, and I thought that maybe I could buy Julia's old three-speed from Katherine. I was wondering if she'd maybe just give it to me when the man threw back his head and spat in my face. He did it a second and third time, but nothing came out, just a sound, *ptoooo*. I guess he was dehydrated from a day of drinking.

As the spit was running down my forehead, I saw a black woman walking toward us. As she neared, I took my bike from between the man's legs and went around him, not riding but walking it. From behind I heard the guy calling me a sissy white boy and telling me to stay out of his way. I took a drag off my cigarette, still not riding, as that would give him satisfaction. Instead I walked, spit on my face, feeling victorious. He'd demanded a cigarette and I didn't give it to him. So doesn't that make me the winner?

October 15, 1983
Raleigh
Last night was the reception for my SECCA show. I wore a new shirt and a black jacket and combed my hair. Lots of people came, and I went outside twice to smoke pot. Though I was high, the show still looked good to me. It was a solid year of work. Now the party's over and both Neil and I are feeling sick.

October 26, 1983
Raleigh
I went to Capital Camera this afternoon to buy slide jackets

and talk to Mrs. P., the wife of the owner. She's from Smith-field and told me that her husband suffers from high blood pressure. "His medication is thirty dollars a month!" she said.

Mrs. P. is very Southern. She calls everyone "honey" and wears half-glasses attached to a chain around her neck. The front door used to be open all the time, but now it's locked and gets unlocked only when customers come—people like Dr. R., who came to drop off the film he'd shot in Europe. He told Mrs. P. that his wife had gotten sick in Paris, and Mrs. P. said she knows all about sickness. "My husband has high blood pressure, and the medication is costing us thirty dollars per month!"

Then she said that she was robbed last week. It seemed she'd forgotten to lock the door, and when she turned around a man put his hands around her neck and demanded all her money. She said she couldn't believe this was happening to her and that she called him "sir."

"I told him he was welcome to all the money and that I hoped he spent it wisely." After she emptied the cash drawer, he asked for a cord or something he could use to tie her up with. "I promised him that if he let me be, I wouldn't call the police," she said. "So he didn't tie me up and I didn't call them."

"But why?" I asked.

"Because I promised."

"Can't there be an exception?" I asked. "I mean, do you really have to keep every single promise you make?"

She said no but that he could have returned or sent one of his friends to rough her up. "I considered calling a private company and having them dust my neck for fingerprints, but I looked in the Yellow Pages and didn't find any such business," she said.

November 4, 1983
Raleigh

I washed walls at Tracy's today. Meanwhile, her maid Julia scrubbed the floors. Julia lives in the Washington Terrace apartments and will not put up with any mess from the people she works for. "It's not worth the fuss," she told me. "I will not babysit, and I will be paid extra for holidays, including Labor Day and Memorial Day."

After Tracy left, Julia called a number of people on the phone. To one person she described a man she had seen wearing a built-up shoe. "No, girl," she said to the woman she was talking to, who apparently had questions about it, "you got to have a thing like that made special, and no, you do not got one foot tinier than the other."

On Thursdays Julia works for the people who live next door to Tracy, a couple with a dog named Domino, who was not in his outdoor pen today. "You think he ran away?" she asked ten or so times before knocking on the couple's door and hearing him bark on the other side of it.

Aside from working for Tracy, Julia and I have WPTF radio in common. We both listen to *Open Line* and agreed that Barbara needs to start putting some of her callers in their place.

November 19, 1983
Raleigh

On Thursday I was accepted into the School of the Art Institute of Chicago and on Friday I received insurance and housing information. I'll leave Raleigh on January 2. It hasn't really hit me yet, all the work I have to do before I go. Leaving. I am leaving.

"What's David up to?"

"Didn't you hear? He left and moved to Chicago!"

103

December 26, 1983
Raleigh
This is my twenty-seventh birthday. I've been anticipating this age for a long time, thinking that when I reach it, I'll make a big change. I seem old to me now.

The Amtrak station is not answering their phone, which is a problem because I'm supposed to pay for my ticket today. My reservation will be canceled if I don't do something fast. I've thrown out a lot these past few weeks and have packed most everything else for storage.

December 28, 1983
Raleigh
This was my last night at the IHOP. I've been going steadily since 1979, just drinking coffee and reading. On my way out tonight I said good-bye to my waitress and left a $2 tip. I didn't cry, though I worried I might.

Also today I got a real winter coat, boots, socks, and gloves. The coat is down and super-ugly. I never thought I'd see the day that I'd wear a down coat. Gretchen came with me. Then I went and paid $183 for my train ticket. I liked the woman at the station and felt bad for hating her so hard the other day when she wasn't answering the phone.

1984

January 6, 1984
Chicago, Illinois

Now I am in Chicago. Everyone came to the train station in Raleigh and saw me off. It was bitterly cold, and I cried as we pulled away and I saw Mom and Joe and Sharon and Dean and Katherine and the Parkers all waving. At the DC station I bought a Coke from a vending machine that talked. That was a first.

My three days visiting Allyn in Pittsburgh were a blur— smoked a lot of pot, snorted a good deal of cocaine, which never really agrees with me.

Tonight was a reception for new students in the dining area of the Art Institute. There was wine and cheese and people in uniforms who emptied the ashtrays. I'm not as hysterical as I thought I might be and am having a good time looking around. Visited the post office and the big main library and the conservatory of music, where Ned Rorem went. I am be-side myself. On leaving the reception tonight, I saw a man sitting on a stool. He'd removed his artificial legs, which were lying on the ground beside him. What a place!

January 10, 1984
Chicago

I looked at four apartments today, the best being 820 West Cuyler. It's a short street, and everyone in the building is from Mexico or Central America. There's trash in the courtyard and on the landings, but the rent is only $190. The living room / bedroom ceiling is covered with plastic to catch the falling plaster. The floors are collaged with different patterns of linoleum, but the bathroom's OK. There are plenty of windows and a kitchen big enough to do all my work in. Best of all, it's eight blocks from an IHOP that looks exactly like the one I left behind in Raleigh, both inside and out.

January 15, 1984
Chicago
After looking at sixteen apartments, some so small I could heat them with a candle and a few that were roommate situations, I came back to 820 West Cuyler. George, the super, told me I can take up the linoleum if I want and remove the flimsy wall that divides the main room in half. The closet's big, and he will replaster the ceiling.

While cleaning it, I found lots of matches, a cap, and a rat-trap. The last tenants left behind a sofa I'll be getting rid of and a framed picture of Jesus spreading his arms as wide as they will go. There are roach eggs everywhere, and the place stinks of pesticide.

January 17, 1984
Chicago
Because I'm basically starting from scratch, I have to take a number of core classes. These are 2-D (basic drawing), 3-D (basic sculpture), and 4-D, which can be video or performance or whatever the teacher, whose name is Ken Shorr, wants. Our first assignment from him is to collect overheard sentences and shape them into a dialogue. Then we're to find a scrap of something measuring four by five feet and slap a

word or image on it. This is right up my alley, and I've already started on it. My scrap will be some of the linoleum I've ripped off my living-room floor.

Ken said that school is one of the few places—perhaps the only place—where we'll find people who are interested in what we have to say. He's sort of a pessimist that way. Before class, I looked him up and learned he was in the Whitney Biennial. I wanted to ask what he'd done to get there, but I had already talked too much in 2-D and 3-D and didn't want to exhaust everybody.

January 22, 1984
Chicago

I pulled up all the linoleum, got rid of the extra wall in the living room, and have started painting the kitchen. Last night, after finishing the cabinets, I went to the little market around the corner for beer and found $45 on the floor in front of the checkout counter. I thought I'd dropped it, and by the time I discovered it wasn't mine, I was back home. First thing today I went out and blew it. I bought:

1. two pounds of goat meat
2. more beer
3. *Fires* by Raymond Carver
4. the *New York Review of Books*
5. hardware
6. groceries
7. a magazine called *Straight to Hell* in which gay men recount true sexual experiences, many of them outdoors and in cars or under bridges

February 13, 1984
Chicago

I sanded the living-room floor and put the first coat of polyurethane on it before leaving for school this morning. At five I returned to find a group of kids playing in the hall. When I unlocked my door they rushed in behind me and ran all over the place. None of them speak English, so I had to scold them in Spanish, which made them laugh.

I can't believe how good my apartment looks now. I've been sleeping in the big closet and will probably continue to do so. That way I can keep the living room completely empty, not a thing in it.

February 20, 1984
Chicago

There's a radio show I've started listening to that's hosted by a woman named Phyllis Levy. People phone in and discuss their sexual experiences—it's fantastic. Last night Debbie called saying that she and her boyfriend spent the weekend experimenting with a vibrator. She came four times—a first. "It was wild!" she said.

Phyllis seemed genuinely happy for both Debbie and her boyfriend. Then Jill called to discuss a fantasy situation, and Frank reminisced about a recent three-way with his ex-girlfriend and the guy she's now seeing. Next came Sue. Her parents are divorced, and during a visit with her dad last week, he came to her bed in the middle of the night and the two of them made love. That was the term she used, *made love.*

Phyllis explained that this is what we call an "incest situation." She was clearly disturbed and suggested that Sue might want to date men who were not related to her. Then Laurie called to say she'd just done the dinner dishes dressed in a negligee. She stopped to answer the phone and returned to find her husband, completely naked, scrubbing the bottoms of the pans. It was, she said, "a real turn-on."

Phyllis was happy for her and spoke briefly about the element of surprise. The program airs on Sunday nights and reminds me every week that I'm not in North Carolina anymore.

February 27, 1984
Chicago

Again last night I listened to *Let's Get Personal* on Q101. The first hour is hosted by a woman who's interested in general problems and miserabilia. She has numbers for various suicide-prevention hotlines and places where people can report child abuse, etc. The next hour, and my favorite, is hosted by Phyllis Levy, who started off by speaking to a man who was born in India. He said that small insects were thriving in his girlfriend's pubic forest—that's how he described it. He was worried that she'd been unfaithful and that these creatures were a sign of that.

Irene called, upset that her brother had started wearing women's clothing. Phyllis calmly explained that this is what we call cross-dressing. It doesn't mean Irene's brother is gay, she said. Plenty of cross-dressers marry and have children. "Is that what's bothering you?" she asked.

Irene said no, the trouble is that her brother is taking all her and her mother's clothes and that they haven't got a single bra or pair of panties left.

The solution, Phyllis said, was to put a lock on her bedroom door and offer to take her brother out shopping.

When Brian, the premature ejaculator, phoned in, Phyllis suggested he try an exercise called "the quiet vagina." Another solution was to masturbate before sex so as to calm his penis down a little. She really has all the answers, Phyllis does.

March 16, 1984
Chicago
There's a big argument going on next door in Spanish. I can make out two words: *whore* and *shoe*. Two men are yelling at the woman. Someone has been slapped. On the ground in front of the building are a number of broken things that seem to have been thrown out the window. Clothes and hangers, a cabbage, mayonnaise.

March 24, 1984
Chicago
Last night I saw a woman drag a teenage boy out of the Sheridan "L" Lounge. She was maybe in her forties and kept slapping the kid across the face. "How many times do I got to tell you to stay out of there?" she asked. "It's trouble." Every so often she'd pause from smacking him and sign something with her hands. He responded with a noise rather than words. That's when I realized he was deaf.

When the slapping stopped, she grabbed the kid's ear and twisted it. Like a dog being beaten by his master, he did not fight back but just took it. A couple of people watching heckled the woman. "Leave him alone!" they shouted.

She shouted back that they should mind their own business. She called them trash, and in response they laughed at her.

March 26, 1984
Chicago
Betty Carter is perfection. They just played her version of "What's New" on the radio. It's on her latest record, and I think I'll buy it for Dad. Female jazz vocalists are just about the only things we agree on. When good music would come on the radio at home, he used to call me into the living room

and make me sit still until the song was over, saying as it played, "Are you *listening* to this? My God!"

April 8, 1984
Chicago
There was a severely handicapped guy at the IHOP tonight. He was with two men and a woman, and I watched as one of the men spooned ice cream into his mouth. Everyone involved was black. The guy in the wheelchair could not talk; he could only moan. I couldn't tell what it meant, though: Was he in pain? Was he unhappy? It sounded like he was being tortured—horrible to listen to. The woman kept scolding him and calling him a show-off. She said she would quit taking him to nightclubs if he kept on acting that way. *Does he think the IHOP is a nightclub,* I wondered, *or is she referring to someplace else?*

April 29, 1984
Chicago
At night in warm weather, the courtyard of my building is crowded with children jumping rope and playing various games. They'd bashed in a piñata while I was at the IHOP, and I returned to find bits of it all over the ground, lying among candy wrappers. This afternoon I was working, and when someone knocked on the door, I answered wearing a hideous rubber mask I'd brought back from Raleigh. I'd assumed a kid had come around, but instead it was the man down the hall, who asked for a cigarette.

April 30, 1984
Chicago
The woman next door came, asking for a cigarette. Four minutes later she sent her daughter to ask for another one. The

next time I just won't answer. All day long I fend off people who want my cigarettes. It's not right that I should lose the battle in my very own home.

May 24, 1984
Chicago
Last night Neil caught another mouse. It was two a.m. and I was in the kitchen working. After presenting it to me, she set the mouse down. He was still alive, and she pounced on him when he tried to make a run for it. She batted the poor thing about, and after a while I started feeling sorry for him. "You're being cruel," I said. "Put yourself in his shoes, why don't you?" I picked her up, and the mouse ran into a hole under the radiator. Looking back, I shouldn't have gotten involved. I went to bed then, and she stayed up to sulk.

May 30, 1984
Chicago
Edith Sitwell said that one of her favorite pastimes was to sharpen her claws on the wooden heads of her opponents.

June 14, 1984
Chicago
I met with a guy named Harry, who's started a refinishing business. I'd hoped I was done with chemical stripper, but he's offering $5 an hour and we'll be working in people's houses rather than in a garage. The interview was held at Harry's apartment, a big clean place, nicely decorated but with the TV on. His wife was at work, and after asking me a few questions, he offered me a beer. Then he rolled a joint, and I thought, *Great, I've found a job.*

June 25, 1984
Chicago
I found a letter on the ground near the neighborhood McDonald's. It reads:

What I think about my mother

My mother is a bitch.
Motherfucker shitty ass.
Haffer goddamn nigger sucker she raisin' witch. Shit.

signed Charlene Moore

June 30, 1984
Chicago
At work Harry told me about his brother Bob, who died a few years ago at the age of twenty-six. Bob had bad luck. He was an epileptic, and a seizure he once had while driving caused a ten-car pileup. Later he fell down some stairs and broke both his legs. Finally he was hit by a train while walking, which is strange because trains don't generally sneak up on people. For the most part, barring a derailment, you know exactly where to find them.

All that was left intact after he was run over were his hands.

August 13, 1984
Chicago
Ken Shorr, the guy I had for 4-D, called a few days ago and asked if I'd be interested in being in a play he wrote. I haven't acted since high school, but it'll be just the two of us and he is terribly funny. I went to his place last night and met his wife and newborn son. They didn't have any ashtrays, so I used a

plate. We talked, and he gave me a script I brought home and read. I already have the first page memorized. I play his father.

August 15, 1984
Chicago
Tiffany was rushed to the hospital in New York the night before last. It turned out she was four months pregnant and the baby was growing in her fallopian tube rather than in her womb. It's called an ectopic pregnancy, and she knew nothing about it until she started hemorrhaging. "Do you have any questions?" the doctor asked before he performed the operation to extract the fetus.

And in a weak voice Tiffany said, "Yes. When can I have sex again?"

You really have to hand it to her sometimes.

August 26, 1984
Chicago
Tiffany's been home for two weeks, and Mom can't take it anymore. Last night they had a fight and pulled each other's hair. Tiffany is twenty-one now. Mom called to tell me about it and to offer me $300 to spend on school clothes. Three hundred dollars!

August 30, 1984
Chicago
Tonight at the IHOP two men were hostile to Lisa the waitress. They had ordered hamburgers and kept pestering her as to their whereabouts. Were those them, under the heat lamp? They better not be!

The men were gay, a couple. Both were in their fifties and one had a mustache. Lisa gave them some lip and they stormed out. I was at the register when one of them returned and told her she could take his hamburger and shove it up her ass. When saying this, he lowered his voice to a whisper and narrowed his eyes.

The two men live near the bowling alley in a basement apartment. I often walk by and see them in there, sometimes lying around in colorful underpants watching TV. Their floor is carpeted and there's a dumbbell in one corner.

September 6, 1984
Chicago
School started, and I had my first writing workshop, taught by a woman named Lynn Koons. There are twenty-five students in the class, and she had us arrange our chairs in a circle. Then she asked us each to recall a vivid image from a dream. *Oh, no,* I thought. *Dreams!*

September 10, 1984
Chicago
Tonight was my first art history class. It's called Artists' Diaries, Journals, and Notebooks. The teacher, Stephen L., explained what we'd be reading and told us we'd have one major paper. I think I might want to do mine on Edmund Wilson, but it's early yet. Before the break we were shown a number of slides, and when we came to a Paul Klee painting, the guy beside me said loudly, "I could do that."

He was wearing a leather jacket, just trying to be funny.

"It's nice to know you think you can paint like that," Stephen L. said. "But I don't really care."

The guy's face turned so red, it actually threw off heat. Now he's branded as the class knucklehead. Between working for Harry, school, and the play, I worry I'll lose my private reading time at the IHOP.

September 15, 1984
Chicago

Harry and I are close to finishing the job on West Armitage. I worked in the living room today, putting tung oil on trim and talking to the painter, Mr. Johnston, who is forty-seven and has nine children and six grandchildren. He's black and wore white pants with no shirt. Mr. Johnston has a huge stomach and told me that he has all kinds of girlfriends. "You don't need to be young or handsome," he said. "You just got to know the secret to unlock a woman's mind."

The secret, I learned, is "Hit 'em."

"The harder you do it, the harder they'll love you," he said. "A woman will always crawl back after a good beating."

He invited me to listen while he called one of his girlfriends on the phone. "Listen here, Joyce," he told her. "I want you to bring that pussy of yours to Milwaukee and Cicero at ten o'clock tonight."

He said the secret is to talk shit because ladies love it—that and beatings. The front door was off the hinges, and when a woman came up the stairs, Mr. Johnston turned to me and winked, as if to say, *Watch this.*

"I'll have to paint your apartment next," he said to her as she passed. "Maybe we can work out a deal." When the woman smiled politely, he stuck out his tongue and made a quick licking gesture. She was in her late twenties and was carrying a bag of groceries from an expensive store. She was dressed in a suit and was so clearly not a prostitute, it was ridiculous. The woman entered the apartment across the hall, and after she had closed the door behind her, Mr. Johnston told me he had her in the palm of his hand, that she was his for the taking. As he said this, I heard three clicks—one lock after another being secured. That's how interested she was.

September 25, 1984
Chicago

There was a long line at the Sheridan L station ticket window this morning. It was raining and I was carrying a big bag with paint and brushes in it. Off to the side of the booth, a black woman stood talking to a policeman. She was in her twenties, maybe, and plump. Her clothes were plain and she was pointing at a man who was standing nearby and calling him a motherfucker. She said it three times, and her voice got progressively louder. She told the cop that she had to get to school, that it started at nine, and that he, the cop, was making her late.

When she tried joining the ticket line, the officer grabbed her. She broke free, and he trapped her in a corner and held his arms out to block her. "I didn't do anything wrong!" she yelled. "I didn't do nothing and I gots to get to school."

The cop twisted her arm, and she kicked him and made a break for the turnstile. I guess her plan was to squeeze in underneath it, but she was too big. The cop grabbed her again, and this time she bit him. "Somebody help me!" she yelled. Again she went for the turnstile, thinking—what, exactly—that once on the other side, she'd be home free?

The cop pulled out his walkie-talkie and recited a code. The young woman was hysterical by this time. Maybe she'd done nothing wrong. What did we know? The line moved more quickly once he got her cornered again. From up on the platform, we could still hear her screaming that she didn't do nothing, that she had to get to school, that she just wanted to be left alone.

October 28, 1984
Chicago

The first night of the play, back in the dressing room, Ken and

I drank a pint of Scotch. The second night it was vodka. He was a nervous wreck both times, but then, he wrote the script and was responsible in a way I wasn't. We had never performed for more than three people and weren't sure where the laughs might come. Plus we'd rehearsed for so long, we'd forgotten certain things were funny. Both shows were sold out, and hopefully they'll be next Friday and Saturday as well.

December 7, 1984
Chicago

There's a woman in my writing class named T. who was pregnant at the start of the quarter and had her baby a few weeks ago. Every so often over the past few months, she'd make a comment, but she's never read any of her writing out loud. I can't help but think she was drunk or stoned today. She said out of nowhere that she would like her story read and that Rose would be the one to do it. "I'm tired of hearing all this average stuff," she told us. "It's time for something good."

Rose started and was stopped by T. a few seconds into it. "You didn't give people time to relax," T. said, slurring her words a bit.

The story, when Rose finally got to it, was about a young woman dressing for a lesbian party. She has recently decided she is attracted to women and wears jeans and cowboy boots. Once dressed, she leaves the house. The end.

T. was angry that the story wasn't longer. "It seemed longer when I wrote it," she said. Then she blamed Rose for reading too quickly and making it sound less substantial. She told the class that she herself is a lesbian and that none of us could relate because we're all afraid to confront our gayness.

People in the class looked at one another, not knowing what to say. The women weren't too keen to learn they were all insecure lesbians masquerading as heterosexuals.

T. criticized people who think realism is using the word *shit*. She went on and on until someone told her to shut up. Then she put her head on her desk and fell asleep. She even snored.

December 25, 1984
Raleigh
For Christmas I received:

> *The Joy of Cooking*
> *Family Dancing* by David Leavitt
> six pairs of underpants
> a shirt from Gretchen
> Fiestaware salt-and-pepper shakers
> a box of pastels
> $2 in cash
> a check for $125

December 28, 1984
Raleigh
Amy, Tiffany, and I sat in the kitchen and talked until three thirty this morning. One of the things we laughed about was an old episode of *The Newlywed Game*. The host asked the wives, "What's the most exotic place you've ever made love?" He was likely expecting "The kitchen" or "On a tennis court at night," but one woman didn't quite understand the question and answered, "In the butt."

1985

January 9, 1985
Raleigh

Since I've been home for Christmas vacation, Paul has been leaving notes on the kitchen counter that say *Please wake me up at 7:30. Signed, David.*

Last night Mom made lemon tarts for dessert. Paul took an empty shell and filled it with cold mashed potatoes. Then he topped it with whipped cream and fooled me with it. Mom is making him put down a $20 deposit every time he takes her car.

January 10, 1985
Raleigh

Amy and I went from her apartment to the A&P. It was late, and as we walked back through the parking lot to the car, an old woman approached and asked us for a ride home. Her name was Eunice, and she settled into the backseat, saying, "Don't worry, baby. I ain't gonna sit on your tapes."

On our way to her place she pointed out landmarks—the Johnsons' house, for instance. She told us that for years she worked as their housekeeper but lost the job when she had to go to New York and check on some furniture.

Eunice said we looked like nice people. That's why she'd asked us for a ride.

"You look nice too," we said. And she promised us that she was.

When we dropped her off, Eunice told us that we should come back in the summertime and visit her. She pointed to a space in her dark yard and told us that in warm weather that's where we could find her, sitting under the yum-yum tree.

February 1, 1985
Chicago

There is a blind black fellow who comes into the IHOP once a week and has a friend who is also blind. Neither of them wears dark glasses, and one of them speaks very formally. Tonight a Bill Withers song came over the sound system, and the one guy said to the other, "It may interest you to know that we can expect a new LP from this gentleman in the near future."

When his chicken arrived, the waitress, Barbara, cut it up for him.

February 8, 1985
Chicago

There was a man at the IHOP tonight who had on two hats at the same time. The base was a stocking cap, and over it was a red floppy thing a woman might wear to a garden party. The waitress, Mary, ignored the guy at first. Then she took his order but made him pay in advance. He wanted coffee with his eggs, and when, after ten minutes or so, he still hadn't gotten it and asked politely when it might arrive, Mary snapped at him and said that she was busy, OK? It made me uncomfortable to watch her be so rude.

Had she had trouble with him in the past? Did it have anything to do with his two hats?

February 16, 1985
Chicago

Tonight I saw police and an ambulance on the corner of

Irving and Sheridan. There was a man lying on the curb, face-down in the snow. Had he been hit by a car? His shirt and jacket were up above his waist and the crack of his ass was showing. Maybe he was dead. I don't know for certain.

February 24, 1985
Chicago

Mary at the IHOP has been on a rampage lately, throwing people out left and right. Tonight two men walked in and she pointed to the door, saying, "Beat it!" One of the guys was thin and the other was obese and wore a V-neck sweater that wasn't long enough to cover his stomach. The thin fellow wore glasses and had been thrown out before.

"You can't discriminate against us," he said. Then he asked for Mary's name.

She refused to give it, and he said he knew the owners of all the IHOP restaurants in America. He said he'd write a letter and she could kiss her job good-bye. Adios.

Mary said that would be fine by her, and when the men took a step closer, two cops seated at a rear table intervened and told them that they had to leave.

"Yeah," Mary said to the larger of the two men, "get the hell out of here, fatso."

July 10, 1985
Chicago

The meal on my flight back from Raleigh was a kind of Oriental barbecue. Across the aisle were two men who complained about having to sit in the back of the plane. They said it was unfair that the niggers got to sit in the front. One of the men had three bourbon and waters. Before we landed, the stewardesses used pincers to hand out hot towels that smelled like they'd been steamed in a dishwasher.

July 28, 1985
Chicago

Odd family at the IHOP tonight. A big, loud husband who announced when he came in that his wife was pregnant and needed some pancakes. Barbara came to take his order and he gave her the once-over. "Looking good, looking good!" He put an arm around his young son and said that eating dinner with his family was one of the greatest joys of a man's life.

My favorite couple sat not far away. They're old, and it took me months to figure out if they were a man and a woman or two women. Now I know that they're brother and sister. The two are very kind and always ask after Barbara's health. Tonight the brother ordered chocolate chip pancakes. Then he picked up the syrup and asked if you pour it over the top, as if he'd never seen a pancake before.

The family man, meanwhile, called out for more butter.

"I've got some here I'm not using," the old brother said. "Needless to say, you probably wouldn't want to eat off someone else's plate. It's clean, though. I haven't touched it."

"That's OK," the family man said. It was interesting how he changed over the course of the meal. As they left he scolded his wife for leaving a big tip. Then he turned to his young son and said, "She just loves to throw my fucking money away."

July 29, 1985
Chicago

Tiffany has moved in with a piano player named Mike. They're living in Queens and selling cocaine to make money. Before this she worked at Macy's for a Belgian chocolate company. I think hers is what you call a checkered career.

August 17, 1985
Chicago

I saw an interview with one of the few surviving passengers of the Delta Flight 191 crash—a woman. She had been visiting with a friend in the smoking section when they went down. Being in the back of the plane saved her life. On the news, she said, "I'm going to start smoking and stop flying." She had a cigarette in her hand and was holding it awkwardly, like the beginner she is.

August 26, 1985
Phoenix, Arizona

Ted's mother is in love with Lorne Greene and has watched all of his television programs, even *Battlestar Galactica*. Now she lives from one Alpo commercial to the next.

Here are a few of the Yellow Pages listings under *Cactus:*

Cactus Camera
Cactus Carpet
Cactus Car Wash
Cactus Catering
Cactus Candy Company
Cactus Chemical Company
Cactus Animal Hospital
Cactus Beverage
Cactus Vending
Cactus Preschool
Cactus Air-Conditioning
Cactus Wren Party Goods
Cactus Wren Mobile Park
Cactus Wren Drain & Sewage

September 8, 1985
Chicago
The woman we've started refinishing woodwork for keeps a
load of reading materials in a basket beside the toilet. These
include *Crochet Fantasy, Charisma* ("For Dynamic Spirit-
Filled Living"), *Medical Abstracts Newsletter, Farm Computer News,* and *Jackpotunities.*

On the street, a prostitute in a jean jacket asked if I wanted
a good date. I'm always amazed when they mistake me for a
straight man.

Tonight at the IHOP I overheard Mary talking to a policeman. She started by saying that she hates Africans. They're
demanding, she claimed, and they don't know how to drive.
She said that she stands behind South Africa and hopes they
do not change their policies. She's maybe thirty, Mary, short
and pretty with an athletic walk.

September 9, 1985
Chicago
Ted H. is my painting teacher. He says "Yeah" to mean "Isn't
that so?" and has gray curly hair. At the start of class he said
that no question was a stupid question. So I raised my hand
and asked if we could use part of the room as a smoking section.

He said "No" twice, and several of my fellow students
whispered, "Good." One of these, a woman, was wearing
a smock with the signatures of famous artists printed on it:
Matisse, van Gogh, Rousseau. She had brought four of her
paintings to class, large landscapes, and leaned them beside
one another against the wall.

Later in the afternoon, Ted took us to the museum and

talked about de Kooning. I like how worked up he got. Signature Smock glared at me the entire time we were in the museum, though I don't know why.

October 1, 1985
Chicago
I read a *National Examiner* article about Christina Onassis, who has apparently gone to a weight-reduction farm. She's trying her best, but still they referred to her as a "lardy lass" and, worse still, "that Greek tanker."

October 17, 1985
Chicago
I stayed up all night and worked on my new story. Unfortunately, I write like I paint, one corner at a time. I can never step back and see the whole picture. Instead I concentrate on a little square and realize later that it looks nothing like the real live object. Maybe it's my strength, and I'm the only one who can't see it.

October 20, 1985
Chicago
On Thursday the Cherokee Nation elected their first woman leader. Her name is Wilma Mankiller.

Kim's husband gets his hair cut at a place called Blood, Sweat, and Shears.

October 24, 1985
Chicago
Before leaving school tonight I reexamined the painting of a briefcase I've been working on and got depressed. It looks like it was done by a seventh-grader. At the end of class I

signed it *Vic Stevenson*. That's the name of the motel manager in the story I'm writing. Between now and my critique, I have to come up with some sort of justification for this painting. Ted, the teacher, is one tough customer and will chew me up and spit me back out again if I'm not on top of things.

October 26, 1985
Chicago

In the park I bought dope. There was a bench nearby, so I sat down for a while and took in the perfect fall day. Then I came home and carved the word *failure* into a pumpkin.

October 28, 1985
Chicago

Critiques get depressing when you realize that everyone's just waiting for his or her own turn. It's a monologue as opposed to a dialogue. "All of a sudden I realized that you don't 'arrive' at Milton Avery, you *pass through him*," a landscape painter said today. This was after she'd pulled herself together. Before this, she'd cried. "I don't want to talk about it, I just want to *do* it."

One guy, Will, shook his painting up and down, insisting that it was not a painting of a beer can but an actual beer can. The longer I'm in school, the more exhausting these critiques become. I went overboard, I think, but it wasn't until later, getting high at home, that I realized how embarrassed I should be. After presenting what I called "my line of products," I read out loud something I'd written about the IHOP. Ted said that my paintings are basically signs. "We do not enter their space, they enter ours." That seems about right.

December 5, 1985
Chicago

I ran up the stairs to the L platform this afternoon and reached it just as the train I wanted closed its doors and took off.

"Sorry, but it just left," said a guy who stood not far away, leaning against the railing. "You just missed it."

I nodded, huffing for breath.

"So, can you help me out?" the guy asked.

"Excuse me?"

"I did you a favor, now you do one for me," he said.

"What favor did you do?" I asked.

"Told you about the train," he said.

That's like me telling someone who's standing in the rain that it's raining. I mean, what kind of a favor is that? I told the guy to leave me alone. Then I sat on the bench, and he stood over me, cursing, until the next train arrived.

December 8, 1985
Chicago

Here is the recipe for Kim's spinach soup:

- One 10-ounce package of frozen spinach
- 2 cups water
- 2 cloves garlic, mashed
- $1/5$ box of spaghetti
- Olive oil
- Parmesan cheese

Add water, spinach, and garlic in pot. Cook until spinach is thawed. Add olive oil—enough to cover surface of water. Break the spaghetti up and cook it separately. When it's finished, add it to the olive oil, water, spinach, and garlic combination and top it with grated Parmesan cheese.

December 26, 1985
Raleigh
For Christmas I got:
  a radio/tape player ghetto blaster
  a wristwatch
  a rubber flashlight
  a hat and neck warmer
  socks
  underwear
  a blank tape
  a file
  two rubber stamps
  a lighter that looks like Godzilla
  a blue checkered scarf
  Back in the World, stories by Tobias Wolff
  oil paints
  razors

1986

January 13, 1986
Chicago

I am trying my best not to spend much money. With nothing coming in, I have to clamp down, so at Walgreens I bought a bar of Fiesta brand soap, which is horrible but costs only 20 cents. I used it last night and still smell like one of those deodorizing pucks they put in the urinals at gas stations.

March 2, 1986
Chicago

Tiffany spent the past five days back in Raleigh with an ice pack against the side of her face. She says that a man, a stranger, insulted her on the street in New York. She insulted him back, and he smacked her.

"That's her story, if you want to believe it," Mom said when she called to tell me about it.

Anything could have happened to Tiffany. She has such an adventurous life.

March 3, 1986
Chicago

Folding clothes at the Laundromat last night, I could feel someone at my back, close but not quite touching. It was a black woman eating an apple. She was maybe twenty-three years old, and as I continued with what I was doing, she talked to me. "What days do we eat meat?" she asked.

I thought it was a riddle at first. I mean, who's the "we" here? I told her we eat meat whenever we want to, or can afford to.

"Can we eat meat three times a day?" she asked.

"Sure," I said. "If we feel up to it."

"Where is there a Catholic church?" she asked.

I told her I didn't know, and she said, "You a lie."

Then she went into the bathroom and stayed there until I left. This is a busy week with me and lunatics, whom I tend to see as either signs or messengers.

March 10, 1986
Chicago

This afternoon I was hit over the head by a hammer. I was on my hands and knees, picking up bits of plaster, and shoved aside the ladder I'd left it resting on top of. When it fell, it felt just the way I always imagined it would. I was stunned. Now there's a bleeding lump the size of a small egg on the top of my head. It's what a cartoon character would have, only it's me.

March 14, 1986
Chicago

At the supermarket a man in his sixties was talking to the maintenance worker about the adult bookstore a few doors down. "So you're in there, after paying three or four bucks for tokens and another fifty cents just for walking in the door. Your movie starts and then some guy sticks his dick through a hole in the wall. And what do I want with that, right? It's disgusting, and the tokens are good for only three or four minutes before the screen turns black. Hell, for a few more bucks I could buy the whole stinking movie. Do you see what

I'm talking about? I wouldn't go into the place, but I got a lot of friends there."

March 18, 1986
Chicago

I voted this morning at an elementary school. The children seemed excited to have so many adults around, one of whom, an older gay man in a leather vest, wore a pin that read DIGNITY.

One of the people I voted for this morning was named Lee Botts. Her campaign slogan is HER BOTTOM LINE IS CLEAN WATER. Someone tampered with the sign she had in front of the school, and now it reads LEE BOTTS. HER BOTTOM IS CLEAN.

March 21, 1986
Chicago

On the L I sat next to a black woman studying a textbook. "How's your math?" she asked as I settled in.

I thought she'd said *mouth,* so I said, "Excuse me?"

She pointed to her book. "Algebra. I could use some help with these problems."

Math is my worst subject, so I apologized, then watched as she wrote and scribbled in her margins.

May 6, 1986
Chicago

I found this excellent bit of advice in *The Amy Vanderbilt Complete Book of Etiquette:* "If you start to shake hands with someone who has lost an arm, shake his other hand. If he has lost both arms, shake the tip of his artificial hand (be quick and unembarrassed about it)."

May 7, 1986
Chicago

I went to the airport today to meet Mom and Aunt Joyce, who had a short layover on their way home from Santa Fe. I'm broke but didn't want to say anything about it, didn't want to be too obvious, but then of course I did say something. We had a coffee, and afterward Aunt Joyce pressed $20 into my hand. Mom slipped me two $20s and a $10. Then she gave me a check, and I left the airport cursing and muttering to myself, because I was angry and embarrassed to be twenty-nine and hinting around for money. I make myself sick.

May 10, 1986
Chicago

Man on the bus with a gray beard and a cheap suit: "I'll kick your fucking ass, bitch." He said this to every woman who walked down the aisle. "I'll kick your fucking ass!"

June 1, 1986
Chicago

I went to an Indian restaurant last night with Rick, Jeannie, and a humorless couple they know from Maine who just moved to Chicago. The husband was fine, actually, but his wife, Liza—what a pain. Before moving into their apartment on Addison and Western, they lived in a tepee. She and her husband are macrobiotic. We all met at my apartment, and after I rolled a joint and some of us started smoking, impatient Liza said, "I'm sorry, but can we talk *on the way to* the restaurant?"

Later I asked why she's so unhappy living here, and she said, "It's too involved to get into with you."

It was fun to make her angry and disgusted and watch her roll her eyes.

133

The Indian restaurant we went to was cheap. It only cost $3 to eat, and I laughed when Liza ordered the potato cutlet.

"Is something funny?" she asked.

"It's just the word *cutlet* used for a potato," I said.

While we ate, Indian prom couples paraded up and down the street. They were kids, and they looked great, so sophisticated. We'd just finished when a woman wandered in and approached our table for money. She wore a scarf on her head, pulled down low enough to cover her eyebrows. "Are youse people familiar with this neighborhood?" she asked. "'Cause I'm scared stiff."

This stretch of Devon Avenue, in the thick of an Indian neighborhood, is the last place to be frightened. "I been to the fire station and all over," she said. "I was outside looking at youse people and crying my eyes out."

She rubbed the back of her hands and tugged at her scarf. "See, I got a baby at home and it hasn't eaten all day. I got to get some formula. The guys at the fire station gave me a couple bucks, but let me tell you, I'm scared. The baby has one diaper left and, see, I'm a waitress. I worked four days but don't get my check 'til Tuesday and I got to get some formula. I been right outside this window, crying my eyes out."

The woman was around my age, and while Rick reached for his wallet, she pulled what she said was a birth certificate from her pocket and flashed it for a second. "See, I got a baby. I'm not lying."

I wondered what she'd do if I offered to buy the birth certificate for $20. Not that I would have, it was just an idea, and such a cruel one it made me blush.

June 7, 1986
Chicago
Finally, Amy has moved from Raleigh to Chicago. After she

sat shell-shocked on the couch for a week, looking out the window at the horrible neighborhood I'm now living in, I took her to apply for cocktail-waitressing jobs. One of the places we went to this afternoon was called the Bar Association. We walked in to find the manager sitting at a table and eating a slice of white chocolate cake. "Here," he said, holding out his fork, "try a bite."

We just stood there.

"Aw, don't be like that," he said. "I don't have AIDS or nothing."

We each took a forkful and told him it was good, which seemed to make him happy.

On our way back to the apartment, Amy bought a lottery ticket at Sun Drugs. She asked the woman behind the counter how these things work, and when the woman explained that hundreds of thousands of people play each week, Amy was disappointed. She thought only a handful of people bought tickets and that her odds of winning were one in ten.

June 29, 1986
Chicago

Now that Amy has a job, it's time for her to find a place of her own. This afternoon we answered an ad we'd seen in the *Reader*. Someone named Jerry was looking for a roommate, and we arrived to find a full-grown man with long oily hair. His teeth were amber pegs, like dried corn kernels. "After you called I was going to clean up, but I watched TV instead," he admitted.

Jerry had collages of wrestling stars hanging on his bedroom walls. He told us he'd made them himself, and then he showed us one of Elvis Presley he was working on. He drank from a coffee mug with the word ME on it, and when not holding it he scratched his elbow a lot.

It seems that Jerry's last roommate drove the gas bill up by using the oven all the time. "She was always baking potatoes," he told us. "All hours of the day. One night she put two or three in the oven and then fell asleep. I got up the next morning and those potatoes was baked, roasted, broasted, I don't know what all, but they was burnt and black."

Amy and I laughed, not about the fire hazard but about someone eating nothing but baked potatoes.

Jerry took it seriously, though. The only time he laughed was when talking about a murder that had recently taken place in the neighborhood. "So it turned out that whoever it was, ha-ha, stuffed the body, ha-ha, into a Dumpster."

He gave us a tour. The kitchen table had what looked like molasses spilled on it. In the living room was a suit of armor and a great many books about Vietnam. He has a statue of Buddha and a baseball cap with THE GENERAL written on it. The T-shirt he was wearing read THE FIGHTING SAMOANS.

One thing we noticed was that Jerry was remarkably calm. He spoke very slowly and usually with his eyes on the TV. There were overflowing ashtrays everywhere. Jerry told us that he works with computers and is very successful, so successful he's looking for a roommate to pay half of his $250 per month rent.

We told him we were going to see a few more places but would keep him in mind.

On our way home Amy told me about a girl in her Second City class named Sue, which she spells S-I-O-U-X. Amy was laughing about it at work with a cocktail waitress named Kim, until she discovered the girl had changed the spelling to K-H-Y-M-E.

"Well, sure," Amy said, cornered. "Khyme makes sense, but *Sioux?*"

July 7, 1986
Chicago
Amy and I were downtown, and when it started to pour we ran beneath the awning of an art-supply shop. A woman the age of a grandmother trotted up shortly after we did. She was small, and as she bent to tie her sneakers, we noticed how tiny her feet were.

"What's your shoe size?" Amy asked.

"I'm a one and a half," the woman said. She wasn't bothered by the question but seemed pleased that we had noticed. "I was a war baby," she said. "There were shortages all around." She winked. "That's what I always tell folks. I have to buy all my shoes in the children's department."

We watched as she tied a plastic bonnet over her hair and headed out into the rain.

July 10, 1986
Chicago
This evening I saw a Doberman pinscher with its mouth taped shut. It was a makeshift muzzle, and I bet it really hurts when it gets ripped off. An hour later, Mom called to tell me that Melina, her and Dad's Great Dane, had been stung by bees and taken to an emergency vet. If anything were to happen to that dog, I don't know what my parents would do.

July 18, 1986
Chicago
I saw a bird swoop down this morning and pick up a wad of chewing gum. Later, on the corner of Magnolia and Leland, I saw a drug deal taking place. The seller looked me in the eye as I passed. Later still, I saw a man rifle through a woman's purse on Kenmore. He looked me in the eye as well.

It's Friday, and horribly hot, so after cashing my paycheck

137

I went to McDonald's and bought an orange soda, which cost 70 cents. Sitting down, I noticed a woman from my bank approaching the counter. Alice Devlin, her name is, and I learned a long time ago to never stand in her line, as she always gives me grief. At McDonald's she ordered a sundae. When it was handed to her, she carefully wiped her plastic spoon with a napkin. She went over it time and time again, as if she'd picked it up off the street. Only when she was satisfied did she hand over her money and accept her change.

July 20, 1986
Chicago

I went to breakfast on the corner of Leland and Broadway, and my waitress had her initials tattooed on her wrist. When my food came, a couple approached and stood on the other side of the window. The man pointed to himself. Then he pointed to the woman beside him and put his hands into a prayer position, begging for my toast and eggs.

September 6, 1986
Chicago

While working I listened to a radio program called *Good Health,* broadcast live from the Plutonia Health and Fasting Center and hosted by a woman named Eileen Fulton, who answers questions and makes comments regarding the way people feel. It is Dr. Fulton's opinion that her listeners need to clean the "toxivity" out of their systems. She says, "You take a bath once a week, right? You take your clothes to the Laundromat when they get dirty, so it only makes sense for you to clean out your insides!"

A pregnant woman called to say she gets constipated. Dr. Fulton set up an appointment immediately, saying that backed-up poisons can ruin an unborn baby. "You need to evacuate and eliminate," she said.

An obese woman called to say that her heels hurt—they throb. Dr. Fulton said, "I know you. I bet you get out of bed at night and go down for a snack from the refrigerator. Am I right?"

The woman confessed, adding that sometimes, when there are no sweets in the house, she'll fix herself a glass of sugar water.

Dr. Fulton calls this suicide. She set up an appointment for Monday at seven forty-five and said she'll cure the sweet tooth with Dr. Fulton's Meal in a Glass.

The Plutonia Health and Fasting Center broadcasts on Saturday mornings.

September 7, 1986
Chicago
Today I listened to Daddy-O. Sometimes he calls his show *The Sunday Jazz Clambake,* but today it was *Daddy-O on the Patio.* He has little nicknames he's given the musicians: Sassy, of course, for Sarah Vaughan. Today after playing "A Cottage for Sale," he said, "Mr. B. is doing fine."

"Who? Why, Billy Eckstine!"

Daddy-O calls the radio station "Dad's pad." I imagine it looks like a den and has in it many pictures of him shaking hands with famous jazz musicians. I'd love to have a den one day. That's why I don't want to live in a loft—it's one big room. I suppose you could carve a "den space" out of it, but it's not the same thing.

September 12, 1986
Chicago
Again today I worked for Walt, refinishing the woodwork

and painting in his basement. He listens to an oldies station and complains that it plays too much Motown. "Even back when they weren't oldies, it seems like they played too much Motown," he said. Walt sings along to all the songs. Today, when the game came on, he switched stations and listened as the Bears went against someone or other. I know nothing about football, so he explained certain things—why, for instance, a certain player shouldn't get paid this week and the definition of *sudden-death overtime.*

Walt is remarried and has a one-year-old daughter. His wife came down in a pink dress, carrying the sweet-looking child in a matching outfit. Walt calls his wife "baby." He told her, "If they ask why we didn't go to the church picnic, tell them it's because we didn't go. Jeez, baby, who would schedule a picnic during a Bears game? Nobody will be there and we need to get this framing done or else we'll be living on one floor for the rest of our lives."

On my way home, riding my bike down Buena Vista, I saw two raccoons on the sidewalk. I've never in my life seen one. I stopped my bike to get a closer look and watched as they climbed up a tree. You could have knocked me over with a feather, seeing raccoons like that.

September 16, 1986
Chicago
A bumper sticker I saw:

> *Bumper to bumper*
> *butt to butt.*
> *Get off my ass*
> *you silly nut.*

September 19, 1986
Chicago
Last week a girl in our fiction workshop told the teacher, Jim, that she didn't know what she wanted to write exactly. She said she was interested in death, so today she turned in a poem about Vietnam called "The Walking Wounded." "I see silhouettes. / Green silhouettes," it began.

Every line had a period at the end. Jim called her poem a list, and she announced that she would not be coming back. She wore leather straps around her wrists.

After class I came home and spent an hour and a half taking my typewriter apart. Something was jammed inside. There are countless tiny screws in there, and it's amazing to me that I fixed it. I feel so proud of myself.

September 25, 1986
Chicago
Yesterday Amy took a cab home from her improv class. She sat in the back wearing sunglasses, and the driver tried to flirt with her, saying, "You've got beautiful eyes."

Later she went to the Laundromat, where she saw a man carefully folding his wet clothes and putting them in the dryer.

September 28, 1986
Chicago
Paul was here until this afternoon. During his visit we went around town on bikes and buses and the L. We took a few cabs, but mainly we walked. Last night he had a meatball sub and today he had a hot roast beef sandwich. He ate a lot of gravy on this trip. Before leaving he told me this joke:

Q. How did they know Christa McAuliffe had dandruff?

A. They found her Head & Shoulders on the beach.

October 2, 1986
Chicago
Dad called at six a.m. It was still dark outside, so I assumed someone had died. Why else would he call me?

It seemed he was on his way from British Columbia to Raleigh and was at O'Hare, laid over between flights. In Canada he'd fished for steelhead trout. He caught five big ones in ten days, but his main haul was stones, which are his new thing. In his suitcase were two twenty-five-pounders, one that he says resembles a human head and another that looks like a fish.

While there he saw an eagle swoop down and snatch a beaver off the banks of a pond. I loved the wonder in his voice when he related this story. My father has a terrific voice.

October 3, 1986
Chicago
A woman on *All Things Considered* did a seven-minute story on the idea of home that involved a number of different people. Mr. Rogers talked about the house he grew up in. He said that the bedrooms were upstairs and described the furniture and the hallways. It was layout information. Then came an old woman who talked about her father. She said that he was a kind man and that he had been beaten to death while working as a scab at a bakery. The woman received the news and remembered thinking, *If anyone has to die, why not my mother?*

In those days, she said, dead bodies were put on ice and displayed in the family's home. Her father's casket had a leak. "I remember the ice melting and dripping and forming a puddle on the floor, and I will remember it until I die," she said.

"I'll remember seeing it and thinking, *Here is my father. He is on ice in the living room.*"

I found some Xeroxed papers from Adult Children of Alcoholics that included the following Checklist for Hidden Anger:

Procrastination in the completion of imposed tasks
Perpetual or habitual lateness
A liking for sadistic or ironic humor
Sarcasm, cynicism, or flippancy in conversation
Frequent sighing
Overpoliteness, constant cheerfulness, an attitude of
    "Grin and bear it"
Smiling while hurting
Frequent disturbing dreams
Overcontrolled monotone speaking
Difficulty in getting to sleep or sleeping through the
    night
Boredom, apathy
Slowing down of movements
Excessive irritability over trifles
Getting drowsy at inappropriate times
Sleeping more than usual, twelve to fourteen hours a
    day
Waking up tired rather than refreshed
Clenched jaws while sleeping
Facial tics
Grinding of teeth
Chronic depression
Chronically stiff neck or shoulder muscles
Stomach ulcers

These people have got you coming and going. You can't be happy and you can't be miserable. You can't yawn, laugh, or sigh. I am sarcastic, sometimes have a hard time sleeping, get tired at school and work, and have facial tics. Four out of twenty-two isn't bad.

Here is the list of telltale attitudes:

We judge ourselves harshly.

We take ourselves seriously and have difficulty having fun.

We are approval seekers and fear personal criticism.

We feel isolated, different from other people.

We focus on others rather than looking honestly at ourselves.

We are attracted to people who are rarely there emotionally for us.

We guess at what normal is.

We live from the viewpoint of victims.

Is seven out of eight bad?

October 5, 1986
Chicago
Lately Neil has stopped sitting down. She hovers, but her ass never touches the floor. I lifted her tail yesterday and discovered an awful mess. She's balding back there, and it's all very raw-looking, so this afternoon I took her to the Uptown Animal Hospital. At first we were alone in the waiting room. Then a woman came in with two Persian cats in a carrying case. One was named Wiener and the other was Schnitzel. A few minutes later a man arrived with a dachshund that was wrapped in a blanket and was named Schnapps. As I was leaving after seeing the vet, a well-dressed woman walked

in with a white poodle and announced that it was time for Gucci's distemper shot.

October 9, 1986
Chicago

A list of things that I could paint on a cat:

a log
a telephone receiver
tonic
a list
a trophy
a tongue

October 13, 1986
Chicago

In sculpture class we looked at Arte Povera slides. One was of a pile of potatoes with bronze ears lying on top of it. We saw Richard Serra and Eva Hesse pieces. Everything looked dirty and depressing to me. There is an odd chatterbox in our class who speaks as if she's known the person she's talking to for years, and like it's just the two of them in the room.

The teacher was discussing discipline, and the chatterbox interrupted, saying, "I know what you're talking about because I used to be a dancer. I studied dance...well...let me go back. See, I always did art, but at the start the pieces were made of wood. I feel like I put them on the back burner, with dance, you know, on the front one. Even so, I feel like they were related to movement. So anyway, I studied dance for three years and then I moved to New York, which, let me say, wasn't all that great. But I went anyway and nothing happened. I mean that nothing in the dance world was happening for me, and it was very discouraging until I said to myself, *Hey, what about the sculpture?* And I knew then that art was really my first love. It was at the core of everything, so I said to myself, *Better go back to school.* So I moved back here and... yeah, the discipline thing is really important. Now I'm working in metal."

She delivered at least ten monologues this morning, all while smoking and rubbing at the blue circles under her eyes. I sort of love to hear her talk. She's just burning up with her own thoughts. Tomorrow, she said, she's driving to a place to buy aluminum.

October 15, 1986
Chicago
I'm thinking Neil must have a cold. She sneezes all the time now and sleeps on the stereo in the living room. It's cold and drafty there, so I don't get it at all. Early this morning, at around six, I woke up from a bad dream. Then I had a cigarette and took Neil off the stereo. I thought she should sleep with me for a change, but she didn't want to. Now she's sniffling and sneezing, and so am I. We're in the same boat, only I sleep in bed and she sleeps on the stereo.

October 17, 1986
Chicago
I ate lunch at McDonald's and saw a fat wallet fall out of a man's jacket pocket and onto the floor. Broke as I am, I did not think of waiting until he walked away and then taking it. Instead I said, "Hey, you dropped your wallet."

He said, "Oh," and looked at me as if I were the one who'd taken it from his pocket.

Tonight at the coffee shop a telephone number fell out of my library book and a man pointed it out to me. It was not an important number, but still I pretended that this guy had saved my life. He did not seem to care.

October 19, 1986
Chicago
A man approached me on the street, saying, "Sir?"

I told him I'd already given away all my change, and he said, "No, I don't want money. I want a job. I need one."

I told him there was a labor pickup on Broadway and Wilson and that he might try there early in the morning. The fellow was black and had nice clothes on. He was a few years older than me and said, "I have experience in accounting." This last word was whispered, which was strange.

I told him that I didn't know anything about accounting.

"Well, can you give me some money, then?" he asked. "I'm hungry. Can you buy me something to eat?"

I said no, and he continued, "What if I come to your place and you fix me something?"

October 22, 1986
Chicago
Today we had a critique in painting class. One guy who spoke a lot has bangs down to his chin. He wears medallions and paints his fingernails black. I'd written him off as being too affected, but he was one of the few people to comment on his classmates' work. Now I feel bad for having judged him.

Another person I noticed was Don, who is also in my writing class. He's a little older than me, and I'm sort of fascinated by him. Ask Don where he's from, and he'll say he's been all over the world. Don introduced himself on the first day as a poet, a filmmaker, a painter, and a photographer.

I might say, "I paint. I take pictures, I try to write, et

cetera," but would never in a thousand years use those titles for myself the way he does.

Don is interesting to me because he treats everyone like a child. He scolds and gives pats on the head. His poetry is about "sittin'" in a hotel room with "nothin'" but his memories and an "ol' trombone." His paintings are equally clichéd—night scenes, mainly. Norman Rockwell with a five o'clock shadow. Don is complex in an odd way. "I guess you could say that I've always been a loner," he says, and, "Really, my concerns are very intellectual." He spends a lot of time telling you how smart he is, which is odd because, if you're truly all that bright, people can usually figure it out on their own.

October 23, 1986
Chicago

I followed a couple down Wilson Avenue last week, walked behind them for two blocks, and the woman said *fuck* eleven times. She was angry at a friend who was supposedly spreading lies about her. "I'm going to fucking talk to that bitch Donna and say, 'Who the fuck do you think you are, spreading these fucking lies? It's none of your business who I fucking fuck, you fucking asshole. I'll knock your fucking teeth down your fucking throat if I ever...'"

I would have followed them longer, but I was carrying heavy groceries.

October 27, 1986
Chicago

At the Kentland Western Pancake House in Kentland, Indiana, we sat beside a table of high school athletes. They'd just come from a football game and were eating fries and talking about the coach. One thing about him, they all agreed, was that he wears loose shorts and always wants to sit on the desk. When the coach does that, his balls hang out. You don't want to notice them, but you pretty much have to. They're just this guy's hairy balls, and you don't look at them because you're interested or anything, but how can you not notice them?

November 2, 1986
Chicago

On my way to work I stopped at George's, ordered a cheeseburger, and sat down. The place was empty except for me and a woman my age who wore tight blue slacks tucked into her boots, an expensive-looking sweater, and a coat with a jeweled medallion pinned to the lapel. She asked for the barbecued chicken and said to me, "Did you order fries? If not, you don't have to because some are coming with my chicken and I don't really want them."

I told her thanks, but I was already scheduled for some. When her order was ready, she brought it to my table, though there were a dozen unoccupied ones. Eating messy food like barbecued chicken really made her feel primitive, she said. Then she told me she lives on Dakin Avenue, in a building called Melissa-Ann, which sounded to her like a snack cake. She said she was a graphic designer and guessed I was an English major. "Don't tell me," she said. "I bet you're at... DePaul."

A mother walked into George's just then and scolded her children for dawdling. "I could have cooked the fucking food myself in the time it's taking you to order it," she said.

"Don't you hate it when parents curse and don't treat their children with respect?" the woman who lives on Dakin asked.

I told her that my mother's new favorite word is *fuck* but

149

that she can't figure out its place in a sentence. "She'll say, 'I don't give a fucking darn what you think.'"

The woman who lives on Dakin considered this. She tore her chicken from the bone with her fingers. I enjoyed her company, and I think she enjoyed mine, but we never introduced ourselves.

November 3, 1986
Chicago

On the radio, someone was talking about cranes. The ones he'd studied had been taken from their mother at birth. At first they were raised by hand puppets, then later by men who were dressed like cranes. *How does a man dress like a crane?* I wondered. *And are birds really dumb enough to fall for it?*

November 20, 1986
Chicago

Two women got on the train this morning and commenced to beautify themselves. They both put on makeup, then one of them sprayed her hair, which was flattened down on the back and sides and stood up on the top. One strand wouldn't cooperate, so she went at it again and again, filling that car with that terrible smell and all the while talking to her friend.

November 22, 1986
Chicago

Ronnie's aunt Tessie used to take her to the Salvation Army in the Bronx and switch price tags. Tessie would pick discarded numbers off the floor of the butcher shop, saying, "Hey, what about me? I was here long before the rest of you." Once, Ronnie and Tessie were in line at the grocery store. The kid in front of them asked his mother for some candy, and she answered, "No, it'll ruin your appetite."

The child started crying, and Tessie butted in, saying, "So let him chew on it and then spit it out. Go ahead, give him some candy."

Eight years ago we visited her and her husband. Tessie made a big Italian dinner and later approached us, whispering, "Hey, youse don't happen to have any marijuana, do you?"

We said yes, and she asked for a joint, which she wanted to save for later. Here she was, my mother's age!

She died of a heart attack last week, and Ronnie wrote to tell me about it.

November 25, 1986
Chicago

I stayed up all night rewriting my new story, which is better now. At two I heated up a couple of frozen potpies and made some crescent rolls. They came in a tube, but still I formed them on the baking tray. I thought I'd take a break from typing and eat in the living room in front of the television, so I put the food on a tray and then tripped while carrying it. The potpies skidded across the floor and flipped over when they hit the baseboard. Rather than cleaning it up right away, I let Neil eat as much of it as she wanted. I just took the crust and continued on to the living room, where I watched a rerun of *The Odd Couple* that guest-starred Marilyn Horne.

When the show was over I went to clean up my mess and found that Neil had gotten most of it. If she were a dog, she'd have gotten all of it, but I'm happy with her as she is.

November 28, 1986
Chicago

Yesterday was Thanksgiving and today the Christmas season officially started. To celebrate, we went to Daley Plaza and watched them light the big tree. A speaker announced that we had several important guests. One was Ronald McDonald, and another was someone named Mistletoe Bear. The third was the mayor. It was nice watching with Lisa, who arrived on Wednesday night. Amy and I went to the airport to collect her. O'Hare was packed. We met Lisa at her gate, and as we walked her to the baggage claim, Amy did this bit where she pretends she's super-popular. "Hey, Sandy, great haircut!" she shouted at a stranger while waving. "Jim, I'll call you!" "Hi, Nancy. Gotta go." "Mike, yes, this is my sister."

She has two friends in town from Raleigh, Jan and Sherri, and they joined us all for Thanksgiving. Tonight we went to a bar around the corner called Sharon's Hillbilly Heaven, a big mistake, as the girls were all dressed up. After we walked in, an older man started talking to Lisa. He was driven off by someone much younger who had glasses on with thick lenses. I tried to step in, and the guy turned on me, saying, "Hey, back off. I was talking to the lady."

Meanwhile, Amy was cornered by a pimp named Dwayne. "You're my little shortcake, aren't you?" he said. He told her he knew all the ladies in Uptown and asked if she liked riding the love stick.

An American Indian woman watched them talk, and as she stomped past, Dwayne called, "Hey, baby, you leaving? Don't do it, babe, don't go."

November 30, 1986
Chicago
Yesterday in Lincoln Park a man asked us for money. "I'm a nice person, really. I'm not a bad guy, just a hungry guy. Can I have some money from you?"

I rooted through my pockets for change but couldn't find anything. As we walked on, the man shouted after us, "I thought you were nice people, but you're not. You're real sons of bitches. Go to hell. May you fall down where you live."

December 4, 1986
Chicago

There is a deaf man with a goatee in my painting class who can't speak and is much older than everyone else, in his late forties, maybe. His work is cheerful and surrealistic, Magritte-like trains steaming over the ocean, two dolls having a conversation. The man has no idea of the noise he makes. During critiques and slide lectures, he drags tables and chairs across the room. Steve has two deaf uncles and said that one used to drive through Cleveland with the radio playing full blast. Sometimes it was just static.

December 8, 1986
Chicago

It was foggy today, and dark by three. By five, delinquents were breaking into cars. They're shameless in this neighborhood. All are white with greasy bangs brushed to the sides of their heads. They all wear Windbreakers and sneakers. Delinquent style is timeless. Real trouble doesn't walk around with a ponytail. It doesn't have a Mohawk or special shoelace patterns. Real trouble has a bad complexion and a Windbreaker.

I am making Jeannie's baked mostaccioli and cheese. You need:

- 1 pound of mostaccioli
- Spinach (I use frozen)
- 3 eggs
- Cheese (Muenster)

- 1 cup of milk
- Butter
- Parsley

Cook the spinach and the mostaccioli and mix them together. Add eggs, cheese, and milk. Put it in a buttered pan and dab some butter on top, along with some parsley. Bake it at 350 degrees for half an hour to forty-five minutes.

December 10, 1986
Chicago

Today we started painting critiques. The deaf man put his work up at the front of the room, and while he did it, he farted. Then he handed out pieces of paper we could write our comments on.

December 15, 1986
Chicago

An Asian woman approached me at the IHOP tonight. Without asking, she sat at my table, snuggled up beside me, and said, "Have you had your hug today?"

I pulled back because I am not a hugger. Never have been. When someone wraps their arms around me, I shut down and stand there with my eyes closed, waiting for it to be over.

"I don't think I need a hug today," I told the Asian woman. She moved to the next table, where a black man was eating pancakes and looking at a magazine. She did the same thing to him that she'd done to me, and he said, "Would you please leave me alone?"

I'd seen the woman at the IHOP before, trying to sell flowers, and both then and now she was almost eerily cheerful. You have to at least give her that.

After the black man rejected her, she moved to a large group of Mexicans. All the seats at their table were taken, so she squatted on the floor. They couldn't understand what she wanted, and when she asked a second time, the waitress came and threw her out.

December 17, 1986
Chicago
I read a funny article by Patricia Marx called "Getting Along with the Russians." She says, "Education, not force, is the effective way to change the Russians. If we want a three-year-old not to put his hand on a hot stove, we do not beat him unmercifully. Rather, we *teach* him that a stove is hot, by pressing his hand to the burner for a minute or two."

She goes on with soft approaches and offers harder ones if plan A fails. "Continue to send the Russians wheat, but package it in cartons filled with so many Styrofoam pellets that Russia becomes a big mess." "Give them broken headsets at the UN."

We had our final critique this afternoon. I read a brief short story by Joy Williams and then pinned first- and second-prize ribbons to my paintings.

December 22, 1986
Raleigh
Paul missed a class and borrowed a weight lifter's notebook so he can catch up. Written on the front and back covers in Magic Marker are:

Born to be wild!!!
Break a sweat!
Pump iron, then your mate.

Once you go around, there's no turning back...so raise
   hell.
Lift for life.
Love conquers all.
Grunt power.
If you raise hell you're gonna burn your feet.
Doobies!

1987

January 13, 1987
Chicago
The deaf man has shaved off his goatee and is in my new painting class. Our teacher, whose name is Judy, started the day by showing slides, mainly of famous artists in their studios. We saw Matisse, Braque, and Renoir. When she got to Picasso, the deaf man became excited and tried to say something, perhaps "Picasso." The teacher wasn't sure how to handle it. She smiled, and just as she asked him to sit back down, he farted.

January 18, 1987
Chicago
In the mail we received a video guide of new releases. One movie is called *Never Too Young to Die*. The copy reads, "A vicious hermaphrodite wants to control the country, and only two people stand in his way. [*Only two?*] The resulting 'battle of the sexes' will blow your mind with a heady mixture of powerful heavy-metal music, state-of-the-art weaponry, martial arts, and espionage that makes this exciting action flick a winner."

Times have changed when a hermaphrodite wants to control the country and only two people stand in his way. If he were a black or Hispanic hermaphrodite, he'd probably have a harder time of it.

April 26, 1987
Chicago

A woman at the IHOP tonight got up from her chair and crossed the room to eat french fries off the plate of a person who had just left. She was stylishly dressed and had a suitcase with her. Everything on the menu was too much, she moaned. It sounded like she was trying to watch her weight, though she was surely talking about the prices. Four chocolate chip pancakes were out of the question, she said, "so how about you sell me two?"

The waitress said short stacks just come in buttermilk, so the woman ordered a plate of french fries, which she ate with ketchup. Then she took syrup and poured it onto her spoon, the way you might with cough medicine. She had multiple spoonfuls of all the various flavors, one right after the other. In my nine years of going nearly every night to the IHOP, both here and in Raleigh, I have never before seen anyone drink the syrup. She had to be crazy.

May 5, 1987
Chicago

I told Dad I was disappointed that I wouldn't be graduating in a cap and gown—the Art Institute doesn't swing that way—and he said, "I've got your old cap and gown from high school. Want me to bring them when we come up?" Then he said, "Do you think it will still fit?"

A person would be in pretty serious trouble if his graduation gown no longer fit. It's like outgrowing a tent, basically.

We had our final critique in sculpture class today. It was dull, which is good, as it'll give me less to miss. I'm sad to be finishing school. I liked being in college. It was respectable to be a student. You get discount admissions all over town, and it makes you work.

May 6, 1987
Chicago

Today I worked for Marilyn Notkin. She had company coming and needed her storm windows removed, and knobs applied to her bathroom linen closet. I was taking out one of the windows in the sunroom when I broke it. Then I dropped one of the porcelain knobs she had special-ordered for the linen closet. "I guess this just isn't our day," she said when I confessed. It was the "our" that got me. It was my bad day for breaking things and her bad day for hiring me. "You don't need to pay me," I said.

She insisted on giving me something and settled on $7. I honestly would have felt better if she hadn't paid me anything.

May 20, 1987
Chicago

Mom came for my graduation and stayed with me after everyone else had left. It was nice having her. We went out to eat with Amy every night, and she gave Neil lots of attention. I'd wake up and find them both in the kitchen, Neil in Mom's lap while she smoked and drank coffee. She slept in my office and took naps on the sofa. This afternoon she left, and now I'm not sure what to do with myself. I'd looked forward to everyone coming, and now it's over.

On Saturday, when the whole family was here, we got dressed up for cocktails and dinner. Lisa, Gretchen, Amy, Tiffany, and I were walking past the vacant lot on Leland that's always full of drunks and drug addicts. Any time of day or night they're there—white, black, American Indians, but strangely no Mexicans. They have fistfights, they build fires

159

David Sedaris

and pass out. As we walked by on our way to the L, a drunk woman fell in behind us and put her nose in the air, bringing up the rear in what she saw as a snooty parade.

Then someone yelled out, "Hey, they're people too!"

May 22, 1987
Chicago
This morning a Jehovah's Witness woke me up. Someone buzzed her into the building, and she came to my door with a small child and two copies of *The Watchtower*, which I paid 40 cents (printing cost) for. The child saw Neil in the background behind me and said, "Once we had a cat, but it scratched the baby, so we had to get rid of it."

May 23, 1987
Chicago
My recipe for Koto Kai Pilafi:

Pour a little oil into a pan.
Wash a quartered chicken and rub it with garlic.
Dot it with butter, big dots or small—whatever.
Add 3 tablespoons of tomato paste and half a cup of water, and put it in the oven at 400 degrees.
Cook the chicken on its side for 15 minutes and then turn it over and cook the other side an equal amount of time.
Add 2 cups of water and 1 cup of rice and cook it for another half hour at 350.

May 24, 1987
Chicago
Last week, after being drunk for two days, F. came to. It was Sunday, and the last thing he remembered was Friday night.

160

He woke up naked with no furniture left in his living room. The front door was open, and there were piles of shit on the floor.

May 27, 1987
Chicago

Jehovah's Witnesses came again this morning, this time a pair of young black women. I told them I already had both current issues of *The Watchtower,* and they gave me some information on their next big meeting. If I were to become a Witness, then I could go door-to-door just like they do.

June 3, 1987
Chicago

This afternoon I found a $50 bill in the foyer of the building near the mailboxes. It was folded thin and full of cocaine. Some of it spilled when I opened it up, but there's still plenty left. So that's $50 in cash and around $80 worth of cocaine— $130! If I find $50 every day, I won't need to get a job.

June 7, 1987
Chicago

I dared myself to lean too hard against one of the living-room windows yesterday, and it broke and cut my elbow up. Later in the afternoon I took the empty frame to the hardware store, where they said it would cost $30 for new glass. That seemed exorbitant to me, so I was walking back home by way of the empty lot when an American Indian woman grabbed on to it, saying she'd been looking for a window frame just like this. "I need it," she said. "Hand it over." Her face was strikingly flat, and for a second all I could do was stare at it.

The woman was holding a beer bottle and put it down so

she could grab my window frame with both hands. "Turn it loose," she said, and the several drunk people behind her cheered her on. Then a man who was slightly less drunk told her to let it go. "Leave him alone, Cochise," he said. "This here's a working man."

I haven't worked in more than three weeks, but it was nice to be mistaken for someone with a job. Today I took the frame down a different street to the L, where I thought I'd try another hardware store. Right near the station a man asked me for money, and when I walked by he shouted, "Watch where you're going with that thing, asshole! You almost killed that girl. You almost hit her with that window, you fucker."

I said, "What?"

"You just about hit that baby, you son of a bitch. I'm going to kill you. I'm going to teach you a lesson you'll never forget, you little fuck. You can't get away from me."

The guy was really beside himself, and I'm lucky I was so close to the ticket window. I worried he'd panhandle enough money to reach the platform before the train arrived, but luckily he didn't. And what baby? I didn't see any baby.

Why did I have to break that window, and on a dare, for God's sake?

June 11, 1987
Chicago

I got a few days' work painting for Lou Conte, a nice guy in a high-rise. On Tuesday afternoon the doorman in his building chewed me out for riding in the elevator. He said, "How did you get upstairs this morning? How?"

The main elevator is burled walnut. It was very clean, and riding in it, I wondered why anyone might ever think to deface anything so beautiful. Not that it *was* defaced.

The doorman marched me around back to the service entrance. He said, "Our tenants don't want to come home and find people like you in the lobby."

I just happen to be a college graduate, I wanted to say. But of course I didn't, as it never works to get huffy in these situations. If I have to, I'll just take the nice elevator from Lou's floor, then change to the service elevator on two. The service elevator is like riding in a cat-food can.

There were two men at the IHOP tonight. One was brokenhearted and did not give the other guy a chance to talk. His topic was getting over Beth. "The relationship didn't *fall* apart," he said. "It was *torn* apart."

June 13, 1987
Chicago

We went to Betty's Lounge for a drink last night. It's never crowded, and when we arrived, there was only one customer. She looked like a grandmother and wore rimless glasses and a straw hat with fake flowers on it. The woman was drinking beer and playing pinball, fighting the machine but never calling it names. I was watching her when three other women came in, two of them wearing feed caps. The bartender singled out the one who was bareheaded, saying, "I'll close up shop before I ever sell to a nigger, and that's what you are: a white-faced nigger."

All three women appeared to be drunk. Two of them adjusted their caps while the third one said, "You can't talk to me that way, you son-of-a-bitching asshole."

The bartender told her to leave. Apparently she'd shot a friend of his named Doug, with whom he had once worked at an ice factory. He said he would not serve any bitch that would shoot a man in the back with his own fucking gun, shoot him while he was shaving, no less. "How many years did you get, bitch?"

"Your mama's a fucking bitch," the woman said.

The bartender lit a cigarette and threw the burning match on her.

Then the woman started to cry. She said that Doug deserved to die and asked how the bartender would like it if someone pushed *his* head through the basement window and kicked *his* ass up and down Magnolia Avenue.

The bartender said she deserved it.

"Why, you bald-headed...you white-haired bastard," the woman said. "I'll shoot you too."

"You ain't never going to get the chance to kill me, nigger, 'cause I'm never going to turn my back on you," the bartender said.

The woman stepped toward the door and called the man more names. She said she didn't want to stay in this dump anymore. "Come on, girls!" she shouted. "Let's go down to the Wooden Nickel."

But her friends didn't join her. They stayed. After she left, they ordered drinks and told the bartender that they never liked that bitch in the first place. Never.

June 14, 1987
Chicago
Geraldine Page died yesterday of a heart attack. I heard about it on the radio. She was one of my favorite actresses.

I went to the beach at Montrose Harbor and sat on a towel for a while. People there barbecue and then dump their hot coals on the grass and drive away, leaving everything else behind. They throw garbage into the lake just to watch it float. Children swim in the shallow water and pull soiled Pampers up from the bottom. What I like about Montrose Beach is that all the loud music is in another language.

Bad teenagers hang out in the alley behind our building, and whenever they see me on my bike they call me Pee-wee, after Pee-wee Herman, because I have an old one-speed that cost $8. It gets on my nerves, but if I had a better bike they'd just steal it.

June 16, 1987
Chicago
I had an elaborate fantasy yesterday after the kids called me Pee-wee again. I kept thinking how great it would be to follow them home, buy their apartment buildings, and evict them. I don't know what I would do with the buildings after I bought them. I wasn't thinking that clearly.

June 19, 1987
Chicago
I ran into Walt on the L this morning. He owes me $450 and said he was just going to call me the other day because Gail, his wife, is always saying, "We need to pay that David Sedaris."

I actually don't hold anything against him. I miss Walt and Gail. Walt said that last week she got a profit-sharing check for $10,000. That was why he planned to call—to pay me. He said he took the check to the bank but lost it along the way. It was physically big, he told me. "I folded it in my top pocket, and wouldn't you know!"

He called the bank to cancel it, then he called New York for a replacement check, but the woman whose job it would be to write it was on vacation. "Wouldn't you know it!"

At around five, I took the L home. A woman near me had a

three-year-old child on her lap, a girl, who looked at me and said, "Mommy, I hate that man."

Hours later, walking up Leland, I heard someone running up behind me. It was a guy who lives in the halfway house next door. He is black and wore a long-sleeved shirt buttoned all the way to the neck. The man called me sir and asked how I was doing.

"All right," I said.

He told me that he had a taste for a steak sandwich and asked me if I'd buy him one. You can't pull money out of your pocket on Leland Avenue. It's like ringing a bell, so I said no and he ran across the street to ask a woman the same question.

Later still I saw two men sitting in a car in front of the halfway house. They had the door open and were listening to the radio. As I passed, one of them asked me for a cigarette.

"I don't smoke," I told them. Then I thought of the guy who wanted a steak sandwich and of the little girl who hated me and thought, *What the hell.* I handed the guy in the car one of my cigarettes, and he scowled at me and said, "Fucking liar."

June 21, 1987
Chicago
I listened to a radio tribute to Arch Oboler, the creator of *Lights Out,* a scary program that aired in the '30s. They interviewed him at his home in Studio City and then they played a few of his radio dramas, starting with "Cat Wife," about a woman who hangs out with her friends, drinking and gossiping. Her husband calls her a cat, and then she turns into one.

It was a fifteen-minute story dragged out to half an hour. Boris Karloff played the husband and would say, "You,

Linda, are nothing but a cat. A cat, do you hear me? You remind me of a cat. When I think of you, a cat comes to mind. You...cat, you. You belong in an alley with your friends, yowling and carrying on. Cat."

When Linda turns into a cat, Boris Karloff feels responsible. He tries to keep it a secret and murders two people who discover the truth. Then Linda claws his eyes out and he shoots himself by accident.

June 22, 1987
Chicago

When John Tsokantis was growing up in Greece, he learned to play water polo and smoke. He told me that when kids misbehaved in class, the teacher would send them to the corner, where they had to kneel on a pile of rocks.

I like the kind of man John is. He watches things closely and then does nothing with the information. His English has improved since I met him four years ago, shortly before he had an aneurysm. The other night at a pizza restaurant he played a game of picking out the thirty spies hidden in the landscape of his place mat. I couldn't find even one, but then he explained it. "Is not the whole thing," he told me. "Only the heads of the spies."

July 11, 1987
Chicago

Last night I watched a made-for-TV movie called *Consenting Adult*. It was another of those programs about how people with station wagons solve problems. In this case the problem was the son, who turned out to be gay. Marlo Thomas played the mother, and after learning the truth, she pulled her car off the side of the road and wept. It was silly, and watching it I wondered why such movies always concern the upper middle class. If they were a minority family, the show would be a situation comedy and everyone would laugh it off.

July 16, 1987
Chicago
I went to the library and passed a street musician who had a live weasel in his guitar case. It was on a leash and was taking a nap. There was a girl at school who had a weasel, though she called it a ferret. She said it was sweet and would burrow under the covers while she was sleeping.

   If there was a weasel in my house, I'd move.

July 26, 1987
Chicago
When Steve was six years old, his family lived in Hollywood and he appeared on *The Pat Boone Show,* which had a segment involving kids and the adorable things they sometimes come up with. He remembers saying, "A doctor or a fireman," but can no longer remember whether he was asked what he wanted to be when he grew up, or who he wanted to sleep with.

September 13, 1987
Raleigh
Amy said loudly to Paul's girlfriend yesterday, "Hey, did that bleach ever work on your mustache?" They were in a crowded ladies' room, and everyone turned to look at Angie's upper lip.

   Later she said to Mom in line at the grocery store, "It's great they gave you your license back so soon after that DWI."

September 20, 1987
Chicago
Before I left Raleigh, Mom walked the dog up the street and back. It's part of her exercise, and she went as far as the Andrewses' old house, where Melina peed in the driveway. Just then a boy drove up and told my mother to get the fuck off his property. He called her a bitch and a cunt, so Mom returned home, dropped off the dog, and went back up the street, where she told the kid that he couldn't talk to her that way. "Yeah?" he said. "Well, how'd you like it if I shit in *your* driveway?"

Mom said Melina was only peeing, but peeing and shitting were the same to this kid. Again he called her a bitch and ordered her off his property. Then he threatened to come to our house with his Doberman pinscher.

"Do you have a Doberman pinscher?" Mom asked.

He said no but that he could just come alone and pee in our driveway.

Mom said it was good that he didn't have a dog and that she wouldn't put it past him to pee in our driveway. She told me this in the kitchen as she poured herself a drink. Then she made me promise not to tell Paul because he would make trouble and as a result Melina could wind up dead.

I can't keep a secret to save my life, so she said that if I *do* tell him, she'll never help me out again.

Help means money.

My lips are sealed, which is a pity. Paul would have gotten inventive revenge. He's not the type to pour sugar in someone's gas tank. Rather, he'd steadily chip away at this boy and his family. He'd be patient, and just when they thought it was over, he'd start again. It would go on for years until they begged for mercy. That Mom felt safe telling *me* about it is a real shame. An embarrassment, really.

November 2, 1987
Chicago

I bought an old newspaper photo of a suicide note left by a man named Wilbur Wright who hanged himself in the county jail. "I can't go on," it reads. "Life isn't worth anything without you forgive me. Bobbye I love you more than you'll ever know. May God watch over you and our baby. Bill."

November 3, 1987
Chicago

Those boys were on the street again tonight, three of them. They are ten, maybe twelve years old. One is chubby and wears glasses. Tonight they yelled, "Nerd! You...prick."

I'd never have talked that way to a grown-up when I was their age.

November 4, 1987
Chicago

I saw a bumper sticker the other day that read I LOVE KILLING COMMUNISTS. The word *love* was replaced by a heart shape I'm guessing they'll put on the typewriter keyboard any day now, right beside the exclamation point. The bumper sticker was on a Ford Fairlane on Montrose Avenue.

November 7, 1987
Chicago

I saw a family—a mother, father, and ten-year-old boy—walk down Leland Avenue today. It was raining, and when the mother told her son to put up the hood on his Windbreaker, the boy said, "Aww, lemme alone. My fuckin' hair ain't wet."

She responded, sweetly, "Maybe not, but it *will* be."

November 14, 1987
Chicago

Barbara went to clear the dishes off the table behind me at the IHOP tonight. A couple was sitting there, both in their sixties, and they started smoking the moment they'd finished.

"Was everything all right with your meal?" Barbara asked.

"No," the woman said. "No, it was not. The meat was all tough and the vegetables was cold."

"Well, why didn't you say anything?" Barbara asked.

And the woman said, "We was hongry."

November 16, 1987
Chicago

Steve Lafreniere loaned me a few copies of a St. Louis newspaper called the *Evening Whirl,* which comes out daily and is completely devoted to black-on-black crime. Criminals are pictured on every page beneath headlines like "Fiend Sneaks In While Parents Are Asleep, Sodomizes Their Two Sons" and "Mean Pastor of Church Dates Two Brothers, 10 and 11, He's Caught."

This man rapes two kids, and the paper calls him *mean?*

"It was revealed how the sex mad faggot tagged one boy that he especially adored and wrecked him. He would tie him up by his hands and body and go to work on his victim like a greedy hog that had missed a meal. He caught the boy like a rooster running after a hen and dragged him into the office and oh, Glory! What a session, oh, my!"

There is a short article in one issue headlined "You Don't Know Who in the Hell I Am, Do You? I'm Mr. Muckity Muck with the Big Buck. Mess with Me and You'll Have No Luck."

Another article is titled "Andy Gray Said, 'I Am Freakish. I Love My Own Sex and I Like 'Em Young. If They Yield to Me I'll Give 'Em Some Tongue. I Can't Help How I Was Born, I'm Gonna Have Fun and Live, Right On!'" It says in this article that Mr. Gray "snorted and cavorted with other men."

This paper is not to be believed. An annual subscription costs $35. The ads are placed by lawyers, funeral homes, and bail bondsmen.

November 17, 1987
Chicago
Police caught the guy responsible for smashing windows and painting swastikas outside Jewish businesses on Devon Avenue. He's out on bail now, and this morning's paper included a picture of him. What strikes me is that he has a very small mouth, smaller than a baby's. I mean, tiny. If you wanted him to suck your thumb, you'd have to grease it up first. The article says he belongs to a skinhead group and has tattoos, which is strange, I think, because Jews in concentration camps had shaved heads and tattoos. You'd think the anti-Semites would go for a different look.

December 27, 1987
Raleigh
Tiffany left this morning. Last night we sat around in the basement with company and she told us that she often gets gas trapped in her neck. She pointed to a spot beneath her ear, saying, "It's right here."

I never heard of such a thing.

She spent most of her vacation on the telephone arguing with black men who are a mystery to us. Some we've met once or twice, but she never tells us the nature of their relationships. It's not normal to spend hours in your room crying over misunderstandings with people who are just friends. She left herself out of a lot this Christmas. Every night has ended with Amy, Gretchen, Paul, and me sitting on one bed or another and laughing until four in the morning.

1988

January 3, 1988
Chicago

It was cold when I returned to Chicago yesterday—eleven degrees. I took the bus into town and was surprised when the driver kicked someone off. It was a belligerent man who'd been arguing with him over what seemed to me like nothing. After a few minutes the passengers started putting their two cents in, and not long afterward the guy was thrown off. "I hope you freeze to death," the driver shouted after he'd closed the door.

The first Chicago baby of 1988 was born a few minutes after midnight. A suburban limo service had promised a special ride to the child and its parents, and other businesses had made similar offers. On the news tonight they showed the mother and father receiving a box of fine cigars and a dozen roses before getting into the backseat of a Rolls-Royce. According to the reporter, the two are not married. Both are sixteen years old, and black, and from the West Side. They looked very happy.

January 6, 1988
Chicago

It is bitterly cold out tonight. I was on Irving Park Road walking past Graceland Cemetery, on my way home from the

IHOP, when a van pulled over and the driver motioned to me. I ignored him, and he followed slowly behind me and honked. When the window came down, I saw that the guy was missing a few teeth and that he wasn't much older than me. He asked where I was going, and when I said, "Home," he asked if he could do anything for me.

That stretch of Irving is usually busy with prostitutes. If he thought that's what I was, then the rules have definitely changed since I left Chicago for the holidays. Here I was, wearing two coats, two hats, and glasses. I thought of accepting a ride but said that I was fine walking. Get into a car with a stranger on that stretch of Irving and you can't really complain should something awful happen.

January 11, 1988
Chicago

I ran into Shirley on Broadway and Irving. She was my neighbor on Cuyler, the only other native-born American in the building. Shirley wears an overcoat, a housedress, and slacks all at the same time. She has only one visible tooth, and it's on the bottom. I asked about Ray, the man she lived with, and she told me he'd passed away on August 30, of cancer or something. Ray was always drunk. He wore ski caps, like Shirley does, and women's glasses.

"He died on me" was how she put it. She said that her brother had died on her too. Then she laughed, like they were off somewhere, hiding together.

January 13, 1988
Chicago

David G. was on Wilson Avenue, walking behind a large woman in a thin winter coat. The pawnshop hadn't shoveled their sidewalk, and there was only a narrow path in front of it, bordered by snow-covered ice. Two Mexican girls were coming from the other direction, and just as they reached the start of the path, the large woman shouted, "Out of the way, bitches. This is *my* country."

January 14, 1988
Chicago

Last week on Montrose and Magnolia I noticed a flyer for a missing cat named Brutus, and this afternoon in a vacant lot I think I found him: big and black, with ragged ears. He was dead, and frozen solid.

I called the number on the flyer and told the woman who answered where she could find the body. "I hope I'm wrong, but I'm pretty sure it's Brutus," I said.

She asked if the dead cat had nappy ears and I said yes. What I didn't say was that I think the body had been kicked up and down the street. It was scuffed, and a lot of the fur had been worn away. The woman sounded very distressed on the phone. The poster mentioned a $100 reward, but I didn't bring it up, figuring it only applied if Brutus was returned alive.

January 17, 1988
Chicago

There's a Wieboldt's not far away so yesterday I ducked my head in. The store sells dress shirts for $6. They sell a line of denim jackets that have *Love* and *Peace* already written across the backs of them. One of the cashiers, a teenage boy, wore a Gucci sweatshirt and had a sketchy mustache. He was smoking, and when a customer stepped forward to pay, he laid the cigarette on the counter, with the lit end hanging over the edge. When it fell to the floor, he sighed and stepped on it.

Half the shelves in the store were empty, not because it's

a popular place but because no one restocked them. They're exhausted over at Wieboldt's. Like the ALDI grocery store further down Broadway, their motto is "Leave us alone. Let us smoke in peace, for God's sake." Goldblatt's is even worse. All of the mannequins in their front windows are missing their fingers.

January 27, 1988
Chicago

At the underground Jackson L stop, I came upon a group of three rappers. The song they were performing was about AIDS, a message to all "fags, fairies, and dykes" that they are "history." They will die and everyone will be better for it. One rapper said in an aside that he hoped there wasn't anyone with that shit standing next to him. A big crowd had gathered to listen, and they loved it. Everyone laughed and applauded.

I received a letter from Susan Wheeler, who's in New York now, temping at a company that makes dental rinses. For Christmas her mother gave her a beautifully wrapped empty box, three pairs of queen-size panty hose that are way too big for her, and $32.

January 28, 1988
Chicago

I called about a job writing for a young person's cable show. The receptionist answered, saying, "Youff C'moonication."

"Excuse me?"

It took me a while to realize he was saying "Youth Communications."

I eventually got through to the guy in charge who told me I didn't want the job. He said he'd just had two people walk out on him and I'd no doubt be the third. I said all right and hung up.

February 3, 1988
Chicago

I got a job at a place called Jay Roberts Antique Warehouse. They had a help-wanted ad for a wood stripper, so I went in and talked to the owner, who asked me some questions about furniture. I start next week on a trial basis for $6 an hour.

February 10, 1988
Chicago

I started my job at Jay Roberts and learned I'm replacing a guy who made $11 an hour. I was told this by Earl, who makes $15 an hour. I was hired to refinish furniture, but the first thing I did was shovel snow. Then I swept, moved dressers from place to place, and cleaned brass. While moving dressers I saw a throne made out of horseshoes.

Earl said that five refinishers have quit since December. "Don't tell Jay I told you," he said.

February 11, 1988
Chicago

At the end of the day Jay Roberts handed me a check and told me it just wasn't working out. Earlier, at lunch, the furniture repairer, Lorenzo, asked me where I live. I told him, and he asked if there were a lot of faggots in Uptown. There were three other people in the room, and they all laughed. Lorenzo said that faggots destroy everything because they're perverted and only look out for themselves. He said that they're selfish and don't devote themselves to family.

I asked if he had children and he said yes, why else would he work six days a week? Before I went to Popeyes

I asked if anyone wanted anything, and Lorenzo told me to bring him a woman with big tits. He said he had one last week who almost tore his dick off. That's how much family means to him.

I will never walk down that block again.

February 16, 1988
Chicago
Reasons to live:

1. Christmas
2. The family beach trip
3. Writing a published book
4. Seeing my name in a magazine
5. Watching C. grow bald
6. Ronnie Ruedrich
7. Seeing Amy on TV
8. Other people's books
9. Outliving my enemies
10. Being interviewed by Terry Gross on *Fresh Air*

April 5, 1988
Chicago
At the IHOP I sat behind a pregnant woman in her midtwenties and her companion, who was in her seventies and walked with a cane. The pregnant woman is expecting her baby on July 4 and said she's hoping Mike can get his shit together before then. He's the baby's father and also an actor. Right now he's playing the part of someone named John Deering. "Mike doesn't act, he *becomes*," the pregnant woman said. She told her friend that normally that's fine, but when he becomes John Deering he freaks out that he's got a baby on the way. A few weeks ago he moved out of their

apartment. She goes over to his new place and uses the computer but only when he's at rehearsal.

The older woman lit a cigarette and said that in her opinion, Mike was being irresponsible.

The pregnant woman sighed. "I'm just hoping he gets his act together, maybe after the play is finished."

Yesterday on the radio I heard a young woman address a few of the hardships she's faced since her husband walked out on her and her two young children. Because he disappeared, she's still married and thus ineligible for welfare in the state of Virginia. She's college educated, but the children are young, and she can't leave them alone. When she tries to get aid, the people at Social Services tell her that she's pretty, which means what, exactly? That she could become a prostitute, or find a wealthy boyfriend? She said that her five-year-old got sick, and that when he sat on his potty seat, his intestines came out.

I dropped my screwdriver when I heard that.

April 29, 1988
Chicago
At the library I got a biography of Dorothy Parker, and on the L, I dipped into the middle of it, where an old man reaches under the table for a lit cigarette. As he bends, his arthritic knees pop, and Parker stretches out her hands, saying, "Ahhhh, there's nothing I love more than a good crackling fire."

May 8, 1988
Chicago
They hired a waiter at the IHOP, a guy named Jace. He was OK at first, but now he brings in a portable TV and sits at the worktable smoking cigarettes and watching it. He tells customers it might be a twenty-minute wait before he can take their order, and one after another they leave. Last night there

were three occupied tables. It was me, a couple, and a heavy man who waited for fifteen minutes before getting up to complain. Later at the cash register, Jace apologized for taking so long. "Sorry," he said. "But I was watching a bullfight."

A bullfight?

May 29, 1988
Chicago

I got so sick of being called Pee-wee that I bought a new bike with the money I earned painting for Gene. It's like the one I had in Raleigh, a Frankenstein bike, made of different bits and pieces. The brakes are new, and the pedals. It's been painted umpteen times and there's a *Playboy* insignia on it.

June 7, 1988
Chicago

I checked *The Oxford Book of Canadian Short Stories* out of the library. One of the entries in it is titled "The Day I Sat with Jesus on the Sundeck and a Wind Came Up and Blew My Kimono Open and He Saw My Breasts."

June 10, 1988
Chicago

The poet Elaine Equi was supposed to teach a writing class at the Art Institute this fall. Instead, she and her husband are moving to New York, so Jim phoned this afternoon and asked if I might be interested. It doesn't mean I'll get it, just that I've been invited to apply.

Adrienne started teaching a few months ago in Denver and wrote that it leaves you with a constant feeling of deceiving people. That you know nothing they don't, or couldn't learn on their own if they cared to.

June 13, 1988
Chicago
Frank, the super of the building I'm working in this week, is full of jokes. "Hey," he said, "how come Puerto Ricans don't pay with checks? Because they can't write that small with spray paint." Another joke was about a Polish man who, forced to shit in the woods, was advised to wipe himself with $1. In the end he winds up with shit on his hands and four quarters up his ass.

June 23, 1988
Chicago
Frank told me that the metal disk on the floor beside the bathtub is a cover for the drain and that when it clogs, you unclog it with a product called Clear Out. He then pulled down the neck of his T-shirt and showed me a half a dozen welts on his chest. "I opened a jug of it once and it spattered, so be careful," he said.

Next he showed me a scar on his arm. Here he'd used Clear Out to remove an embarrassing tattoo. Now he has only one, a heart on his upper arm that reads *I Love Patty.*

I asked who Patty was and he told me she was his first wife. I asked if that made things difficult with his second wife, and he told me that Patty and their three kids all died in a house fire while they were still married in 1977.

House fire sounds different than just regular *fire* for some reason. It sounds meaner, hotter. He has one daughter left and told me that since the fire, he has gained two hundred and fifty pounds.

June 27, 1988
Chicago
Someone shit on the floor of the foyer I'm working on. Luck-

ily Frank got to work before me, so I didn't have to clean it up. It's so sad to see human shit out of context.

June 28, 1988
Chicago

I got the job teaching a writing workshop at the Art Institute, and I owe it all to Jim, and to Evelyne, who typed up my résumé. My class will meet on Thursdays at one o'clock, hopefully in the Fine Arts Building on Michigan Avenue, where we can sit around one big table. I love the rooms there but not the lights, so maybe I can bring in lamps to make it more appealing.

On Thursday I need to fill out forms and order books. I can make people read things! I'm thinking I'll assign Flannery O'Connor's *A Good Man Is Hard to Find,* Tobias Wolff's *In the Garden of the North American Martyrs,* and an anthology called *Sudden Fiction* because everything in it is short and it'll make writing seem possible. They're all great books, but between now and the start of school, I have to figure out why they're great.

As a teacher I'll have faculty meetings and cocktail parties. I can hardly wait. It's only one class, but still I plan to buy a briefcase and play the part for all it's worth. Now I can refer to all the Art Institute teachers as my colleagues. Dad is super-proud of me.

July 4, 1988
Chicago

We took a cab home from the Hotel Belmont and the driver scolded me several times. "Hey, buddy, don't be crawling in my taxi." Then he got mad at me for running my fingers along the track where the window meets the top of the door. "You're nervous," he said. "I know you. You're going to ruin all the rubber up there with your nervous touching. See that

No Smoking sign back there? See how it's all worried around the edges? Nervous people done that too."

Ronnie was catering a banquet where the guests were drunk and annoying. A man asked her if she was Italian and when she told him yes, he said, "I thought so. All Italian women have mustaches."

I'd never noticed that Ronnie had a mustache, but still it upset her. When she got home she told Blair, who said she'd probably feel a lot better after a shower and a shave.

July 8, 1988
Chicago
I saw a man being handcuffed under the Sheridan L stop. He'd been beating a woman who wore a tight red pantsuit with an image of a cat stitched on each leg and the word *Cat* written above them. Her face was puffy from the blows, and she stood there threatening the handcuffed man, who tried to break free and kick her.

"Look at what you done now," he kept saying.

July 10, 1988
Chicago
New American Writing published my story "Firestone" and sent me a check for $15. One of the things I bought with the money is a terrarium I saw at a yard sale. I was thinking I could put hermit crabs in it. I thought of a hamster as well, but they really stink up a room if you don't keep on top of them.

July 15, 1988
Chicago
At the IHOP a boy had an epileptic seizure. I'd never seen one and didn't tonight either. I knew something was going on

behind me but didn't turn around to look until the boy was asleep on the floor. He was snoring and his mother stood over his body while his sister ran to use the pay phone. Firemen came, and then an ambulance. An EMT guy woke the kid up gently, saying, "Terry? Hey, buddy. Hi, boy. Say, buddy, do you know what day this is? Do you realize you're at the International House of Pancakes? Do you?"

They put him on a stretcher and told him several times to relax. When they wheeled him by, I saw his face. He looked like someone had woken him up in the middle of the night and told him to get packed because it was time to move. He was black, and very light-skinned. Do black people become pale? Why don't I know that?

Last night Gretchen wore high heels, and the minute we got home she kicked them off, saying the sound was driving her crazy. "I swore to myself I'd never have a roommate who wore shoes like this," she said.

It's been nice having her here. Every day she goes to the beach to revive her tan, and every day men fuck with her. They call out concerning all the various parts of her they'd like to have access to. Men on bikes, on the street, on the train. I forget how much crap women have to put up with. Last night when she was walking down Devon, a group of six boys called out, "Wooooo, baby. C'mere."

She walks on.

July 22, 1988
Chicago
I've been working on a new story and have pages of IHOP notes spread before me that I can't read. One says *gammerstrayer.jermei.*

Oprah had a show about people who have forgiven the unforgivable. One girl forgave the fellow who stabbed her twenty times and then stabbed her father, a minister, to death. She had pleaded for a stay of execution, as had the man whose grandmother was stabbed to death by a gang of teenage girls. I remember when that case was all over the news. The grandmother who was murdered taught a Bible studies class.

A woman on the panel forgave the man who killed her son while driving drunk on Christmas Eve. He's a frequent visitor at her home now.

There were two other guests, a woman who would never forgive the man who raped and drowned her sister, and a black woman who was shot in the stomach by gang members who then molested her daughter. She said she could hear the girl crying out, and Oprah said, "Did you help her?"

"No," the woman said, perhaps feeling put on the spot. "I was shot and bleeding profusely." She explained that she still has a bullet lodged in her kidney and doesn't see the sense in forgiving anybody. "Hate is what's kept me alive," she said.

In today's paper I read about a six-year-old girl who was stabbed seventeen times by her mother's cousin. He was look- ing for money, apparently. I'm always struck by how many times people get stabbed. It seems like it's never just once or twice. It must be one of those activities that, once you get started, you just can't stop. The girl lived, but according to her grandmother, after the stabbing she developed a mean streak and is bossy now and picks fights.

July 29, 1988
Chicago
The subject on *Oprah* was profound handicaps. Two of the guests were parents of a teenage boy who weighs only thirty-six pounds. He is blind and dumb and now has impaired hearing due to an ear infection. He doesn't have any thoughts that they are aware of, and he lives at home.

The father explained that the government will only pay SSI if you make under $17,000 a year. He advocated for a national catastrophic health plan and that was fine, but he wouldn't stop talking about it. He said his daughter has diabetes and that his other daughter almost had cancer. Again and again he interrupted his fellow guests, and in time I grew tired of him.

In the middle of the show, Oprah brought out a twenty-four-year-old man. She said, "Jimmy, here you are. You have no arms. You have no legs. What keeps you going?"

Jimmy was optimistic and spoke about his life at the university where he studies child psychology. He kept saying that: *the university.* He said that his roommate in the dorm keeps the TV and radio and computer on the floor so he can get to them. Jimmy's neck was thick and muscular. He wore a suit with the arms and legs pinned up.

Another guest, a young woman, had all her limbs but they were too small. She could walk but needed crutches for long distances. Forks she could manage, and light loads. She said she wanted to die but didn't have the wherewithal to commit suicide.

Jimmy said he just wanted to help people. Once, when he was talking, they identified him at the bottom of the screen the way they often do on talk shows (*Judy: seeks revenge; Marco: loves women*). His read *Jimmy: happy to be alive.*

A couple in the audience stood to talk about their twenty-

187

seven-year-old son who had the mental capacity of a newborn baby. The husband was handsome and in his late fifties with a West Side Chicago accent. "I ain't fed my boy in twenty years," he said. "I'm ascared to."

I think I'm the ideal viewer for a show like this. After watching, I felt so lucky, like it's a blessing just to be broke and have bad teeth.

I worked in Linda's garage today, and at one point the kid who lives across the alley came over to me, asking, "Are you a boy or a man?"

July 31, 1988
Chicago

This afternoon I went to Montrose Beach, which was quiet and not nearly as packed as Foster. It rained yesterday, so the sand was hard. I'd been there for an hour, reading, when two men and three children moved near me. One of the men was missing his left hand. His arm was fine until a few inches above the wrist, where it tapered to a point. He sat on a blanket while the other guy took the kids into the water, all of them fully clothed, some with long pants on, even.

While they horsed around, the man with one hand turned on an enormous radio and tuned it to a mastermix station where the songs are not sung so much as bleated. Bleated and repeated. After a few minutes of this, a fellow in a tank top came over and asked that the music be turned down. The radio was so loud I couldn't hear their argument, but at the end of it the one-handed man lowered the volume.

When his friend came back, the one-handed man related what had happened. He made a fist with his good hand and held the other arm straight out like a lance. "I was just about to hit that asshole," he said. "I tolt him, 'This is a free country, isn't it? Isn't this a public beach?'"

The wet guy looked off toward the water, trying to pick out the person who'd told his friend to turn the music down. He said it was good to bring up the free-country business. He'd have said the same thing.

August 7, 1988
Chicago

Late last night a group of drunk white boys ruined their car and three others just outside my window. The crash was loud. I was in the sunroom at the time, thinking of ways to make money. The windows were open, and I heard one boy say to another, "Get going, asshole. Fucking *leave. Drive,* you fucker."

The guy behind the wheel tried to take off, but his car was too damaged. I called the police and called them again after one of the boys ordered two others to remove the license plates and the stickers. If you want the cops to come in Chicago, you really have to put the word *gun* in your sentence. I called a year ago and said it and they were here within two minutes—three cars of disappointed police officers.

The boys took off with the plates and stickers and I went to the corner, where a group of neighbors were gathered. It was two a.m., and I stood with a black bicycle thief, his friend, and a family of five with Southern accents. The little girl was named April, and like everyone else in her group, she was barefoot. One of her teenage brothers had a big cross tattooed on his forearm. Then there was her mother and her grandmother, who said, "Them boys was drunk. I mean, *drunk.*" She reached for a cigarette, then called to her grandson, "Skeeter, you got my lighter?"

When the cops finally came, the grandmother told them

that the boys had been drunk and that she'd had a time of it earlier, trying to keep everyone's prints off everything.

By this morning the drunk boys' trunk had been jimmied open and all four tires were gone. Once a car gets a flat in this neighborhood, it's considered abandoned and is stripped.

August 12, 1988
Chicago
Amy made it into the Second City touring company. They chose six people out of two hundred fifty. Nothing can keep her down. Amy's success means success for the whole family. I'm so proud I'm splitting open with it. She has something extra. Anyone can see it.

August 15, 1988
Chicago
I listened to AM radio church shows while I worked yesterday. One preacher denounced feminine men. "Now, when God took Eve out of Adam, He took *all of her* out," he said. "He didn't leave any behind. Then I see these men with the weak elbows and wrists, dressing like women, and I say, 'No.' I say 'No' to that."

I've pretty much decided to take Neil to the vet tomorrow. She shit all over the house this weekend and then peed on the rug. She's seventeen, so I can't really write this off as a phase. Her shit is liquid. Food just goes in one end and comes out the other.

August 16, 1988
Chicago
We took Neil to the vet today and on the way there she peed on me. She peed on my lap and then she just sat there. She didn't even try to get away from the urine. She's being cremated now, and I'll get the ashes in a few days. I'd always

expected her to die at home. The vet said that's what everyone wants. He examined her, her shrunken kidneys, her bad breath, which indicates severe digestive troubles, and asked if Neil had stopped being a pet. "Has she withdrawn?"

I said yes. She quit cleaning herself six months ago, and from then it's gone from bad to worse.

Now my life is post-Neil.

August 20, 1988
Emerald Isle
Names of beach houses I saw today:

Clambaker
Crow's Nest
Dune Castle
C&C by the Sea Upstairs
Skinny Dipper
God's Gift
Buck's Stop Here
Captain's Country
Skipper's Chip
Sea Mist
Sea Shape
Pelican's Perch
Footprints
Duck Inn
Breezy Outlook
Tip Top
The Scotch Bonnet
Rip Tide
Beach Nut
Lazy C
Summer Love

August 23, 1988
Emerald Isle

At the dinner table, Mom fed the dog a piece of steak off Dad's chair, and he called her a big dummy. He was wearing a pair of shorts that hadn't been washed in weeks so I didn't see what the big deal was. No one did but him.

September 5, 1988
Chicago

Tomorrow I go to school to have my ID picture taken. Teachers wear them on lanyards around their necks so they'll have something to fool with when they get nervous. One week from tomorrow, I'll have my first class, and I'm still working on an outline.

Tonight I remembered that I don't know anything about point of view, or about anything, really. So far I've gotten along OK, but as the teacher, you're kind of supposed to be on top of it. My greatest fear is having someone like N. in my class, the editor of the school paper. He writes articles about the nuisance of cigarette smoke and City Hall's feelings about artists' spaces. Were he in my class, he could easily point out my inadequacies. I can point them out too, of course, but I'm not the student, and I worry that in defending myself I'll sound too desperate.

September 6, 1988
Chicago

Tomorrow is the cocktail party for faculty, and today I found a $5 bill on the street. I'm thinking I'll spend it on magazines. One thing I'll buy is this week's *New Yorker*, which has a Joan Didion "Letter from Los Angeles" in it.

September 8, 1988
Chicago
Last month, Evelyne's electric bill was $345.
   Kim's was $109.
   Shirley's was $280.
   Mine was $35.

September 9, 1988
Chicago
I came upon two evangelists on State Street this morning, both conservatively dressed white women in their late thirties. One handed out pamphlets while the other preached. "Oh, just look at that," she said into her microphone as a young woman walked by. "The way she's dressed, she's asking for it, begging to be raped. And when she *is* raped, she'll deserve every single minute of it and eventually burn in hell."

It seemed harsh to me, her judgment. If the young woman had stopped to listen, would she have been redeemed?

September 13, 1988
Chicago
I realized I was a teacher when I felt warm during class and got up to open the door. Later on there was noise in the hallway, so I got up and shut it. Students can't open and close the door whenever they feel like it. For my first day I wore a white linen shirt with a striped tie, black trousers, and my good shoes. At the start of the session, I had nine students. Then one dropped out, so now I have only eight.

September 22, 1988
Chicago
I played my class a taped speech given by a woman named Nancy Sipes. It's about selling Amway, and while (my sister)

193

Amy and I think it's just the best thing ever, one of my students thought differently and dropped the course during our fifteen-minute break. Then I was down to seven, but luckily two more students added the class, so now I'm up to nine.

September 24, 1988
Chicago
I started a small job for Malik, the Indian man at R.J. Paints who has dark brown spots in both his eyes, not far from the pupils. All I'm doing is stripping a door. To make less mess, I took it off the hinges and carried it outside to his small backyard. I worked alone until three women in saris stepped out and took seats in lawn chairs. They'd ask me a question in English and then speak among themselves in a language I wasn't familiar with.

One of the women told me she studies chemistry at Northwestern and asked me if I was a student.

I said no, I was a teacher. Then she said something to the other women in their language and they all laughed. She asked how much I made teaching one class, and that drew even more laughter.

One of the women, the oldest of the three, was a card. Her friends doubled over at her wry observations. I worried I might ruin their afternoon in the sun with my harsh-smelling chemicals, but once it had been established that I made the least amount of money, I became invisible, and they carried on as if I weren't there.

September 26, 1988
Chicago
This morning Malik answered the door in what was either a pair of pajamas or an Indian about-the-house suit: a knee-length shirt with a Nehru collar and a loose pair of matching

trousers. His neck, face, and chest were blotched with powder. I couldn't tell if it was fresh or if he'd worn it to bed. In the afternoon I met his five-year-old son, who was very sweet and asked kind questions.

At Mitchell's restaurant, Amy and I sat next to an insane woman who was missing her front teeth and who had shredded her napkins and place mat. The paper littered the floor around her, as did torn-up bits of pancake. She spoke in three distinct voices, one of them rough and deep, like Linda Blair's in *The Exorcist*.

After sitting for a while, talking to herself, the woman got up and went to the bathroom. She was in there for a long time, and when Amy couldn't stand it any longer, she went to see what was going on. The door was locked, but she could hear the woman on the other side, cursing in one voice and defending herself in another. Five minutes later she came out, pushed her bangs away from her face, and said to the waitress, "Sorry 'bout the mess, love," in an English accent, as if she were Hayley Mills and had just spilled a glass of wine.

After she left, the manager said, "Go check the washroom. She walked out of here too happy."

The waitress ignored him, so Amy went in and reported that there was water all over the floor. The john was packed with toilet paper, paper towels, and part of the *Sun-Times*. All the soap had been bitten in half, and there were crumbs in the sink.

September 27, 1988
Chicago
This afternoon Professor Sedaris addressed a dead audience. Even S., the mother of two who answers questions with questions and is usually confrontational, said nothing. I drowned

in the silence. Then I babbled, hoping someone would maybe stick an oar in just to shut me up.

"Sometimes that just happens," said Sandi, a fellow teacher, when I saw her in the office.

Jim says that maybe next semester I can teach two classes, but right now that sounds like a nightmare. It would make me eligible for health insurance, which I'll need after I slit my wrists. What did I do wrong today?

October 1, 1988
Chicago
Charles Addams died two days ago.

On Friday I worked for Malik, who answered the door in a breezy skirt, shirtless, and with more splotches of baby powder on his body. His son Zeshan kept me company, as he was home from school with a cough. When his mother gave him medicine, she said, "Zeshan, you gut to take dis because I hate people what cough."

The boy described the medicine as "ugly." His voice is raspy and I like how reasonable his questions are. He's only five but told me he has four children, the oldest of which is nine years old. I want this kid. If he were mine, though, he wouldn't be so charming.

At three o'clock, Zeshan's sister Najia came in with three other girls, cousins from upstairs. Everyone was very excited because one of them had won a goldfish at school.

If any of the children in my building got a goldfish, the excitement would come from watching it twist to its death on the gas burner, but these kids were genuinely innocent. It was like a first-grade primer, a chapter titled "The Goldfish Excitement." I return on Monday and look forward to it.

October 3, 1988
Chicago

At the departmental potluck, I kept my mouth pretty much shut, afraid that if I spoke, everyone would realize that I don't know what I'm talking about. Not that I didn't ask a few questions. A couple of teachers talked about throwing people out of their classes—troublemakers. Their talk made me realize the subtle ways I'm being taken advantage of by certain students. I'd been looking for the criminal with the livid scar on his face and all the while I'd been getting my pockets picked.

M., the independent-study kid I picked up last week, is a liar and a poor student. I shouldn't have let her in after the third week, and allowing it has marked me as a teacher chump. Teacher chumps get a reputation, as do easy teachers. Come next semester, your class is full of lazy people expecting just to coast along.

October 5, 1988
Chicago

I've been taking great joy in grading papers. My evaluations are typed and, for me, startlingly honest. I read them over late at night and am frequently struck by how mature and wise they sound. "A child raised in a violent sexual environment should know at least three different terms for a dog's balls, and 'thingofabobs' is not one of them."

I write what works and what doesn't. I don't want to embarrass anyone in class or tamp down discussion, so the notes are just for the students.

Today in my box I got J.'s story. It ran one and a half pages and was followed by a P.S.: "My typewriter ran out of ribbon and it's pretty late." Another student, C., gave me torn half pages that were written in the cafeteria, probably while he was having a conversation. Last week he seemed interested, but this week he comes to class without his book and sits there looking mean and bored.

October 24, 1988
Chicago

I met with a woman named Betty who owns a three-flat on North Kenmore and would like to have one of the apartments painted. Someone started the job a few weeks ago but was fired for laziness. Asked to remove the hardware and spray it with gold paint, he left the hinges and doorknobs in place and spray-painted them anyway. It looks beautiful, much better than it would have if he'd followed directions. It's like the knobs are spreading good cheer to the comparatively sober white doors.

October 29, 1988
Chicago

Two well-dressed, white-haired women at the IHOP tonight. I noticed their looks as they walked out, but before that they were just whiny voices at the table behind me. The pair divided the bill right down to the penny. Each owed $3.77. Then they addressed the subject of the tip and decided they should leave 70 cents. Neither said, "Aw, what the hell. Just make it a dollar." That's how tight they were.

One of the women had injured her finger earlier in the day and was concerned regarding its treatment. This was the one named Lil. "I caught it in the door, but I'm holding up," she said. "Most people would have fainted, but not me."

"Finger?" the other woman said. "You're talking about a finger?"

"I almost lost a nail!" Lil said.

"Don't talk to me about one finger," the other woman said.

"I caught three of them in a car door once. Nikki slammed it and it shut all the way!"

"You could see stars," Lil said.

"Three fingers and the door was completely shut," the woman repeated. "And they swelled up terribly and changed color from blue to purple to yellow."

"Sure they did," Lil assured her.

"Anyone else would have fainted. Nikki, for instance. She saw what she'd done and suddenly all the color drained out of her face. She was standing there—"

"I love that raincoat," Lil said, changing the subject.

"I live in this raincoat," the other woman said.

"I live in mine too," Lil said. "Now can you help me put it on, because with this damaged finger, I'm useless."

November 23, 1988
Chicago
I have been a bad employee lately. I went to Betty's with a drug hangover and fell asleep on her floor. I had a terrible headache and woke up several hours later with a carpet burn on my face.

1989

January 5, 1989
Chicago

I weighed myself this morning and tip the scales at 146 pounds. Last April I went on a diet and weighed only 141. Now look at me! At the IHOP tonight, I sat facing the rotisserie on which three chickens turned and dripped juices. Tonight I'll just have a steak and some spinach, then tomorrow I'll have less.

January 9, 1989
Raleigh

Last night I wondered if other teachers get stoned at night. Can I be the only one? Classes start next week and I am not at all prepared.

January 15, 1989
Raleigh

I will never again drink at a party I am hosting.
I will never again drink at a party I am hosting.
I will never again drink at a party I am hosting.

I drank at a party I was hosting. After four beers, I had three screwdrivers, then I started taking bong hits. It was around then that things started spinning. I ate an apple yesterday, and a tiny sandwich. There were fifty people here. I tried to sit down and watch my guests dance, but the sight of them made me nauseated so I stumbled into my office and collapsed.

On the other side of the door I could hear John Smith, who talked about playing Pictionary with a dull partner who didn't know who Henry James was. I listened and tried to get up. Then I decided it was better to just quietly slip away.

January 17, 1989
Chicago

Today was the first day of the new semester, and I'm teaching two classes. There are twenty students in the first one. I asked everyone to list the last three books they'd read (answers included *Jonathan Livingston Seagull* and a Danielle Steel novel) and then I asked what they'd do were someone to give them each $500. One person said he'd get more tattoos; many wanted sound systems; and three wanted plane tickets to warm places.

Because there are so many students, it's easy getting them to talk. One person ate in class, and another said "Shit" way too many times. Before they left, I had them each write a few paragraphs explaining to me how they'd lost their feet.

Something has changed, and now, when I look at my students, I see only people who are going to eat up my time.

Meanwhile, my diet is working. I went down a belt notch and was comfortable.

January 19, 1989
Chicago

This is the last day of Ronald Reagan's presidency, and on *All Things Considered* they asked a variety of people how he had affected their lives. The person I most identified with said that after the past eight years, she will never trust a Republican again. There were many people who cheered him, and a few who hated him in a personal way. One woman blamed Reagan for her parents' divorce. She was from a farm family and said that the stress brought on by the president's agricultural policies ruined the marriage, which under previous administrations had been happy.

A Brooklyn man blamed Reagan for his AIDS, speaking almost as if he'd caught it from him. I hated Reagan but stopped dwelling on it after he became such an easy and popular target. My eyes never welled up when he spoke. They narrowed.

January 24, 1989
Chicago
Names from the phone book:

> Adonis Labinski
> Dolly Branch
> B. J. Beefus
> Eugene Bratman
> Wolfgang Fey
> Freeman Fry

January 27, 1989
Chicago
I was in the coffee shop of the Palmer House, seated at the counter, and reached for my glasses. The guy next to me had set his glasses down as well, and when, by mistake, I picked them up, he let out a little cry and accused me of trying to steal them. The man was in his seventies and though his glasses had plastic frames like mine and were a similar shade of brown, his were aviators. Mine was an honest mistake. I apologized, but still he called the waitress over, saying, "This guy was trying to steal from me."

The waitress talked to him the way you might to a child. "Oh," she said, "I'm sure he wouldn't do a thing like that."

The man, frustrated that nobody recognized the kind of person I really was, lifted his coffee cup and held it close to his chest, as if I might try to swipe that too.

Just then a woman took a seat and the man turned to her and said, "Watch out. This one here just tried to steal my glasses." I glanced over to give her my this-person-is-crazy look, but she was too busy locking her purse firmly between her legs.

January 30, 1989
Chicago

I saw an ad in *Time* magazine for a CD of the biggest country hits of 1961. Songs include:

"Under the Influence of Love"
"I Dreamed of a Hillbilly Heaven"
"Po' Folks"
"Beggar to a King"
"Three Hearts in a Tangle"

Each of these would be a great story title.

February 2, 1989
Chicago

Because Stephanie quit, Mary was back at the IHOP tonight. She worked there for nine years and left three weeks ago to manage a hotel restaurant in Evanston. She told me that she loves it but misses throwing people out and calling the police. That was always her thing. I remember nights when one out of every four people who walked through the door would get the bum's rush. Someone would mutter something under his breath, and she would snatch the menu out of his hand and point to the door, shouting, "I heard that—out!" Not just crazy people and drunks but men and women who never imagined themselves being thrown out of a restaurant.

Tonight the man I think of as the Old Jew paid his bill and asked Mary if she was back working nights.

She said yes, but just for two weeks.

"Well, if you're free sometime, I'd like to take you out," he said.

Mary put her hands on her hips. "Are you kidding? The only place I want you to go is hell. Understand? You can go straight to hell."

The Old Jew looked down at the gum displayed in the case before him and said, "Oh, well. I guess it's just that way with some people."

"Yes," Mary said. "It sure is. It's that way with me."

After he left, I asked Mary why she hates him so much. He's been a regular as long as I have—five years now, though he's never spoken to me and just looks away when I nod hello. The Old Jew eats at the IHOP every night, sometimes alone and sometimes in the company of a nurse. He's been through dozens of them, and I always figured either he doesn't pay well or they get bored. He's got to be in his late eighties, hunched over, the top of his bald head speckled with liver spots.

Mary told me that he used to come in for lunch back when she worked the day shift. One afternoon he told her that his wife had just died and that he wanted to get rid of some of her old jewelry and would love it if Mary would take some.

"I agreed because I know how hard that can be, getting rid of things after someone you love dies," she told me.

That night she went to his apartment and noticed in the living room half a dozen candy dishes, some glass and some silver, all filled with condoms. The Old Jew told her then that actually his wife had died more than eight years ago and that he didn't have many of her belongings left. "Maybe a pair of earrings," he said, but he'd have to get in the right mood before he started looking for them.

Mary said she didn't feel threatened. "I could have beaten him to death with one hand tied behind my back," she assured me. "But ever since then I've really hated him, because sometimes that's the way it is."

I was in front of the Sheridan L stop when I passed a woman cursing at oncoming cars. I'd seen her before. She looks like W. C. Fields would if he wore a red wig. Her nose is bulbous, like his, and she doesn't have any noticeable eyebrows or lashes. When a couple walked past, she said that they were going home to fuck, just like all the other shitheads.

I'm guessing she has Tourette's or something.

I'd taught and was wearing a tie and carrying my briefcase. When I was a student, I always felt better when the teacher dressed up. It suggested that his or her job was a real one. As for the briefcase, I look at it like a safe. Students see me putting their papers into it, and it makes them feel that their stories are valuable, though it is a drag to carry.

As I passed the woman in front of the L station, she said, "Oh, look at him. The little man. Thinks he's a big fucking deal because he's carrying an attaché case." I crossed the street with my head down, shattered because she could see right through me.

February 10, 1989
Chicago
Jackie Disler is a fountain of information. This morning she told me that Hungarians have the filthiest mouths in Europe

and are known to say, "Get that cock out of my face that is covered with shit that you used to fuck Jesus."

According to her, fucking Jesus is a popular insult in that part of the world.

February 13, 1989
Chicago
Tonight at Barbara's Bookstore, Tobias Wolff read from his new memoir, *This Boy's Life*. All the seats were taken, so I sat on the floor in the front and tried to act normal. I was too shy to say anything when I got my book signed, afraid that if I started talking, everything inside me would just spill out. He seemed like a kind person and wore a turtleneck, a plaid shirt, a tweed jacket, and jeans with black socks and running shoes. I have to be his biggest fan.

February 14, 1989
Chicago
Barbara has begun speaking to me. She's from Tennessee, maybe forty-five years old, and has worked at the IHOP the entire time that I've been hanging out there. Tonight she told me that the new waitress, the black woman who started a few weeks back, has been fired for refusing to wear panty hose. Barbara said, "And of course we have to wear panty hose. We *all* do!"

March 4, 1989
Chicago
I read an interview with an obsessive-compulsive woman who said that before she went on medication, she spent eighteen hours a day cleaning her house. After vacuuming, she would go over the carpet with tape in order to pick up dirt she might have missed. When guests visited, she'd make a mental note

of everything they touched and wipe it down the moment they left. She said she'd miss important events in order to stay home and clean her keys or her checkbook, which, how do you even *do?* As for keys, it would never occur to me that mine were dirty, though they probably are. Filthy, actually.

March 13, 1989
Chicago

A man approached me on the Wilson L platform this morning to ask me what I thought of the neighborhood. He said a woman he knew had just moved in and he was worried about her. I didn't want to be the voice of doom and told him that nothing terrible has ever happened to me here, which is true. Then I said that I fully expected something terrible to happen, which is also the truth.

Why live in a place where you expect trouble? He could have asked me that, but he didn't. I'm surprised he approached me in the first place. I look terrible lately. I reek. A few days ago I was behind my desk at school and caught a whiff of urine. Then I realized it was me I smelled—my pants. My students must have noticed it. How could they have not? I'll have to concoct some sort of a story. I could say that I take care of a baby every Wednesday morning and that last week it peed on me.

March 20, 1989
Chicago

I read a story by a Chinese woman whose main character curses her husband by calling him a turtle and a salted egg.

March 21, 1989
Chicago

Last week a manhole cover disappeared from the alley behind my building. I guess people sell them for scrap or something. The city covered the open hole with plywood and put up a sawhorse with blinking lights, but overnight both those things were stolen as well. When I got home from work today, someone rang, and I buzzed in a guy from the sewer department. He asked if I was the manager of the building, and I said no. Then he asked about the missing manhole cover, and I offered to take him out back. It was bitterly cold, and the guy seemed happy to be in my warm apartment. He looked to be in his sixties, about my size, wearing a brown coat and a ski cap pulled low on his forehead.

I went to put on my shoes and jacket and he said, "No rush. Take your time."

We walked through the kitchen, and he stopped and looked at the radiator. "You know how to keep that from hissing? You need to take yourself a skinny nail and unclog that hole right there. That's your problem. But don't do it now because you might burn yourself."

"OK," I said. "Thanks."

"What you want to do is wait until later, then take a nail, a long, skinny one, and ream out that hole. That'll solve your problem."

I thanked him again and then took him to the alley, where we saw that the manhole cover had been replaced. While standing there looking at it, I learned that getting a new one had been the landlord's responsibility. "I love to catch people stealing them," the man said. "You can get sent to prison for taking one of these babies."

He could have walked around the corner to get back to his truck, but instead he followed me into the apartment. In the living room, he paused to look at some drawings. "Did you do these?" he asked. "What are you, some kind of...drawer?" He bent forward and chuckled. "Man, oh, man. These are great."

I always offer coffee to people working in my home. The guy who fixed the stove, an electrician, the cops who came once, everyone. I offer and they decline. I had a feeling this guy would have said yes and then stayed until five o'clock or whatever was quitting time for him. Since he wasn't working in my home, I didn't offer him any, but now I wish I had. I liked him.

March 23, 1989
Chicago

The president of the NRA was on the radio today, speaking before the Commonwealth Club of California. I was working at Linda's, refinishing her banister, and when she came in, we listened together. The guy started defending the sale of assault rifles. It's not the guns that are the problem, he said, but the birds who use them. "These birds who are psychos and should be locked up in the nuthouse. These birds who break into houses and try to rape people."

The guy was very folksy. "Just like my dad," Linda said. "That could be him on the radio!"

Her father is a farmer and she grew up with guns. As a child she shot a robin. Shocked at what she'd done, she tried to set it back in the tree, thinking it might spring to life once it was returned to its rightful place.

The head of the NRA kept using the term *birds*. He said that sportsmen across the country enjoy the responsible use of assault rifles and that a few sicko nut birds shouldn't ruin it for the rest of us. He wasn't particularly articulate, but he believed in his cause and didn't evade questions the way so many speakers before the Commonwealth Club do.

March 26, 1989
Chicago
Walking to the L, I passed two men on Leland, both of them fully grown. One of them asked for a cigarette and the other, not hearing my answer, grabbed my arm. "I said we want a cigarette!" he shouted.

You can't go around grabbing people like that. I'm sick of how trashy it is here. It's filthy and depressing and every day it gets worse due to the warm weather. Living in Uptown, I get the idea that people are basically stupid, cruel, and violent.

The lease runs out at the end of April, and I think I'm ready to move.

In other news, I heard that a man's waist should be twice as thick as his neck.

March 31, 1989
Chicago
The blind man was at the IHOP tonight, eating dinner with a sighted companion who brought up a friend of his who had hoped to open a combination café/theater in the Loop and offer light meals and plays during the lunch hour. "Of course, you'd have your soup of the day and your salads and so on," he said. "I'm talking sandwiches and so forth."

The blind man nodded.

"But it turned out he didn't go through with it," the sighted man said. Apparently the friend didn't have enough money. "So I said to him, 'Well, money's not everything.' Then *he* said, 'Maybe not, but it's about ten thousand goddamn miles ahead of whatever it is that comes in second.'" He sighed, then stole a french fry off the blind man's plate.

I graded L.'s paper today. She always arrives late to class, then settles herself in and starts eating a snack. She likes potato chips in cellophane bags. Then she'll decide to clean out her purse, taking out papers and crumpling them up. A couple of times I've turned to her, saying, "Are we all done now? Got everything squared away?"

Then she'll say either "Yes" or "Almost." Sarcasm is lost on her.

L.'s story was among the worst things I've ever read in my life. How on earth did they allow her to graduate from high school? Even Tomoko, who is from Japan and can just barely speak English, is a better writer. Plus Tomoko is spirited and she tries, unlike L., who just snacks and cleans out her purse.

April 12, 1989
Chicago
Money:

> $33 from Lower Links reading
> $50 honorarium from Randolph Street Gallery
> $83 total!

April 18, 1989
Chicago
This evening I feel fat, stupid, and ugly. I was a lousy teacher again today, completely incapable of holding an opinion. I'll make a statement, then, at the slightest resistance, I'll retract it. How can they respect me?

There are several students in this class whom I don't like. I don't spend a lot of time thinking about it, I just don't like them. Can they tell?

April 21, 1989
Chicago
At the market underneath the Wilson L, I pulled the shopping

list out of my pocket. Just as I realized there'd been money in there too and that I'd dropped it, I turned to see a man swoop down and pick it up off the floor. He had sand-colored hair and a red, boozy face crosshatched with wrinkles. I told him politely that that was my dollar he'd just picked up, and he said, "What dollar? I didn't pick anything up."

"Yes, you did. I saw you."

"You didn't see nothing," he told me.

I followed him to the back of the store, where he grabbed a quart of beer and a bottle of Four Roses. "Come on," I said. "I saw you take my money. Give it back."

This guy was in his late forties, at least, way old enough to know better. If I saw a dollar bill fall from someone's pocket, I'd say, "Excuse me, you dropped something." If there was no one around, I'd claim it as my own, but this was different.

At the register the man untwisted my dollar. Then he took all the change out of his pocket and slowly counted it out. When the cashier told him he was short 10 cents, he turned to me and said, "Give me a dime."

I couldn't believe it.

There were two men behind me in line. One of them rooted in his pocket and handed the man who'd stolen from me two nickels. Then he looked at me with mild disgust, the way you might at a skinflint, and said, "What's a dime?"

May 5, 1989
Chicago

I really need to avoid red wine. I drank it last night at Rob and Lyn's house and awoke hours later with a terrible fire in my throat. My uvula felt like a pilot light. When I got up this morning, my face was very white. I feel fragile today but don't have what I'd define as a hangover. I remember what went on last night. At one point, Rob showed me his computer and explained that you can plug one into a tele-phone jack.

On Tuesday I handed back seventeen papers I'd gotten from the beginning class, including one from L. It's about a little girl who gets out of bed on Christmas Eve to spy on Santa. She never sees him but gets a shiny new bike the next morn-ing. The final line is "I knew that this was going to be a very special Christmas."

It was something a fifth-grader might write, and it made me sad that I was reading it. Her other story, "The New Me," was about a caterpillar turning into a butterfly. I was talking about it to Sandi in the teachers' lounge, and she told me she'd gotten the exact same story from someone else last semester. I looked in the right-hand corner of the title page and saw that L. had just whited over this other idiot's name and then typed in her own. When I confronted her later in the day, she said, "Look, just tell me. Am I going to pass the class or not?"

Man ordering at Butera's deli/prepared-foods counter: "Hey, give me one of them chickens what spins around."

May 9, 1989
Chicago
This morning I made a list of chores that might lift my spirits:

1. Lose ten pounds.
2. Rewrite the last two stories so I can start something new.
3. Paint a picture of a mole.
4. Make myself go out when I don't want to.

* * *

Again this year I made Mom a Mother's Day card. It reads:

> *M is for the Morbid things you showed me*
> *O is for the Other things you did*
> *T is for the Thousand bucks you owe me*
> *H is for the things you found I Hid*
> *E is for the Error of my caring*
> *R is for the Ranch house you call home*
> *Mother dear, I wish that you had shown me*
> *how to shave and how to use a comb.*

May 28, 1989
Chicago

I have seen two fistfights this weekend. One was across the street from Steve Lafreniere's, where two men confronted a skinny guy they'd seen beating a woman. "You ain't supposed to hit girls, you stupid fuck, you asshole," they said as they punched him.

Later, on Beacon, I passed two men fighting over a small bicycle, just pounding on each other.

June 21, 1989
Chicago

Since moving farther north I've been taking the bus to the IHOP. On the way home tonight I sat across from a woman with teardrops tattooed on her face. She had a bad complexion and hard features made all the more jarring by her outfit: a skirt and blouse, the blouse one of those high-collared ones with ruffles that a conservative lady might wear. The skirt was cream-colored. From my distance I could see that the clothes were cheap. I'd seen this woman before, but never sober.

After a few blocks, a man boarded. All the teeth on the right side of his mouth were missing and when he saw the woman, he said, "Doris!" He commented on her clothing and said it was fancy.

"Yes," she said. "I decided to wear a dress for once in my life. Wonders never cease, do they, Roy!" She raised her hand to swipe away her bangs and I saw that there was a tattoo on her forehead as well.

July 4, 1989
Chicago

While on my bike I passed a woman walking with two young children. The little girl had a plastic six-pack ring wrapped around one of her feet, and her mother, noticing it, shouted, "What the fuck are you doing, bitch?"

July 20, 1989
Chicago

There was a shooting in Amy's neighborhood last night. She and her boyfriend, Paul, heard the shots from their living room and figured they were firecrackers until they saw a crowd gathered in front of the house across the street. The man who lives there is very ugly and is missing a hand. In its place he wears not a hook but a pincer that starts at the elbow and is sort of like a crab claw. Eight police cars came. Officers led the man out of the house and started to cuff him, but then they noticed his pincer, at which point they took him by the arm and locked him in the paddy wagon.

On *All My Children*, Erica is being stalked by a dwarf. For a long time they just showed a hand that would draft ugly letters to her and turn off the local news whenever she appeared. I get the feeling I'm supposed to know who this person is, but I've been watching regularly for only four years so I'm at a loss. Meanwhile, on *One Life to Live,* Vicki has been shot in the stomach. Megan watched it happen and hasn't made a sound since. I'll bet anything she inherited Vicki's multiple-personality disorder.

July 21, 1989
Chicago

I was right about Megan. Vicki's shooting triggered her latent inherited multiple-personality disorder and turned her into someone named Ruby Brite, who likes gambling and speaks with a Brooklyn accent.

July 25, 1989
Chicago

Amy gave me her old toaster, which I put in the pantry and forgot about until last night at two a.m. I'd already had dinner, and plenty of it, but still I made two peanut butter sandwiches with canned peaches on them. I don't eat like this when there's no pot in the house, but now I'm back to sucking up everything in my path. Peanut butter and *peaches?* Since when do those two things go together?

July 30, 1989
Chicago

I was standing on Clark Street when an elderly woman approached riding one of those electric carts people take to when they're not quite crippled enough for a wheelchair. "Out of my way, asshole," she said. I moved to the side, and after driving a couple of feet past me, she chained her little chariot to a parking meter and hobbled into the restaurant I had just walked out of.

July 31, 1989
Chicago
Jewel is having a sale on chickens, 49 cents a pound, so I bought several and stood in line reading an article in *New Woman* titled "Infidelity: How to Keep Your Man from Straying." It included several warning signs, as you need to know when your boyfriend or husband is feeling insecure and neglected. You need to take notice when he loses interest in sex, and you have to fight, fight, fight to win him back. The article suggested that a man's infidelity is always the wife's or girlfriend's fault. It never considers that maybe he's just an asshole.

August 7, 1989
Chicago
Anatole Broyard on Jane and Paul Bowles in this week's *New York Times Book Review:* "Their marriage was so open it yawned."

The blind fellow was at the IHOP last night with his father, and I listened as they discussed geography, particularly the states that make up the Great Plains, the Sunbelt, and the original thirteen colonies. Then he asked his dad about New York City, saying he'd heard they have no alleys there and that the people are rude.

"Rudest sons of bitches on the face of this earth," his father said. "It's crammed full of rude people and rich foreigners — Jews, Arabs, Japs — and they make it so you can't afford to shit."

The blind guy has a small voice and is very polite. His eyes are in the far corners of their sockets. Last night I noticed a lot of food stains on his shirt. The blind guy's father, when talking about New York, reached behind himself and used his knife to scratch his back.

August 9, 1989
Chicago

I was at the Roseland Bike Shop, waiting for them to repair my handlebars, when a woman came in. Behind her were two children, a ten-year-old boy, blond with a dirty face, and a teenage girl riding a small pink one-speed. Earlier, apparently, the mother had spoken to the owner, Ken, about his buying it. He'd offered a low price, so the mother and her two children had walked down Broadway looking for a better one. Now they were back.

"I just got her that bike last Crusmus," the woman said.

"No way," Ken told her. "That's at least seven years old. It has a banana seat, for Christ's sake! They don't even sell those anymore."

"Last Crusmus," the woman repeated. She had shoulder-length yellow hair and wore a sweatshirt with DAMN, I'M GOOD! written on it. "I saved and saved to buy her that bicycle. I got it at Woolworth's. You can check with them! I got the papers somewhere at home but'll have to root around to find them." She wiped her mouth with her hand. "I'm a poor woman, Ken."

"Aw, Mom, shut up," her daughter said. "Please shut up."

"I've got me thirteen children—eleven of them living—and seven grandchildren." She looked to be around forty—a very hard forty—but I didn't doubt the thirteen kids. The daughter took off down the street then, and her mother called after her. "Bonnie, Bonnie, you better get back here." She wiped her mouth again. "Don't mind her, Ken, she just thinks you don't want to buy her bike." She turned back in the direction of her daughter. "Bonnie, you better get back here before I slap the shit out of you."

August 11, 1989
Chicago

I was at the liquor store, buying a bottle of Canadian Club as a thank-you gift, when a drunk man approached and told me not to be frightened. He was absolutely hammered, this guy, and said he wanted me to buy him some potato chips, the kind in a large-portion bag—Big Grabs, they're called. I brushed him off, and when I got to the register, out of nowhere he laid the chips on the counter beside my bottle of Canadian Club.

The cashier saw what was going on and snatched the bag away. Then he pointed to the door and shouted, "Out of here, you!"

When I stepped outside after paying, the drunk was waiting for me. He was very angry and got up in my face, demanding that I give him money. I handed him a quarter and he said, "A *dollar* and a quarter."

I needed to unlock my bike, so was in a bind. Drunk or not, this guy had clearly been in a lot more fights than I had. I didn't want to give him $1 because by this point, I hated him, and it was more like getting robbed than doing someone a favor. Luckily, just then a friend of his walked up and said, "What are you, begging for money again, Ronald? Begging? Dogs beg, man."

This gave me a chance to unlock my bike and ride away.

August 21, 1989
Emerald Isle

I was up by eight thirty this morning and we were all out on the beach an hour later: Mom, Amy, Tiffany, and me. Mom was in a terrific mood and talked about her father, who was an alcoholic but a cheery one. Whenever Mom or Aunt Joyce came home late with friends, he'd get out of bed and cook for everyone, make spaghetti sauce, pies, anything anyone wanted. He'd fill the tub with water and let ducklings splash around in it. As a teenager, Mom was allowed two sweaters per winter, but she sweat so badly that they were ruined in no time.

August 27, 1989
Raleigh

I rode home from the beach with S., and on the way we stopped at Pappy's Army Surplus. One of the T-shirts they're selling pictures a handgun and the words SMITH & WESSON, THE BEST IN FEMININE PROTECTION.

While looking around, I learned that last Christmas, S.'s sister-in-law sent her a half-eaten box of candy. The year before that, she gave her a broken jewelry box made of stained glass.

September 22, 1989
Chicago

I went to Barbara's Bookstore to hear Russell Banks talk about his new novel, *Affliction*. I'd read *Continental Drift, Searching for Survivors, Success Stories, Trailerpark,* and *The New World* and liked them all. He wore tan-colored slacks, a striped shirt, a sport coat, and loafers and read for twenty minutes. Afterward I bought the book and stood to get it signed. The first woman in line told Russell Banks that she'd tried to get his phone number from Richard Ford's wife, but since Ford's wife couldn't find it, she'd decided to come in person and give him a list of questions she'd like answered. The man behind her went into a lengthy explanation of why he himself writes and was very particular about the inscription he wanted. I was next in line, and just as I opened my mouth a woman appeared with a paperback copy of *Conti-*

nental Drift and said, "Excuse me, hi! It says on the back that this is a novel about American life. Is that true?"

He said politely that it was not a novel about all of American life, but, sure, it had Americans in it.

I never know what to say when I'm getting a book signed.

September 26, 1989
Chicago

I asked my beginning writing students to compose fan letters, and today we read them out loud in class. Most were sincere in the way I hoped they'd be, but one kid's amounted to hate mail and was addressed to his mother. He wrote about being shit out of her cunt. Then he reminded her that he was not her fucking boyfriend, and on and on. Afterward no one knew what to say.

My fan letter was to Joy Williams.

September 27, 1989
Chicago

Ted called last night. "All my life I've been looking for Mr. Right, and here I've wound up with Mr. Wong," he said, referring to his new boyfriend, James Wong, who is from Hong Kong. Ted's sister, meanwhile, has started playing guitar and singing gospel songs, mainly in malls.

October 10, 1989
Chicago

I worked four different jobs this week—school, Betty, Evelyne, and Shirley—and during the last three of them, I fantasized about moving to New York and living in the apartment of that drug dealer I visited last June. It wasn't huge, just a one-bedroom on the third floor facing the street. In my fantasy, people come to visit me, but I don't have time to see them because I'm so busy. Because of the book I've had published, I am often recognized when I go out. I am very trim and lots of people call me. I don't know how I'd ever get the drug dealer's apartment or, more important, the book. There's still a lot to work out.

October 24, 1989
Chicago

Today in class I wrote *Spotlight on Love* on the blackboard. Then I drew a spotlight aimed at the words to show I meant business. "Today I'd like us to talk about breakups," I said, rightly figuring that everyone had a story to tell.

E. started off by talking about his hometown girlfriend, who he'd just learned had been cheating on him.

"That's because she's trash," I said, trying to make him feel better. "She's a liar and a skunk, and this is how she gets attention." I said that what goes around, comes around, and in time the guy she was seeing now would be cheating on her, just like she cheated on E.

He was glad to hear it.

Next came M. and A., who both had good stories. Then it was J.'s turn and she ran out of the room crying.

K., a young woman who is always tardy and wears lots of makeup, said that she's not currently involved with anyone but is pursuing a guy who is already in a relationship.

Boo. Hussy. Troublemaker. No one came out and said this, but our attitudes conveyed it. I love teaching college lately.

October 29, 1989
Chicago

Mom arrived for a visit yesterday, and we went from the airport to the Palmer House, where we had a cup of coffee. We walked around, we went to Amy's, we took naps, and today we're going shopping.

*   *   *

I was on the L, reading a book, when someone said, "Sir?" I looked up to see the most terribly disfigured person imaginable. He took my breath away, a black man who'd been horribly burned. His head looked like a candle in the shape of a head, the skin slick and dripping down like wax. He was missing both his hands, and there was a can attached to his bandaged stumps. Taped to it was a sign reading NEED MONEY FOR OPERATION.

Man, it scared the life out of me.

November 1, 1989
Chicago

Mom left today at four. She was a big hit with my beginning students. I brought her in for my Ask a Mother segment, and she was fantastic and answered everyone's questions with humor and wisdom.

Last night we went to Eli's for steaks. I was wearing a tie but not a jacket, so I had to wear one the restaurant provided that was way too big for me.

November 2, 1989
Chicago

Paul enrolled in a technical college in Durham and has been assigned an English paper in which he needs to compare and contrast two things. The teacher said it might be good to compare the people of Raleigh to those who live in Durham. "In this town, folks are curious and will allow you to merge into their lane, while in Raleigh they're all too busy and stuck-up," she said.

Paul is thinking that for his paper he'd like to compare mushrooms to acid.

November 21, 1989
Chicago
I've been offered a chance to teach summer school. The class lasts three weeks and pays $2,300. It's five days a week, three hours per day, and I could use the money to move to New York.

December 21, 1989
Chicago
On the last day of class I took my students to the Walnut Room, where we sat by the big Christmas tree and had cocktails. Everything on the menu had a festive name. One item in particular was called something like God Rest Ye Merry Gentlemen California Blush Wine.

Afterward I went with Ben and his mother to the Wagon Wheel Restaurant, where the two of them ate bacon cheeseburgers. His mom could be fifty but looks younger. She wore a knit bonnet, and through it I could see gray hair but couldn't determine how much of it she had. This was the ten-year anniversary of her divorce. At first she thought she'd order the pancakes and have a beer to go with them. Then she changed her mind and went with the bacon cheeseburger, deciding that instead of beer she'd have coffee. Ben's mother works at B. Dalton and earns $75 per week. I liked her a lot.

1990

January 1, 1990
Raleigh

At midnight Gretchen and I were driving down Glenwood Avenue. Someone honked his horn for no reason, and I looked at my watch and realized it was the New Year. A new decade, even, one I am entering with an electric typewriter. (Christmas present from Mom.)

Everyone says, "Thank God the eighties are over," and I wonder if they say that about every decade.

This afternoon I worked on the Clark Avenue rental property with Paul. Last week during the cold snap, Dad set up a kerosene heater that covered everything with soot. The former tenant had left the freezer door open, so it's black in there as well. Paul and I spent a day washing everything down, and then Dad drove over and the three of us painted while listening to the FOXY 107 countdown. Everyone in our family listens to black music, everyone, all the time.

January 4, 1990
Raleigh

Mom reads her horoscope daily, sometimes in two or three different places. It's something she started doing a few years back, and while I don't believe in astrology, still I find myself falling for it. This morning she told me that an older person will be giving me something in return for a favor, and that the gift has the potential to change my life.

Dad is the only older person I know who owes me a favor—Paul and I painted that apartment he owns for free. So I waited for him to give me something. When it became clear that it wasn't going to happen on its own, I *asked* him to give me something.

We were in the kitchen and he said, "All right, hold on. I've got something for you!" He went into the basement and returned a few minutes later with a box of S&H Green Stamps. Some were pasted into books, and some were loose. This was a box he'd brought with him when we moved to Raleigh from Binghamton in 1964. I didn't think anyone honored Green Stamps anymore, but Dad said they're still redeemable in Florida.

"How will these change my life?" I asked.

"Well, I guess that's up to you," he said.

January 23, 1990
Chicago

According to the mother of one of my new students, women whose last names end in the letter A tend to have larger breasts than women whose names end in any other letter. The student, Lisa, had her arms crossed when she said this.

January 29, 1990
Chicago

I'm trying to replace the kitchen faucet for Shirley's tenants and wound up going to the hardware store with a guy named Jack, a carpenter who'd come to give an estimate on the new closets. He's been married three times. His first wife left when their youngest son was only two years old.

I asked why she left, and Jack said she'd fallen in love with some hillbilly's dick. He said, "Fuck it. I don't give a damn what that bitch does. Who needs her?" He told me that she stayed away for three years before coming back to check on the kids.

When Jack's first mother-in-law died, his reaction was "Then fucking bury the bitch." He started drinking heavily when married to his second wife, who was as bad as the first. Now, with the third, he's been sober for five years. The two of them take nice vacations and went to Hawaii once, where whores charge $200 just for a fucking blow job!

Jack uses the word *tits* to mean great. The hotel in Hawaii was tits. That red Camaro is tits. Replacing the valves beneath the sink was not tits. I stood and looked down at him on his back, his big belly exposed, while he cursed. In his own way, he's a nice-looking man. In the late afternoon, we made a second trip to the hardware store.

Jack honked at shapely women as we passed them. "Hey," he'd yell, "turn around, you stuck-up bitch." He wasn't what you'd call the silent type, not at all, and he charges $20 an hour.

February 6, 1990
Chicago

I asked my students if any of them had stolen anything lately, and two raised their hands. R. said he'd taken a sweatshirt at a party because he was cold. A few days later its rightful owner, a young woman, confronted him, and he ignored her. "She was rich and could buy herself another one," he said.

There are a couple of students this semester I have a real hard time liking.

February 10, 1990
Chicago

I went to bed at three thirty last night and had just lain down when I heard a woman yell, "Somebody help me! Oh, God, help me!"

I couldn't see people out on the street, but I could hear them, so I called the police and opened the window, at which point I could make out two shapes. The man kept trying to yank the woman upstairs. She would say no, and after he hit her, she'd scream for help again. Then he told her to suck his dick and gave her what sounded like a real wallop. When I heard her being slammed against a chain-link fence, I stuck my head out the window and told him to leave her alone. "I called the police!" I yelled. "I called them and they're on their way."

He must have heard me, but he didn't stop. Just as I started looking for the baseball bat I don't have—that and my missing courage—the cops came and flung open the doors of their squad car. I heard them call the man a son of a bitch and a motherfucker. They said, "You get your kicks from beating up women, asshole?"

The guy yelled that he wasn't doing anything wrong, and the cops told him to shut up. They handcuffed him, and then they talked to the woman, who wasn't sure she wanted to press charges. Two more police cars came, and a few minutes later they took the guy away.

February 19, 1990
Chicago

I spent all day waiting on Kool-T, who was supposed to deliver a bag of pot at one this afternoon and finally got it to me at nine thirty tonight. First his car broke down on the expressway, then his initial connection fell through. At nine I went over to his place. Then he, me, his wife, and their two-year-old daughter drove across town to some other connection's apartment. It made me crazy to be inside all day. For a long time, I read. Then I graded student papers and wrote to a kid I had last semester who has since left town and wanted my opinion on a story he'd just finished. It was about his dog, Tipsy, having puppies.

At around five I called the mother of the deaf child whose birthday party I was supposed to go to. Then I talked to Lisa and Mom and Amy. Mom told me that Tiffany is dating a mailman, and Amy and I made plans to send her postcards reading "The tests came back positive" and "I need that $10,000 you owe me." At around seven I watched part of a TV show where a kid with Down syndrome sang "Fight the Power" for his high school talent show. On the radio I learned that Keith Haring died of AIDS.

I really felt like I was in prison yesterday.

February 27, 1990
Chicago
It looks like I've got a place to live in New York. It belongs to Rusty Kane, a two-bedroom in the West Village. The couple he's been subletting to is moving out, so he's moving back in and has asked if I'd like to be his roommate. My half of the rent would be $400, which isn't much more than I'm paying here, plus the utilities are included. New York, finally. Or almost. I think I can make it by August or September.

March 3, 1990
Chicago
I hailed a cab at four thirty this morning and got a driver with straw-colored hair. After I got in, he met my eyes in the

rearview mirror and said, "Did you see any pussy out there tonight?"

I told him I hadn't been looking, so some might have slipped by unnoticed.

"You can usually see pussy further south, on Montrose," he said. "But a lot of that is sick pussy. 'Course, it's a little bit cold out there tonight. Cold and late. A lot of that pussy is home now, home asleep."

I'm often talked to like this by taxi drivers, and it makes me think their cabs should be a different color than the others— that way women will know to avoid them. It gives me the creeps that this guy might pick up my sister. Then again, if anyone could destroy him, it would be Amy.

March 22, 1990
Chicago
I taught today. Sometimes I go in with no idea of what to do. I have them write in class and then I go into the stairwell to smoke and try to think of something. Today I told my students about a friend of mine who is going through a breakup. "What do you do when you're trying to get over someone?" I asked.

They gave me the best advice.

April 1, 1990
Chicago
Last night I watched the last half of *A Patch of Blue* on TV. I hadn't seen it in ages and couldn't help but wish that Sidney Poitier were *my* boyfriend. He's so handsome and has such a great voice. At the end of the movie, Selina says that she knows he's colored and that it makes no difference to her. He has arranged for her to attend a school for the blind, and just as the bus arrives to take her away, she announces that she loves him. He feels the same, I can tell, but needs to do what's

best for her. At the end, when he heads alone up the stairs to his apartment, I cried. I'd been wanting to do that all day, had tried most of the afternoon.

"Boo-hoo," I'd said, lying in a fetal position on my bed. I'd hoped it might trigger something, but it felt artificial. And so it was great to happen upon *A Patch of Blue*. I was crying more for myself than the movie, but that's how it usually goes. I cried hard. I sobbed. I went to the bathroom mirror, watched myself cry, and cried even harder. "I loved you," I said to my reflection.

I wished then that someone would call so I could answer in my weary, broken voice.

"Wrong?" I'd say. "No, there's nothing wrong on my end. Why do you ask?"

April 6, 1990
Chicago
Sarah Vaughan died three days ago. I have always loved her.

April 13, 1990
Chicago
I told the beginning students that it's a tradition for the class to buy the teacher a gift at the end of the school year. Then I said I've had my eye on a watch that costs $160. "That's only fourteen dollars each."

After describing it in detail, I told them where it could be found. The end of the semester is approaching, so I'll make a point to mention this again over the coming weeks. I want that watch. I must have it.

April 16, 1990
Chicago
On Greek Easter, I drank Scotch followed by retsina fol-

lowed by ouzo followed by Scotch followed by brandy, and today I feel like I've been raked over by an acetylene torch.

April 18, 1990
Chicago
Again in class we talked about love. A.'s fiancé just slept with her best friend, and she's written them both off. D. was beaten by her boyfriend twice before she left. R. confessed to hitting his girlfriend so hard, he knocked her out. Two students are married, two are engaged, three have mothers who have been married three times, one has children, three are heartbroken, three others can have sex tonight if they make a few phone calls and beg.

April 25, 1990
Chicago
Amy and I decided a few years back to call ourselves the Talent Family. In the fake bio I'm constructing for us, I claim that two of our earlier plays were *A Testament to Tansbury* and *Cassandra, Albeit Cassandra.*

May 6, 1990
Chicago
A bumper sticker I saw on a beat-up car: THIS AIN'T THE MAYFLOWER, BUT YOUR DAUGHTER SURE CAME ACROSS ON IT.

A man at the IHOP tonight lifted his entire steak with his fork and held it before his mouth, chewing off hunks of it.

May 20, 1990
Chicago
Mom called to tell me that, according to my horoscope in the *Raleigh News and Observer,* in two weeks I'll get exactly

what I've been striving for. That's two weeks from yesterday, meaning June 2. She sounded excited, so I got excited as well. Why do I always fall for this?

May 21, 1990
Chicago
Amy and I were leaving the Century mall when a guy approached and asked if we'd take part in a survey for a new candy. We answered two simple questions and thought we were through, but then he led us downstairs to a basement where we were shown a mock-up of the product and interrogated for what felt like hours.

The guy who took down my answers had frizzy hair to his shoulders, and skin that was too white even for a white person. He wore a blue cotton lab coat and laughed nervously after everything he said. He was really a mess. This was a marketing test for a "lite" candy bar called Forever Yours. The pale guy told me it contained NutraSweet and was only 120 calories. One of the questions he asked was "Do you think this product fulfills a continental heritage?"

I was like, "Huh?"

Next he asked if I thought it had a traditional American flavor. I said I couldn't eat chocolate, but that didn't matter as they never offered us a taste of anything. Eventually I said that the whole idea was stupid. If you're worried about calories, then don't eat a candy bar, or eat only half of one.

"Everything's 'lite' now," I said. "And the letters that spell it out are always yellow so our eyes won't get fat looking at the label."

He asked what I thought of the name Forever Yours and I said that it was silly. "Because it's *not* forever yours. You'll eat it, then later in the day you'll pass it, and the experience will be over. It has a beginning and an end. There's nothing timeless about it."

The guy then asked if I was married, single, or divorced. This was perhaps his way of gauging how jaded I am regarding the word *forever*.

May 25, 1990
Chicago

Katherine Anne Porter's *Collected Letters* has been released, and the *Times* review included one she wrote to Hart Crane. "Your emotional hysteria is not impressive, except possibly to those little hangers-on of literature who feel your tantrums are a mark of genius. To me they do not add the least value to your poetry, and take away my last shadow of a wish to ever see you again.... Let me alone. This disgusting episode has already gone too far."

Ouch.

June 4, 1990
Chicago

Amy's neighbors were kicking a ball on the front lawn her boyfriend, Paul, had recently seeded, so she opened the window and politely asked them to play somewhere else. "We're trying to grow grass," she explained.

"You're trying to grow it *now?*" one of the kids asked, as if she could put it on hold for a while.

June 18, 1990
Chicago

Summer school started this afternoon. They said they'd cancel the class if I had fewer than twelve students, then they changed it to seven. I started the day with eight. One was absent, two added at the last minute, and one dropped out, so now I'm at a relatively safe nine. That'll be $2,300 ($1,900 or so after taxes) I can add to the $1,000 I already have saved for New York.

June 26, 1990
Chicago

Amy and I went to Hoffritz to find Dad a Father's Day gift. Our original idea was to buy him a knife, but in the end we spent $72 on a vibrator. It's a Panasonic with a long stem and a thickish disk on top, designed so you can reach behind yourself and work out the kinks in your back and shoulders. We also figured he'll use it on his dog.

"Our father's going to love this," Amy said to the saleswoman as we laid the vibrator on the counter.

The woman smiled.

"The next time we see him, though, I bet his front teeth are all chipped."

The smile faded.

June 28, 1990
Chicago

A few days back, at the library, I found the new biography of Jackson Pollock, who was surprisingly naive. On the advice of a Park Avenue "healer," he started drinking a combination of bat shit and ground beets, this to establish a "proper balance of gold and silver in his urine."

In 1951 the doctor put him on a special diet for his alcoholism. No dairy and plenty of fresh fruits and vegetables. The only meat permitted was fowl, which had to have been shot within the past two hours and had to be wild—"Eat no bird that can't take off at fifty miles per hour." Meanwhile, he could still drink as much alcohol as he wanted. The trick, the doctor explained, was to balance out the metals in his body.

*   *   *

Jean Detzer came by the other night, and she and Evelyne swapped stories about the Academy of Orthopedic Surgeons and the time they'd spent working there as meeting planners. American hotels have a rule that you can't display a cadaver in any room where food is being served. "How archaic," Jean said. "I mean, really. In this day and age!"

Perhaps the rule had something to do with wakes, but for whatever reason, it was instituted, and both Jean and Evelyne have broken it. Evelyne once traveled with half a woman, a cadaver from the waist up, that she named Tracey and had to smuggle into a convention. Jean once sneaked an entire dead body into a meeting room at the Fairmont. She said they dressed the dead man in a suit and mussed up his hair to make him look drunk. "Then we carried him in supported by two sober doctors." She took a swallow of her Scotch. "The only hard part was finding two sober doctors at the convention."

June 30, 1990
Chicago
As I passed three teenage girls on the street yesterday, one was saying, "Don't you just hate it when you meet a guy and he's got the personality you always dreamed about but is ugly? I swear I hate that shit."

July 2, 1990
Chicago
Before leaving for class this morning I found out that I won another literary award. It's $1,000 for "The New Music" from the Illinois Arts Council, which gives the same amount to the magazine that the story was published in (*ACM*). This was the final day for claiming the prize so I let my students

go early and rushed out to get my money. I'm as shocked as I was the last time. "The New Music" was written two years ago, right after I graduated.

July 7, 1990
Chicago
I finished the Jackson Pollock biography and started a new one about Hattie McDaniel, who played Mammy in *Gone with the Wind* and was married four times, once to a man named Wonderful Smith.

July 12, 1990
Chicago
For the third time this week, a man approached me and asked if he could have $1. He pointed to a van and said that it was his. "It broke down and if I don't get to work, I'm in big trouble."

Each time it's a different guy, but it's always the same van. A scam, obviously, but even if the story was true, who goes to work with no money in his pockets? What if you ran out of gas?

When I taught my night class in the Fine Arts Building, I was often asked for money by a woman who said she'd been robbed and needed to take a commuter train to one of the northern suburbs. Even the first time I saw her I thought, *Really? You can't call a friend or a family member? You're honestly going to hit up total strangers for your fare?* Like the men with the van, she was always well dressed and acting frantic.

July 26, 1990
Chicago
Last night I read at the Park West as part of the Orchid Show,

and it seemed pretty full to me, maybe five hundred people. I'm hoping that a year from now I'm not regretting my decision to leave Chicago. It was always my dream to read in such a fancy place in front of such a big audience. Now I want a bigger audience, but in New York.

One of the other acts last night performed a rap number with two other guys. Backstage he'd hogged the dressing room and made a big deal out of having a manager. Then he got out there and I saw that his fly was down.

July 30, 1990
Chicago

I read in an interview that David Lynch used to go to Bob's Big Boy in Los Angeles. Every day for seven years he'd have a milk shake and six cups of coffee and take notes before going home to write. I sure will miss the IHOP when I move to New York. Every night Barbara carries a menu to my table and says, "Just coffee this evening?" Every night I cross my fingers as she hands me my change at the register. Every night as I leave, she says, "Take care." The few times she hasn't said it, I've worried I'll get hit by a car while riding my bike home.

At the IHOP I go through phases of sitting in different booths. I can look at the one in the very back and think, *I remember those days.* I recall sitting near the front where I could hear people on the pay phone. Each phase lasts about six months. I always stay at the IHOP long enough to smoke three cigarettes. I never have four. I love for things to stay exactly the same, but I can't have this IHOP *and* New York.

July 31, 1990
Chicago

Again tonight on Addison a man approached me and said that his van had broken down. "I need you to give me a quarter," he said, as if that's what it would cost to have the thing towed and repaired.

August 7, 1990
Chicago

Today was my last day of teaching at the Art Institute. The summer-school class was so sweet, one of the best. I brought my black-and-white Polaroid camera and Ben stepped in from the office and took group photos, one for each person. Students read their stories out loud while we ate cake. We all said how much we'd liked one another.

Seeing as I had my camera on me, before leaving the IHOP tonight, I took a picture of Barbara, who has worked evenings on Mondays, Tuesdays, and Wednesdays the entire six and a half years I've been coming here. In the background of the photo I took are the rotisserie chickens, the ones what spin around.

August 13, 1990
Chicago

As a going-away present, Amy gave me some sort of a paw. It's mounted on a thin slice of mahogany, and beside it, written in pencil, is *1888*. I thought it maybe belonged to a sloth, but the fingers are splayed. It's like the hand of a Dr. Seuss character. Amy really is the best gift giver. "It's beautiful," I told her. "Every time I look at it, I'll think of our paw."

She gave it to me at the going-away party. It was held at the Quinns', and when vegetarian Janet saw it she flew off the handle. How dare I bring this into her house? Did I have any idea what this animal had gone through, etc.? She put a sort of curse on me. This morning she left to attend massage school.

August 17, 1990
Chicago

I passed a fight on Broadway near Belmont tonight, a chubby white guy and a black kid who was maybe fifteen. The white guy seemed a little crazy and I got the idea that the kid and his friends had provoked him into being just that much crazier. At one point he screamed, "Go back to nigger town, nigger!" The black kid took off his belt and charged, swinging it above his head, but the white guy just grabbed it. The two friends, meanwhile, hung back and laughed.

August 28, 1990
Raleigh

Dad, Paul, and I spent eighteen hours in the front seat of a Toyota pickup truck. Eighteen hours through Illinois, Indiana, Kentucky, Ohio, Tennessee, and North Carolina. At one point I fell asleep. Paul reached into my Dopp kit then, got out my shaving cream, and covered a good three-quarters of my face before I woke up. Later he elbowed me in the ribs while I was pouring coffee. It went from the thermos to my bare legs and burned me. If I tried to read a magazine, he'd take the page and crumple it up. He dumped a cup of water over my head. He grabbed the skin beneath my arm and twisted it until I begged for mercy. The three of us were crowded together side by side. It was hot, but I never lost my temper. It was all funny to me, and I laughed while Dad drove and we all three listened to the radio.

August 30, 1990
Raleigh

I told Melina, my parents' Great Dane, that we were going to have her put to sleep on Saturday, and Dad got super-angry. As if she could understand me! So I said to her, "OK, we'll wait until Monday." This made him even angrier, and he ordered me to leave his house.

Yesterday I told him I'd ridden my bike to the grocery store and bought a chicken.

"No, you didn't," he said. The chicken was right there on the counter, along with the receipt, but still he insisted for absolutely no reason that I hadn't bought it. He refuses to be wrong.

August 31, 1990
Raleigh

> *I would rather be a Klansman*
> *In a robe of snowy white,*
> *Than to be a Catholic priest*
> *In a robe as black as night;*
> *For a Klansman is AMERICAN*
> *And AMERICA is his home,*
> *But a priest owes his allegiance*
> *To a Dago Pope in Rome.*

That's a 1925 Klan song verse in the Jean Stafford biography I'm reading. Like many good biography subjects, she became a mess toward the end of her life. One of her last ideas was for a recipe book called *How to Cook for One While Drunk*.

September 7, 1990
Emerald Isle
Mom left the beach a day early. Paul drove her. She seems to be in poor health lately. She coughs and hacks a lot more than usual. The sound of it brings out the worst in me (said the guy with a cigarette in his mouth). It's bad, though. We

call her Mount Vesuvius. She spent a lot of time indoors on this trip.

September 19, 1990
Raleigh
A joke Dean told me:

> Q. What is it in the air in San Francisco that keeps
>   women from getting pregnant?
> A. Men's legs.

September 25, 1990
Raleigh
Last night Dad predicted that six months from now I'll regret ever having left Chicago. He's been a real terror lately. An hour later he yelled at me for picking up a meatball with my fingers. It was on a dish in the refrigerator and he accused me of touching a lot of them before deciding on the largest. I think he worries that I'm spreading AIDS. He doesn't like me drinking out of anyone else's glass either.

Dad doesn't pay attention when you talk to him, so Paul's taken to throwing the term *IRS* into his sentences. Then it's suddenly: "Hold on a second, what did you say?"

October 2, 1990
Raleigh
I'm in the breakfast nook, drinking a cup of coffee, when, out of nowhere, Dad wants to talk. "I have something important I need to discuss."

Then he decides that he has to take Melina for a walk. Ten minutes later, he returns and slams a coaster on the table— which is made of Formica, not wood—and anyway I have my cup on one of the ten catalogs that arrive in the mailbox every morning. Then we go to the A&P and the entire time we're in the car, he talks to the dog instead of me. As we walk into the store, he confides that his biggest regret is that Melina never got to have sex, that he ruined all that by getting her spayed.

At the A&P he walks around eating things—free samples, pieces of fruit he should be paying for, whatever's open. He charges into the back room, demanding the freshest tomatoes and discounts on wilted lettuce. He berates the cashiers and bag boys. On the way home, he finally gets to what he'd wanted to talk about: Paul. "That guy is going nowhere fast," he says. He predicts that he'll become an aimless alcoholic and I remind him that Paul is only twenty-two and deserves to live a young person's life.

"Aw, baloney."

October 5, 1990
New York

Before leaving for the train station, Mom and I watched part of a *Today* show segment about monkeys that are trained as helpers for handicapped people. They showed a quadriplegic fellow in an electric wheelchair instructing his little servant, Lisa, to pick up a cassette tape off the floor.

The monkey did as she was told, and when the guy ordered Lisa to put it in the machine and press Play, she did that as well. Sometimes, to demonstrate their love, the monkeys will stick their filthy hands into the mouths of their masters, who are completely paralyzed and can't swat them away.

When the time came, Mom drove me to the station. The train was there waiting, and when we said good-bye, her eyes welled with tears. I had a terrific time with her this past month. I sure do love my mother.

And now I am in New York City. The train took eleven hours, and during that time I accidentally walked in on three people who were sitting on the toilet, two women and one man. Once every hour I'd go to the bar car for a cigarette and listen to the drunks, who were always saying something like "When I say you're a friend, you're a motherfucking friend. I'm not bullshitting you, man."

I took a cab from Penn Station, and Rusty was waiting at the apartment when I arrived. It's much bigger than I'd imagined. The neighborhood is too beautiful for me. I don't deserve it. Or, OK, my block I deserve. It's more industrial than the ones around it, and we look out at a parking lot for trucks. Two short blocks away, though, it's perfect. Tree-lined winding streets, restaurants and coffee shops. It's enchanting. I can't picture myself in any of those places, but still. How did I get to live here? Rusty says that some of the apartments in the area are going for a million dollars. I'm not sure about that, but I do know that a ginger ale costs three dollars. Three dollars!

At two thirty a.m. Rusty took me out on his motorcycle, and we went all over. At six thirty I went to bed, and three hours later I got up. First I heard a siren, then trucks, then car horns, then every noise in the world. I can't get over it. I walk down the street and I can't get over it.

This morning I went to the nearest supermarket. Chicken was 89 cents a pound. Other things—Wesson oil, orange juice, butter—were generally 15 cents more than they should be.

October 7, 1990
New York

Everywhere I go in New York, people are selling electrical tape. They sell it in stores, on the sidewalk, on card tables, and at street fairs. There must be a terrific demand for it here.

*   *   *

On Rusty's TV, on a cable channel, I saw a nude woman say, "I want to wipe my pussy with your face, motherfucker." On TV!

At last night's Feature (gallery) opening, I heard someone whisper, "Is she the one who sets herself on fire?"

I saw lots of chicken today for $1.50 a pound.

October 11, 1990
New York
Today I saw a woman with no legs who said, "Can you give me a dollar, sweetheart? I'm trying to buy an electric wheelchair."

I think beer is expensive here. A six-pack of Bud, for instance, is $6. For Bud! So tonight I'm drinking Schmidt's for $2.89. Lily told me that an ounce of pot goes anywhere from $320 to $400. I felt bad in Chicago paying $60 for a quarter.

I haven't worked out my coffee situation yet. Each night I try somewhere different. Chock Full o'Nuts has too many distractions, so the best place so far is the Bagel Buffet on 6th Avenue. The IHOP gives customers a whole pot. It's awful coffee, but at least you don't have to flag someone down every ten minutes. Plus you could sit at a booth for as long as you needed to and they never hustled you out. At the Bagel Buffet, you get a paper cup of coffee for 60 cents so it's just $1.80 for three cups, which I can afford if I cut back a little in other places. Now I need a library card.

October 14, 1990
New York

Tonight on 6th Avenue I saw a completely naked woman. She was black, disturbed, and her breasts hung down to her waist. I saw her yesterday in the same spot, but dressed and yelling, "I'm getting drunk!"

I previously enjoyed walking down 6th, but tonight it was rowdy and humid and someone threw a bottle that smashed on the sidewalk ten feet away from me. Who threw it? The nice thing about crowds is that someone can throw a bottle and you don't take it personally.

I saw two more people without feet today, one before and one after I walked to the Central Park Zoo. It's not nearly as big as the one in Lincoln Park in Chicago, or as well stocked. For example, they have ants at the Central Park Zoo. From watching the original *Cat People* movie, I was expecting panthers, but the wildest things they had were polar bears. Then there were penguins, monkeys, bats, and tortoises, which really made time when the guy showed up with their food. It was funny to see them run, their necks stretched out, their eyes bulging.

At a store called Gay Treasures on Hudson Street, I heard a man in his mid-fifties talk to the cashier, who was around the same age, about his new boyfriend. "He spanks me raw at least twice a week. Last night he used an umbrella!"

"He should have stuck it up your ass," the cashier said.

The customer leaned forward. "Who said he didn't!"

October 15, 1990
New York

I screwed up my courage this afternoon and called Philip Morris. Rusty then told me that I wanted *William* Morris. They're the talent agency. Philip Morris is the cigarette company.

I walked around today and saw a man get chased and kicked in the ass for taking an apple from a fruit stand. Tonight it's cool and the air is dry. The city smells like burned coffee.

October 19, 1990
New York
Lily has been painting and doing light carpentry work in the town house of an antiques dealer. He has a little dog named Crumpet that acts pitiful and lame when it wants food and attention. She told me about him at a falafel restaurant in the East Village, and then I told her about my downstairs neighbors, who have been complaining about the sound of my footsteps. "Because of them I now go barefoot when I'm at home," I told her. "*And* I tiptoe."

A woman sitting near us finished her meal and said to me on her way out, "Listen, you pay rent too. There's no need for you to tiptoe around your own apartment."

October 21, 1990
New York
Every day I get the paper from the same trash can on Abingdon Square and look through the want ads. Tomorrow at nine I'm applying at UPS. Then Lily is paying me $20 to help her carry a ladder. So for days, I can feel resourceful. I hope that UPS hires me. Even if it means I have to work through Christmas, I want a job so I can buy things.

October 22, 1990
New York
I went to 43rd and 11th to apply for the driver's helper job at

UPS. It was maybe ten o'clock when I arrived and there were a good three hundred people in line ahead of me. Many of them were dressed in suits. Others looked like they had just been passing by and saw the sign. While waiting for my interview, I listened to the two men in front of me. One said that his wife had just had a baby and that he'd lost his job because a friend had borrowed his driver's license and had a wreck. "So it went on *my* record," he said.

You can't tell that story to a potential employer. They don't want a guy with crummy friends who ask you to do things like loan them your license.

The UPS interviews were conducted by ten people. Some of them—a Japanese man, a black woman—talked to applicants for a long time and wound up scheduling callbacks. I got stuck with a white guy, Mr. Hardball, who did not even shake my hand.

At five I met with Lily, who paid me to help her carry a ladder. We picked it up on Canal Street, at the loft of a guy named Hugh and his two roommates, Scott and Leslie. Their place was spacious and homey, like a log cabin. Hugh had a wet bar in the shape of a tree stump. Leslie was making an apple pie and they were listening to *All Things Considered*. Hugh is handsome, a nice guy. Gay. Lily and I walked the ladder to a studio apartment on the corner of Jane and Greenwich and she gave me $20. For the first time since arriving in New York, I feel like I've plugged a leak.

October 24, 1990
New York
"Macy's Herald Square, the largest store in the world, has big opportunities for outgoing, fun-loving people of all shapes and sizes who want more than just a holiday job. Working as

an elf in Macy's SantaLand means being at the center of the excitement..."

So I called and have an interview next Wednesday at eleven o'clock.

October 25, 1990
New York

Lily and I saw a dead man on West 11th. He had jumped from a sixth-floor window, landed on a car, and rolled into the street, where he was lying in an ever expanding pool of blood. You could see that on the way down he'd hit a tree. I wondered if, at the last minute, he'd changed his mind and tried to grab hold of the branches, many of which were broken now. A crowd formed and some boys who'd seen him jump claimed to have heard his skull crack. People passing said, "What happened?" and the two kids, celebrities now, acted as spokesmen.

Tonight I paid $5 to watch an Irish performance artist at Margo's gallery. It's the money that kills me because this was just the worst—it's like she followed a formula:

1. Show slides.
2. Arrange your various props on the floor.
3. Use them one by one.
4. Don't say a word.
5. Incorporate blood.

It was insufferable. The props included a mannequin's head, feathers, a mound of soil, a shovel, a bell, a few vials. After arranging them just so, she used them, one after another, for an hour. If you're going to perform wordlessly, you need to wow people with your movement or your music or lighting, but she was not graceful or clever or well prepared.

She rolled herself in paper; she fell to the ground. I was so relieved when it ended that I applauded—a mistake, as I don't think things like this should be encouraged.

October 28, 1990
New York
On Friday night I met Lily on Jane Street and we carried the ladder back to Hugh's place on Canal. I was excited to be there and decided to have a crush on him. We sat for a while and drank a beer. Scott and Leslie had put up a bird feeder, which was fine until the birds got sloppy with the seeds, and rats showed up. I wanted to stay but had to leave to meet Gretchen, who'd arrived from Providence and needed to be picked up at her friend's place on 103rd Street.

October 31, 1990
New York
This afternoon I sat in the eighth-floor SantaLand office at Macy's and was told, "Congratulations, Mr. Sedaris. You are an elf."

I return tomorrow at nine thirty for my training schedule, but in the meantime, me and the others who were hired were shown a chart from last year. A third of the names had stars beside them. Those, we learned, were elves Santa had invited back for a second or third year. A woman named Marianne told us she'd had more than her fair share of bad elves. There are various ways of being categorized as bad. "Parents can get cranky," Marianne said. "Children can get cranky. But an elf cannot get cranky."

November 14, 1990
New York
Everyone on earth knows I'm an elf. Everyone. Today I went

to Feature and met a woman who was talking to Jim and Hudson. I looked around at the show then, and heard her quietly ask, "Is the little elf still here?"

Hudson gave me flyers for the reading next week. It starts at eight thirty, but I'm supposed to be there by seven forty-five. I have elf training until six that day, so I will need to have my clothes laid out.

November 20, 1990
New York

I read last night at the Kitchen. There were around eighty people there. Hugh came, and Lily. The audience took things pretty seriously, which was disappointing. I was hoping for laughs.

November 23, 1990
New York

This was the official opening day of SantaLand and I worked for eight hours. I started the morning at the Magic Window, then spent time as an exit elf, Santa elf, maze elf, and counter elf. The Santas wear wool suits. They sweat and get heat rashes on their asses and knees. Most of them sit on pillows.

I get an hour for lunch and a twenty-minute afternoon break. Today I ate in the cafeteria with a she-elf whose husband is a female impersonator. Hmmmm.

November 25, 1990
New York

I was a photo elf yesterday when two men, both in their mid-twenties, came to visit Santa. They didn't want to sit on his lap or have their pictures taken. Instead, they just wanted to be sensitive. When asked what they wanted for Christmas, one of them said, "I'd like it if some homeless people could have a decent meal."

His friend nodded in agreement. "Right on."

I stopped listening and fooled around with some stuffed animals on the mantel. When I turned back around, the men were on their way out the door. "And, hey, Santa," one of them said. "Look after our boys in the Gulf, will you?"

He said it with such gooey poignancy. Santa and I laughed merrily after they'd left.

The elf I share a locker with, Keith, invited me to his Bible-study group tomorrow night.

December 7, 1990
New York

Lily and I saw a warning poster outside a small theater that read THIS PLAY WILL LEAVE YOU FEELING SAD AND EMPTY.

I led a five-year-old boy to Santa's door and said, "Look at all the toys my master has."

The kid was small but sophisticated. "I've got more toys than that. To tell you the truth," he said, "I'm very spoiled."

I got yelled at twice today, once when I was working as an entrance elf. The job amounts to hustling up visitors, and I thought I did a pretty good job. "Patronize Santa," I said. "Behold his chubby majesty. Santa was born and raised in a small home. Hail him. Santa's patience is beyond your comprehension. Come test it."

I'd been at it for ten minutes when a manager came by. Then he went and rounded up two other managers and the three of them brought me to the desk for a scolding. I wasn't saying anything nasty or sexual, though. I just heightened the discourse a little.

December 10, 1990
New York

Walking home I passed two men on 14th Street who were working with long poles, one of which hit me in the nose and drew blood. The man who hit me found it funny and laughed.

"Hey," I said. "That really hurt."

He laughed all the harder and I asked if now I could hit him in the nose with a long pole so we could be even. I told him he had to apologize, so he did, but it really doesn't count because I had to ask for it.

Today a Japanese child came and played his violin for Santa.

December 29, 1990
Raleigh

Tell people you live in New York, and I've noticed they'll offer half a dozen reasons why they *don't* live there: the crowds, the high cost of living, the crime. I'm not suggesting they move or anything—far from it. It's funny how defensive certain people get.

1991

January 2, 1991
New York

I took the Carey bus from LaGuardia and was crossing 42nd Street when a guy said, "Hey, big man, how about giving me one of those cigarettes?" He was a good six inches taller than me, so I pointed that out and asked why he'd called me big man. "Did you think I'd find it flattering?"

"Hey," he said. "That's just the way I am."

I said, "Fine, and this is the way I am."

As I walked away he called out after me, "Hey, it's just a fucking cigarette."

"Well, you know me," I called back.

In front of Grand Central, a big black guy asked did I want a taxi, and when I said yes, he grabbed my duffel bag and proceeded down the street. I followed and watched as he hailed a cab, threw my bag into the backseat, and demanded a tip.

I took my bag out of the backseat and hailed another cab. The driver told me that he hates those self-appointed porters. When he hears one of them shake a passenger down for a tip, he rolls down his window and shouts, "You don't owe him shit! Don't give him nothing."

January 7, 1991
New York

I found a *PlayGuy* magazine in a trash can on West 4th

Street and read the letters section, where a college student wrote that six months ago he began drinking his own semen. "The kinkiest thing I ever did was the time I saved up a seven-day output of my cum and put it in a bottle. I went to the cafeteria for dinner, got a salad, pulled my little bottle out of my pocket and put it on the table. When a couple of P.E. majors asked what it was, I told them that it was a high-protein salad dressing my mom had sent me. Several of them asked to share my dressing, which I gladly did. I could barely contain myself as I watched these guys pour my cum on their greens and eat it. Now, some people might think my antics are a bit much. But I enjoy it and it feels good. Isn't that what sex is all about?"

"I enjoy it and it feels good" doesn't really justify his actions, in my opinion. Then again, he can't honestly have done this, can he?

February 5, 1991
New York
Elaine called last night with a possible job. I'd be working for an Italian woman named Alba who runs a small press and is looking for a personal assistant two days a week, for $10 an hour. I think it involves typing, which might be a problem. On the phone she was enthusiastic, so we'll see.

February 7, 1991
New York
This afternoon I met with Alba at the Chelsea Hotel, where she rents a room she uses as an office. She's a trim woman, pretty. Nice clothes, nice accent. When I arrived, she was talking to another trim and beautiful woman, an American, who was planning to attend a twenty-four-hour chanting seminar led by a noted Buddhist. She said she really, really needed to

chant and throw out some good energy, that the world would be a better place for it.

After the American woman left, I looked at a book Alba and her business partner had recently published. I remarked that it was beautifully bound and printed, and Alba sighed, saying, "I am tired now of beauty."

My understanding is that the press is more or less a hobby for her. There are parts she enjoys and parts she avoids. I would take care of what she avoids. I admitted that I type with only one finger and have never in my life touched a computer.

The last person who worked for her was paid $10 an hour. She offered me $7. I said that wasn't enough and she told me she'd be talking to some other people.

John Smith is in town and last night we went to the Tunnel Bar. Just before leaving, I stepped in to use the bathroom, which is just one toilet in a room. There is a sink as well, and standing beside it was a fellow I'd seen earlier. He asked my name and then said, "I'll tell you what I'm going to do, Dave. Do you like having your toes sucked?"

I wanted to say, *That's Dav*id. *Nobody calls me Dave,* but I was so shocked by his question I couldn't do anything but look down at my feet.

"I was watching you in the other room, Dave, and stepped in here hoping we could talk. Now here we are, talking."

I turned to leave and he put his foot in front of the door, blocking it. "Just hear me out, Dave, because I think you're really going to like what I have to say. What size shoes are those you're wearing?"

I told him they were a 7½ and that my feet are perfectly flat.

"Good," he said. "Small, flat feet equals big cock."

That's the most ridiculous equation I've ever heard, I thought.

"I bet you've got a very veiny cock, don't you, Dave?"

"No more than anyone else," I said. "I mean, I don't know. I never thought about it."

"It's got a lot of blue veins, doesn't it, Dave?"

"I don't—"

"Let's just say that it does, OK, Dave?" He told me he was going to take my shoes off and start by sucking my toes, slowly, and that his upper teeth would tap just slightly against my nails—not biting, mind you.

"We don't even know each other," I argued. "Besides, I'm here with a friend visiting from out of town."

"No problem," he said. "I'll do everything to him that I plan to do to you."

He wouldn't unblock the door until I promised to take it up with John, who was standing out front waiting for me and who said, "What took you so long?" when I finally found him.

February 11, 1991
New York

I took part in three Orchid Shows at P.S. 122. They were all sold out, and the audiences were kind and responsive. On Friday Andy from *One Life to Live* was in the audience. She plays Max Holden's sister and gave me her autograph, which read, *To David. You were wonderful. Please write for our show.*

I can't believe it!

A number of bookers for clubs were there, and the head of P.S. 122 invited me back. Then there were guys, most of whom were dandelions. That's my name for men with short hair dyed yellow. They almost always have two pierced ears and wear leather jackets. The uniform makes them unappealing to me. That's what's good about Hugh. He's his own person, lookswise.

After last night's event I came home and found $350 worth of traveler's checks I'd never cashed. I was paid $100 per night for the shows, so if I budget, I can pay rent and last at least a short while longer.

February 24, 1991
New York
Today the United States began its ground war in Kuwait. Saddam Hussein said the American troops would drown in their own blood, but they met no opposition and took five thousand prisoners. It's strange to see the war from New York. I've noticed a surprising number of yellow ribbons and posters of American flags with the words THESE COLORS DON'T RUN printed beneath them. Then too you hear "No blood for oil" a lot.

March 3, 1991
New York
I have to get these sculptures off to the Renaissance Society, and I asked Hugh over to take a look and advise me on finishes. He is very handsome, a hard worker, thoughtful. His dad was a diplomat so the family left Kentucky when Hugh was a kid and lived in Ethiopia and Somalia and the Congo. He lived in Paris for five years after graduating from college and is here now, painting.

Hugh looked at the sculptures and said, "Just oil them."

Then we joined Lily, Hugh's roommates, and another couple at a place in Little Italy. Someone or other knew the bartender, who charged us $20 for $150 worth of drinks. Hugh and I flirted all night. Is that the right word? I drank out of his glass and got him to say that he hated me, which usually means the opposite.

At the end of the night he said he'd call me later this week. Then he left with Scott and Leslie. I left with Lily in the opposite direction, and when I turned around to look at him, I saw that he'd turned around as well. It was romantic.

March 15, 1991
New York

The *Village Voice* came out with me in the Choices section. "North Carolina transplant David Sedaris reads his wry, hilarious stories and diaries, withering social comedy leavened by an emphatic eye for the soulful ridiculousness of our behavior." I'll never know why they chose me, but still it's nice. I got the name of the guy who wrote it and have already sent a thank-you letter.

March 16, 1991
New York

I'm down to $190 and am starting to panic. In this situation, I have no business buying pot, but that's what I did. Scotch too.

March 19, 1991
New York

I worked today for Alba. The person she hired instead of me didn't pan out, so she called this morning and I was at the Chelsea Hotel by noon. She'd planned for us to spend the day going through the files, but then Cy Twombly invited her to lunch, so I was here on my own. I went through the papers she wanted me to go through and filled out a quarterly tax form. I've never in my life done anything remotely close to that. In the end I called an accountant twice. Then I phoned the New York State tax board and asked them what was 8¼ percent of $25. The woman said, "I'm sorry, ma'am, but we can't tell you that."

Eventually Alba returned from lunch. We were supposed to bring boxes to the house she just bought, a whole house on Bleecker Street, but then Herbert Huncke came to visit. I understand that he's famous, but I've never read any of his writing. The guy is old and in poor health. He spoke slowly and told a dull story. Then a young guy came by and I didn't much care for him. He dropped a lot of names and seemed annoyed that I didn't already know who he was.

March 21, 1991
New York

On this, the first day of spring, I am able to shop around and find chicken for 59 cents per pound, coffee for $2.99 a pound, and spaghetti on sale—two boxes for $1. Tonight I'll have chicken with some squid-ink linguine Hugh brought me. It's black.

This spring I am, if I'm not mistaken, in love.

I've started working for a Kentucky man named Jeffrey Lee who is painting a master bedroom at 77th and 5th. I saw splendors today—things I had no idea existed. This apartment is vast, ten rooms, maybe more. Huge rooms with fireplaces and windows looking onto Central Park. The owners are a couple in their mid-forties who have no children. They've built a special bathroom for their dogs with a floor that flushes. The two came in this afternoon with their decorator, who lives not far away, in Claus von Bülow's old apartment. We went over at the end of the day, and I couldn't believe my eyes. In the living room, or whatever you call the room next to the living room, she had a door-size Sargent painting. Just hanging there.

Jeffrey Lee wears a big beret and smokes Lucky Strikes and has anxiety attacks. His brother died of AIDS and now he has it too. I asked how he controls his fear of dying and he said, "Drugs"—prescribed drugs, and Jack Daniel's.

March 26, 1991
New York

I waited for Alba for forty minutes this morning, standing outside her door at the Chelsea. She arrived wearing a tailored suit and worrying that it made her look frumpy. In the end, she changed, then did different things with her hair. Alba can't wait in line at a restaurant or the post office—she doesn't have that kind of time. I worked for a few hours, and then she borrowed $50 from the guy at the front desk and we went to an Italian place called Intermezzo that had a $4 lunch special. I paid for my own meal—fine, but I also didn't charge her for the time I spent waiting, and this when I'm getting $3 an hour less than the last person who did my job.

I wouldn't mind but I'm broke right now and could have made a lot more money working for Jeffrey Lee today. I have to do something about my finances. I don't want Hugh to think I'm shiftless and I don't want to scare him away by relying on him. I've always counted on things to work out, and they usually do, but the stakes are higher here.

I'm surrounded by people who have more money than they know what to do with, and none of them have earned it.

March 27, 1991
New York

I received an offer for the Citibank Citicard, which promises me instant cash privileges if I need to spend time in a hospital. If I lose both hands and feet, I am entitled to $20,000 under their "cash benefits for accidental dismemberment" clause. If

I lose one hand or one foot, I get half that, but if I lose one hand *and* one foot, I'm back up to $20,000.

April 3, 1991
New York
Jeffrey Lee says *ish* a lot.

"How do the curtains look?"

"Ish."

He can pay me $200 on Friday so I can pay Rusty the rest of the rent money I owe him. So far with Jeffrey Lee I've earned maybe $650. I've earned another $100 with Alba and I have $80 in the bank. So I'll be rich. Ish.

April 9, 1991
New York
I read last night at the Knot Room. The opening act was a singing duo, the guy on ukulele and the woman on violin. Their first song was called "Everyone Here Is White Tonight." When they finished, eight people left. That happens all the time. People leave after their friends are done. After the exodus, there were maybe twenty audience members left, but it's a tiny room so it didn't feel empty. Alba came, which was sweet of her.

April 13, 1991
New York
I worked today for David Donner, a marketing analyst who paints apartments on the side. He's been hired to do a one-bedroom on 29th and Lexington and I'm helping for $11 an hour. We met on the sidewalk outside the building this morning because the doormen were giving him such a hard time. They're the worst, these guys. They take loads of shit from the tenants and then heap it on whoever's less powerful.

The service-elevator operators were just as bad. They say we're not allowed to work on the weekends and that if they knock on the door and find us painting, they'll cut off the electricity.

He's tireless, David. Five minutes for lunch. His regular assistant is on vacation. I asked what he was like and David used the term *workhorse* three times. At first he was very terse, but he loosened up as the day went on and told me that his dad is a veterinarian. You'd think that would spell pets, but his mother didn't want animals walking through the rooms of their house unescorted, so they had none.

We worked eight hours, and he paid me in cash at the end of the day.

April 18, 1991
New York

Alba spent the better part of the day crying. I asked what was wrong and she said, "Everything." I felt bad for her.

April 21, 1991
New York

I worked with David Donner again today, which is Sunday. The doormen were on strike, so they brooded outside the building as opposed to inside the building. In their place are private security guards who issued David and me passes we need in order to exit and reenter.

I went out at one to buy lunch and was in the lobby when one of the striking doormen stepped in and called me buster, as in "You're going to have to clean up those footprints, buster." He pointed to something I could barely see.

So I said, "All right, can you give me something to clean them with?"

He told me to go upstairs and get something. "Would you

make a mess like that in your own home?" he asked. And again, I could barely see what he was talking about. And wasn't he supposed to be outside on strike?

"I'm a very clean person," I told him.

He said, "I'll have you thrown out and make sure you never come back. I'll take that goddamn card of yours and tear it to pieces, you hear me, buster?"

People in the lobby turned to see what the fuss was.

"Goddamn you, you're out of here," the doorman said.

I went upstairs and returned with a damp rag. Then I got on my hands and knees and cleaned my faint footprints off the carpet. Boy, my blood was boiling. It was pouring when I went out for lunch. On my way back in, the security guard asked to see my pass, which was complete bullshit as five minutes earlier he'd seen me crawl in front of him on my hands and knees. So I had lunch in one hand, an umbrella in the other, and as I searched in my pocket for my pass, I get yelled at for dripping water onto the carpet. I don't know where to begin with these assholes, I really don't.

April 25, 1991
New York
Today we moved the office from the Chelsea Hotel to Alba's house on Bleecker Street—four full floors and two basements. She hired movers, two nice Colombians who have a company called Going. I don't think Alba understands the thoughts of people who are working. If you've carried a big TV up four flights of stairs, you don't want a lot of hemming and hawing about where it goes—you just want to set it down. At one point I suggested that if she was going from the first to the third floor, it wouldn't hurt her to carry a little something up, a magazine, maybe, or a coffee cup.

She told me that she was not a lazy person, and then she went up empty-handed. Later she had a fit when one of the floor refinishers broke a mirror. It was the type you'd put on the back of a closet door, nothing valuable or hard to replace, but still she went bananas, throwing her purse against the wall, throwing down the book she was holding. "Fucking fuckers!" she shouted. "How dare you do this to me. You broke that mirror. It's my first day in this house and now I am stuck with the fucking bad luck you have made."

"I thought you told us you didn't want this mirror," one of the guys said.

Alba yelled that that wasn't the point. "It's here and it's broken and now I have to suffer."

When he reminded her that she didn't break it and that perhaps the bad luck wasn't hers, she got even angrier. It was an amazing tantrum.

May 16, 1991
New York

Alba dictated a letter today, which, when typed up, made no sense whatsoever. I don't understand how someone can use the word *contemporary* twice in one sentence that runs for nine lines and then get upset because I misspelled *completely*.

June 22, 1991
New York

After Bonnie and Clyde were gunned down, souvenir hunters mobbed the car, taking with them shards of windshield glass, upholstery, and even hanks of human hair. One fellow was caught attempting to saw off Clyde Barrow's ear. I read that somewhere yesterday.

June 25, 1991
New York

Tiffany was hit by a car this weekend while riding her bike. This is the second time it's happened, and again she went to the hospital. There's no great damage—she's just scraped up is all. Now she's planning to sue and has hired herself a shyster lawyer. He told her to make twenty visits to a chiropractor he frequently works with and says they'll aim for a $5,000 settlement, of which he'll retain a third. It seems she'll spend her share on the appointments, won't she? Plus the lawyer told her to take a week off from her job, and that's another financial setback. Tiffany never mentioned a thing about it. It was Mom who told me. She's furious.

June 26, 1991
New York

I began a writing class at the Y tonight, and though the teacher hasn't a knack for generating critical discussion, I still get a kick out of her. At one point she read a poem by someone I'm not familiar with. "History has borne him out to be something of an anti-Semite and a racist, but he *was* funny," she said. Our homework assignment is to write a story in the form of a diary entry.

June 27, 1991
New York

In addition to the house on Bleecker Street, Alba has two apartments on 7th between C and D, one in the basement and another on the ground floor. I emptied out the former this afternoon with the help of a mover named Patrick who drives a big van and wears plastic-framed glasses. It must be hard having someone who never lifts a finger telling you all day to be careful, to not scratch the walls or drop something, etc., but he was good at tuning it out.

Patrick is maybe five years older than me. He lives in Chelsea and pays $650 for three rooms. At the end of the day I gave him my number and told him to call if he ever needs any help. It turns out he can use me on Saturday morning and will pay $10 an hour.

June 29, 1991
New York

I worked today, hard, for Patrick the mover. It was a thirteen-hour shift, and I left with bruises on my thighs. It reached 97 degrees this afternoon, and at times I could wring water from my shirt. That said, between the payment and the tips, I made $155. I also drank seven Gatorades.

Our first job was a double, two people moving to two different places. One of them had packed in plastic bags, while the other had used huge boxes, which is always a mistake, especially when you're moving into a sixth-floor walk-up.

Joining Patrick and me today was a guy named Willie, who lives with his parents in Queens and was once thrown into prison in Argentina. As for the people we moved, it was amazing to watch them walk up the stairs of their old and new apartments completely empty-handed.

What was great was driving all over town: Harlem, the Upper West Side, Chelsea, the Village. Patrick says, "Let's ride." At one point we went to his apartment on 16th Street, which was really dirty and messy. On our way back to the van, he told me that Alba had not tipped him. Even worse, after we'd unloaded all of her stuff at the house on Bleecker, she tried to talk him down on the previously agreed-upon price. She's leaving for Provincetown tomorrow, so no work this week.

July 10, 1991
New York
My writing class is held at the Y on 63rd Street. *One Life to Live* is filmed just three blocks away, and tonight, while passing the studio, I saw the actor who plays Max Holden talking to two fans.

After commenting on the stories we turned in last week, our teacher advised us to "throw all taste and decency out the window" and use lots of violence in our next assignment.

Walking home, I fell in behind two black women, one short and one tall. Some little bitch kept phoning the short woman's house, and she'd had it. "When I get mad, I don't argue," she said. "I swing."

July 15, 1991
New York
Hugh and I were on the subway when two women boarded. One was obese, and she pointed to the far end of the car, saying, "Oh, look, Dorothy, two seats together!" The two of them walked over and then the heavy woman sat down, filling both the seats.

August 1, 1991
New York
I worked for Alba again today. She's preparing to leave 7th Street and is kindly giving the basement apartment to the writer Herbert Huncke and his twenty-one-year-old protégé Jason. I asked the kid where the two of them met and he said, "At the methadone clinic."

In our past encounters, Herbert was almost grotesquely polite. He's a charmer, always begging and borrowing money for drugs. He'd hoped to move into the apartment tomorrow and complained that it wasn't in the state he'd been promised it would be in. So that was my job today, to paint it: shitty latex on shitty, unprepared walls. Herbert wanted the floors done in black enamel, but Alba had already bought white and didn't feel like exchanging it. This put Herbert in a foul mood that soured as the afternoon progressed.

The place needed to be finished by tonight, and at seven, Alba asked the two men to help. Jason suddenly remembered an appointment he was late for, and Herbert angrily dunked the latex-paint roller into the enamel. The roller was ruined by that point, so he started painting the floor, a dumb thing to do when the walls weren't finished. When I mentioned this, he turned on me, saying, "What do you know, office boy?"

Office boy? *Me?* He doesn't know how to work a roller and *I'm* the know-nothing? Herbert had a tantrum. Then he asked for turpentine—"turps," he called it—and I told him we didn't have any.

"Then how do you expect to wash your hands?"

I told him I planned never to wash my hands again, and he stormed off and sat in the front window. There he crabbed at the people who passed by. He yelled at a guy who touched the sewing machine Alba had left on the curb, hoping someone might take it. He yelled at a neighbor whose gate squeaked. "You ought to oil that damned thing."

"You ought to oil your fucking head!" the man shouted back, apparently unaware that he was talking to a very important petty thief and heroin addict.

August 4, 1991
New York

The day before yesterday, Patrick and I moved a humorless waiter from 171st Street to 110th. The guy said that he'd had both Milton Berle and John Gotti as customers and that the latter had left him no tip. We didn't like the waiter, but he was much better than Lola and Raoul, the idiotic club kids we moved last night. She's from Nigeria, he's from Israel, and between the two of them, they hadn't a single box. Who moves without boxes? They had vases of flowers, plates, all the things you'd find in an apartment, just sitting there. Unbelievable. Lola was very beautiful and must have had money in order to afford all the expensive clothing I handled. She had a little lapdog named Poochie that yapped nonstop. The entire job was a nightmare. I'd carry something to the truck and she'd say, "No, not *that* lamp. Take it back upstairs."

And Raoul was just as bad, all "Come here *now*" and "You *must* listen to me."

August 20, 1991
New York
Before moving people, I talked to Tiffany. Then Mom called to say that Lisa and Bob's wedding will take place in a dry county. Bob's parents don't approve of cigarettes, so she said we'll have to drink and smoke in our hotel rooms.

September 20, 1991
New York
Amy is in town to do our play so we were together last night when Mom called and told us that she has lung cancer. She phoned from the hospital, her voice stuffy-sounding due to a tube she had in her nose. We are all of us shocked. The surprise isn't that it's lung cancer over any other type but that she has it at all. It made sense that Mrs. Steigerwald, Mrs. Rury, and Uncle Dick had cancer. Not that they were deserving of it, but you could picture them in waiting rooms. I always felt certain we weren't that kind of people. It's silly, but that's what I'd told myself.

The tumor is lemon-sized, but it hasn't spread, which is

good. On Monday the doctor will present a treatment plan, and she'll let us know what it is.

After Mom hung up, Amy and I talked to Lisa and Tiffany. Paul doesn't know yet. She hasn't told him. On the phone, she said it very simply: "I have news for you. I have cancer."

This is the last day of summer. The temperature was in the low sixties, crisp. Before rehearsal I went to the new apartment on Thompson Street and watched for a while as Hugh chipped away plaster and exposed the brick wall beneath it.

September 24, 1991
New York

Mom called to say they have outlined a course of treatment. Surgery's been suggested, but first they have to make her strong enough to withstand it. They have her exercising, trying to improve her breathing. It's hard to imagine Mom jogging or riding a bike, so for the time being, she's just walking. Meanwhile, she's going through her jewelry, setting things aside for each daughter. She said she's not stepping into her grave but just managing her time, and that since I don't wear jewelry she's sending me a thousand dollars. Lately, what with the play, I worry about money until my gums bleed. So it will come in handy.

Next week Mom and Eleanor are going out wig shopping, which is scary. She told me she's still smoking, but only four cigarettes a day. Afterward she sprays the bathroom with perfume so that Dad won't smell anything. She has a collapsed lung, so it's not a great idea for her to go to the mountains for Lisa's wedding, but still she's determined to make it. "I've talked about this with Tiffany and Gretchen and I don't want any of you smoking at the wedding dinner, not at the table. Bob's people don't like it, so the least you can do is to step outside."

October 14, 1991
New York
Lisa got married on Saturday afternoon on top of Eaglenest Mountain. I'd worried it might be sort of hokey, but in fact it was nice to be outdoors and in such a beautiful place. Lisa wore white but not a wedding dress. She and Bob stayed someplace nice and the rest of us were at an Econo Lodge in Waynesville. It was on a highway, but across the road was a pleasant cemetery we could walk to and get high in a circle of stone crosses tall enough to actually crucify people on.

This morning Mom has her first appointment with the radiologist, and tomorrow they're doing a scan of her brain. Wednesday they're looking at her bones, and she's just taking it as it comes. All weekend she was sneaking cigarettes, asking for a drag off mine or Gretchen's or Tiffany's.

October 15, 1991
New York
All day I had a terrible headache, so I went and had my hair cut at a place on 6th Avenue that I'd passed several times but never entered. The barber was Italian and really took his time. All the magazines, I noticed, had naked women in them, *Playboy* on the soft end, and on the hard side, *Pink in Film,* which had on the cover a woman wearing a strap-on penis.

While I was gone, the play continued. William said that the shows went well but that the audiences were on the small side, six to eight people per night.

October 16, 1991
New York
Amy and I walked up 8th Avenue to Intermezzo, where Hugh and his friend Sue were having lunch. "*Here* you are!" Amy

shouted. "Just what do you think you're doing? You can't afford to be eating here, not when I've got a five-month-old baby waiting in the car. And wine too! You're drinking wine! I hate being your sponsor, I really do."

Everyone stared and Hugh turned bright red.

Afterward I went to Macy's, where I filled out umpteen forms, peed into a jar, and had my eyes tested. This year, as a returning elf, I'll make $9 an hour. Regular Christmas help gets only $6.

October 28, 1991
New York

Last night was the final performance of the play (*Jamboree*). The house was packed so we brought in extra chairs. Unfortunately we brought too many, meaning that, once again, we had empty seats. In the end the audience numbered sixty-four, which was great, the biggest so far.

Afterward we struck the set and then came home to cook chicken, which we ate at three thirty in the morning.

The night before that, I performed at P.S. 122 as part of their Avant-Garde-Arama. The house was sold out, and though we were told to limit ourselves to twenty minutes, most people went on much longer—a trio of girls, for instance, who slowly rolled a hundred oranges across the floor.

I'm having a bad run as far as readings are concerned. I was bad at the Nuyorican and bad at P.S. 122. Next Monday I'm at La MaMa, and then Ward-Nasse, followed by a benefit, followed by two weeks of Orchid Shows, and then another gallery. I stretch myself too thin and wind up with tiny houses.

November 1, 1991
New York

Hugh and I moved into our new apartment last night, but I screwed up and we won't have phone service until the twelfth, and that's if we're lucky. I thought they could turn it on from some office somewhere, but instead they have to make a special trip that should have been scheduled weeks ago. I was supposed to do this last month but I didn't. I fucked up.

After paying this month's rent and giving Rusty the money I owed him, I'm left with $40. I might make some at La MaMa this week, but without a way for people to call me, I'm screwed.

November 3, 1991
New York

Amy and I met Jeff and Tina for a drink last night at El Teddy's, the fancy Mexican place in Tribeca that sometimes feels exciting and sometimes feels awful. Last night it was the latter. I was standing in front of a woman who was seated at the bar, waiting on friends, and said to her, "Excuse me," as I reached over and dunked a tortilla chip in salsa. I then put it in my mouth and was chewing away when she said, "Hey, you got tomato stains on my pants."

I looked down and watched as she stabbed at the red spots with a wet napkin. She was super-angry, like this was the last straw. Her friends weren't showing up, the place was too crowded, and now some idiot had spilled salsa on her new tan slacks.

"Oh, gosh," I said. "I'm terribly sorry about your pants." With the letter *p*, a shard of tortilla chip flew from my mouth right into the corner of her eye. I couldn't believe it.

"Jesus fucking Christ," she said. "Now you spit on me!"

She wanted me dead, and it only got worse when her

friends showed up. I caught her pointing at me, the creep who ruined her outfit and then spat on her.

November 5, 1991
New York

I talked to Mom this afternoon, called her from Alba's phone. She's lost six pounds this week. The chemo and radiation make her nauseated and she recently finished a meal after going five days without one. She checks her comb for hairs that have fallen out but so far hasn't found any. I'd expected her to be down and depressed, but she was full of good hospital stories.

November 9, 1991
New York

It costs 10 cents to enter the children's zoo in Central Park so I bought a ticket and saw a litter of albino mice gathered around their mother. There were twenty-two of them, newborn and hairless, pink like pencil erasers. Later I walked to the library and came away with the new Ronnie Milsap biography. "Your mother's twin," I said to Hugh when I got home, though of course she looks nothing like him. Ronnie Milsap is blind. His grandfather's name was Homer Frisbee.

Our neighbor Helen came to the door this morning holding a takeout carton filled with chicken. *Hugh* was written on top of it in big letters. The other day she brought him a pound of sausage. The day before that it was a turkey meat loaf and a gallon of milk. Hugh gave her a dozen roses, but she returned them, saying she's allergic. It seems important that no one ever repays her, that the other person is always in her debt. Last week she accepted a few flashlight batteries but that was a first.

"What do you say?" she growled after handing me the chicken this morning. "You say, 'Thank you, Helen.'"

She's something else, this woman.

I worked for Alba, who was sick, throwing up all day. At a party last night she had eleven Bellinis, those peach-and-Prosecco cocktails. These were followed by three tallboys. Yikes. You'd think an adult would know better: Beer on wine, you're fine. Wine on beer, stand clear. But eleven Prosecco cocktails should not precede anything, not even a twelfth.

November 14, 1991
Raleigh
Mom died last night, suddenly, of pneumonia brought on by her chemotherapy. Amy called to tell me, and now we're all in Raleigh. Dad gave us the option of seeing her laid out at the funeral home, but I was afraid to go. We all were. How strange to be in her house and see her things—the half-worked crossword puzzle, her mail and stockings. She didn't expect to die yesterday, did she?

When it happened, Hugh and I were in our kitchen in New York. He was making manicotti and talking about a wooden chicken he'd bought when I got socked by the weirdest feeling. I thought that Hugh was going to die, and I must have said something because he accused me of being dramatic. I can't believe this has happened.

November 21, 1991
New York
The other night we were visited by Father Regis, the new priest at the Greek Orthodox church. He came to get an idea of what our mother was like and took a cue from the unfinished thousand-piece puzzle spread out across the dining-room table.

For the past few days we've been working on it—just something to do with our hands as we sat around talking. "Oh," the priest said when he saw us. "I see you're finishing this in memory of your dear departed mother, God rest her soul."

He made it sound so hokey.

November 22, 1991
New York

I had elf training today, from one to four. The filmstrips about safety and theft I remember from last year, but there was a new one about shoplifting narrated by a guy in prison. The walls of his cell were scarred and ugly, and after he spoke we heard from the cashier who had seen him steal and alerted security, thereby earning a $500 bonus.

For most of the day I sat beside Richard, whom I met last year. He's older than me but lives with his parents. All his talk is about cute guys.

November 23, 1991
New York

I really outdid myself last night. After three martinis, five beers, and two joints, I fell asleep on the kitchen floor. There was a sofa three feet away, but I couldn't manage the walk, I guess. I've been getting high since Thursday, and the drinking is out of control. Since waking up I've felt like shit—headache, hot flashes, chills—and to make it worse, I spent the day on a scaffold, helping Mark and Lily paint a restaurant. I was hoping that maybe I'd fall, get amnesia, and forget that I drink.

December 2, 1991
New York

Someone threw up outside of SantaLand and covered it over

with a paper bag. I saw the bag lying there on the floor, and when I picked it up I got vomit on my hands.

December 22, 1991
New York
SantaLand is filthy now. I loaded a large bag with trash this morning: disposable diapers filled with crap, cans, bottles, mittens, destroyed bits of the various displays. Yesterday a woman had her son pee into a cup, which of course tipped over. "That's fine," I said, "but Santa's also going to need a stool sample."

December 31, 1991
New York
Before catching the plane to Raleigh on Christmas Eve, I worked. We were packed, and I photo-elfed for five and a half hours before getting my break. At the beginning I was paired with Santa Howard. He always asks the children what they plan on leaving him, and I laughed when a kid hesitated a moment before saying, "Matches?"

Actually, for a pipe smoker, it's not a bad little gift.

Christmas was hard. Luckily Hugh was there to help with the cooking. When Mom was around, we'd remain at the dinner table for hours, but this year we all scattered the moment we finished eating. Included in this year's gifts were many things our mother had bought us, mainly from catalogs, which was rattling.

Dad wants to talk about her death—he needs to—but unlike the rest of us, who yak incessantly about our feelings, he has no vocabulary for it and is reduced to the clichés you'd find on a sympathy card. It's like not knowing a language.

He also doesn't know how to shop.

1992

January 13, 1992
New York

Looking into the future lately, I see nothing but a mess. I think I peaked in 1988, and it's all downhill now. How awful, to decline this way. What makes young people young is that they see themselves going up, up, up. Not me, though. I'm old now.

January 15, 1992
New York

From nine to three I moved furniture and from four to eight I sanded floors, so I'm beat but glad to have worked and made $90. In the morning I was with Richie and learned that he lives with a man named Herman who is gay and has AIDS and owns a satanic-supply shop. Herman has a thing for convicts and is currently courting one of the defendants in the Howard Beach case. Richie, who has been in prison himself, lives rent-free and takes care of the dogs. He has a voice like Jackie Gleason's, so it surprised me to learn that he was gay. It seems he has appeared in several pornographic movies. "I'm a top," he said. "I know everybody says that, but I really am."

January 20, 1992
Bridgehampton, New York

I woke up to snow this morning. While Hugh and Lily painted, I continued the Elvis Presley biography. Toward the end of his life, they practically needed a crane to lift him out of bed. He was so doped up and obese and out of it. His windows were covered to keep things dark. Drugs had paralyzed his colon, so he had to take lots of laxatives. Often he shit in his sleep. His bedroom smelled awful and he hated taking baths and showers. He was just this lump, apparently, not mean or cruel. Reading the book, you can't help but feel sorry for him. If I were that wealthy I'd probably be the same and take drugs until I died.

Lying in bed last night, I imagined that Elvis said to me, "David, I need your help."

So I said, "All right," and together we turned his life around. Elvis used to eat a pound of bacon every morning along with a six-egg Spanish omelet and biscuits. At night he'd have many cheeseburgers and loads of mashed potatoes with gravy. He'd talk and watch TV while he ate, and when his food got cold he'd call out for more.

February 9, 1992
New York

Hugh sat me down today and said, gently, that while I whine and sulk, I don't do much of anything when it comes to finding steady work. "Do you think that someone's going to knock on the door and offer you a job?"

And I said that of course that's what I thought. Doesn't he know anything? I don't make things happen—that's not my way. Rather, I wait around and settle for whatever comes along.

February 10, 1992
New York

Admin Asst Dream Job
WORK FOR A STAR Gal/Guy Friday
all around exec asst.

Answer fan mail
Admin duties. Lite typing
MADEMOISELLE 16 E 40th St

I saw this in the *New York Times* and thought, *Honestly, that is my dream job—answering fan mail at* Mademoiselle *magazine.* I shaved, threw on clean clothes, and went to apply, not feeling intimidated the way I normally do but thinking, *Out of my way. This is mine.* I suppose I wondered who at the magazine got fan mail, but it didn't really matter. Whatever the letter, I'd answer it. Mainly I pictured Hugh's face when I greeted him with the news: "I got a job, and it's perfect."

When I arrived at the office and saw fifteen other people applying, I still wasn't worried. The application asked what experience I had and listed various computer programs. Did I know Lotus? Quark? Would I be interested in paying $70 to take a class in either one of these? The room was big and we sat on a built-in sofa as the movie *The Fabulous Baker Boys* played on two TV sets. I heard the receptionist call someone's name, then say, "You can step in now for your typing test."

Furious clattering noises came from the place where the test was being administered, and I thought, *Fuck.* After thirteen years, I can still only type with one finger. I'm fast with it, but I can't lift my eyes from the keyboard. Taking a test was out of the question, so I approached the receptionist. She asked what job I was applying for, and when I said answering fan mail, she said I needn't worry. "Just sit back down."

When I was called for my interview, the woman, whose last name was Pizza, told me that the job was already taken. "But have you temped before?" That's when I realized this was Mademoiselle Temporary Services, not *Mademoiselle* magazine. I told her I hadn't taken the typing test and she said sometimes companies just wanted someone to answer the phone. That said, they'd probably want someone with a nice voice and the face to go with it.

"Thanks anyway," I said.

When I got back to the apartment, the phone rang. It was Dad, who told me I should try to get work as a model. I told him he was being ridiculous and he said no, he'd just been at the barbershop and saw a *GQ* magazine with a guy on the cover who looked just like me. So I went to the newsstand and found a copy and the person on the cover was not a model but Gary Oldman.

February 11, 1992
New York

On Friday at two thirty I have an appointment at the World Trade Center, a part-time job moving furniture around in an office. I get these little fantasies going. Passing some place or other, I'll think of working there, and then suddenly it's as if I have the job. And it's a great place. Everyone's friendly and terrific.

I passed the Duplex on 7th and Christopher and saw a sign announcing that Wednesday was comedy night. So I came home and called to ask how it worked. Did they audition people? The guy told me to phone back the next day and talk to Colette, who runs something called Stars of Tomorrow.

Hugh says if I do it, he'll leave me. Meanwhile, Mike Tyson has been convicted of rape. I've always thought of him as the sexiest guy in the world, so it's hard to imagine him forcing himself on anyone.

February 12, 1992
New York

I applied for a job at an Upper East Side sandwich shop.

The woman I spoke to was named Charlotte, and I was the fifth person she'd interviewed. I don't know who the first one was, but the three who went before me were all from Pakistan.

"Why do you want to work with sandwiches?" Charlotte asked.

And I thought, *Well, I don't, really. It's just that I need a job.*

Next I went to 5 & 10 No Exaggeration. It's a combination antiques store/restaurant. Waiters are required to wear wing-tip shoes, suspenders, and bow ties, and it's a smoke-free business. I don't know why I bothered, really. New York restaurants want waiters who look like models. If you're not pretty, you don't stand a chance. Then there's the no-experience problem.

This is Lincoln's Birthday, so the library was closed.

March 1, 1992
New York

Patrick and I moved furniture from Jericho, Long Island, to Park Slope in Brooklyn. We were near the drop-off point when I noticed what smelled like a candle burning inside a pumpkin. Then I saw smoke coming from the back of the van and we pulled over. One of us had apparently thrown a lit cigarette out the window that blew back in and settled on a moving quilt. It burned through two layers but luckily didn't reach the tabletop. The people we picked up the furniture from in Jericho, an older couple, had a spotless house. What's odd is that they had brass knockers on all of their inside doors—to the bathrooms and bedrooms, the closets, everything. "Be careful," they kept saying. "Watch the corner! Watch the stairs!"

The couple in Park Slope were in their late thirties and had a baby. They smiled a lot, were nice. Brooklyn is covered in graffiti. Absolutely covered.

March 19, 1992
New York
Hugh and I went to Westport, Connecticut, and picked up two tuxedo cats that used to belong to the actress Sandy Dennis, who recently died of ovarian cancer. On the train back to New York, two black teenagers were discovered hiding in the bathroom. They'd snuck on without paying and were shocked when the conductor asked them to hand over their Walkmans, saying, "Those should about cover the price of the tickets."

"You don't understand," one of the kids said. "These aren't our Walkmans." He said that they belonged to friends and that they went to a really tough school where every day someone got shot and killed.

"That's not my problem," the conductor said.

"But...," the kid said. "But..."

The conductor said they'd have to get off at the next stop, 125th Street.

The other kid spoke up then, saying, "But we want to get off at Grand Central."

"Look," the conductor said, "you can either get off at One Hundred and Twenty-Fifth Street or go to jail."

To this, the first kid said, "Which one?"

March 22, 1992
New York
Patrick stayed up late last night and watched a show about termites, which don't eat wood but apparently just store it in their cheeks or whatnot. Then they bring it back to the mound, where they use it to mulch mushrooms. Can this be true? I'm so gullible sometimes.

March 23, 1992
New York

According to the book I'm reading, Judy Garland was once singing "Over the Rainbow" at the Greek Theatre in Los Angeles when a moth flew into her open mouth. She couldn't spit it out in the middle of the song, so she just parked it in her cheek until she had finished. Again, can that be true?

June 15, 1992
New York

Normally in the morning, Hugh drinks tea and eats a piece of fruit. Most often it's an apple, but this morning it was a banana that had been sitting too long on the shelf. The peel was bruised almost black, and inside it was the color of pus, all slick and nasty-looking. I'd just brushed one of the cats and couldn't help but take the hair and arrange it just so on Hugh's seeping banana. Then I sat back and winced. It truly was disgusting. Obscene, really.

June 21, 1992
New York

A few weeks back, my *Interview Magazine* mention came out, and this morning I received a postcard reading *Dear Mr. Sedaris, You are very cute and I love what you have to say about the world. It is a crazy place, but you make it well worth it. Your admirer, Jean Snyder.*

The card is just what I needed. It's nutty, sure, but how nice to know that some stranger is thinking of me.

June 23, 1992
New York

At Coney Island we passed a sideshow booth that featured a two-headed baby represented in four mammoth paintings.

In the first he was in diapers, shaking a rattle. Then there he was, taking his first, astonished steps. In the third painting the baby seemed on the verge of a decision, one head delighted, and the other one wailing. The fourth should have been the first but wasn't for some reason. It showed the baby swaddled in a bandanna, delivered by a stork that had sunglasses on.

I had to see this for myself, so while Hugh waited out front, I bought a ticket and went inside. There, I found the two-headed baby, not playing patty-cake or scribbling on walls with a crayon but floating in a jar of formaldehyde. Three of the four pictures I'd seen were absolute bullshit, as he couldn't have been more than a few hours old when he died. Even in a jar, that kid has outearned me.

June 24, 1992
New York
The postcard I received the other day, the one from a stranger, was false. Hugh wrote it, not Jean Snyder. She was someone he went to school with as a child in Beirut. It seems he typed the postcard, attached a used stamp, and extended the cancellation marks with a pencil. I really have to hand it to him sometimes.

July 3, 1992
New York
I stopped at a discount store on Broadway this morning hoping to buy some floor-wax remover for one of my cleaning jobs. It was the kind of place that sells everything but under a different name. For instance, they have an all-purpose spray, but it's called Fabulous instead of Fantastik. They don't sell Ajax, they sell Apex. The store is owned by men in black turbans who asked that I check my bag on entering. I did, and when I didn't find what I was looking for, I returned to collect it.

"You stole something," the security goon at the counter said.

This same thing had just happened a few weeks ago, so I was furious. "Are you accusing me of shoplifting?"

"You have something in your pocket," he told me.

"Really?" I said. "You pretty sure of that?" I emptied my pockets, front and back. "Does your store sell keys to my apartment? Do you sell half packs of cigarettes and books of matches from a restaurant in Providence, Rhode Island? Or, hey, maybe I stole my own wallet!"

The man said, "I can accuse you of anything I want."

Later I felt bad for emptying my pockets. I hear people all the time shouting, "You think I stole something? Call the police." I always wonder why they're making such a big deal out of it. *Why not just prove you haven't stolen anything?* I think.

Both times this month I've proven myself innocent, but the security goons never apologized. They just said, "Hmmmm," and on leaving, both times, I condemned their entire race: Fucking Koreans. Goddamned...whatever people who wear turbans are.

Both times I was accused, I was dressed for cleaning apartments, wearing shabby clothing and smelling like Ajax, or Apex, I guess they'd call it. Does this mean I should wear a suit when running out for supplies and change back into my rags after returning to work? Of course, this is nothing. If I were black, I'd get this several times a day. And I'd be really angry all the time.

July 5, 1992
New York

I woke up to someone crying, "Ma, Ma! Help me, Ma. Open the door. Ma. Ma. Open the door." It went on for hours and the voice was odd-sounding, not like a child's but more like a man's.

I asked Helen and she told me it's Franny, the Italian woman who lives downstairs and will turn one hundred years old on Monday. Her daughter lives on the same floor and looks after her with the help of a hired Jamaican woman who comes at night and on weekends. When the daughter leaves town, Franny gets worse and screams for her mother, her brothers, her sisters, all dead. When Helen went down this morning, Franny told her to go fuck herself.

"Can you beat that!" Helen said. "The language on that one. A hundred years old with a mouth like that."

July 23, 1992
New York
I worked with Patrick, who told me that last week Richie was arrested and then released on a $100,000 bail his father paid by putting up his taxi medallion. According to Richie's story, he was coming out of a bar when two men tried to rob him. They started fighting, and after the first guy ran off, Richie hit the second in the face with a beer bottle—hit him so hard, in fact, that the bottle broke. The police pulled up to find Richie standing over the bleeding, unconscious body, and it got worse when the guy, who is now expected to be blind in one eye, fell into a coma. I would never attempt to rob Richie. First off, he's huge. He's strong and he isn't afraid of anything. You can tell that just by looking at him.

August 15, 1992
New York
I went to France with a passport so new it was still warm and five books about serial killers: Robert Berdella, Billy Lee Chadd, Henry Lee Lucas, Jeffrey Dahmer, and Ted Bundy.

The worst of them smiled when their mug shots were taken, though it has to be said they were all pretty bad. Interesting was how many were disappointments to their mothers, who were hoping for daughters rather than sons. One of the five (I can't recall which, as they all ran together) was sent to school in a skirt and bonnet. That sounds so old-fashioned, a bonnet.

While in Normandy we drove through the countryside, sometimes with a mission and sometimes aimlessly. The villages looked like I thought they would—tidy yards, stone houses, window boxes spilling over with flowers. Hugh's house is in La Bagotière, a hamlet. Maybe twenty-five or thirty people live there, nobody fancy. The Gs across the road raise sheep, horses, chickens, and rabbits. They're in their mid-sixties and live with Madame G.'s mother and Mr. G.'s sister Brigitte, who has Down syndrome and spends her days at an outdoor table laying down dominoes. She wears very thick glasses and though she doesn't talk much, she'll hold out her hand if you hold out yours first. The teenage boy next door is mentally retarded, as is Sandrine, two doors up. That's a lot for a hamlet this size, one in every ten people.

Hugh's house is stone and he guesses it's maybe three hundred years old. As of now there's no running water or electricity. I spent my week helping him empty it out and clean it. Plumbers and electricians came by and I didn't understand a single word any of them said. We stayed a half a mile away in a house owned by Hugh's friend Genevieve, a pharmacist, and her husband, Momo, who holds some sort of elected office.

When the week was over, we went to Paris. There are any number of stores there that time seems to have forgotten. At one of them I bought five rubber noses. That's one for every serial killer I read about while I was in France.

August 20, 1992
New York

Today I did a cleaning job for a forty-two-year-old named Tommy who was short and slight and answered the door in his robe. He wore socks as well, and the toes of them were pulled forward and flopped around when he walked. At the start of the day he sent me to the storage place to buy twenty-five boxes. These were added to the thirty he already had, most of which were half full of things he had failed to unpack during the three years he'd lived in his apartment. One particular box contained a $2 bill, a place mat illustrating various sources of vitamin C, a book titled *How to Be Funny*, several manila envelopes, and dozens of lists and scraps of paper with messages such as "I am denying myself food in order to grow as a person" and "Hunger is a state of mind" written on them.

In the afternoon he sent me to his new apartment, where I measured the windows and then went to the hardware store to buy child guards for them. "Do you have kids?" I asked.

He said no but was worried he might have friends over, and that some of them might fall out the windows.

"Do you have a lot of blind friends?" I asked.

Tommy has fifty identical stainless-steel plates, and three times a day he broils himself a steak. In his freezer were two hundred portions of fish, each labeled with the date and what kind it was: *1/18 cod, 2/29 red snapper,* etc. I asked and he explained that he had gone through a seafood phase before turning to steak. In his closet were dozens of pairs of suspenders, many of them neon-colored, along with bow ties and hats. He is an only child. His father died "from drinking," and his mother lives in Massachusetts. He asked me to return tomorrow and help him some more but, either fortunately or unfortunately, I'm already scheduled to work with Bart.

September 4, 1992
New York

Walking down 8th Avenue, I fell in behind two muscled gym queens. When a car alarm went off, one of them turned to the other, saying, "That's the Puerto Rican national anthem."

"Really?" the other guy said. "That's actually their anthem?"

September 5, 1992
New York

Yesterday the man Richie hit with a bottle died; this according to Patrick, whom I worked with today. Richie was out walking one of Herman's dogs when the cops stopped and asked him what it was like to be a murderer. In response, Richie punched one of the policemen in the face and knocked him out. That got him arrested again. The guy can't stay out of trouble for the life of him. He's sweet when he's sober, as sweet as they come, but he's already killed two people. The first murder occurred when he was a teenager. Now he's, what, thirty?

September 27, 1992
New York

I went to Walker's with Marge and two friends of hers, a guy named Dan who's fluent in sign language and a woman named Pat who just got her master's in dance history. We got to talking and I learned that her dad was a radio celebrity at WABC from the early 1940s until the mid-1970s. The family lived in New Canaan, Connecticut, and every Christmas morning his show was broadcast live from their living room. Pat received cards and letters from listeners and rode to Manhattan in a chauffeured car to watch her father emcee *Circus of the Stars.* Once, her dad came home from work in a helicopter, and she remembers the young trees bowing in the wind generated by the blades. Pat was, at the time, "horsey," meaning devoted to horses. She went on to say that her father was an alcoholic and was married six times, her mom being wife number five. The drinking didn't bother me, but the umpteen marriages and the thought of all those stepsisters definitely tarnished the beautiful picture I had formed in my mind.

September 29, 1992
New York
Patrick's truck broke down, so he's applying for welfare. He told me that over the phone today, and then he added that Richie's murder charge had been dropped. After we hung up, Hugh's friend Leslie called. She's a buyer for Barneys and leaves tomorrow for Milan and Paris. One person talks about welfare and the next about the terrible Donna Karan collection.

October 9, 1992
New York
While cleaning this morning, I listened to a radio call-in show hosted by a woman who helps people find things. Not missing objects but merchandise and services. The first person to phone in was looking for denim boots. She said she's been searching everywhere and wanted some phone numbers so she can call around before coming into the city. "I have a few pairs already, but let me tell you, once they start to fray, there's not a thing in the world you can do but buy another pair! I've got regular denim boots and stonewashed and they're both on their way out. I swear, if I can find another place that sells them, I'll buy a hundred pairs."

October 13, 1992
New York

Hugh is in Boca Raton, Florida, for a job, staying at a Days Inn. I call and ask for his room and am connected with a Vietnamese woman. We exchange a few words, and I phone the front desk again and say that I enjoyed talking to someone from Southeast Asia but that now I am ready to speak to Hugh Hamrick. They then connect me to the room of Lisa Gold, who is doing the job in Boca Raton with Hugh. I call back and tell the operator that it was great talking to Lisa. Though she lives only ten blocks away from me in New York, we rarely see one another, so I appreciated the opportunity to catch up. Now, though, I wouldn't mind talking to Hugh Hamrick in room 412. Jesus.

October 15, 1992
New York

The new Pakistani cashier at the Grand Union is named Dollop.

October 27, 1992
New York

In Saugerties, we had a waitress who was for Bush. "I'm voting for him because my generation does things like that," she said. "My ex-husband is a shithead and a bastard with a big government pension and he'll vote this way or that. But me, my best years were when Republicans were in office. You know what I'm saying?"

October 31, 1992
New York

We went with Ken and Taro to see the Halloween parade. My favorite costume was a very thin, dirty Santa carrying a plastic bag of discarded cans. He was accompanied by a filthy Ronald McDonald.

November 25, 1992
New York

Helen went off this morning on the Korean grocers on the corner of Spring and Thompson. "One day they charge me forty cents for an apple and the next day it's fifty cents. For an apple, the bastards! The girl behind the counter asked if I was going to cook a turkey for Thanksgiving and I said, 'What's it to you?'

"She says, 'My mother's not going to make one.' And I said, 'Yeah, well, your mother's a lazy bastard.'"

December 3, 1992
New York

I got a call a few weeks back from a fellow named Don who had read my SantaLand story in the *New York Press*. He taught a high school equivalency program in the basement of the Fulton projects and asked if I might visit his class. "The kids are bound to love your writing, but reading it in front of the actual author will likely make them nervous," he said. "So if you don't mind, I'll tell them you're a graduate student who's come to observe my teaching style. Then, when they're finished, maybe near the end of the session, I'll reveal your true identity."

He gave me the address, so this afternoon I showed up and was introduced as James from Columbia University. Copies of the SantaLand story were distributed to the students. Then Don said, "Eddie, would you like to start?"

Eddie, a twenty-two-year-old with razor-nicked eyebrows and letters tattooed on his knuckles, began. "'I was at a cuff...a cuff...at a...I was at a cuff...'"

"Sound it out," Don said. "Come on, Eddie, you can do this."

I had felt uncomfortable around these students. Loud and powerfully built, they had spent their break threatening one another and yelling out the windows at passing girls. They were all so volatile and mean-looking, but faced with the page, they were powerless, like children. Once someone had finished his paragraph, he'd put his head down on the table-top or walk away to see what was happening outside. Then someone else would be called on. " 'Snowball just . . . leads elves on, elves and Santas.' "

How odd it was to have my experiences recounted in these voices. *What were you doing while I was wandering the maze or having nickels thrown at me?* I'd wonder, looking at some-one in a hooded Gang Starr sweatshirt. *And what was I doing when you got that teardrop tattooed on your cheek?*

It took well over an hour to complete the reading. Don con-gratulated the group on a job well done, then folded his arms and leaned back in his chair. "All right," he said. "So, if you could *meet* the person who wrote this, what would you ask?"

The guy next to Eddie put up his hand. "I'd ax, Yo, is you a faggot or what?"

December 15, 1992
New York
Ira Glass called to say that *Morning Edition* would like to broadcast my "SantaLand Diary." They'll pay me $500 and give him $200 to produce it. So tomorrow I go to a recording studio.

December 24, 1992
Raleigh
Yesterday morning my story aired on NPR's *Morning Edi-tion.* Ira and I had been on the phone the night before, trying

to decide which cuts to make. I have an allergic reaction to my voice, but the singing was all right. Hugh's friend Marian phoned after the 7:40 broadcast and said how much she liked it. A minute later I got a call from a switchboard operator who was late for work on account of sitting in her parked car and listening to me. She said she'd already phoned NPR to say good things but thought she'd reach out to me as well. They played the story again at 9:40, and then I was called by William, Allyn, and several strangers. The moment I'd start talking to someone, call-waiting would act up. At ten I left for the first of today's four cleaning jobs, and when I returned at six, my machine was full of messages, most of them from people I don't know who'd looked me up in the phone book. A woman from Oregon called, a guy who runs a theater in Philadelphia, a writer for a TV show; two NPR stations left messages saying they were flooded—their word—with calls from people wanting to get in touch with me. A stranger from Rochester called, stuttering, asking for a tape. It was all I ever wanted. Then Hugh and I left for the airport.

1993

January 16, 1993
New York

Helen's forty-two-year-old nephew was a public-school teacher and today he died of AIDS. I said I was sorry to hear it and Helen said, "The bastard. Thought he was Mr. Big because he had an education, but where's him and his college degree now? In the ground, that's where. The last time I saw him, I called out, 'Tommy!' but he kept on walking. I say, 'Fuck you, Mr. Smart.' Yeah, we all know how smart he was now."

February 24, 1993
New York

This was an amazing New York day. In the morning I met with Geoff Kloske, the editorial assistant from Little, Brown who called a few weeks back to ask if he could read my manuscript. He's only twenty-three, a kid, and has a grandmother in Jacksonville, North Carolina. We had coffee and afterward he took me to meet his boss, Roger, a big, good-looking chain-smoker who said that he, too, liked my manuscript and hopes to get back to me within a week or two.

Afterward I went to our play rehearsal (for *Stump the Host*). We open a week from tomorrow.

March 8, 1993
New York
The night before the play opened (at La MaMa), William dropped out, saying he wasn't having much fun. "And if it's no fun, why bother?"

I spent some time panicking and then decided to take the part myself, seeing as I know the lines. So I performed on Thursday, Friday, and Saturday. Opening night we had fourteen people in the audience. On Friday, there were forty, and on Saturday we were sold out. Meryl has extended our run, and thankfully Paul Dinello has agreed to take over my part. Hugh and Amy say, "Oh, you know you love being onstage."

But they're wrong. I don't. Not like that, anyway.

March 9, 1993
New York
Roger Donald called from Little, Brown to say he would like to negotiate a two-book deal. To celebrate, I bought a denim shirt and thought it amazing how quickly one's life can change. I never thought I'd want a denim shirt.

March 13, 1993
New York
I met on Thursday afternoon with Don Congdon, the agent Roger Donald recommended. He proposed lunch and took me to Le Madri, an Italian place near his office and the fanciest restaurant I've been to in New York. Don is in his late seventies and was very elegantly dressed. A fine suit, a Pucci tie, a topcoat, even a black beret. The maître d' knew him. "Right this way, Mr. Congdon."

Our waiter poured olive oil onto a plate and then gave us bread, which I guessed we were supposed to dip into it. I had thinly carved steak arranged into a turban with grilled radicchio and endive. Don had pasta that he didn't finish.

While eating, I learned that he represents William Styron, Russell Baker, Ellen Gilchrist, and Thomas Berger. He represented Lillian Hellman for a production of *The Little Foxes* in, I think, Russia, and Frank O'Connor. He told stories about wandering through the Village with J. D. Salinger, whom he called Jerry, and recounted the night the two of them went to hear Billie Holiday. I heard of the time Don was arrested by the vice squad during Prohibition, and then something about Dashiell Hammett. The problem was that it was all about the past. That said, I liked his language, especially his old-fashioned slang.

April 30, 1993
New York

Between cleaning jobs, I bought a coffee and sat in Union Square Park to read for a while. The benches there are sectioned off with armrests—this to prevent people from stretching out and sleeping, I imagine. I'd just lit a cigarette when a guy approached—wiry, around my age, wearing soiled white jeans and a Metallica T-shirt. His hair fell to his shoulders, he had a sketchy mustache, and he was carrying a paper bag. *Ex-convict,* I thought. It was a snap assessment, but I'm sticking by it.

The guy asked for a cigarette, and when I handed him one, he took it without thanking me. Then he pointed to my bag of cleaning supplies, made a sweeping gesture with his hand, and said, "I'm going to sit down there."

There were plenty of other benches, so I said no.

"Goddamn it," he said. "I told you to move your fucking shit."

I got up and left, knowing that if I hadn't moved my bag, he would have thrown it. If, on the other hand, I *had* moved it, he would have sat beside me and continued asking for things. All afternoon I thought about it and wished that I knew how to fight.

May 2, 1993
New York

Yesterday I rode my bike across the bridge to Brooklyn. On the way back, I got a flat tire, so I was beat by the time I returned home. This morning I looked in the mirror beside our bed and saw a whale—a fur-bearing one—looking back at me. A very tired fur-bearing whale with a cat beside him. The cat looked familiar.

May 12, 1993
New York

Bart and I went to Long Island City to clean the loft that was used to film a recent Marilyn Chambers movie. The crew finished yesterday, and I went, expecting to find a lot of semen. On our way, Bart told me that many years earlier, while working in fashion, he was sent on business to Tucson. One thing led to another and on his second night, he wound up drunk and stranded. It was downtown, late, and as he tried to find a cab, a car stopped and offered him a ride. The people inside were Mexican, so he brought out all his high school Spanish, saying, *"Muchas gracias"* and *"Su automóvil es muy grande y bonito tambien."*

The driver passed Bart's hotel and took him into the desert. There the group of four beat Bart beyond recognition. They broke his nose. They held him down and kicked him in the ribs and stomach. They drove Bart's bloody face into the dirt, and when he ran away, he fell into a cactus. One of the men had taken his room key, so while Bart crawled bleeding across the dark road, they went to his hotel and stole everything. Afterward his nose was so swollen he couldn't wear glasses. The medical report stated his blood-alcohol level, and when his boss learned of it, he fired him.

The loft was the entire floor of a building owned by an interior decorator. A pale fellow with a ponytail gave us a roll of paper towels, some Windex, and a spray bottle of oil soap. It wasn't much, but aside from two sofas and a copper bathtub, the loft was empty. I swept for an hour and a half and then mopped for an hour and a half.

While mopping, I imagined that I was in the navy and was cleaning a battleship. When that wore off, I pretended that this was *my* loft, though it lasted only a few minutes, as who wants to live in Queens? The only thing I came across was a small triangle of fabric attached to some fishing wire. It was smeared with makeup, so I guess it was—what, a costume?

May 20, 1993
New York

This morning Bart told me about a woman he used to clean for. "The filthiest house I've ever seen," he said.

I asked how filthy and he told me that the first time he vacuumed her carpet, he collected $38 in change. He knew the exact amount because he kept it.

June 10, 1993
New York

At around midnight Hugh and I took a walk, ending up at the park on Thompson and Spring, where we sat and ate some ice cream. As we were doing so, two young men came around the corner. One of them said to the other, "I need to talk about this shit *now*." To punctuate, he used his elbow to smash the window of a parked car. The guy's friend walked to an empty table, and after standing there for a moment and rubbing his elbow, the guy who'd smashed the window joined him.

I came home and called the police, who said, "Would you like to leave your name, ma'am?"

The police always think I'm a woman.

June 19, 1993
New York

I talked to Paul this morning. While on the phone, he told me he was scrubbing his toes with a pumice stone, trying to rub away some Magic Marker.

"Why do you have Magic Marker on your toes?" I asked.

He told me that on Thursday night he'd attended a Live After Five concert on the mall in Raleigh. There he had five beers. These were followed later by shots in some bar, and that's the last thing he remembers. The next day he was covered with Magic Marker. His friends did it, and though it's a pain to wipe off, he still feels lucky. "The last guy who passed out had a bull's-eye painted on his butt and a Cheeto stuffed up his asshole."

June 21, 1993
New York

Amy has moved into a new apartment in Chicago, and last night she called to tell me about it. She lives above a husband and wife, a couple in their mid-forties who are taking care of their infant granddaughter, Amber. The woman, Brandi, has a shag haircut and several tattoos, one of which reads *Brandi loves*...The name has been rubbed out. Her son is twenty-five, and his wife walked out on him after the baby was born.

"And you never saw her again?" Amy asked.

"Oh, she came around once, but my son beat the shit out of her and tolt her never to come back," Brandi explained.

The son is now planning to marry a thirty-year-old prostitute. "I tolt him, you find a good piece of ass, you should stick to it."

Brandi has trouble sleeping and often comes up to complain about the noise Amy makes. Yesterday she said, "If you don't turn down that radio I'll break your legs."

June 22, 1993
New York

Last night I went to the park to buy some pot. I told Hugh I was walking to the store for milk, but my long absence must have tipped him off. I came home to find a sign taped to the front door of our apartment that read NO DRUGS. He'd put up the chain and I explained through the crack that I *had* gone for milk and run into Dale on the way back.

"And what did you two talk about?" he asked.

"Oh, this and that." The only Dale I know is an obese, ragged-looking dog Hugh and I saw in the park a few months ago. It was me who decided that's what his name was, and I refer to him all the time. "I got another letter from Dale," I'll say. "He told me to tell you hello."

I should have thought of another name, as this did nothing to get me back into the house.

July 1, 1993
New York

Because of the radio, the *New York Times* is doing a profile on me. Yesterday the reporter called Amy, who said, "I'm not telling you shit about that son of a bitch until he pays for that abortion he made me have."

July 2, 1993
New York

I was drunk and stoned, watching the twenty-four-hour *Twilight Zone* marathon at three a.m., when a commercial came on. The man in it pointed his finger at me and said, "What are you doing watching TV this time of night? You're drunk, you're stoned, you're a wreck, and you're destroying the lives of everyone around you."

It was like he could see me.

1994

January 8, 1994
New York

Stitches (our play) opened Thursday night to an audience of fifty. La MaMa can squeeze in 120, so this wasn't so bad. Friday was sold out, as was tonight. The *Times* came last night; tonight it was *Newsday* and the *Voice*. I want to tell them we were just joking. It's not a real play, it's what comes from doodling while you're holding a bong. Whatever they have to say, it's out of my control now and in the hands of the actors. My job is to play the host and greet people at the door as they enter.

January 11, 1994
New York

It seems that Amy and I have pulled this off. Today the reviews came out in the *Times, Newsday,* and the *Voice*. *Newsday* was great and said good things about everyone, especially Amy. The *Times* criticized the play for being too long, but other than that the review was fantastic. La MaMa has extended our run and said that several producers have called about possibly moving us to a bigger theater. I can't believe people took us seriously. Amy and I got everything we wanted from this show: the Talent Family name used in reviews, big crowds, an extension. Since opening week, we've cut out seven minutes and rewritten two scenes. This is just the happiest day.

January 18, 1994
New York
The *New York Daily News* review came out yesterday and reads, in part, "As any nine-year-old can tell you, there's nothing quite so funny as a face hideously deformed by bungled plastic surgery, unless it's the spectacle of an amputee trying to play the guitar. For those of you who are forever nine, the greatest gross-out in New York right now, the show in the worst possible taste—is *Stitches*."

January 30, 1994
New York
Six people walked out of the show Friday night. They were all over the age of sixty, and noticing them in the lobby as they collected their tickets, I thought how nice it was to have such a wide range of ages in the audience. As they left, I heard one of them on the stairs, saying, "You'd have to be a moron."

February 26, 1994
New York
I went to the corner to buy Helen some cigarettes and when I returned she sat me down to discuss the Winter Olympics. "Did you see it on the TV? That Tonya Harding? I never liked her. She's a street fighter is what she is, a dirty snot. Nancy Kerrigan I like, but not that street fighter."

Tonya Harding really is something else. I resisted the story until I saw a picture of her. With her fierce makeup, she looks like a child's drawing of an angry babysitter. Whatever else, she's succeeded in capturing my imagination. She doesn't strike me as mean. Rather, she's seems like the type to whom everything is unfair.

February 28, 1994
New York

Helen knocked this morning and asked me to mail some shit for her. Literally. "It's a stool sample," she said.

April 4, 1994
New York

On the radio today I heard a story about an American living in Singapore who was convicted of spraying graffiti on parked cars. As punishment, he's been fined and sentenced to a caning. An official described the process: "A pad is placed over the kidney so as not to cause serious damage. We tell the men to aim for the buttocks."

American diplomats are trying to appeal the punishment, but I think it's reasonable enough. Spray-paint cars and the least they should be able to do is spank you.

April 19, 1994
New York

At the library I found *Pimp: The Story of My Life* by Iceberg Slim. It's the kind of book you have to read from the beginning, otherwise you can't understand the slang. One chapter is titled "To Gain a Stable," and in it he teaches you how to turn out a whore by breaking her will. (He suggests beating her with a straightened-out coat hanger.)

April 22, 1994
New York

All Helen talks about is her pain. Every time I see her she goes on and on and I'm tired of it. Other people's pain is uninteresting. My own, though, is spellbinding. I went to bed at midnight and didn't fall asleep until seven a.m. My knee hurt so much I couldn't do anything but moan. While awake I read an entire issue of the *Source,* which bills itself as "the Magazine of Hip-Hop Music, Culture, and Politics."

My favorite bit was an interview with Warren G. "I was finished with almost the whole album, but I took everything back," he said. "Now I can have DJ Pooh and QD3 and Bobcat and all of them see how it sounds compared to what I had. I ain't with all that bullshit, you know the shit how motherfuckers be trying to punk motherfuckers and shit. I ain't with that shit."

May 5, 1994
New York
As part of the publicity I'm doing for the book (*Barrel Fever*), I was interviewed and photographed for *Avenue* magazine. The talking part I'm fine with, but I hate having my picture taken. First the photographer had me pose with Dennis (my cat) while wearing a cat mask. Then she had me pretend to hang from the antlers in the living room. Next I was told to close the louvered doors on my neck and then to hold my freeze-dried turkey head up to my nose. Just as she was running out of film, the photographer said, "Can we try something silly?"

May 10, 1994
New York
Walking down Broome Street I saw a couple massaging their Labrador retriever's asshole. Then the man stuck his finger in and coaxed out a clot of shit. He wasn't wearing gloves or anything. Dog people.

May 14, 1994
New York
I met with Dawn Erickson at a café tonight. Though we've

written back and forth, we hadn't seen each other since Kent State in 1976, and because she doesn't smoke and has never had a drink or taken any drugs, she looks just the same. I learned that she still designs fabrics, that she travels a lot, mainly alone, and that her mother has cancer. Her father died fourteen years ago in a skydiving accident. She still doesn't drink coffee, so she just had water.

Afterward I went to the Grand Union and was shopping for dinner when a young man touched my arm. "Hey, watch where you're going. You almost hit my baby in the head with your basket."

"I'm sorry."

The guy had a shoulder-length mane of carefully styled hair and wore a pair of sweatpants with the back torn out. I thought I was seeing fur underwear until I realized it was his hairy ass showing. "You almost hit the baby," he repeated.

I said, "*Almost*. But I didn't, right?"

He was just looking for a fight. In fact, I'd been nowhere near the baby. I watched from behind as he got in line and then listened as he accused the cashier of overcharging him. The manager was called and I wondered how anyone could go out in public like that, with his ass hanging out. I should be OK with it, but it's never the ass I want to see.

June 21, 1994
New York

They were boarding my flight to Indianapolis yesterday when a Russian man in a wheelchair rolled up, accompanied by his family. "Can't he walk?" the gate attendant asked.

When she realized that none of them spoke English, she repeated herself, only louder. "Can't he walk at all?"

As I passed the man, I noticed that his pant legs were empty, that he either was an amputee or had been born this way. "Well, could he walk if he tried?" the gate attendant, who was not nearly as observant as I am, asked.

July 1, 1994
New York
Today I cleaned for the Rs. They're nice people but incredible slobs. Every week I find something new the son has decided to use as an ashtray. Today it was a paper cupcake jacket. I mean, really. What's wrong with a saucer? Another thing they're big on is dropped change. This afternoon I found pennies in one bathtub and dimes in another.

July 9, 1994
New York
It's hot and icky here so Hugh and I went to the air-conditioned Museum of Television and Radio and watched TV all day. First came an hour-long tribute to women in comedy. During this we sat behind three elderly women, one of whom kept turning around and scolding me for resting my knees on the back of her chair. I did this once. That was it, I swear, yet she kept nagging me. A fly could have landed on this woman's seat back and she would have felt it. The third time she turned around I told her to fuck off. I don't think she heard me, but still I was ashamed for having said it.

July 11, 1994
New York
On the news we saw a story about brown tree snakes in Guam. They're long, these things, and aggressive, and not too bright. The report showed a human baby one of them had tried to eat. The child weighed fifteen pounds; the snake, two. They come up through people's toilets sometimes, and one bit a man on the testicles (!).

According to the report, the snakes are spreading. One was found in Texas. When things get bad in New York, I remind myself that at least there are no snakes here. Rats, but no snakes.

July 15, 1994
New York

Hugh and I went to Dixon Place and now I want to be reimbursed for those two hours of my life. We'd gone to see Lily sing and play guitar and had she been the only one on the bill, it would have been fine. Sadly, there were several other acts. The first and worst was a woman named Estelle. I wouldn't call her a dancer; rather, she pranced while a second woman read a poem and a third batted pots and pans with a stick. The three of them wore something akin to war paint. If they were trying to scare the enemy, it didn't work. If they were trying to entertain the audience, it didn't work either. Estelle twirled in circles. She skipped and flailed her arms and then threw herself onto the floor. Unfortunately, she picked herself back up and began again from the top. It was my worst nightmare of performance art.

She was followed by a thin, bearded troubadour. "This next song is about illusions and falsifications," he said at one point. "I think you all know what I'm talking about." He had either a great voice or a terrible one. I couldn't quite tell which.

August 25, 1994
La Bagotière, France

Hugh and I left Scotland yesterday afternoon and got back to France almost twenty-four hours later. The first leg of the trip involved a bus from Pitlochry to Edinburgh. I sat behind a pair of young women and a very fat baby girl, who I'm guessing belonged to one of them. The two took turns holding her. I watched as the first put the child on her knee and pushed chocolate candies into her tiny mouth with her fingers. Then she handed her to her friend, who poured some Coca-Cola into a baby bottle and had the kid suck on it until she vomited. After that, she was handed back over for a candy refill. The baby wore several gold bracelets and rings, and I wondered how she'd ever get them off her ever-expanding wrists and fingers.

October 4, 1994
New York
This afternoon David Rakoff and I went to see *The River Wild*. It was preceded by a very lengthy preview for the new Warren Beatty movie. The thing went on and on, and just as it ended, David turned to me, whispering, "I understand the remaining seven seconds of this film are remarkable."

Later, at dinner, Paul D. tried to tell us that cows are nocturnal but that farmers force them to stay awake during the day. That is so funny to me, the idea of keeping a cow awake.

October 31, 1994
New York
As research for the new play (*One Woman Shoe*), Amy and I went to the welfare office on 14th Street. We'd wondered what we might say if anyone asked why we were there and decided on "They told us to come back on Monday."

But nobody asked.

I got the idea it's possible to spend all day in the welfare office without being asked any questions. After entering the ground-floor waiting room, we joined a line that never moved. Out of six windows, only two were open, and the woman behind one of them was dressed for Halloween as a cat, with ears and whiskers. There was some confusion as to what the line we were standing in was for. The woman ahead of us had no teeth and had brought a wooden crate she used as a chair. Sometime later a Hispanic woman tried to sneak her friend into the line and the toothless woman called for security. "I know who's in front of me and I know who's behind of me," she said, "and she wasn't no way in front of me or I would have seed her."

Other people chimed in, but the Hispanic woman stood her ground, claiming that her friend needed to cut in line because she has asthma.

"Oh, yeah, well, my baby's got asthma too," a black woman said.

"Oh, really, where's the baby?"

The black woman pointed to her stomach. "In here."

The Hispanic woman's friend was booted to the back of the line. Like a lot of other people, she was dressed in spandex pants. These she wore with a T-shirt that pictured a number of cartoon pigs fucking in various positions.

Everyone in line seemed to have a story about a misplaced form, a missing check, a stolen wallet. Everyone complained about the staff. "They make it hard, hoping we'll just give up and go away. The bitches is acting like the money come outta they own pockets."

"Someone tolt me they're hiring at UPS," a woman said to one of the few men in the office.

"I ain't working for them because I'm a certified chef," the man said.

People limped and had their arms in slings. One man walked like he was a marionette worked by a novice, his legs bent almost to a kneeling position.

The office was filthy and everyone ignored the NO SMOKING signs. There were crumbs and cigarette butts on the floor, the noise of fights and crying children. The seats were all occupied by exhausted-looking people, some sleeping, hardly any of them reading. "I've been here since nine this morning!" There were white people, black people, Puerto Ricans, Japanese, an Indian family—the mother talked like she was channeling a spirit, while her daughter stared straight ahead. Loudspeakers would call out a name, but the person was hardly ever there. People seemed to know each other. They socialized. So much time spent waiting.

There were signs everywhere. TAKE THE NAME OF YOUR CASEWORKER, REMEMBER TO KEEP YOUR APPOINTMENTS. The signs were all marked with graffiti. Men would approach waiting women, and the women would ignore them, sometimes surrendering their seats to get away.

A woman with braids left the line every so often to spit in the trash can. A grown man suckled a pacifier and dribbled saliva all over his hands. He would lift his shirt, walk in a circle, then stare at the wall as if it were a mirror and laugh. It felt wrong to be there. Amy and I could leave anytime we wanted to. The others either could or couldn't, depending on how you think about it. Which brings us back to the play.

December 14, 1994
New York

I went to a deli on 2nd Avenue and 73rd Street for lunch and waited behind a seventy-five-year-old woman with wild gray hair and sad, poorly fitting slacks. She ordered a bit of chicken salad and when the clerk asked for her definition of "a bit," the woman turned to me and rolled her eyes. "See, they don't know because they can't talk English. I want to make myself a sandwich at home. I got bread at home, but they don't understand."

December 27, 1994
New York

Christmas afternoon, Dad pulled out his film projector and a half dozen Super 8 movies from the late '60s and early '70s. I recall him standing in front of us with the camera back then, but, like the photos he takes of us on the stairs every year, I never knew what became of them. Two friends of Lisa's had dropped by, and though nothing could be duller than watching someone else's home movies, none of us cared. The moment we saw Mom, we forgot about our guests. They mumbled something on their way out— "Merry Christmas," or maybe "Your kitchen is on fire," whatever.

I never knew my mother had been captured on film, moving. The first reel was from St. John in 1972. Mom, Dad, Aunt Joyce, and Uncle Dick. We see the island. Boats. More island. More boats, and then there's Mom, who waves goodbye before ducking into a thatched hut. Then the camera is handed to someone else, and we see Dad pull her out. He is young and handsome—he is always handsome. When he points at the camera, Mom buries her head in his chest. Then he lifts her chin and they kiss.

Watching this, Dad stomped his foot on the floor, the way you might if you just missed the bus and knew that another wasn't coming for a long while. He rewound the film and replayed it a second time, then a third.

"Again," we called. "Play it again." To see them both on an island, so young and happy. I couldn't believe our luck: to have this on film!

1995

January 9, 1995
New York

I cleaned for Judith today. Her full-time housekeeper, Faith, showed up half an hour late so I waited outside and was joined by Mary, the young woman who comes once a month to trim the cat's toenails. She used to work at an animal hospital and has, she said, "a houseful of critters." First, there's a ferret whose goal in life was to escape his cage and murder the guinea pigs, which he did. She loves birds but only if they can fly freely through her apartment. She also loves cats and found a way to make everyone happy by adopting a blind one. That way it can hear the birds but not catch them.

Mary told me it's illegal to have a monkey in New York City because they carry human diseases. That said, she's treated two of them. "These were people who won the lottery," she said. "They got the money and the first thing they did was buy their son the two capuchins he wanted." The monkeys went from living in the son's room to living in the garage, and eventually they wound up in a shed far from the house. They were bloodthirsty, apparently, and before they were banished, the son was regularly treated for injuries.

January 11, 1995
New York

I followed two men on the street. One was telling the other

that he hates it when Danielle holds his hand. "'Cause there might be some other piece I want to talk to. You know what I'm saying?"

January 24, 1995
New York

The review (of *One Woman Shoe*) came out in *Newsday* and it's good. The guy said that after a while he didn't know what the hell was going on but didn't care, he was laughing so hard. He said it was stronger and more satisfying than the "woefully erratic *Stitches,*" which is funny. Last year they wrote a love letter to it, and now it's erratic. The *Times* review comes out on Thursday.

January 26, 1995
New York

We got a wonderful review in the *Times*. Rakoff called late last night to read it to me and I thought he was kidding. It changes things, a review. First off, it kills the element of surprise and leaves the audience with a "prove it" stance. It fucks with the cast as well. Everyone was off tonight. One moment bumped into another, and the show felt way too long. We were excited by the great review, but by the end of the night we were depressed.

July 7, 1995
New York

Someone stopped Mitch on the street last night and said, "I need another seventy-five cents so I can buy a cheeseburger. How about helping me?"

Mitch said, "Get it without the cheese," and continued walking.

September 18, 1995
New York

A woman phoned at eleven o'clock last night and asked if she could speak to Rich.

I said there wasn't a Rich here.

"OK," she said. "Is this the game we're going to play?"

"Game? Listen—" I said.

"Rich is having his roommate cover for him, is that it?"

"There is no roommate. Listen, this is David Sedaris and Hugh Hamrick—"

"Rich? Is that you, you shithead?"

"There is no Rich," I repeated. "You have the wrong number."

"You think you can fuck with me, Rich? You have no idea who you're fucking with."

"That's just it," I said. "I *don't* have any idea. None whatsoever. This is wasted on me."

She hung up then, hard.

1996

January 1, 1996
New York

Amy's New Year's resolution is to make more Asian friends. She hopes to find them at community meetings and small restaurants. I think that's great, to have a goal.

Hugh's friend Sue, who's from Georgia, had a New Year's Day luncheon and served ham, collard greens, and black-eyed peas, traditional Southern food meant to bring good luck and prosperity. She cooked the collards with a penny. I told Amy about it and now we're trying to think of other recipes that call for change.

January 24, 1996
New York

It really is torture to sit around the house and write all day. I'm thinking it might motivate me to finish the book faster, the thought that after it's finished I can return to housecleaning. The problem is that I haven't even started the book yet. Today I wrote a letter to Karen Dobragosz, a girl I went to high school with. She sent me a Christmas card over a year ago, so I responded to it. Check. Then I read a thirty-five-page story written by a guy in Colorado named Robert. He sent it to me weeks ago and called last night asking why he hadn't heard from me.

His story was not easy to read. All the characters said things like "Whattya doin'?" and "Nuthin'."

Then I wrote two letters of recommendation. It doesn't sound like much in terms of progress, but I sat at my desk from noon until six thirty. Practically.

January 30, 1996
New York

Helen called me over to give me a chicken quiche but really to complain about the excessive heat. The landlord suggested she keep her windows open, but she says that if she does, it'll let all the air-conditioning out. It makes no sense to have that running in the winter, but she does, along with the heat and three fans.

February 8, 1996
New York

In the paper there's a story about a fifty-five-year-old cancer patient who paid her twenty-year-old neighbor to kill her. The kid went with strangulation, but she revived and then tracked him down, claiming that because she was still alive, he had to give her the money back. They argued, and he beat her to death with a power drill.

February 12, 1996
New York

According to an article I read this morning, Scouting was invented to rescue boys from the clutches of their mothers and schoolteachers. The fear was that they'd turn out gay, or *deviant,* as they said back then. Parents were advised to be on the lookout for boys who willingly took baths and kept diaries. Guilty and guilty again.

February 27, 1996
Albany, New York

William Kennedy and his wife are a waiter's worst nightmare. At dinner last night they ordered their drinks neat. Then, when they arrived, they asked for a bowlful of ice. Mrs. Kennedy wanted her salad without onions, while he asked for his without tomatoes or cucumber. She ordered her entrée without broccoli and potatoes and asked instead if her fillet could be served with just spinach. William asked for his pasta without the mushrooms.

When her order came she frowned down at the plate, saying, "Oh, no. I don't think I want this. Just bring me a sirloin steak, rare."

The two of them ordered from busboys and called the hostess over at one point to ask for a club soda. They weren't malicious, but I can't imagine that either of them ever worked in a restaurant.

April 14, 1996
New York

I saw Helen yesterday for the first time since late January. She'd called me over to fix her mop, and I arrived to find her without her teeth in. "You're fat," she told me. "You need to take some of that blubber and give it to Hugh. He's got a skinny ass."

May 13, 1996
New York

A man called last night, saying he had read my book and asking if I could come clean his house. I offered to give him Bart's number, but he reiterated that he wanted me. In exchange, he said, he would give me four stories I could put in my next book. I told him my book wasn't about other people's stories, and he got snippy and yelled, "Then why the hell don't you screen your calls?" before hanging up.

June 21, 1996
New York

A stranger called from New Jersey to ask if I'd written a movie he'd just seen. I told him no and he talked for a while about this and that. He offered a cure for writer's block, which was odd, as I hadn't mentioned anything about it. It turned out he's a painter who is having a hard time finishing a portrait. That was the day my typewriter broke. I couldn't work so just sat in the rocking chair and listened to him.

August 6, 1996
La Bagotière

Things are moving along at the house. Not only do we have water, but now there's even a washing machine. This saves us from doing laundry in the tub, which always took forever, especially the wringing-out part.

I'm continuing to put new vocabulary words on index cards. "What does that mean?" I keep asking Hugh as he's talking to people. "How do you spell it?" He lost his patience a few hours after we arrived.

In the morning we went to the small city of Flers and ran into R. and her husband, P. They're a fit and attractive couple fifteen years older than us who feel that their friends should be equally youthful and good-looking. After she'd kissed me, R. put her hand on my stomach and pinched my cheek, saying that I am fat and pale. "Look at me!" she sang. "I am very bronzed! P. and I have been watching the Olympics. The black people run as if they're being chased by tigers, so now we are doing the same thing! Every morning we jog in the forest. Then I go home to bronze myself." She invited us to lunch, but I begged off. Three green beans and she's full.

September 9, 1996
New York

I walked so long and hard in Paris the other day that my overgrown toenails rubbed against one another and started to bleed. Before leaving for the airport, I went to cut them and, finding no clippers, I used a pair of Colette's poultry shears. That is exactly why you don't want people staying in your apartment when you're not there, or even when you are, really.

October 10, 1996
New York

Amy's been called for jury duty and she phoned from the courthouse, saying, "It's a rape case and I hope I get it. The guy is really cute!"

November 18, 1996
New York

I was on the number 6 train early yesterday evening, coming from 59th Street. The car was crowded and I stood before a group of three men. All were black and in their late twenties and all were dressed in similar-looking bomber jackets. The fellow in the middle was the heaviest of the three, and as we got under way, he nudged me and pointed, saying, "Hey, you. There's a seat over there. Ax that lady to move her bag so you can have it."

"That's OK," I said. "I'm fine standing."

He pursed his lips and mocked me for his friends. "I'm fine standing." They laughed, and he continued. "I can't stand this shit with everyone putting they germs in my face. Fuckers.

They's all faggots and lesbians, faggots and lesbians, the whole city is turning faggot. Yo, man, I'm going to ax you one more time to sit the fuck down." He took his foot then, placed it against my thigh, and pushed me.

"Why are you doing this?" I asked. "I mean, what difference does it make whether I stand or sit? What's it to you?"

He said that I was blocking his view and that he wanted to look at the girl seated opposite him. So I moved down the car a few feet, wondering why he couldn't have said so in the first place and hating him with all my might. It sickened me to hear him sweet-talking the young woman who was now back in his sight line. "You are one beautiful lady, has anybody ever tolt you that?"

He went on and on, and against all the advice I was telepathically sending her, she responded. No, she wasn't married, she said, but she did have a man in her life. Yes, she would take his phone number, but she wasn't promising anything. He called it out, and I was a fool not to write it down. If I'd had a pen on me, I'd be calling him night and day until he was forced to change his number. "Yes," I'd say. "We met on the train and you said you wanted to get together. Don't you remember?"

November 26, 1996
New York
Hugh left this morning to spend Thanksgiving with his mother, Joan, whom I've taken to calling Maw Hamrick. I'm on this kick lately where I pretend that she's one of my closest personal friends. Whenever I hear Hugh's key in the door, I pick up the phone and act like I'm in the middle of a conversation with her. "Well, sure," I'll say, "I know it's hard, but we'll get together some other time, when it can be just me and you, without Hugh to bother us. Oops, hold on...I think

I hear him coming." I claim to receive gifts and checks from her and have been writing fake letters in which she says she wishes I were her son instead of him.

It doesn't get to him because it's so ridiculous. In truth, she'd much rather hang out with Hugh than with me. Joan was here last month for a few days and spent her mornings drinking tea and reading the international section of the *Times*. It's the last part I'm likely to turn to, but having lived in Africa and the Middle East, the Hamricks love nothing more than to discuss foreign policy. They're forever mentioning some crisis in Karachi or Ghana, and they know the first and last names of countless ambassadors and attachés. They're so far removed from my own family.

November 29, 1996
New York

I went to Amy's apartment for Thanksgiving and left for home, drunk and stoned, at three a.m. She had a good-size crowd, and charged her guests $5 for the chance to wear a Pilgrim hat and have their picture taken with her rabbit, Tattle Tail. Eight people took her up on it, but in the end, not one of them paid. Lately I'm trying to be a better listener. This involves asking questions such as "Tell me, Louis, do you have a lot of candles in your house?"

Louis works with Amy at Marion's and his thing is to tell huge lies and then allow himself to be interrogated. Last night he said he was the world's first rapper.

"Really, the first?"

"Yes," he said. "And it was hard because no one believed that it would catch on and grow into this big sensation."

"Did people make fun of you?" I asked.

"Oh, yes, everyone."

"And did that hurt?"

"It hurt a lot. An awful lot."

An old neighbor of Lisa's was recently caught having sex with his Labrador retriever, and when I told Louis about it, he asked if the dog could get pregnant.

"Are you serious?" I said. "How old are you?" That's one of those things you think about when you're a child, the possibility of a half boy/half pony. If it were possible to cross-breed like that, the world would be full of talking goats and sheep who could shear their own wool.

November 30, 1996
New York

Helen called offering me some gravy. I told her our refrigerator was full and she launched into her suspicion that our seventy-five-year-old neighbor is creeping into her apartment while she's asleep. It makes no sense, but she's convinced that something is going on. She then recounted her recent fights with the people at the corner grocery and the construction crew renovating the apartment upstairs from her. After that, she talked about her nephew and the reasons she didn't go to her daughter's house for Thanksgiving. Her monologue went on for twenty minutes and ended with "So if you don't want my gravy, go fuck yourself."

December 18, 1996
New York

We met last night for the first read-through of the play (*The Little Frieda Mysteries*) and I felt bad for everyone in the room. What I'd written was so clunky and full of exposition, I wouldn't blame any of them for trying to back out. One scene between Amy and Chuck (Coggins) has potential, but the rest will have to be scrapped.

At the copy shop on Prince Street an hour or so before our

meeting, I stood in line behind a woman with dyed-black hair. She was taking forever, color-Xeroxing photos of herself, and said to the guy behind the counter that though she pays next to nothing in rent, she's looking for a new apartment. "I've got two lizards on Thompson Street, but they're not getting any light."

1997

January 29, 1997
New York

On Monday, *The New Yorker* arranged for Amy and me to have our picture taken by Duane Michals. This so they can run it in the Goings On About Town section. I was a big fan of his when I was in my early twenties, all those photos with the cursive writing along the bottoms of them. Amy and I promised ourselves we wouldn't do anything stupid, and an hour later we were sitting on top of a battered piano with our arms in slings.

Mr. Michals was what you might call a wild card, and at the end of the session, our mouths ached from fake laughing. "Did you know that Flaubert had a second career as a gynecologist? He wrote a book about it called *Madame Ovary*."

Years back he had been shooting an upside-down model who accidentally kicked him in the head with his heavy boots and crushed his skull. Now there are metal plates in it.

February 3, 1997
New York

The New Yorker is taking the Shouts and Murmurs piece I wrote for Valentine's Day. Chris sent the galleys by messenger, and, reading them over, I noticed four repetitions of the phrase "we're hoping." I pointed this out on the phone yesterday and he said, "Man, you're like a self-cleaning oven!"

328

February 4, 1997
New York

I had a horrible experience today with a photographer named Chris, who'd come to take my picture for some magazine. We were trying to prepare a tech rehearsal of the play, and because we were so busy, I asked if we could meet at the theater. Chris thought it might be nice to use the basement hallway so we went downstairs, where he and his assistant set up their lights and umbrellas. I'm finding it progressively more difficult to have my picture taken, especially now, when there always has to be a gimmick. The idea is that you have to be humiliated in order for your personality to shine through. You need to hang from the ceiling by a hook or crawl on your hands and knees through a puddle of something.

Chris started the session by handing me a package of stage cigarettes he wanted me to cram into my mouth—the entire thing. "I'm catching some reflection off the packaging," he said. "So can you lower your head a little?"

Normally I just do what they tell me, figuring the quicker I surrender, the sooner I'll get out of there. Today, though, I snapped. "I can't do this," I said after taking the package out of my mouth. "It makes me feel silly."

"If it makes you feel silly," he said, "you need to find another way to do it. If I give you a wacky idea, you should give me one that's even wackier."

I told him it wasn't my job to out-wacky him, that I'm not a comedian or even an actor, for that matter, and that I saw nothing wrong with just a normal photo of me standing up or sitting in a chair.

And that was pretty much the end of that. He told me about some other "difficult people" he'd worked with, and I defended them all. I mean, really. How is it that someone wants to tie you to the railroad tracks, and refusing makes *you* the bad guy?

I told him about the photographer I had last week who wanted me to spit onto a pane of glass and then press my face against it.

"That sounds interesting," Chris said. "What was his name?"

I told him I didn't remember, and he nodded, saying, "That tells me everything I need to know."

February 15, 1997
New York

Tiffany arrived yesterday for a short visit. She's on mood stabilizers and they seem to have made a significant difference. She listens to people now and doesn't get angry quite so easily. I took her with me to Little, Brown and introduced her to everyone. Hugh made a rack of lamb for dinner and then we all went to the play and out for drinks afterward. She's especially entertaining when talking about Ludovic, the French guy who stayed with her for a while. "He said to me, 'I like you, Tiffany, but I don't love you.'"

She'd responded that here in America, if you don't love someone, you don't tell them; rather, you just say nothing. I wish I'd written it down verbatim. It was so funny the way she said it.

March 5, 1997
New York

Dad came to town for the book-release party, and I woke him this morning at four. A short while later I accompanied him to 6th Avenue, where he caught a taxi to Penn Station. It was still dark, and a lot of remarkable people were out: a man screaming about shitty black criminals, a sobbing woman, the drunk super from across the street. Funny how normal it all seems to me now. Before getting into his cab, Dad shook my hand and told me to be a good boy. He said it as though I were seven years old, as if he didn't know that I had grown up. It made me so sad.

March 28, 1997
Iowa City, Iowa
Someone told me that Minneapolis, where I was yesterday, is the slimmest city in the United States. I don't know if that's true, but it did have a Laundromat called the Spin Cycle. I also passed a gift shop called the Caardvark. I did a reading at a gay bookstore called a Brother's Touch. It was what I'd feared it might be, lots of rainbow-striped flags and wind socks. My mike was set up in the magazine section, so behind me were pictures of all sorts of men, some in jockstraps, some with gags that looked like Ping-Pong balls in their mouths. What killed me, though, was the incense, which was coconut, I think.

March 29, 1997
Atlanta, Georgia
The Cedar Rapids airport was decorated for Easter. They'd put plastic grass, marshmallow chicks, and plastic eggs atop the X-ray scanner, and I was looking at them when one of the guards, a young woman, asked to check my bag. She found the bottle of Scotch that Little, Brown had sent me and said, "I'm sorry, sir, but I'm going to have to pour this out."

I thought that maybe this was a rule in Iowa, but then her boss stepped over and said, "No, Tanya, you don't pour it out. You just need to smell it and make certain it's not gasoline."

"Really? I've been pouring it out for the last two months!"

"Well, you shouldn't have been," her supervisor told her.

The woman named Tanya opened my bottle of Scotch, held it to her nose, and winced. "Now I got liquor on my hands," she said. "Great!"

Her supervisor rolled her eyes. "Oh, just go over to the fountain, add a little water, and have a drink," she said, sighing. "It'll do you some good."

April 13, 1997
Portland
This morning at the Seattle airport I saw a kid, maybe ten years old, jerking his head every fifteen seconds or so. It was like seeing myself as a boy. His father said, "Aaron, I'm warning you..." I wanted to rush over and scoop the kid up.

May 10, 1997
New York
I finished *Nickel Dreams,* the new Tanya Tucker autobiography. Every time she used the phrase "my new friend," I pulled out my pen, knowing there would be a great name coming. The book is full of them, my favorites being Peanutt Montgomery, Sonny Throckmorton, Michael Smotherman, Dave Dudley, and Sheila Slaughter.

May 17, 1997
La Bagotière
Mr. G's new colt is sick so we went to the barn and watched as he milked the mother. He then fed the baby from a bottle, eventually taking the nipple off and pouring the milk down its throat, saying, "Come on, now, drink." His wife then shoved a thermometer up the colt's ass and together they force-fed it some paraffin oil—all this because the vet charges extra on weekends.

Coming from New York, I find it really shocking to spend time around animals. The baby geese are in the garage, their backs bare and bloody from where they've plucked one another's feathers out. Lambs are in their pen. They're friendly, the babies, but already their coats are caked with dirt and shit. In the pen next to theirs, a nine-year-old ewe sits on all fours facing a bowlful of mush. All her teeth have fallen out, so she can no longer graze or eat hay or pellets.

June 19, 1997
New York

I was watching *The Simpsons* last night when Tiffany called. She'd just spent a month in Raleigh and it was strange listening to her talk about it. "Then Gretchen wanted me to change the hat on her taxidermied beaver, and I said, 'Are you *telling* me or *asking* me?'"

She was particularly bothered about a lamp and how she needed Dad to put it in his car and bring it to her at Paul's place. "This is about *respect*," she kept saying as I looked at the TV screen with the sound turned off, wondering what I was missing.

June 27, 1997
New York

Last night I talked to Paul, who lamented, "I ain't seen pussy in so long, I'd throw stones at it."

I wished it weren't too late to add that line to our play. Then I noticed that we're listed in the special children's section of *Time Out*.

"*Our* show?" Amy said when I told her about it. "The one that includes the pot-smoking and cursing and has the line 'Psssst, Glen. Hey, Glen, you want a blow job?' in it?"

I'll worry about it tomorrow.

June 28, 1997
New York
As if Amy didn't have enough to do with learning her lines, one of her friends has invited herself over to cook eels. I don't know how she gets herself into these things.

She was in the drugstore today and saw a female police officer open a bottle of base makeup, cover a blemish in her nose, and then place the bottle back on the shelf. A cop!

July 1, 1997
New York
We did a read-through of the play for fifteen people from Lincoln Center and when we finished, John, the man in charge of the festival, stood up, saying, "Well, I don't care what anyone says. *I* liked it."

Afterward I walked through the park for a while, thinking. On my way back home a woman, very thin with a missing front tooth, entered my subway car and said, "Can I please get a little fucking attention?" When no one looked up, she called us a bunch of stuck-up snobs. "You'll give money to those other bitches. You'll help them but not me, so fuck you."

She got up in someone's face and the young woman gave her money, as did the next person she confronted. "Well, that's just fucking great," the woman said. "Fucking great, shitheads."

July 6, 1997
New York
Last week Amy gave Hugh and me a large plastic tankard of industrial cooking oil for deep-fat frying and this afternoon I carried it to the Laundromat, having mistaken it for the nearly identical tankard of detergent—same size, same color.

The only difference was the spout. That's what stopped me from pouring a cupful of it into the top of the machine. If I had, the best thing to do would have been to walk away, buy new clothes and sheets and towels, and never return to that Laundromat again. I'm guessing stuff would be pretty much ruined after going through an oil cycle.

July 11, 1997
New York

Last night was one of the happiest of my life. The play was sold out, every seat taken, with folding chairs set up at the back of the theater. I had no idea our *Times* review was out until Amy called to tell me about it. Then I heard from Drew, the choreographer, who read it out loud to me before I could stop him. It's as if I wrote it myself as a joke. They mentioned Hugh's set and his inventive direction. "Vulgarity just shouldn't be this funny, but it's being ridiculed, reveled in."

Really, we ridiculed it?

I hoped they'd praise all the actors equally, and it hurts that they left out Toby and Sarah. I can't understand their choices, but it's a glowing review. After last night's performance, the Lincoln Center Festival people took us to dinner at a swank restaurant. I was so certain this play would fail.

July 28, 1997
New York

Last night I watched *Alien Autopsy: Fact or Fiction,* a ten-minute program stretched out to an hour. "Is this genuine film footage of a visitor from another planet, or just a cruel hoax designed to prey upon our worst fears? We'll be back in a moment."

I kept waiting for the actual autopsy, but for the most part we saw the same shot over and over: a doctor in a protective outfit gesturing with a fountain pen toward the alien's flesh wound. The alien itself looked like a child in a Halloween mask, its genitals blurred out with one of those scramblers. Interviewed were several people who had witnessed the Roswell crash fifty years ago. An unstable-looking woman said she was threatened by government officials to keep silent. "We saw the saucer on the ground and two little people who were crying and trying to resuscitate a third alien, who looked like he was more than likely dead. Then the two live ones ran over and clutched this metal box. I don't know what was in it but remember thinking, *That box means something to those two aliens.*"

July 29, 1997
New York
Ben Brantley wrote an overall review of the Lincoln Center Festival in yesterday's *Times*. "'Astonish me,' Diaghilev's much-quoted artistic dictum, is the imperative brought by the sort of people who attend self-defined 'cultural events' like 'Les Danaides'...But only the Sedarises' 'Incident' provided astonishment. This brother-and-sister playwriting team has an unparalleled ear for American cultural clichés and an equally fine hand for twisting those clichés into devastating absurdity."

The news of the review was ruined by a call from a *People* magazine photographer. They're running a story about the book, and she phoned saying she'd like a picture of me either wearing a towel or peeking out from behind my shower curtain. This is what happens when you choose the title *Naked* over, say, *Quiet Dignity.*

August 31, 1997
La Bagotière
Hugh and I awoke to the news that Princess Diana has been

killed, literally hounded to death by photographers. I've been listening all morning to the BBC. Correspondents interview one person after another, one of them an "agony expert" who said it's often very painful when people die.

October 3, 1997
New York

Tiffany called collect this morning, sobbing and saying that she can't leave the house. It happens every so often. Other days she *can* leave but still wakes up crying. I feel bad for her but can't understand the problem. Isn't there some kind of medication for this? She talks about Mom, about the school she went to twenty years ago, all this stuff from the past, over and over.

October 5, 1997
New York

Hugh and I went with Amy and Mitch to see *Kiss the Girls*, the worst thing I've seen in a long time. It was another of those "I think we've got a serial killer on our hands" thrillers. I sat beside a stranger, and twenty minutes into it we were nudging one another and rolling our eyes. Making it worse, I had to sit through another endless preview for *Titanic*. Who do they think is going to see that movie?

October 18, 1997
Columbus, Ohio

I was met at the Columbus airport by a fellow named Rick, who was kind and positive and announced with genuine excitement that he was taking me to a restaurant called Johnny Rockets for lunch. "You'll totally love it," he said. "It's a fifties-style place where the waitresses chew gum and offer to draw things on your hamburger buns with plastic ketchup squeezers. They sing sometimes, too, and give you a nickel so you can play the little jukeboxes they have on the tables!"

It sounded awful to me, but I didn't want to disappoint him, so we went, my teeth gritted. When the waitress did indeed offer to sketch something on my hamburger bun, I requested a swastika and then wished I hadn't.

"Or a face," I said. "A happy face would be great too."

Rick, bless him, reminded us that before it was taken over by the Nazis and turned into something ugly, the swastika was a Celtic symbol of good luck.

After lunch he took me to Target, and I learned he'd recently won a year of free groceries by entering a sweepstakes at Big Bear, a local supermarket chain.

October 20, 1997
New York

Women are angry in New York tonight. On the corner of Houston and Thompson, I heard a black woman yell at her boyfriend, "Because let me tell you something, motherfucker, I don't *need* you."

Continuing south down West Broadway, I fell in behind a white couple, the woman walking several steps in front of her boyfriend. "Don't you *ever* fucking shush me, you asshole, especially in front of an employee."

Apparently he'd been trying to make a dinner reservation and asked her to pipe down so he could hear the hostess on the pay phone he was using. This was clearly the wrong thing to do. She went from being shushed to complaining about the stupid way he goes about giving and receiving information. "Like whenever we get into a cab and you ask the driver how he's doing tonight. And nobody fucking *cares* how he's doing, least of all him. All he wants is the goddamn address and there you are, trying to be his best friend, so don't shush me."

He didn't do much in terms of defending himself, and I got the idea that dinner would be one long tirade. It's pretty rare to go from a fight to a pleasant meal. Maybe he could have said, "You know something, you're right. I apologize. That was thoughtless and I'll never do it again."

I followed them for blocks, hoping he might take this approach, but he never did. It irritated me, the way she kept snapping her fingers to make a point. I wondered what he was doing with her, but by the time we hit Broome Street, I wondered what she was doing with him.

October 23, 1997
New York

I think it's strange that neither of Hugh's parents bought the *People* magazine he's in. His father says, "I'm not wasting three dollars. Just tell me what the article says." His mother leafed through an issue at Target, then phoned to say, "I've got better pictures of you at home."

Any other parent would have bought a dozen copies. It's not like getting a set of encyclopedias. I mean, really.

November 20, 1997
New York

Paul called from Raleigh and told me he had two black eyes. Apparently he started a fight with a guy in a bar, a guy who was much taller than him, and stocky.

Me: And when did he stop beating you?

Paul: When he was done.

November 26, 1997
New York

Walking back from the movie theater, I cut through that little pedestrian area between 3rd and 4th Streets. There, a

David Sedaris

white man, a guy around my age, was sitting on a bench and screaming, "Are you fucking deaf? I asked you what time it is."

He was yelling at a group of three young women, one of them Japanese. When none of them answered, he got up off his bench and followed them. "Hey, you. That's right, Jap, I asked you a fucking question."

One of the women turned around then. "I'm sorry," she said. "I didn't realize you were talking to us."

"Don't fucking apologize!" the man screamed. "Just give me the fucking time."

This happened a few hours ago, yet I can't stop thinking about it and hating myself for being such a coward. The correct answer to the man's question was "It's time for you to learn some fucking manners." He wasn't a lunatic, but you could tell he'd spent some time in prison. I wonder what he'll be doing for Thanksgiving, then I wonder where he learned how to ask people questions.

November 29, 1997
New York
I went to have my hair cut and sat in the chair beside a man who'd just gotten out of jail. The barber asked what he'd been in for and he answered, "Aggravated assault. I had to beat up some Italian woman because she didn't know how to keep her mouth shut."

I thought the barber, who was Italian, might slit the guy's throat, but instead he just turned the TV up.

December 20, 1997
New York
I bought a half dozen books this week on horrible diseases, some for me and some to give to Gretchen for Christmas. My

favorite picture is of a woman with horrible arthritis. Her fingers are twisted and tapered, almost like carrots, yet her nails are beautifully manicured and painted. She's working with what she has. The same is true of the gum diseases viewed through lipsticked mouths.

December 26, 1997
New York
Continuing our tradition of seeing movies about black people on Christmas Day, after opening presents, Dad, Lisa, Paul, Amy, and I went to see *Jackie Brown*. Last year I think it was *The Preacher's Wife,* and the year before that *Waiting to Exhale*. We really wanted to see *Soul Food* this year, but the only screening was at nine a.m.

Afterward, over dinner, Dad mentioned a woman we used to know from church. "I saw her not long ago, and golly, she looked just like a man," he said. "She's got a beard and everything, like a bristled hog."

When Gretchen scolded him, he said that he hadn't meant that as an insult. "The hairs of a bristled hog are used to craft some of the finest brushes there are, both for painting and shaving! I used to have one, as a matter of fact."

1998

January 1, 1998
New York

I went to Helen's to deliver the tangerines she'd asked for, and she answered her door looking like an old Mafia capo, in big dark sunglasses. "I fell and broke the regular ones," she told me. We hung out for a while in her kitchen, and before I left she gave me a nutmeg-colored pantsuit she thought Amy might wear. "All my friends have fat asses, so I don't have nobody else it would fit. Tell her to wash it in Woolite or, what the fuck, tell her she can wash it in any old shit."

January 2, 1998
New York

A young woman called, saying, "Who is this?" I asked who she was calling for and she said, "What number is this?" After I told her she said, "You don't have to yell at me." Then she said she'd call back in a few minutes and hung up.

Several hours later a man called and asked if I was David Sedaris. "Me and a bunch of friends bought you a present and want to come over and give it to you."

I said it wasn't a good time and suggested he call me back tomorrow. How dumb is that?

January 7, 1998
New York

I went to deliver Helen her chicken cutlets and she sang "I Got You, Babe" in honor of Sonny Bono, who died two days ago in a skiing accident. "I like that Chastity," she said. "And her father was very understanding when she tolt him she was lesbian." I stayed for an hour and she recounted the various fights she's had this week. "I'm not a troublemaker. I just stay out of it now." Before I left, she gave me another pantsuit to give to Amy, one with a studded top. It's hard to imagine Helen in it, but she swears she used to wear it to church. "The monsignor said, 'Hey, hotshot, where's your horse?' I tolt him it was in the garage. Ha! You laugh, but that's what I tolt him."

January 20, 1998
New York

The woman below us, Franny, died last night, a few months shy of her 106th birthday. Helen told me about it and said, "My mother died when she was forty-six! I remember asking her, 'Hey, Ma, what are you going to give me for my birthday?' She said, 'I'll give you something you'll never forget.' And she did. She died."

That Helen. Everything has to be about her.

January 21, 1998
New York

I called my agent Don to discuss the Little, Brown situation and he began by talking about Mary Todd Lincoln. Then he moved to Abe Lincoln and then to FDR. The mention of Bill Clinton heartened me, as we were finally moving into the present decade, but then he went back to *Collier's* magazine before finally saying it's best to just sit tight and let Little, Brown make the next move.

January 24, 1998
New York
I listened to a lot of talk radio today. The president is caught up in a sex scandal that could ruin him if it's proven he encouraged the young woman to lie to the grand jury or who-ever it was who needed to be lied to. One station offered a prize to whoever could give the scandal the best name. I'm sick of attaching the suffix *-gate* to everything, though it's hard to sneeze at either Fornigate or Tailgate, the top two contenders. Who knows what will come of it.

January 26, 1998
New York
While straight men watched the Super Bowl on NBC, the other networks fought it out for the women and homosex-uals. *Funny Girl* was on channel 9, and the Bette Midler remake of *Gypsy* played on channel 2. Meanwhile, channel 13's *Nature* special was devoted to cats. Hugh and I switched back and forth from musical to musical to the mother calico teaching her young to hunt. It's a lesson that Dennis, our cat, apparently slept through.

February 10, 1998
New York
Helen called me over to rub some Tiger Balm into her back. Our mutual neighbor Joe had offered to do it, but she turned him away, saying she didn't want to get raped. "I'm not into that," she told me. "Especially in my own bed." The other night she confided that her real name is Elena, and that her childhood nickname was Rocky because she got into so many fights. She sent me home with some spaghetti sauce that had chunks of chicken breast in it. Hugh threw it in the garbage, just as he threw away the veal she gave me the day before yesterday.

February 13, 1998
New York

A German publisher has offered a nice advance for *Naked* and Don thinks we should take it. "That's what the Japs coughed up," he said.

February 15, 1998
New York

Helen called at eight a.m. and then again three hours later. "Get over here. I made you the chicken with the potatoes and peas." I went and she told me about her latest fight with the deli on Spring and Sullivan. Their delivery boy is deaf and Helen's accusing him of stealing her pen. It seems a simple enough mistake. The kid probably used it and then accidentally stuck it in his pocket. I think of how confused he must have been when Helen lunged at him, demanding it back. She later called the deli, saying, "That freak ain't allowed in my house no more. He wants a tip? Let him keep the fucking pen!"

She accuses the Grand Union deliverymen of stealing canned goods from her order and selling them on the street. That's how paranoid she's gotten.

February 16, 1998
New York

Lots of domestic violence on *Cops* tonight. A young woman is punched in the face and her boyfriend goes bananas when officers enter his trailer to arrest him. He's strong, and it takes three men to bring him down. Meanwhile, his girlfriend is screaming, "I only want to talk to you, baby." To the cops she pleads, "He didn't mean to hurt y'all. He was askaird."

As the boyfriend is taken away, he yells, "I ain't never gonna forgive you for this, Randi. When I get out I am going to fuck you up."

She answers, "Do you want me to pay your bail?"

"See," the guy says to her as he's pushed into the car, "they don't know what you're like. They don't know how you talk to me, how you make me have to beat you up."

"I'm sorry," she cries. "I'll get you out tonight."

February 22, 1998
New York

They're broadcasting the closing ceremonies of the Winter Olympic Games in Nagano. This means I can return to writing without having Hugh yell every five minutes, "David, get in here—hurry!"

I sat him down the other night and explained as gently as possible that I do not care about ice-skating. I do not care about Michelle Kwan or Tara Lipinski and would be happy if I never hear the words *triple lutz* or *double axel* again. I told him that on Friday and walked into the kitchen an hour later to find him in tears. "It's heartbreaking," he said, watching his beloved skaters.

Last night he called me in to watch Michelle Kwan do her final routine. The competition is over, but they're allowing the skaters to come back and do whatever they want without fear of judgment. They don't let the bobsledders do it, but apparently the ice-skaters have a lot of fans like Hugh, who can't get enough. Right now they're killing time with a soft-news segment explaining that "rice is very important to the people of Nagano." The narrator is taking his three-minute story and stretching it out to ten. The secret is to t a l k v e r y s l o w l y.

March 4, 1998
New York

I called my drug-delivery service and they sent a young white man named Luke. Like all of them, he arrived on a bicycle and knocked on the door with four different grades of pot. I complained about the construction noise coming from the hotel they're building next door, and he said, with sympathy, "Oh, dude."

I asked where he lived, and he said Williamsburg. "It's like a party place but really laid back."

Luke was like a parody of a stoner. I think that's what I liked about him. I'd hate it if the person selling me pot in the middle of the day was super-articulate. That would make me feel like even more of a loser.

March 13, 1998
New York

Helen fell this afternoon and I watched the paramedics carry her down the stairs. According to Joe, she'd been up on a chair changing a lightbulb and may have broken her hip. Her daughter arrived, dressed in a fur coat, and said, "You must be Dave, the one she drives crazy. Welcome to the club."

March 19, 1998
New York

Hugh goes through phases with the *New York Times* crossword puzzle. He'll do them religiously for a few months and then drop off entirely. Sometimes I'll look over his shoulder and whenever I get a correct answer, I'll feel so smart and capable. Before she died, Mom started doing the crosswords from the *Raleigh News and Observer.* She bought a book of easy puzzles and it broke my heart to find them in the bathroom wastebasket. Three-letter word for "Placed out of sight," and she'd have written *put* instead of *hid.*

I never cared about puzzles one way or another until this weekend, when I completed the crossword in this week's *People.* The clues were, I'll admit, pretty simple. "All ___ ___

Family." "Singer once married to Sonny." It was on a fifth-grade level, but after I'd finished, I couldn't stop staring at it.

I showed it to Hugh and then went through the recycling pile on the curb and found two more *People*s. I love getting stoned and doing the crossword, but they're even better first thing in the morning.

March 27, 1998
New York

Ken Shorr is in town and dropped by this morning. We went for a coffee on Sullivan Street and were sitting at an outdoor table when an elderly man approached and asked if we could help him lower a plant into a hole he'd just dug. It was a strange and unexpected request, so we said yes and allowed him to lead us up the street and into a building I must have passed five hundred times. It had an elevator, and he pushed the button for the basement, explaining that this was his son-in-law's apartment. "He's Chinese," he added, "and is composing an opera. I hoped the maid could help me with the plant, but unfortunately she's not strong enough."

In the basement, we walked down a dark narrow hallway and into a clean-smelling apartment. It opened onto a small backyard, where the man gestured to a good-size tree, its roots contained in a sizable burlap ball. It must have weighed three hundred pounds, and he needed it carried up four steps and then dragged to a hole six feet away.

Ken and I tried to lift it, but it took all we had and within seconds it was back on the ground with us over it, panting. "I can't believe...your maid couldn't...handle this on her own," Ken said, gasping for air. "Mine could carry two...trees and still manage to...breast-feed...the children."

The man blinked.

On the second try, we got it up a single stair. Then another and another. On nearing the hole, we realized that it was way too shallow. Someone needed to make it deeper, but it wasn't going to be either of us. The man was so frail that it might have taken him hours, so we said nothing and lowered the tree into the too-shallow hole, where it looked pathetic.

March 28, 1998
New York

Hugh and I went to visit Helen in the hospital and throughout our half-hour stay I wondered if we didn't have the wrong room. She's been literally defanged, and without her teeth, it was difficult to understand what she was saying. "How are you?" Hugh asked.

She pointed at the wall and told him to open the refrigerator.

Her hair has grown out since I last saw her. The copper-colored henna is gone, and she looks a good twenty years older. She later told her daughter, Ann, that two men had stopped by. She didn't recall our names and had no idea why we'd come.

March 30, 1998
New York

Because I was in a bind with my BBC story, I devoted most of my day to defrosting the freezer. In the afternoon I called the delivery service to order some pot, and an hour later a guy named Stogie came to the door. After counting my money, he looked at the papers on my table and said, "Hey, are you David Sedaris? My wife really likes you." He asked if he could have my autograph and I was so flattered. I mean, here he was, a big-time pot dealer, and *he* wanted *my* autograph? It was sweet of him to ask, and his attention made it much easier to finish the BBC story.

April 10, 1998
Hanover, New Hampshire
I was met this morning by a woman named Georgia who took me across the river to do a radio interview in Vermont. Afterward we went to a restaurant where she seemed to know everyone. On leaving after our lunch, she introduced me to an eighty-year-old Japanese American woman named Bea who said, "We just got back from our annual Good Friday March for Peace!"

Bea, I learned, lives part-time in a local Quaker retirement community. "The rest of the year we live on the farm."

"You farm?" I asked.

"Oh, yes, have for decades. My husband and I are tied to the land."

I asked what she farmed and was slightly disappointed when she said, "Christmas trees." Because, come on, that's really not the sort of thing that forces you out of bed at five a.m. I could be wrong, but don't Christmas trees pretty much take care of themselves?

April 15, 1998
New York
I passed the Black Israelites on 7th Ave and 50th Street this afternoon. These are the people who wear outlandish robes and talk about how much Jesus hated white people. I was walking along, minding my own business, when the guy with the microphone called me a cracker faggot.

April 17, 1998
New York
Rakoff was on *As the World Turns* today, playing a talent scout for the Visage Modeling Agency. His lines included "Are you kidding, I'd never miss a Rebecca Drake fashion

show. I'm simply mad for her work." I'd never seen this particular soap opera before but will watch as long as he's on it. On Monday he'll appear again and say, "Excuse me, miss, but do you think I might look through your portfolio?"

April 20, 1998
New York

On my way home tonight I passed a fistfight taking place in front of the pizzeria on the corner of Spring and Thompson. I'm not sure who started it, but the kickboxer won, literally hands down.

April 27, 1998
New York

I'm reading a book Amy suggested by Maria Flook. It's about her sister, who took off at the age of fourteen with a fifty-year-old man she met at a bowling alley. He led her to Norfolk, Virginia, where she started working as a prostitute. At one point, the two of them go off to steal a fur coat. They're in the store and he tells her to wait by the door while he stands beside "the Jewish piano." That's what he calls the cash register, the Jewish piano. It's such a good book.

May 7, 1998
La Bagotière

On my way to Ségrie-Fontaine I passed three teenage girls lying on their backs in the middle of the road. It was a dumb place to relax, as they were surrounded on both sides by winding curves. I walked by, and then two of them stood and asked if I had a cigarette for their friend. I indicated that mine were menthols and they said that was fine.

Teenagers in Normandy always seem so innocent—even

when they're hanging out in a village square, they always smile and say hello.

Hugh passed the girls an hour later on his bike and they stopped him to ask if he was English.

"American," he told them.

When they learned that he lives in New York, they asked if he'd ever seen Leonardo DiCaprio. "Well, yes," he said. "As a matter of fact..."

I was there, too, and remember it clearly. DiCaprio was with a beautiful young woman, stepping out of a cab in front of the Museum of Natural History. He tried to pay with a $50, and when the driver said that the bill was too big, the movie star stood in line at the hot-dog cart and got change there. That's what being famous gets you in New York: change.

The girls asked Hugh what other famous people he'd seen and he said something unsatisfying like "Oh, you know."

I keep a list of the stars I see, but even without it I'd have made things up, just to get a reaction out of them. I would have given them the New York they imagine, the one where you can't leave your house without seeing Madonna and Michael Jackson breast-feeding their babies. If you were going to give these girls one star, though, Leonardo DiCaprio was definitely the one. Hugh got back on his bike and as he took off, the girls resumed their position on the road, so small-town, it must hurt.

May 12, 1998
New York
Helen died the other night at six o'clock, five days after being transferred to a Staten Island nursing home. At the funeral parlor on Bleecker Street, I met her sister, Minnie, who had a voice as deep as a man's. "We used to call Helen

'Baby Hippo' because she was always so fat in the hips and rear," she said.

Hugh told her that we thanked Helen in all our play programs. "She's the one who gave us the sewing machine we used to make curtains."

"That was *my* machine," Minnie said. "You should have been thanking *me*, not her."

The sisterly resemblance was striking.

May 23, 1998
New York

My friend Doug is visiting from Los Angeles. He's been single for as long as I've known him and went out recently with a guy who took him to bed and whispered, "Let's pretend we're cousins."

"It's one thing to act like you're somebody's brother or to role-play a father-and-son fantasy, but how do you pretend to be cousins?" Doug asked.

For the rest of the afternoon we came up with possible dialogue, standouts being "Isn't it funny how our dads look so much alike?" and "How come I call my mother Mom and you call her Aunt Sharon?"

June 6, 1998
Chicago

A joke told to me by the media escort Bill Young:

Q. Did you hear about the Polish lottery?
A. You win $1 a year for a million years.

He then said, "The good thing about French drinking water is you know nobody's taken a bath in it."

June 10, 1998
Birmingham, Alabama
I was outside the Atlanta airport having a cigarette when I saw a mentally ill person wander over and search the ashtray for salvageable butts. He hobbled, wearing what looked to be too-tight shoes, and his pockets were bulging, I guessed from all the ashtrays he'd visited before this one. I was seated on a bench and as he stood in front of me, I looked at the tag on his knapsack.

Name: E Dog
Street: My Street
City: My City
State: My State

June 14, 1998
Nashville, Tennessee
While waiting for my flight, I took a seat beside an elderly man and his six-year-old granddaughter. Just before our boarding was announced, the girl climbed into his lap and pounded on his colostomy bag. "Is that your wallet?" she asked in a singsong voice that told me she knew very well what it was.

"Oh, May-June," the man said wearily, "you know it ain't my wallet."

"It's all filled with poody," the girl said. "When you go home, will you throw it down the toilet?"

"Prob'ly so," the man said, no doubt counting the seconds until one of them—it didn't matter which—got on that plane and flew far, far away.

June 21, 1998
San Francisco
In Los Angeles yesterday I met a former book publicist.

"Why did you quit?" I asked.

She sighed. "I was tired having authors call and say, 'My shower cap's too tight.'"

A joke told to me by a media escort, Frank:

Princess Diana and Mother Teresa are in heaven, and the latter isn't too happy. "It isn't fair," she says. "All those years I lived in squalor, devoting myself to the sick and suffering. All *she* did was attend cocktail parties and model clothes, so how come *she* has a halo and I don't?"

Then God says, "That's not a halo, it's a steering wheel."

June 29, 1998
New York

This morning I began my French class at the Alliance Française on the Upper East Side. There are eight students ranging in age from a woman in her mid-fifties to a boy who looks to be around fifteen. I worried I might be the worst, but that honor goes to an Australian who accepted a phone call during class, braying, "*Bonjour!* No, it's me. I'm in French class!"

Our teacher is a beautiful, mournful-looking Parisienne with long brown hair. It's an intermediate rather than a beginners' class, so I assumed that everyone, like me, had studied a little before signing up. One of the students is Japanese American, and when the teacher asked her a question in French, she answered in English, "What? Are you asking me what I do? I guess I'm a student, OK?"

June 30, 1998
New York

Don called this afternoon just as I was getting ready to leave. I said I'd phone him tomorrow and he suggested I try at around twelve thirty. "Tell Cristina it's you, and if I happen to be gassing to somebody, I'll get off the blower." I love how old his slang is.

July 1, 1998
New York

Today was my second French class, and I got to play Fabienne in the *"Comment trouvez-vous Paris?"* dialogue we were asked to memorize. She's a brooder, Fabienne, and I worked hard to master her inflection, especially her line "Me, this town. I don't like it. I prefer my Normandy."

The Australian didn't show up today, but the Japanese American student was there. When the teacher asked her to play the role of Carmen, she shook her head, saying, "I don't think so."

The Brazilian guy hadn't done his homework either—just didn't feel like it. The teacher, Cécile, is very shy and blushes easily. It took all she had to say, softly, "The next time, you should come prepared."

Last night Hugh helped me with my memorized dialogue and this afternoon I started on our next assignment, in which Jean-Claude bitches about the subway.

July 10, 1998
New York

Rosalie transferred to our class last Wednesday because her previous teacher wasn't challenging enough. She's clearly the best student, and is always well dressed and quick to help the rest of us out. This as opposed to the Australian, who Rollerbladed to class, arrived late, and then opened the window because she was cold. She didn't ask—just did it.

July 20, 1998
New York

Class was strange today. We spent ten minutes on the future tense before switching to reflexive verbs. The teacher asked if there were any questions and someone asked where she had learned her Spanish. She told us her husband is Puerto Rican, so she'd picked it up from him. Then someone asked how long she'd lived in Paris. I then asked where she lived before moving to Paris, and when she said Morocco, everyone started in. "Where do your parents live? What does your father do?"

The Brazilian who never does his homework turned on us then, saying, "What you're doing is very rude."

Sharon explained that we meant no offense and that Americans are sometimes too open. I added that to us, her life was very exotic, and we were just curious. I mean, really, it's not like we asked whether she uses a tampon or a pad.

August 3, 1998
La Bagotière

Hugh, Dennis, and I flew TWA from New York to Paris, and the plane was either half empty or half full, depending on how you look at it. I sat beside a stylish woman from the Upper West Side who was maybe sixty and who said after takeoff, "All right, I'm going to tell you one story and then I'm going to shut up."

The story was about a tattooed passenger on a crosstown bus who had a boa constrictor beneath her blouse, wrapped around her like a bandage. It was good, and as I listened I thought of the coming year in France and wondered when I'd next understand everything a stranger was saying to me. The New York class helped some. At de Gaulle we got a cab driven by a cheerful black man who spoke with great passion about two accidents he'd witnessed earlier that morning. It took an hour to reach the Montparnasse station, where we caught the train to Normandy. We boarded early, and as I stepped out onto the platform for a cigarette, an old woman asked if I would carry her bag up the stairs. I did, and she tried to give me 5 francs. Of course I turned it down, but seeing as I no longer have a job and have no working papers, I probably should have taken it.

We're fine here for the month of August, but then I need to start French school, which will mean finding an apartment in Paris.

August 21, 1998
Paris

At the Alliance Française yesterday afternoon, I took a placement exam: twenty-five multiple-choice questions and a short essay in which I had to describe a party. Without the class I took in New York I'd have been lost, but between that and all the strange vocabulary words I've memorized over the past few years, I think I did OK. "The party was held at the home of my Uncle Robert who lives beside the sea with a hairless cat. My family attended and ate a lot. I drank too much and my face got swollen."

After I had finished I approached a desk where a well-dressed middle-aged woman held a plastic sheet with holes punched in it over my multiple-choice test. "Very good," she said. When it came to my essay, she pulled out a pencil and slashed away at all my misspellings and grammatical mistakes. Then she looked up and asked if I had used a dictionary.

"Me?"

It made no sense to her that someone on my level would know and be able to spell a medical term used for facial swelling. I explained my "ten new words a day" program and she laid down her pencil, saying, "Good for you! That is an excellent way to learn."

Meanwhile, the apartment we're renting won't be ready until the middle of September, so it looks like I'll be going back and forth from Normandy.

August 31, 1998
Paris

The train from Normandy was crowded with people returning from their vacations, and when we arrived in Paris, the station was a madhouse. There must have been eighty people in the taxi line, all of them dragging big, heavy suitcases. Cabs were scarce and it took an hour to get one, mainly because people kept cutting to the front of the line. First it was an obese woman with an equally out-of-shape child. Then came a family of four, the grandmother being led by the hand. Somebody made a comment and she shouted, "I'm blind."

Apparently it's a rule that the disabled get to go first in the taxi line. This seems fair, seeing as the buses and subways are inaccessible, but then it got out of hand, and a dozen more people headed to the front. Either the train from Lourdes had just pulled up or owning a cell phone and a little too much gold jewelry are now considered handicaps by the French government.

September 1, 1998
Paris

I've really lucked out in terms of a French teacher. The woman won't give her age, but I'm guessing she's in her late forties, funny and expressive. I'm the oldest student and the only American. The others are Japanese, Thai, Polish, Argentinean, Italian, Egyptian, and Chinese. Today's class started with sentence structure. Then we went through the alphabet and stopped whenever we came to the first letter of someone's name. I went third and was instructed to introduce myself and give my nationality, occupation, marital status, a short list of likes and dislikes, and my reason for living in Paris.

A surprising number of students disliked the sun and adored smoking. A Japanese girl said she hated mosquitoes and the teacher made fun of her, saying, "Really? I thought everyone loved them."

Unlike my New York teacher, who would occasionally at least try to explain something in English, this is all French all the time. By the end of class, my brain felt like it had been kicked.

September 3, 1998
Paris
Last night I worked on my homework for three hours. This morning I got up early and spent another four and a half hours on it. I wondered if I was maybe going overboard, but all that time did nothing to prepare me for today's lesson, or for the teacher.

My fellow students have begun forming camps. The Poles sit together, as do the Japanese, Koreans, Thais, and an inseparable couple composed of an Italian girl and an Argentinean musician, who announced during his introduction that he likes to make love. I was surprised by the number of people who hadn't done their homework or who handed in scraps of paper written on the Métro. The teacher exploded, calling us liars and good-for-nothing shits. She stormed across the room, berating those who had already had absences. Apparently people enroll just to get their student visas. Then they either come to class or stay home, try their best or give up and stare out the window. If

I'm not mistaken, this was her attempt to frighten them off. No one could do anything right today, not even the sweet, pretty Yugoslavian girl who has no one to bond with. I cringed when the teacher yelled at her.

At one point she asked us a number of true-or-false questions regarding the *passé composé*. Everyone agreed to the final one, and when I questioned it she marched across the room, raised my hand, and said, "Bravo. He's the only one in the room who's not sleeping. He's the only one who caught it!"

I felt the hatred of my classmates and slunk down in my seat. Then, too, I'm the only one who typed his homework and handed it in fastened with a paper clip. She told us to keep our sentences simple, and I didn't quite obey. But why write "I went to the store with a friend" when, without relying on the dictionary, I can say "I visited the slaughterhouse with my godfather and a small monkey"?

September 7, 1998
Paris
We got a new student today, a Moroccan who's clearly the best French speaker in the room. She correctly and confidently answered one question after another until the teacher shut her down by saying, "This is not your little occasion to show off. This is for people who *don't* know the language."

Later, when I handed in my homework, the teacher took the stack of papers and said to me, in front of everyone, "What is this, a detective novel?"

Meanwhile, I got back yesterday's assignment with *Excellent* written on the last page. It meant the world, as I'd put a lot of time into it.

September 10, 1998
Paris

I can't figure this woman out for the life of me. Today she came to class apologizing for not having graded our homework. In hopes that we might forgive her, she brought in a chocolate cake and a roll of paper towels. "Come, don't be shy. Eat!"

She was kind and funny for close to twenty minutes, and then she started losing her patience. Today's lesson involved the future tense. We were given an in-class assignment, and as we wrote, the teacher moved from desk to desk and screamed at us. When she got to me, she looked at my paper, bent down, and attacked it with her eraser, digging away at my mistakes and saying, in her best English, "I hate you." Later I mispronounced a word and she said it again. Mine was the last answer of the day, so I was left being the dunce. It's a horrible feeling. I'm the one who allows everyone else to leave the room thinking, *Well, at least I'm not him.*

September 11, 1998
Paris

In class the teacher picked on the former flight attendant from Hong Kong, then on Yasser and the pretty young Yugoslavian woman. Toward the middle of the class, she asked us to turn to our homework assignments, and when I pulled my typed sheet from its folder, she snatched it away and held it above her head, shouting, "When I tell you to do a book assignment, you're supposed to do it *in your notebook*. How many times do I have to tell you that?"

I pointed out that I had also done it in my notebook. It was all there, written in pencil. I'd only typed it up thinking we might be expected to hand it in.

This is where she should have apologized. Instead she just said, "Oh."

Later we broke into groups to practice the future tense. I was with Anna from Poland, who works as a nanny for a family with three rotten kids, and the former flight attendant, who started class last month and has no idea what the teacher is saying.

September 13, 1998
La Bagotière

I spent all weekend working on my homework. The teacher wants an essay about the future, something along the lines of "One day I will be rich and successful." But that's for kids. Instead, I wrote, "One day I will be very old and reside in a nursing home. Toothless, bald, and wrinkled, I will wake myself three times a night, and with the help of my nurses, I will go to the toilet. I will eat nothing but gruel and once a month will bathe myself in tepid, cloudy water. I will regard my long, yellow toenails. I will have no visitors because all of my friends will be in their coffins. When I am old I will lie on my bed and stare at the ceiling. From the next room I will hear my ancient French teacher throwing chalk against the wall. I will say, 'Stop. That's enough!' And she will criticize my pronunciation."

September 14, 1998
Paris

The teacher threw a lot of chalk today, but none of it at me. We have a new student, a German au pair, and I wonder what she must think, watching people get yelled at and hit with things. Our last homework assignment was handed back, and though I'd technically made no mistakes, she still found fault with it. I'd written, for example, "You will complain all the time, day and night." Her comment read, in angry red pen, "Pick one or the other. You don't need both."

September 15, 1998
Paris

The teacher was a kitten today. She picked on no one and for a brief while we all loosened up. Our homework for Thursday is to finish reading a comic strip and identify the vulgar language.

September 17, 1998
Paris

We had two new students today, an Indonesian who loves to travel and a fifty-year-old American named Janet who, when asked her profession, said, "*Je suis* a hairdresser." She answered most of today's questions in English and while the teacher let her get away with it, tomorrow I imagine she'll be hit with both barrels. Today we moved into the tense you use when ordering someone around.

September 18, 1998
Paris

We had a substitute today, a casually dressed woman who did not give her name. She asked what we'd been assigned for our homework, and just as we were telling her, the teacher walked in and apologized for being late. She said something to the substitute like "You can go now," but the woman had no intention of leaving, so the two of them went at it.

"You were late," the substitute said. "The rule is that after fifteen minutes, someone else takes the class."

Our teacher said she had the lesson all planned, and the substitute interrupted her and said, "Time is time."

They went back and forth until eventually our teacher surrendered and stormed out of the room, telling us to have a nice weekend. It was fun watching her fight with someone who could defend herself.

Our lesson had to do with the imperative, the tense you use when making demands. To illustrate it, the substitute made me her slave and insisted that I kiss everyone in the room except her.

Later we were told to come up with a list of commands for students learning French—you must do your homework, you must not daydream, etc. I raised my hand. "You must dodge the morsels of chalk thrown by the teacher."

The substitute seemed confused. "But no, the teacher does not throw chalk."

"Ours does," said the Korean guy next to me.

"When?" the substitute asked.

"All the time," I said.

The Thai woman in the front row turned around then and hissed at me. After class I was approached by her and Polish Anna, both of them furious and convinced that now our teacher is going to get fired.

I tried to say that if I got the teacher fired, I could just as easily have the substitute fired for making me kiss everyone, but it came out a mess.

Anna said she's had her share of nice teachers but never learns with them. The strict ones are the best, she said, and the Thai woman agreed.

I felt like a total shit then and even worse after talking to the Italian, who said that I was clearly the teacher's favorite. I asked what gave her that idea and she said, "Because she told you that she hated you."

September 21, 1998
Paris

The teacher returned, and the Poles and Koreans breathed an audible sigh of relief. I was happy as well until she gave us three homework assignments, these on top of the two she had given us earlier. I've spent hours on them already and still have to write an essay on an American holiday. It's a lot of work, as I'll have to double-check all my spelling in the dictionary.

September 25, 1998
Paris

The teacher was a real wildcat today. We got a new student on Tuesday, an Israeli. He talks a lot in class and she laid into him for it. "This is not your own private session. Why don't you think before you open your mouth?"

Still he continued on, not the least bit intimidated.

The teacher threw a lot of chalk and said to me at one point, "Teaching you is like having a cesarean section every day of the week."

Later, related to the exercise we were doing, she asked each of us, "Are you afraid of me?"

The Israeli said, "I have no fear at all of you."

I said pretty much the opposite, and she used a word I didn't catch. It wasn't *coward;* I know how to say that. She used a word I wasn't familiar with and added, "Every day you sit there and tremble."

September 27, 1998
Paris

I bought nothing at the flea market today but stopped to admire a human skull from the sixth century. It's on a stand, the head of a child, crazed with tiny lines, and exquisite.

The woman selling it gave me the price, which amounted to $6,000. It seemed extravagant, but then, how do you value a skull? The way it is, I could buy either a decent used car or some kid's head. It's twice the cost of Hugh's computer and half the price of a hysterectomy.

September 28, 1998
Paris

Polish Anna and I spoke after class today. She works as an au pair and told me that her mistress is currently in the hospital. The woman is six months pregnant and just learned that the fetus's legs are only two inches long. "That means," Anna said, "that he will have to be pushed always in a rolling chair, and this is very difficult here in Paris."

Based on this news, the woman has decided to terminate her pregnancy. This is interesting, as I don't think you could abort that late in the United States. I'm sure there are always extenuating circumstances, but I don't think that this—tiny legs—would be an acceptable reason. Would it?

September 29, 1998
Paris

This was the last class before our week-long break, and the teacher baked a cake and organized a little party. Anna brought bread and cheese, the German made a potato salad, and the Japanese girl brought in seaweed crackers. A lot of people didn't show up, and because there were so few of us, we got to sit around and ask the teacher personal questions. It was fun watching her talk with her mouth full. After she finished, she pulled out her cigarettes and offered them to everyone. I lit one of my own and she told me, using a word I'd learn from Manuela, that menthol cigarettes are tacky. She talked about American hypocrisy and puritanism and asked why my people were so caught up in our president's sex life. The others got involved and said, essentially, "Yeah, you, what's your problem?"

October 2, 1998
Paris
This morning while cutting cheese Hugh sliced off the tip of his finger. That sounds like a sentence I'd write for class, but it's true. He worried he was going to pass out; my big fear was trying to phone someone for help. There's a small, Arab-owned market a few doors from our apartment building, so while he wrapped his hand in a rag, I ran down the street to buy Band-Aids, remembering along the way that I had no idea what the word is. I'd tried to buy some at a pharmacy last year in Normandy, but my French was so bad I couldn't even describe them. In the end I drew a picture and the woman looked at it, responding with what I guessed was "This is a drugstore. We have no surfboards here." It really was a bad picture. My next attempt was even worse and resembled a flying carpet. In the end, I gave up, figuring my blisters would heal on their own.

This morning at the market I was able to say, in French, "My friend cut his finger so I am looking for a morsel of rubber." The sentence kind of falls apart at the end, but still it did the trick. The man handed me a small, $4 box of Band-Aids and I left realizing that everything in that store costs $4: a can of tomatoes, a box of rice, a jug of laundry detergent—it's all the same price.

I returned home, grateful that Hugh was still conscious, and when I repeated what I'd said at the market, he corrected me. It seems he did not "cut his finger" but, rather, "cut of himself *the* finger."

He applied the Band-Aid, cleaned the bloody knife, and went back to making lunch while I watched from the doorway, hoping he might stab himself again so I could return to the store with both the reflexive verb "to cut of oneself" *and* the proper word for Band-Aid.

October 8, 1998
Paris

I have two homework assignments to hand in, and though I could make it easy, I just can't stop myself from having fun with it. One of the assignments involves accepting or rejecting social invitations. When asked if she wants to join Henri for a run around the lake, Natalie could reply, "With pleasure!" Instead I'm having her say, "That would be different. I'll just put on my leg and we'll be ready to go!"

I'm liking the teacher a lot more since the new semester started. The class is smaller, and the students are a bit older. It's a good group. I like the Italian lawyer who isn't afraid to admit when he's lost. The Colombian gets a lot of grief, but it's his fault for not doing his homework.

October 9, 1998
Paris

After class I took Amy to a pet shop on the Right Bank, where we saw a miniature potbellied pig for $300. He was the size of a house cat and stood in his cage urinating a puddle. Amy can't believe I didn't walk out with him; she was mad, practically, and kept saying, "It's not expensive," as if that's the only thing that would stop a person from buying a pig and keeping it in his third-floor apartment. I tried imagining him as a pet, but all I saw were his sharp hooves scratching my beautiful floors.

October 10, 1998
Paris
Just as Amy told me and Hugh that she's never heard anyone in Paris say "Excuse me," she got hit in the knee with a Coke can, and the boy who threw it called out in French that he was sorry.

October 12, 1998
Paris
Today the high school students went on strike. There were tens of thousands of them marching down the boulevard in front of the school and we could hear their chants all afternoon. The kids were marching in support of their teachers, who'd had a strike of their own a few weeks back. I'm not certain what it was about, but someone told me that the government had wanted to cut some jobs. Walking home from class, I was surrounded by teens with messages painted on their faces. They stopped to chide customers walking into stores and scolded the merchants for not closing in support of their cause.

October 13, 1998
Paris
Today the teacher called me a sadist. I tried to say that was like the pot calling the kettle black but came out with something closer to "That is like a pan saying to a dark pan, 'You are a pan.'"

October 16, 1998
Paris
I noticed that the teacher was wearing new glasses today. This led to an explanation of the difference between *nouveau* and *neuf.* The former is apparently new to you, while the latter is

factory-fresh. I did some homework on the train but still have to type up a paper on the differences between New York and Paris. We're learning to compare things, to say that someone is less tall than her neighbor, more intelligent than her brother, as ugly as her father. I no longer dread school the way I did a month ago but am really going to have to work if I want to keep up while in America for my tour.

October 22, 1998
Paris

Yesterday, there were more student demonstrations. Because the high schoolers want more teachers, they sometimes need to overturn cars and destroy phone booths. After class I sat in the Luxembourg Gardens for a while, reading *Mama Black Widow,* a novel by Iceberg Slim. I'm all for any book that uses the words *pulchritudinous* and *hungry pooh hole* on the same page.

October 23, 1998
Paris

One nice thing about school is that it's made Friday meaningful again. I now feel that, having gotten through five days of homework, I have something to celebrate. Last night's assignment was to write something about a movie. I chose Robert Altman's *Nashville* and spent six hours on my one-page paper. It's the articles that kill me, that and words like *drifter,* which translates to "one who travels without a goal."

Meanwhile, today we took a test that involved multiple choice and an audio exam. It was hard and made all the harder by the teacher, who wandered around the room with a lit cigarette that smelled so good, I found it nearly impossible to concentrate. The audio test was discouraging in that a

371

French twelve-year-old could have passed it with no problem. Then, too, I hadn't taken one since Kent State twenty years ago. After we finished, the teacher invited us all to the cafeteria for coffees. Everyone smoked, and it was nice to sit together outside of class.

November 23, 1998
San Luis Obispo, California
At five thirty this morning, the SuperShuttle came to take me from Ronnie's apartment to the San Francisco airport. There were three other passengers on board, but the only ones awake were me and the driver, who was listening to talk radio. The theme was alien abduction, and the guest, a man named Dr. Reed, claimed to have been taken at a picnic ground. He was not at liberty to discuss its location; this, he said, on the advice of his lawyer, who told him it might hurt his case.

"I don't get it," I said. "Is he suing the aliens or the campground?"

"Most likely the campground," the driver said. "Chances are this isn't the first time a thing like this has happened. They should have posted signs."

This is not what you want to hear from a man responsible for four lives.

"The reason this show comes on at five a.m. is that they don't want regular people listening to it," he said. "They don't want us to know."

Alcohol and telephones do not mix. On Saturday night I called Paris from the Heathman Hotel in Portland. I'd figured it might cost $30, but I hadn't spoken to Hugh in weeks. It was late, and I was drunk and feeling lonely. I had only vague memories of the call the following morning when I was presented with a bill for $156. I'm still trying to remember what we talked about, but I can't recollect much aside from the news that Dennis (the cat) is eating a lot.

November 27, 1998
Phoenix

Ted's boyfriend James loaned me a cookbook called *Imperial Dishes of China,* and I found myself reading it as though it were a collection of beautifully titled short stories. "A Hundred Birds Paying Homage to the Phoenix" stood out, but nothing compared to "Monkey Heads on a Pine Tree." In France I often leaf through recipes in search of words I think might come in handy. It's how I learned the verbs for "to simmer" and "to chop." *Imperial Dishes* was in English, but still I feel I came away with something. Here were instructions such as "Rinse the lips twice in cold water" and "Remove the penis and carve it into bite-sized pieces." Mental pictures aside, it was disturbing to read such things in the form of a direct order. "Scald the vagina and remove any remaining hairs," for example.

As literature, *Imperial Dishes* was outstanding, but as an actual working cookbook, I think it left a few too many holes. A homosexual's notion of bite-sized penis is no doubt dramatically different than that of, say, an Orthodox rabbi's. It's just not specific enough. When told to "arrange the camel paw attractively," my first question was "How?" Camel paws don't even look attractive on camels. Where do you buy these ingredients in the first place? If you can't find a camel paw, can you use a donkey paw instead? Do donkeys even have paws? And what's an acceptable substitute for a vagina? It's frustrating, but that's what I liked about *Imperial Dishes of China.* It made me think.

December 4, 1998
Paris
I returned to French class after five weeks away and the teacher kissed me.

December 10, 1998
Paris
As a homework assignment I need to write a letter from a man to his wife. The two are on the brink of divorce—the teacher's idea, and a good one, I think.

Today in class we read an essay about social change in France. The teacher is outraged over a new program that will allow friends and roommates to enjoy the same tax rates as married couples. Single people pay a lot here, as the government wants to promote marriage and childbirth. The new program was designed to give gay couples the same rights as married people, but instead, the government, afraid it might appear to be condoning homosexuality, has opened it up to any two people living under the same roof: roommates, a mother and her middle-aged daughter. It's cowardice, the teacher says.

December 12, 1998
Paris
The unemployed have gone on strike—at least that's how I understood it from listening to the radio. The teacher explained that, seeing as they have no jobs, they can't actually walk off them. Instead, they're holding a protest and insisting on a Christmas bonus with their unemployment check. She's in their corner and said it's unfair to punish children just because their parents were thrown out of work.

The information desk at the Louvre is also on strike, demanding better working conditions. By this, do they mean a public so well informed, they won't have to pester the employees with questions?

December 13, 1998
Paris

I took a walk last night and ran into Richard, who lives in a grand Left Bank apartment overlooking the river. We talked for half an hour or so, and he told me about a friend of his, a journalist, who each week buys $60 worth of magazines from a kiosk near the Café de Flore. She was there with a male friend recently, a photographer who wanted to see if one of his pictures had been used in the latest Italian *Vogue*. The guy started leafing through it when the newsagent said, the way they do here, "This is not a lending library."

The journalist said she would pay for the magazine, and when she pulled out her wallet the newsagent said, "Why don't you go get fucked up the ass by a nigger."

So much stuff goes over my head here.

December 14, 1998
Paris

For homework we're supposed to write about gift-giving practices in our home countries. I don't actually understand the assignment. We read an essay in class, the teacher asked how flowers are wrapped in Japan, and then she told a story about her husband's Greek grandmother spitting into the mouth of a newborn baby.

December 15, 1998
Paris

Yesterday the teacher held up my essay on social change during the 1960s and pronounced it "a remarkable document."

I made plenty of grammatical errors but gained points on the structure. Today I turned in my paper on social customs. In it I wrote that on the eve of an American man's wedding, it is customary for his parents to cut off two of his fingers and bury them near the parking lot. The groom has eight hours in which to find them, and if he does, it means that the marriage will last.

December 22, 1998
Paris
This was the last day of class until the new semester begins in January. We presented the teacher with the lighter I had had engraved and the carton of cigarettes I had collected money for. She seemed to appreciate both. The lesson was hard, and we broke off fifteen minutes early to eat cake. The room had a nice, festive atmosphere until the Hong Kong student confronted the teacher, saying, in English, "How come you no pass me? How come me alone and not nobody else?"

Personally I like this student, if only because she's so bad. She'll occasionally come to class or do her homework, but only if she's in the mood. Her French doesn't sound much different from her Cantonese, and as long as she was around, I was never the worst one.

December 24, 1998
Paris
As our cab left for the train station this morning, my father turned to me and said, "Ask the driver if it's going to rain all day."

I don't think he cared what the answer was. He just wanted to see if I could ask properly, not that he's any judge. He doesn't speak a word of French, but that hasn't stopped him from criticizing me.

"He said that yes, it's going to rain all day," I said.

My father nodded. "It's coming in from the west. Rain always comes from the west in France."

This is going to be a long eight days.

December 31, 1998
Paris

Last night, shortly after dinner, my father's head caught on fire. He was leaning toward a candle, examining a scratch on the table, and seconds later I noticed the flames, which encircled his scalp like a brilliant crown. He looked like a happy king, content that all was well throughout the land. Just as he realized what was happening, Gretchen bounded over with a cloth napkin. Dad retreated into the bathroom and spent ten minutes examining the damage with a hand mirror. This morning we went to buy him a hat.

1999

January 1, 1999
Paris

Dad ate dinner last night with his airplane ticket in his shirt pocket. With it was a slip of paper upon which he had written the estimated taxi fare to Charles de Gaulle, including the amount he planned to tip the driver. He wore a tan shirt with epaulets, a scarf, a sweater, and a Windbreaker. He wore a hat. The poor thing was more than ready to leave and would have gladly spent the night at the airport—not in a hotel but just sitting in a chair, waiting. It's not France he dislikes, exactly. I think he just hates to be away from his TV.

January 4, 1999
Paris

School started today and we got two new students. One's a pregnant Chinese woman who is married to a Frenchman and hopes to name her baby Beyond, and the other is a German fellow who moved here for love. The rest of us introduced ourselves, and then we all recounted our Christmas holidays. I said that half my family came and stayed for sixteen days, and my classmates audibly drew in their breath. Then I said that I received nine cartons of cigarettes and that before my father left for home, his head caught on fire.

Next came Milton, who got drunk on New Year's Eve and fell on his face, breaking a few blood vessels. When Polish

Anna's turn came, the teacher accused her of getting drunk as well, even though she denied it. The teacher has this thing about Poles and alcohol.

January 7, 1999
Paris

In French class we're studying the *gérondif,* which is used when someone is doing two things at once. As part of last night's homework we were instructed to write six sentences along the lines of "She sang while vacuuming." It was a simple and unrewarding exercise until I turned to the *Pocket Guide to Medical French* that Amy gave me for Christmas. The book is full of terrific phrases, everything from "Do you feel paranoid?" to "Have you noticed any unusual discharge?" I spent a lot of time constructing sentences for the assignment, my favorite being " 'Has anything else been inserted into your anus?' The doctor posed the question as he examined the wounded sphincter."

The teacher collected the papers at the end of class and, as usual, took a moment to skim through what I'd handed her. Things like this can go either way. The paper is grammatically correct, but something tells me I may have missed the mark here.

January 14, 1999
Paris

The teacher was extremely unhappy with the other day's homework and entered the room as if it were a boxing ring. When she's angry, nothing can please her. She didn't warm up until the last half hour of class. We'd listened earlier to a series of recorded phrases and were instructed to match each one with a picture. A kid's voice shouted, "We won!" for example, and we matched it with a drawing of a boy raising his arms in victory. This somehow led her to tell us that in Greece, you indicate the number five by holding your palm toward your face. Palm outward means the equivalent of "Fuck you."

In both Greece and Turkey, nodding yes means no, as does closing your eyes. She and a friend went to Istanbul once and couldn't find a room to save their lives. Finally, at midnight, they entered a hotel and asked if there was a vacancy. The desk clerk nodded, and, delighted, they brought in their bags. In the end, she said, the man let them sleep on the roof.

She brightens up eventually, the teacher, but you have to clear the path. Today, every time I thought she was coming out of it, Ralf would ask a question pertaining to something we had supposedly learned months ago. Then she'd furiously write on the board, turning to say, "*Now* do you understand it?"

Ralf would squint and think a moment before saying, "No," and off she'd go again. Twice she told Luis to shut up, and I got scolded when we were asked to identify the class of people represented in a comic strip she gave us. I said I thought they were working class. When asked why, I pointed out the Jesus snow globe displayed atop their television set.

"That shows what you know," the teacher said. "The French proletariat would never decorate their homes with religious iconography." Or at least I'm guessing that's what she said.

"OK," I said. "They're low class."

That's when she really tore into me, saying she never again wanted to hear language like that from us. She'd just the other day taught us three different words for "farting" along with the phrase "Go fuck yourself on a pole," but "low class" is out-of-bounds?

My fellow students began to guess. Were they middle class? Retired class?

"No!" the teacher shouted. "For God's sake, they're *working* class."

I had given that answer twenty minutes earlier, but I guess she dismissed it when I mentioned the snow globe. It was just that kind of day.

January 18, 1999
Paris

Again the teacher was in a foul mood. She called me a misogynist because, in an essay on my dream house, I said that every evening, once the sun set, I'd decide whether I wanted to sleep with one of my three hundred wives or a camel. She later told me, in English, that she hated me. I had used *falloir* in the subjunctive rather than the *imparfait,* so I guess I deserved it.

January 20, 1999
Paris

Today the teacher told us that a ripe Camembert should have the same consistency as a human eyebrow. It was just a little something she threw in. All week, as part of our homework, we're supposed to listen to the radio and talk in class about what we heard. Luis brought up the forty-some bodies that were just discovered in Kosovo and the teacher listened, then said, "Now tell me what happened that was even worse."

January 22, 1999
Paris

Doing laundry in Paris has to be planned a week in advance, as it takes that long to work up the change. It shouldn't be that difficult, but cashiers here act as if their money drawers can only accept deposits. In New York you'd see signs reading NO CHANGE WITHOUT PURCHASE, but here they should read, simply, NO CHANGE. Every time you pay for something, they shake you down for the exact amount. If the thing costs, say, 185 francs, and you hand over a 200-franc bill, the person will frown at it and say, "Really? You don't have a hundred and eighty-five?"

At the grocery store, I've had several cashiers say, "Didn't I see something smaller in your wallet?" The other day one of them snatched my coin purse out of my hands and simply took what she wanted. On top of that, the checkout people sit rather than stand. They don't bag your groceries like they do in the States, and everything is scanned rather than entered manually into the machine. Their only job is to make change, and they refuse to do it.

January 24, 1999
Paris

It's nine thirty p.m. and I haven't left the apartment all day. Eleven and a half hours ago I started my homework and there's still no end in sight. Every word is checked in the dictionary, every verb tense is reconsidered, and it takes forever. I still have eight questions to answer, three personal sentences to write, and a story to finish.

January 25, 1999
Paris

I spent a total of seventeen hours on my homework. The hardest part was a story the teacher started and asked us to finish. Her opener went like this: "At midnight I decided to leave the party and walk twenty minutes to the train station where I could get a taxi. It was dark and the streets were deserted. I was nervous and hurrying along when I heard a car roll up from behind with its headlights off."

My completion reads "Surprisingly, the trunk was not uncomfortable. There was a pillow there, and a woolen blanket. The floor was carpeted and smelled like pizza. Yes, it was dark, but relatively spacious. While lying there, I would often reflect upon my life before I came to live in this trunk. I'd been walking to the train station when this car stopped behind me. It was dark, but still I could see that the driver was handsome and well dressed. He sensed my nervousness and said, 'Come on, then, give us a smile.'"

In my story she lives in the trunk for twenty-two days and falls madly in love with the man who put her there. Eventually they come to *tutoie* each other through a little hole, and everything's great until he abandons the car at the airport, with her still in the back. A steep ticket is issued for illegal parking, and when she is held responsible, she cries.

January 26, 1999
Paris

Before I left the apartment this afternoon a woman knocked on the door and asked if I wanted to buy her carpet. I don't know if she lives in the building or just walked in off the street, but either way, the answer was the same. I'm not a big carpet person, but rather than getting into it, I just said no and then hurried to class, where the teacher read my story about her being locked in the trunk. Her delivery was good, but she kept pausing to call me a misogynist.

"No," I corrected her, "I'm not a misogynist, I'm a misanthrope. I hate everyone equally."

January 28, 1999
Paris

I went this afternoon and bought a ticket for *You've Got Mail*, which here is called *Vous Avez un Message*. I guess I mispronounced something, as the guy behind the counter loudly mocked me to his associates, all of whom laughed. Handing me my change, he said, "We charge extra to tourists."

If he'd said they charge extra to Americans I might have pointed out that American movies are what keeps his theater in business. As it was, I said nothing and quietly burned for the rest of the day.

February 11, 1999
Paris

A very small man came to the door this morning and used a verb I wasn't familiar with. His face was smeared with something black, as were his hands. *Coal?* I wondered. Luckily Hugh was home and explained that the verb meant "to ream out." The man said that by law our furnace vents and chimneys were to be reamed out once a year, and with that he scrambled up onto the kitchen counter, then climbed on top of the refrigerator. Once there, he reached into a vent and came away with a fistful of soot, saying we should have it cleaned for insurance purposes.

The man's top teeth were rotted to stubs, but the bottom ones were white and even. He came up to my shoulder, that's how small he was. Once we agreed that he should do it, the little guy left and was replaced by his assistant, who was young and handsome. He wore a one-piece work suit over his clothes—the kind that mechanics wear—and the rear end was torn open. Like his boss, his hands were black and his face was smeared. I was enchanted and asked if he could do the fireplaces as well. While he worked, I did my homework, pausing every now and then to ask or answer a question. Did I know, he asked, that the same verb, "to ream out," was also used for sex acts?

"You're kidding," I said. "How interesting."

We talked about his love of football and cats and his hatred of the English. It cost the equivalent of $130, but now I can build fires.

February 26, 1999
Paris

Today was the last day of class. Next month the teacher goes to Brazil, and then she has to work a few months in the office. She kissed several students good-bye, but I slipped out the door. I would have liked to thank her, but everything feels different since my article ("Me Talk Pretty One Day") came out in *Esquire*. I wish I hadn't published it. I meant it at the time, but since then things have changed. She's still moody, but I think she's a good teacher. I can see that now, whereas I couldn't before.

March 13, 1999
Reston, Virginia

This evening for the first time in seven months I got to watch some episodes of *Cops*. They weren't the best ones, but at least I'd never seen them before. Last night's hotel in Alabama had thirty-eight stations, including the Animal Planet Network, which offered something called *Wildlife Emergency*, a sort of *ER* for wounded creatures. The first segment featured an eagle with possible lead poisoning. "Katie, I want you to draw some blood and get this guy into X-ray, ASAP."

I thought, *OK, it's an eagle. It's on stamps and coins so I guess it makes sense to go all out.* Next came a possum with a broken jaw, and again the doctors leaped into action. I was wondering why they didn't just put it down, but that would be another show—*Mercy Killing*, maybe, or *When Animals Die.*

Later that night I watched a British import called *Vets in*

Practice, which follows the goings-on of four attractive veterinarians. Pete was presented with a parrot suffering from an ingrown toenail, and then we cut to Brian, who had his arm embedded to the elbow in a cow's asshole and talked briefly about his relationship with his girlfriend. We saw Ellen, who had recently amputated both wings of a goose and was now reintroducing her back into society. "I'm worried about Denise," she said. "Worried that the others won't accept her."

The show cut to a commercial and the announcer said, "Coming up next, Allison treats a cat and her kittens for fleas."

March 23, 1999
Chicago
I haven't had a drink in forty-eight hours. This is not an accident but a concerted effort, and a very difficult one. I'd have to double-check, but I'm pretty sure I've been drunk every night for the past eighteen years. At the airport yesterday, I felt, if not good, then at least proud of myself. I've long assumed that everyone can tell I'm an alcoholic—strangers, even, the people you present your boarding pass to or buy a newspaper from. If it shows in my face that I drink, mustn't it eventually show that I don't anymore?

March 24, 1999
Chicago
Again last night I lay in bed unable to sleep. It was my third night without a drink and I was trying to remember what's so good about being sober. One thing is that I'll be able to walk through Paris at night. Hugh and I went out for coffee once, and I've wobbled to the Pont Neuf on New Year's Eve, but otherwise I've always been too drunk. I can't walk

straight or go any real distance because after seven beers and two Scotches, I need a bathroom every three blocks or so. So on the plus side, I can start getting out more. My fear is that I'll find it even duller than sitting at home.

April 4, 1999
Paris

Yesterday afternoon I went to the grocery store and bought a half a rabbit, never making the connection that this is Easter. It's a little like eating reindeer for Christmas, or Founding Father on the Fourth of July. My half a rabbit was prepackaged—cut into pieces and arranged in a Styrofoam casket, much like a quartered fryer. I was out of the house while Hugh was cooking and didn't realize until later that when they say half a rabbit, they really *mean* half a rabbit. I was serving myself seconds when I noticed half the rabbit's head lying in profile at the bottom of the pot.

They must have sawed this thing right down the middle. I examined half the rabbit's brain and wondered which variety of thoughts it included. Was this the half that instinctively warned it to run away from dogs or the half that held childhood memories or grudges against other rabbits? I prodded it with a fork, realized I could have eaten it by accident, and had half a mind to become a vegetarian.

April 6, 1999
Paris

The inevitable finally happened, just as I knew it would. My French teacher faxed Andy at *Esquire* to say my article has had the effect of a bomb at the Alliance Française.

"Maybe she means that in a good way," Hugh said.

I tell myself I'm not going to think about it and find I'm able to distract myself for up to fifteen seconds at a time. In my story I failed to mention her wit, and her skill as a teacher. That is what I have to apologize for, my laziness.

April 8, 1999
La Bagotière
Due to the bombings of Serbian targets, there's a lot more anti-American graffiti in Paris. Yesterday on the way to the train station I passed a wall reading USA = GROSS CONS ("big assholes") and the other day in the Métro station I read FUCK OF US. I love it when it's not grammatically correct. "That's fuck *off,* thank you very much."

April 17, 1999
Paris
Hugh and I spent the weekend in Normandy while his mother, Joan, stayed behind to take care of the cat. Before I left, she bought a bottle of wine and I warned her that she might want to pick up a decent corkscrew, because Hugh's is worthless. Every time I use it, I wind up pushing in the cork with a screwdriver.

I returned to Paris this afternoon and shortly afterward Joan walked through the door with a sackful of groceries and a new corkscrew, the type with the two prongs. "Boy, you were right about Hugh's," she said. "I couldn't get it to do anything." I pointed out that she'd just bought an exact replica of the corkscrew we already have, and she knit her brows. "What are you talking about?"

She opened the drawer beside the refrigerator and pulled out a palm-size plastic disk attached to a shallow coupling. "I thought *this* was Hugh's corkscrew," she said. "The circle part fits over the top of the bottle, but when I tried turning it toward the arrow, nothing happened."

This was for me one of those adult moments involving a

choice. Do you shrug your shoulders and say, "I couldn't get it to work either," or do you tell the woman she spent the weekend trying to open a wine bottle with the broken knob to the dishwasher?

April 30, 1999
Paris

This evening a man knocked on the door of our apartment and said, "Hello, I just got out of prison, may I come in?"

I'm not sure if he was legally required to introduce himself like this or if it was his own idea. Either way, it was a case of honesty getting you nowhere.

"Hugh!" I called. "There's somebody here to see you."

The ex-convict was attempting to sell a series of Magic Marker drawings he'd matted into little cardboard frames. They were geometric designs, the kind people sketch when they're trapped on the phone with a relative or, possibly, a parole officer. When Hugh told the guy we weren't interested, he became hostile. "You're all the same," he spat. "You think that just because somebody's been in jail they're not good enough to come inside and sit on your furniture."

He called us a number of names I've only recently come to understand, and then he banged on our neighbor's door and insulted her as well. This is the third time this month that somebody has gotten into the building and come knocking. It used to happen every so often in New York, but there I never gave it much thought, as I'd been able to fluently lie and talk my way out of whatever someone was selling. Last week I was visited by two Catholic nuns collecting money for what I can only hope were new uniforms, and a few days later a small elderly woman came by wondering if I wanted to buy her bath mat. "Look," she said, "it's dry and clean. Perfect for the feet!"

May 8, 1999
London, England

Over dinner I stupidly asked if Vanessa did anything that got on Steve's nerves. I meant it as a joke, but Steve answered seriously. He complained that she always leaves the caps off bottles, and just as I thought that was that, he started in on a list of other things. Vanessa tried defending herself, and when it got awkward, I suggested that Steve put a lid on it.

"Do what?"

I learned then that in England, one says, "Put a sock in it." The phrase originated in the early part of the century. Gramophones had no volume control, so to lower the music, you put a sock in the horn. I also learned there's a woman at the BBC named Jonquil Panting.

Why is it you so rarely see a woman with a hearing aid?

May 17, 1999
Berlin, Germany

I flew from Paris on Air France and was seated across the aisle from the fattest man I've ever seen in my life. He was German, dressed in a T-shirt and shorts with an elastic waist. They brought him an extender for his seat belt and when he sat, his stomach pressed against his folded-up tray table. The guy was on the aisle, while his friend took the window. In order to fit, he had to raise both armrests. Half of him invaded his friend's space and the other half was repeatedly battered by the food and beverage carts that struggled to get past him. When breakfast was served, his tray had to be placed on his friend's table. The fat fellow ate his food and then asked for two additional rolls. The only thing I touched was my coffee, and though I could feel the guy's eyes on my food and had no problem with him taking it, I didn't know how to offer without saying, in effect, "Hey, you're fat. Why don't *you* eat this?"

May 18, 1999
Cologne, Germany
Harry Rowohlt, the fellow who translated my book into German and is reading with me on my tour, told me that when someone on the bus or at a nearby table in a restaurant talks on a cell phone, he likes to lean over and shout, "Come back to bed, I'm freezing."

May 19, 1999
Cologne
Yesterday at five a woman arrived to take my picture. She was in her late fifties and because her English was weak, we spoke in French. During our time together I learned that her husband had recently died of lung cancer and that she was grateful to have no children. She said that her mother is in her nineties and has recently started to pee in her pants.

When we had finished I said good-bye and walked to a supermarket I had passed earlier in the day. You don't have to know French to feel at ease in a French grocery store. Many of the words are recognizable to an English speaker, so you're not likely to mistake cat food for tuna. In Germany, though, it's not so easy. I was standing in the soap aisle when a young woman approached, pushing her shopping cart with her chin. She was in her mid-twenties, and attractive. The first thing I noticed was her beautiful shoulder-length hair. Then I realized that she had no arms. It didn't look as if she'd lost them in an accident, at least not recently. Her ease suggested she'd been born without them.

Next to me were the shampoos. The young woman stopped, and after considering them, she slipped off a shoe and reached up to the shelf with her bare foot. It was level with my chest, but she seemed to have no problem grabbing the plastic bottle and putting it in her cart. I didn't see her paying for her groceries but imagine she was just as skilled at opening her wallet and presenting the cashier with both bills and change.

The hotel offered a buffet breakfast that included what looked to be a tray of flattened meatballs. I asked what they were and Gerd said, "I believe you would call them little hamburgers."

Every time we go out to dinner I find something in my food. On Monday night it was a bit of tinfoil and today it was a rubber band. As long as it's not glass or a thumbtack I don't really care. I'm just wondering what it might be tomorrow.

May 20, 1999
Stuttgart, Germany
It rained yesterday so we all bought umbrellas. Mine is brown and is patterned with little flowers that Tini identified as edelweiss. I'd been in a crummy mood, but by lunch it blew over, and I enjoyed the company of my two hosts. Together we walked through the old part of town, where I saw a man with two canes doing tricks with a soccer ball. Later, at the restaurant, I saw an empty wheelchair parked beside a table for two. It was strange to see. Either someone didn't need it all that badly, or one of the two people wanted a little change. After leaving, we came upon a bronze statue of the man who invented the Bunsen burner.

June 18, 1999
Paris
Today I saw a one-armed dwarf carrying a skateboard. It's been ninety days since I've had a drink.

June 19, 1999
Paris

Abe went to Eastern Europe and stopped in Paris on his way back to San Diego. We were at the zoo, watching the monkeys, when he told me about a recent *E. coli* outbreak in Romania. A couple hundred people got sick and the government sent an agent to investigate. The source was eventually traced to a baker who'd been tainting his breads and pastries with the human feces they found stored in a plastic bucket hidden in his walk-in cooler.

"My only question," Abe said, "is why did he keep the bucket of shit in the refrigerator? I mean, what, did he worry it would go bad?"

June 22, 1999
Paris

My friend Barb claims that when asked to justify his behavior, Ted Bundy responded, "Well, there are *so many* people."

July 7, 1999
La Bagotière

Genevieve is taking care of her granddaughter, Edwidge, for the week. The girl is two years old and has a new doll, a Barbie clone who talks when tapped on the stomach. The tape track is short, so she speaks very quickly. "Hello, my name is Linette. Do you like my dress? I love to play with you!"

A year ago I wouldn't have been able to catch any of it, but now Linette and I understand each other just fine. As a rule I speak a lot more French in Normandy than I do in Paris. Small talk's more important in the country, so I have to be ready to engage at any moment. Today the butcher and I discussed the possibility of him buying a new car. Later I talked batteries with Annie at the market. As for the baker, she's formally off my list. I liked the old one, the woman with the walleye, but her replacement is too impatient. I was looking at ice cream bars this afternoon when she came from the counter and said firmly, "Hey, *I'm* the one who takes care of that."

I apologized and she pointed to a sign taped above the coffinlike freezer. "People get their own and they leave the door open. Then the ice cream is ruined and I have to throw it all away."

As far as tongue-lashings go, I've had plenty worse. She's just never been terribly pleasant.

July 17, 1999
La Bagotière

Someone called to tell me that John Kennedy's plane has gone down off the coast near Martha's Vineyard. We talked for a few minutes and all the while I wanted to ask, "Who *is* this?" She was French, but I couldn't begin to identify her voice. At first I thought she said *Ted* Kennedy's plane. Then I realized she'd said John, and I had to sit down. He always seemed like such a decent guy, a genuinely good person with excellent manners. I saw him a few times in New York, once on a bike and then again at a restaurant in SoHo, seated at one of the outdoor tables. A car with New Jersey plates pulled over and the woman driving sent her daughter out to get an autograph. "Tell him he's good-looking," the mother said.

The train from Paris was packed. A young man across the aisle from us slept, taking up both seats, and when a fellow in his sixties scolded him, the kid said, "Why don't you just shut up."

July 25, 1999
La Bagotière
A sample dialogue from my *Teach Yourself Slovene* book:

> Gospod Skak: *Kako gre?*
> Sara: *Dobro, hvala.*
> Natakar: *Oprosti, je to tvoja denarnica?*
> Sara: *Prosim?*

Ironically, the shortest chapter in the book is titled "Why Learn Slovene?"

July 30, 1999
Ljubljana, Slovenia
Hugh and I spent yesterday afternoon in central Ljubljana, and after three and a half hours I was so desperate to spend money I considered taking out insurance. If forced to buy a gift for someone, it would be a toss-up between an American-made notebook with a pony on the cover and a pair of those flesh-colored pads you use to protect your nose from the bridge of your glasses.

By the end of the afternoon all I'd bought were two plums and a pizza that came topped with canned peas, corn, and diced potatoes. These were referred to on the English-language menu they gave us as *vagatbles.* What they meant, I think, was *Macedonian vagatbles.*

July 31, 1999
Ljubljana
Last night at dinner Nancy mentioned a diplomat named Outerbridge Horsey VI. Afterward I complimented Yassa, the housekeeper, on her English. She is perhaps in her late forties, and blushed, saying, "No, I think I am speaking like a Negro."

August 4, 1999
Paris

In Venice I got a haircut at a little place not far from the hotel. The barber spoke no English, and because I'd left my phrase book back in the room, we just nodded to each other, me indicating, I'm guessing, that he should just go wild. The result is a hard, mousy-brown dome that sits on my head like a helmet someone tossed from a few feet away. After leaving, I tried to soften it, but nothing worked, so I had to walk around like that until after dinner. We ate at an out-door restaurant someone had recommended. Beside us sat a family of Germans—a man, his wife, and their daughter, who looked to be around thirty. They were just finishing their meal and had ordered another round of drinks as we arrived. The man lit a cigarette, then, with no apparent shame or self-consciousness, he farted. Ten minutes later he did it again. The table to our other side started laughing and looking our way, thinking that Hugh or I had done it. They were American and while it would have been easy enough to set them straight, it always looks like you're lying when you try to deny it was you who farted.

August 8, 1999
La Bagotière

I got a letter from my father and realized it's only the second one he's ever sent. Regarding my break with French school, he writes, "I do believe that you need to continue your study on a formal, regimented basis. GET WITH IT!!! Having a good command of any language reflects class. Anything else is not cute, it's pathetic." He then suggests that for my next reading in Germany, I switch from my book to the Bible, "vis-à-vis Noah and the ark, and observe the response you get from the audience—ha!" In the next paragraph he tells me that I should read in Athens. "In the old outdoor theater just below the Acropolis, the Herod Atticus Theater built in the second century A.D.!!!"

Because he so rarely writes, I'd never known he was the type to use exclamation marks.

September 21, 1999
Paris

To celebrate my six months without a drink, we went with Ronnie to Le Parc aux Cerfs. A Scottish woman sat at the next table and in time joined our conversation. She was, we learned, a psychologist, in town for some sort of training session. I wouldn't describe her as drunk, but she seemed at least tipsy and said a lot of strange things. She asked Hugh, for instance, if I was wonderful to love, which isn't a question you'd expect from a stranger, or from anyone, really.

September 24, 1999
Paris

Ronnie was tired so after dropping her at the apartment to take a nap, I walked to La Maison du Chocolat to buy a gift for the Gs. The shop wasn't crowded and the saleswomen acted as though they remembered me. Afterward, proud of the day's French and just generally pleased with myself, I crossed the street to the Métro station and experienced one of those moments of extreme joy, the kind that result from something small and make you grateful that you never committed suicide. And it was just then that a gnat flew into my eye, a big one. I tried looking into the window of a parked car, hoping I could spot it, but the reflection wasn't strong enough. Near me, two teenage girls stood on the sidewalk selling cigarette lighters to raise money for a class trip. They doubled as can openers, but still, lighters! You'd never find kids doing that in America. Instead, they'd have to sell things like candy bars.

I told one of the girls I had something in my eye and she opened her purse and held up a small hand mirror. I bunched up my sleeve and eventually caught the gnat on the wet, wadded-up tip of it. It was so sweet of her to hold up the mirror. I bought a lighter for much more than its asking price, and she told me I was *très gentil*.

October 3, 1999
Paris
A year ago I would have begged Hugh to accompany me to the hardware store, but now I go on my own. On the first of yesterday's two trips I said to the clerk, in French, "Hello. Sometimes my clothes are wrinkled. I bought a machine anti-wrinkle, and now I search a table. Have you such a table?"

The fellow said, "An ironing board?"

"Exactly!"

A few hours later I returned. "Hello. Sometimes I drink tea in a hotel. I now search the little thing, a stick to make boiling water." He taught me the word for "heating element," but I've since forgotten it. The one I bought came in a little carrying case and will hopefully last longer than the one I got last spring in Germany.

October 4, 1999
Zurich, Switzerland
Last night after the reading, Gerd and Tini took me to dinner at Kronenhalle, where we were seated beneath the Picasso. I ordered the Wiener schnitzel, which was huge. The waiter served me half of it, and when I was ready for the other half, he heated it up on the traveling stove he'd parked beside the table. The Swiss Tom Jones was eating a few feet away,

having just returned from what our waiter called "a beauty center." He was in his late sixties with a tan, a face-lift, and hair implants. His date was in her twenties, which, I was told, is nothing new.

While eating, I learned that under German law, Gerd is forbidden to continue selling my book under its current title, *Nackt*. It's been used before, apparently, and the author of the earlier book is suing the publishing house for 40,000 marks, which is interesting. In the United States I could call my book *Gone with the Wind* if I felt like it, but not here. Thus we're changing the title to *David Sedaris's Nackt*. So there.

October 8, 1999
Regensburg

The movie *Groundhog Day* was released in Germany with the title *Eternally Weeps the Groundhog*. That is so beautiful.

October 9, 1999
Paris

Yesterday in Düsseldorf, Harry told me the following joke: Aliens land on earth and cut open the head of a German, finding inside a dense network of circuits and chips. It's all too complicated so they close up the German and open the head of an Austrian, which is much simpler and houses nothing but a thin wire running from one side of the skull to the other. They snip it, and the Austrian's ears fall off.

He's alarmingly forthright, Harry. Over lunch I asked what he did with his morning. "First, I took a shit," he said. "Then I inserted a rectal suppository for my hemorrhoids, and then I made some phone calls in the nude."

While he was doing all that, I had gone downstairs into what I thought was the breakfast room of the hotel. It was different from the others I'd been in this week. Instead of many tables, there was just one long one, and the five people seated around it were casually dressed, some still in their robes. They made a little commotion as I entered and took a seat. "Just coffee for me, thank you," I sang.

The oldest of the five, a man in his fifties, said something in German, and when I told him that I didn't understand, he left the room and returned with a teenage girl who explained to me that the dining room was one floor down. I was, it seemed, in the kitchen of the hotel owner.

October 12, 1999
New York

Before leaving Paris, I passed the Greek man who lives across the hall, and for the second time this week he said, *"Bonsoir, madame."* The first time he said it I assumed that I'd misunderstood him, but apparently I hadn't.

October 18, 1999
Pittsburgh, Pennsylvania

Before leaving Boston I went to Tiffany's place in Somerville. The apartment was all right the last time I was there, but now it looks abandoned, like the occupant took a few of the larger pieces of furniture and left the rest behind. It was filthy, junk stacked everywhere, cigarettes ground out into the floor. It would take a solid week to clean it and still it would have looked like a dump. Sections of wallpaper were torn off, and areas are painted in different colors—a patch of blue, some yellow. As I was leaving she told me they'd found some cancer in her uterus, and that she'd soon be going in for surgery. She made it sound like a minor inconvenience, something hardly worth mentioning.

October 22, 1999
Nashville

At the book signing after last night's show I met a woman named Franda, a blending of her parents' names, Francis and Brenda.

October 24, 1999
Davis, California

Politely ask Paul not to do something, and he ramps it up to previously unimagined heights. One of Amy's pet peeves is change on her floor. She said something about it when Paul came to visit, and before he left he scattered $20 worth of pennies, dimes, and nickels throughout her apartment. To top it off, he coated all her doorknobs with toothpaste and peed a little on her bed.

October 25, 1999
Seattle, Washington

A volunteer picked me up at my hotel and drove me to the Sacramento airport. She was plump and gray-haired, in her sixties, I guessed, and she smelled of shampoo. Her husband had died a few years ago and she moved to town to be closer to her daughter, who is adopted and in a wheelchair. The woman started telling me about the disease her daughter has when we came upon tens of thousands of tomatoes scattered across the road. "Farm-truck accident," she said, then got back to her earlier topic. The woman enjoyed talking, and I enjoyed listening to her. Everything was great until we reached the airport, which had recently been remodeled. After circling twice, she stopped in front of terminal A. There were signs out front for American and United but not for Alaska Air, which is what I was scheduled to fly on. "I'm not sure we're in the right place," I told her.

At this she sighed and popped the trunk. "Listen," she said, sounding suddenly weary. "Lots of airlines go to Seattle. I'm sure you'll find something."

She said it as if I go from city to city and just buy my tickets at the counter.

Here I'd listened to all these stories, and this was how she was leaving me? After she drove off, I asked a skycap where I might find Alaska Air. "See that flag?" he asked, pointing off into the distance.

I did. It was the same size it is on a stamp. That's how far away it was.

"Alaska Air is two buildings beyond it," the skycap said.

I cursed the woman as I walked to the distant terminal with my heavy suitcase, and I cursed her again in the long, unmoving line I joined upon my arrival. For good measure, I even cursed her adopted daughter, the one in the wheelchair with an incurable disease.

October 26, 1999
Ashland, Oregon

In Seattle I moved the sofa in my room in order to unplug a floor lamp and found half a joint lying on the carpet. A year ago I would have smoked it. Pot is still incredibly tempting to me, but I quit it when I quit drinking. Otherwise what's the point? I smelled the joint I found beneath the sofa. I examined it, and then I put it back for someone else to find.

November 6, 1999
San Diego, California

You can walk across the border from the United States into Mexico, but coming back you have to state your citizenship and show papers if you're not an American. Abe and I parked in San Diego and the moment we crossed into Tijuana we were swarmed by children holding cups. They didn't hold them the way most beggars do, as if they were full. Rather they held them sideways, as if they were pouring something out. As we walked down the street everyone called out to us. "You want titty? You want pussy?" "I got pussy, eighteen, nineteen, twenty years old. Tell me what you want." "Taxi?" "Hey, dog, check it out." "You want to party?" "Hey, guys, before you get drunk, check this out!"

Lining the sidewalks were countless prostitutes, young women, mainly, wearing cheap, unflattering miniskirts. All of them had the same mid-1980s hairstyle, the bangs trained in an arc over their foreheads while the backs and sides fell to their shoulders. Their tops had shoulder pads and their shoes broke my heart. They smiled as we passed, but the men did all the talking. "You want pussy?" I guess you'd go to a hotel or something.

On our way to dinner, Abe stopped at a fruit and vegetable stand for a snack. Everything on offer was rotten. It stank, but the guy behind the counter was very friendly. We went into a cathedral that was lit with fluorescent tubes. The floor was covered in linoleum and in one of the little alcoves I could feel the heat from a hundred burning candles. I'd never noticed that candles give off heat, perhaps because I'm not a Catholic.

November 17, 1999
Paris
I went to get my trousers hemmed by the Turkish woman on the rue Monge.

> Me: Hello. I bought two pairs of pants and they are too
>   long.
> Her: You need to grow.

Me: Ha-ha. It is too late for that.
Her: Do you want to try them on?
Me: Yes, please. Why not!

I went into the changing nook and took my pants off. The woman was using a steamer and every time she turned it on, a gust of hot air parted the curtains, exposing me in my underwear.

Me: Oops. Oops. Oops.

November 24, 1999
Paris
You never know when someone might tell you he believes in angels. "Oh, they do too exist," he'll say. "I've seen them!"

People might be more sensible in France, but back in the States I hear it all the time. Someone will claim to live with angels. They swear there's one in the backseat of their car. If you see devils, they lock you up, but in America, if you see angels, they put you on morning TV.

2000

January 8, 2000
Paris

In the mail came two issues of a gay-lifestyle magazine its founder is hoping I might contribute to. It's not my kind of thing, but I got a kick out of the letters to the editor, which are startling when you substitute the word *white* for *gay*.

> *Dear Hero,*
>
> *I am a white man living in Kansas and your hot magazine came as such a relief. Finally a publication for people who are proud to be white, and want to know what other white people are up to. It's nice to know that I am not alone. White people have come a long way, but we've got a lot farther to go. There's no white pride parade in my town, but in the meantime I'll keep my fingers crossed, and continue reading your great white magazine!*

February 22, 2000
Paris

Last night I watched a bleak Luis Buñuel documentary called *Land Without Bread*. Made in 1932, it focused on a remote Spanish village somewhere in the mountains. They showed a traditional wedding where the groom rode a horse and was instructed to snatch the head off a live rooster that hung up-side down suspended by a rope. Most everyone in the movie was barefoot and slept in their clothes. Families lived in one room and earned what little money they had by selling honey made by hateful bees that stung a donkey to death. It showed a mountain goat losing its footing and fatally tumbling down a cliff.

I wished I could go back in time and give these people shoes and beds and sackfuls of rice.

February 23, 2000
Paris
Last night for the first time in three or four years, I opened my mouth in front of the mirror. The advantage of keeping it shut was that my teeth looked however I wanted them to. I knew they were messed up. I just wasn't prepared for all the gaps. According to my new French dentist, my bottom teeth have shifted and pushed the ones on top out of alignment. When I opened my mouth in front of the mirror, I discovered that I look like a donkey. I look like a jack-o'-lantern, like a poster child for orthodontia. Color-wise they're not as dingy as I ex-pected, so that's some consolation.

If I look out the window near the dining-room table I can see a wheelchair chained to the fence that separates the courtyard from the neighboring building.

February 24, 2000
Paris
Last night the BBC aired a program on a proposed bill that would end sexual discrimination. I came in as the reporter was interviewing a member of an exclusive men's club where the sign on the front door read NO DOGS OR WOMEN.

"Well," the man said. "It's inconvenient, but these things happen. For example, I just came from a restaurant that had a ban on cellular phones!"

March 9, 2000
Paris
Last night at nine I was in a theater at Les Halles watching *The Talented Mr. Ripley* and this morning at nine I was lying on a hospital gurney with an IV in my arm. At eight a.m. I was fine and then, wham, a kidney stone. Hugh is in Normandy, so I had to find a hospital on my own. I used the phone book, and after deciding which one to go to, I looked in the dictionary. I always referred to a kidney as a *rognon*, but it turns out that's an animal kidney. A human one is *le rein*. I'd also been using the word for *rock* rather than *stone*, though in this case, I just say *calcul*.

While riding the Métro I gave serious thought to passing out, or at least pretending to. People would have come to my aid. I'd have been taken care of. With this much pain, though, I couldn't possibly have faked being unconscious.

The drugs they gave me at the hospital were delicious and served in an IV. The effect was immediate, like turning off a spigot. I haven't been fucked up since I quit drinking. For the past 353 days, I've been the same from the moment I wake up until I go to bed. The IV made me remember why I so love drugs. It also reminded me that when I'm on drugs, I only want more.

March 15, 2000
Paris
Hugh returned from New York with a present. I'd hoped for a carton of cigarettes, but instead it's an iMac computer, the kind that Amy has, but blue instead of orange. I tried to be

grateful but am actually having a hard time working up much enthusiasm. It seems inevitable that everyone eventually will have a computer, but I'd hoped to put it off as long as possible. Hugh taught me to turn the thing off and on, but that's enough of a lesson for today.

March 24, 2000
Paris
Hugh and I went to dinner with my French agent Michelle Lapautre, her husband, René, and Mavis Gallant, whom I met last fall through Steven. I didn't expect her to remember me, but she did. She even remembered what we'd talked about. At one point she asked about Hugh's mother and her relationship with the man she came to Paris with a few years back, the one who was happy just to sit in his hotel room and watch CNN. "He sounded dreadful," Mavis said. "Oh, I just *hate* people like that. Skip ahead and tell me how she finally got rid of him. Did she write him a letter? Did she say it to his face? Tell!"

March 25, 2000
Paris
Hugh printed out my French medical story. I don't like the way the pages look, but I suppose I'll get used to them, just as I'm adapting to the laptop he bought me. It's so different. On a typewriter, when you run out of things to say, you get up and clean the bathtub. On a computer, you scroll down your list of fonts or make little boxes. It scares me to say it, but I think I'm going to miss my laptop while I'm away. Suddenly I can see what everyone's been talking about for the past fifteen years.

March 26, 2000
New York

On the plane from Paris I heard a man say, "The first thing I'm going to do when I get home is order a Big Gulp. I'm going to supersize everything!" He said he'd been thirsty the entire time he was in Paris, and though I'd never thought about it, if you're used to carrying a trash-can-size cup filled with crushed ice and soda, I suppose it would be hard to spend a few weeks in Europe.

March 30, 2000
New York

I met Ken Simon for lunch. Putnam is located in the Saatchi building, and while he finished making a phone call, I waited in the reception area. Three Mexicans came in while I was seated there, each of them holding a large platter of food. A young woman was paged, and a few minutes later she approached the three, saying, "Did you guys bring the extra tuna salad?"

She spoke very quickly and I could tell by the Mexicans' faces that they had no idea what she was talking about. They wore the same lost, dopey expressions I wear half the time in Paris. It was clear they didn't understand her, and in response the woman spoke faster. "OK, guys, why don't you set up in conference room B."

The men remained where they were, and she interpreted this to mean that they didn't do setups. "Oh, guys, come on, I am super-busy today."

The men didn't seem to realize they were in a publishing house. The highlighted list of *New York Times* bestsellers meant nothing to them, and again I identified completely.

April 6, 2000
Key West

The way I see it, there are at least four separate Key Wests. One consists of people with gum disease who carry parrots on their shoulders. The second is gay; the third is young people with tattoos; and the fourth is made up of tourists. I saw the creepy Key West yesterday afternoon when I walked to the end of Duvall Street to buy a correcting ribbon. Every other storefront was an emporium for T-shirts, the worst of them reading:

I Love to Fart in Key West
Spring Fucking Break in Key West
My [Aunt/Grandma/Parents/etc.] Bought Me This
    T-Shirt Because [He/She/They] Love[s] Me
Shut Up and Fish
Farting Is Just My Way of Saying I Love You
Just Do Me
God Created Adam and Eve, Not Adam and Steve
Queen of the Fucking Universe
Bad Dog's Guide to Pussy
Why Go to High School When You Can Go to School
    High
If Assholes Could Fly, This Place Would Be an Airport
I Say No to Drugs but They Don't Listen
Dry Skin? Free Hand Lotion [with an arrow pointing
    down to crotch]
Out of My Mind—Back in Five Minutes
Real Men Don't Need Viagra
I'm Not *a* Bitch, I'm *the* Bitch
The Only Time My Wife Stops Talking Is When Her
    Mother Starts
I Used Up All My Sick Days So I'm Calling in Dead

Shut the Hell Up
Fuck You

April 23, 2000
New York
Amy and I were near her apartment, walking up Charles Street, when we passed two teenagers graffitiing a mailbox. Like everyone I've ever seen tagging public property, they were white and middle class. I don't think black people even do that anymore. They just get blamed for it. One of the boys said hello and when I scowled, he followed with "Do you dis-approve? Well, you can just suck my dick."

I didn't respond, and for the rest of the evening it bothered me. I doubt I could have said anything that would have stopped them, but still, I wish I'd tried. Then I wish I'd shot them.

April 29, 2000
Paris
This evening at dinner I watched an aggressive American cou-ple tell a group of French people to put out their cigarettes. Occasionally, when tourists ask for the nonsmoking section, the waiter will remove the ashtray from their table and say, "Voilà!"

Tonight the waiter simply shrugged, so it was up to the Americans to clear the air themselves. To make things just that much more insulting, they ordered their neighbors around in English, saying, "We're trying to eat here," and "Don't you know that cigarettes are bad for you?"

Having been driven out of the United States by people like them, it pleased me to watch the American couple disappear into a bank of thick blue smoke. You can't just march into someone else's country and start telling everyone what to do—even the Marines have to practice a little diplomacy.

May 8, 2000
Paris

In 1976 Dawn Erickson taught me that, in order to ensure good luck, you're supposed to say, "Rabbit, rabbit," on the first day of every month. It has to be the very first thing that comes out of your mouth and you have to say it out loud or else it doesn't work. I'd never been particularly superstitious, but ever since she told me, I've made it a point to follow her example. Everything I have can be attributed to "Rabbit, rabbit," including Hugh, who started saying it himself shortly after we met. This is a big help, as he's got a good head for dates and is always the first one to wake up. He says, "Rabbit, rabbit," I repeat it, and then I go back to sleep, confident that I'll be safe for another thirty days. When he's away I'll leave notes on the bed and the medicine-cabinet mirror to remind myself that it's the first. This generally works, but when it doesn't, the doom settles in and I spend the next month running after buses and scraping shit off my shoes.

On the thirty-first of March I was in New York, staying with Amy. She has a dwarf rabbit named Tattle Tail that's been trained to use a litter box and roams freely throughout the apartment, happily chewing through the phone and cable-TV wires. Her feeding mat is in the bedroom, surrounded by the dozens of pictures and gewgaws people tend to give you when you own a rabbit. I logically assumed that I had it made on the "Coming Month of Good Luck" front, but when I woke at seven a.m. with Tattle Tail chewing on my eyelashes, my first words were not "Rabbit, rabbit" but "Get the fuck away from me!"

Hence the kidney stone.

May 15, 2000
Paris

I called Lisa last night. Bob picked up too and I talked to both of them until it was time for his pies to come out of the oven. After he got off the line, Lisa told me that the previous day she'd accidentally put a used Kotex through the wash. It went through the dryer as well, and when it came out, Bob held it up, saying, "These aren't supposed to be laundered on their own, are they?"

Lisa said she guessed not, and Bob asked why she'd washed just one of them. "I looked for the other and couldn't find it anywhere."

"The other?" Lisa said.

"Shoulder pad," Bob said. "Isn't that what we've been talking about?"

He handed her the fluffy clean Kotex, still warm, and she put it in her dresser drawer until he left the room. Then she transferred it to the garbage can.

June 7, 2000
Raleigh

Last night I wore my Stadium Pal and learned that unless you're lying helpless on a hospital bed, you really don't want anything to do with an external catheter. The advice on pulling back the pubic hair should appear in large print, and it's best to first test the sealing adhesive on something less sensitive than a human penis. I'm not sure I can describe the pain of removing this thing. I only know that, when I finally threw it into the garbage can, the condom part was lined with several layers of what used to be my skin. Then there was the bag, which closes with a valve that has to be shaken after it's emptied, just like a penis, the result being that I got urine on my socks and the cuffs of my trousers.

Another drawback is that the Stadium Pal stinks. At a football game there might be other odors to cover it up, but in a hot bookstore there's nothing but the scent of paper, which just isn't enough. I won't wear it again tonight but will give it another try later this week. It's nice to be able to pee in your pants, but nothing's worth the agony of peeling this thing off at the end of the night.

June 15, 2000
La Jolla, California

I was met at the airport by a media escort named Patty, who is fifty-two and could easily pass for a guy trying to pass himself off as a woman. The mannishness comes from her sloppy use of base makeup—that and her hair and, well, her posture. Patty smokes cigarettes, drinks, and rolled up the dope she found last year lying on the ground at a baseball stadium. She has eight cats and lives with a roommate who attracts snakes with the compost heap she keeps in the backyard. "There's a reason they make belts and wallets out of those things," she said. "They're tough as shit. You ever try to decapitate a rattler with a shovel?"

Patty sells real estate on the side and is constantly being sued over nothing. Last year a client with a history of screwing people over caught her toe on a carpet nail and tried to collect $200,000. "Can you beat that!" she said.

Realtors can no longer advertise that a house is located within walking distance of a school—it's unfair to childless couples. *Family room* offends the singles, and *master bedroom* smacks of slavery. She's a great storyteller and I enjoyed hearing about the twenty years she spent tending bar, her two marriages, and her run-ins with people who won't allow her to smoke. What luck to have an escort

414

who'll discuss her drug use. I'm enchanted. Patty goes to sixty baseball games per year.

June 28, 2000
Boston

The best thing about Boston is Sally Carpenter. No media escort has ever made me laugh as hard as she does. We drove to Somerville yesterday afternoon and went out to lunch with Tiffany. She had recently made the mistake of going to Walden Pond with a younger woman, and Sally said, "Oh, you should never wear a bathing suit around anyone who's still in her twenties. My last vacation was to Sanibel Island, where everyone was in their nineties. At first I thought they were all looking for shells and then I realized that they were stooped over due to osteoporosis! God, it was marvelous."

July 8, 2000
La Bagotière

It took most of the day to rewrite and cut my new story so I went on my afternoon walk armed with two pages of the simplest words I could find: *ruiner*—"to ruin"; *flatter*—"to flatter." The night before, Hugh quizzed me, demanding that I use two or three words together in a sentence: "The complainer crawled to the information desk." "Does the lesbian bother you?" It was a good format and I had to surrender only twice. I've got two self-improvement campaigns going on at the same time, and luckily they seem compatible. While walking I learn new words, and while riding my bike I talk to myself in French, often pretending that I'm on one of those rapid-fire issue shows that seem to run for hours on end.

Last night David (Rakoff) was playing down his skill as a reporter, imitating himself in an imaginary interview. "Yes, so you hid Jews in your attic?" he said. "So tell me, where did you keep all of your stuff?"

July 9, 2000
Paris

Last night after dinner, David and I returned to the Hôtel Costes to have a drink in the lobby. He's writing about the fashion shows and thought it might be a good idea to listen in on a few conversations. The bar, or series of bars, encircles the courtyard restaurant, and passing from one area to the next, I realized that I'd never seen such a good-looking group of people in my life. There were no exceptions. As David said, the place made the recent Prada and Gucci ads seem like documentary footage. This was a gene-pool convention, an ark of beauty. I felt ugly and uncomfortable, so we ran over to the Tuileries and shot pellet rifles, pretending the balloons were our own physical flaws. I won a dart gun and a deck of cards. David won a model airplane and then we walked around for a while. I got to come home, but David had to return to the hotel and pass through the lobby.

July 13, 2000
Paris

All week David's been imitating an Englishwoman who's one of the editors of *Harper's Bazaar*. I haven't met her, but it's a moneyed, self-satisfied accent that sounds pretty good to me. Every day he memorizes another perfect bit of dialogue that I force him to do over and over. Yesterday's went something like this: " 'So of course again last year Yves offered me something from the collection. He thought I might like the wedding dress, but I much preferred the smo-king, which was brilliant. I mean, the line! It was like this!' She holds out her hands and moves them up and down as though she were running them along the sides of my office trash can. 'And I remember saying to Jean Paul—whom I adore because my husband's name is Jean Paul—I said, "A cut like this could support an army, couldn't it?"'"

What makes the stories so funny is that they lead to nothing. The cut "could support an army." What does that even mean?

July 14, 2000
Paris

Yesterday afternoon Rakoff and I had lunch at Le Petit Saint Benoit. It was his first time, and my last. Once, with Steven, they were nice, but on every other occasion I've felt rushed and bullied by the staff. Yesterday we were waited on by a black-haired woman in her thirties who blamed Rakoff when the table she was yanking caught on the edge of her shoe. We were seated against the wall, meaning that when we eventually left, we had to inconvenience a total of seven other people. They really pack them in there and when the place is full you feel as if you're eating on a plane. The bill came to 185 francs, and when Rakoff placed 205 francs on the tray, the waitress had a fit, insisting that he'd overpaid.

"The extra," he said, "the extra is...well, it's for you." He had to apologize for leaving a tip and basically beg to be forgiven.

August 9, 2000
La Bagotière

I called Dad last night and he said, "If you're riding a bike I'm hoping it has a big, wide seat, otherwise you'll get testicular cancer like that Lance Armstrong." I said I wouldn't be riding a hundred miles a day for the next twenty years, and he told me it didn't matter. "I want you to go out tomorrow and get yourself a nice big seat, damn it, and while you're at it, you should have your prostate checked."

He said it as if the bike shop employed a full-time oncologist. We talked for about forty minutes and toward the end he launched into his Vote Republican speech. "Don't pull a fast one and pretend that you know anything, because you don't. You don't have a clue about what's going on in this country, so just do me a favor and vote for Bush."

Dad says Al Gore will tax his estate 55 percent and leave us with nothing. He refuses to die during a Democratic administration. It's a point of principle. He asked about this and that and when I told him my book had been number two on the *New York Times* list he said, "Well, it's nowhere near that now. I think on the *Wall Street Journal* list it's either a nine or a ten."

I think I hurt his feelings with this book. Every time it's mentioned he changes the subject and talks about the Republicans.

August 10, 2000
La Bagotière

I started on the new play, knowing that what I've written will probably be thrown out by next week. Whenever I have nothing to say, I wind up with two characters talking over one another. Last night I was thinking about how I've always liked the supportive dialogue in *Death of a Salesman*. Biff says he'll go into the sporting-goods business and his father interrupts and says, "Sporting goods! You'll knock 'em dead," or something along those lines. Every time Biff starts a sentence, his father interrupts to encourage him, and the effect is pathetic.

August 12, 2000
La Bagotière
It's scary, but when riding my bike I tend to think of all the people who are too lazy to exercise. I've become the exact sort of person I hate. The least amount of effort makes me self-righteous and I decide that everyone else should suffer just as I do. I'd probably be a monster if I ever quit smoking.

August 14, 2000
La Bagotière
Hugh went to Ségrie-Fontaine to see Jocelyn, who heard a rumor that I am retarded. It's being spread by a woman in the village of Taillebois who's seen me "looking at pictures and talking to myself." *"Il n'est pas normal,"* she says.

What she thinks are pictures are actually my index cards, and I'm testing myself on French vocabulary words, not having arguments with the little demons perched on my shoulders. The woman said that I'm not dangerous, which I guess is good. Apparently I'm one of those retarded people who can wander off for a few hours but still manage to find their way back home. "He always says hello," the woman reported. "But still, he isn't normal."

I've been dieting for two weeks now, and while my stomach feels a bit smaller, I seem to have lost the most amount of weight in my forehead. It's tight as can be. I'm guessing the loss is due to the constant mental strain of thinking about food. Yesterday I rode my bike for two hours, winding up a few miles beyond La Forêt-Auvray. They have a nice square in front of the church and I sat down to have a cigarette. A group of English people had just left the restaurant and I listened to them make plans for the following morning. One woman seemed to know her way around better than the others and advised everyone that a trip to Caen would definitely cut into their day. She must have said the phrase "cut into the day" at least a dozen times. It was one of those occasions when it's automatically assumed that you are French, so you can eavesdrop all you want without the speakers growing self-conscious. While on my ride I was passed by numerous cyclists and none of them returned my hello. This is sort of a relief, as it means I won't have to say it anymore.

August 19, 2000
Alghero, Sardinia

My suspicion that the four stars beside the name of the Hotel Carlos V were decorations turned out to be correct. Our room is large, with tile floors, clinical overhead lights, a plastic shower stall, and a little TV bolted to the wall. It's air-conditioned, though, and there's a nice terrace overlooking the good-sized pool and the sea. We went down for breakfast this morning and tried our luck with the hot drinks machine. The milk seems to be an optical illusion. It comes out of the spout but disappears as soon as it makes contact with the coffee. On leaving, we saw the Italians bringing their cups up to the bar—which is apparently what you need to do if you want a real latte.

When Dario drove us into the city of Alghero, Hugh said, "Oh, it looks just like Mogadishu." I haven't been to Mogadishu, so to me it resembles Utah but with a beach. Manuela and Dario are in the next town over, staying at his parents' place. It's a boxy, one-story house set in a grove of olive trees. There's greenery, but it's all sage-colored. I'm used to the walls and hedges in France, and the landscape here strikes me as mean. It's dry and dusty and full of things that can hurt you. Packs of wild German shepherds run around at night. There are lizards and snakes. Even the birds seem to have a chip on their shoulders.

We went to the beach yesterday afternoon with Manuela, and it was packed, wall to wall. The crowd didn't bother me. Rather, I enjoyed being pressed against so many people. The women behind us, all in their fifties with dark, leathery skin, rattled on and I guessed they were trashing somebody. When people speak Italian, I always imagine that they're either gossiping or relating the details of a close race. There were many women in bikinis, but no one was topless. A lot of the men wore tiny swimsuits. The water was warm (*L'acqua era calda*) and you could see to the bottom. I went out beyond the boats with Hugh but got dizzy and nauseated after the first two hundred feet. It's the bobbing up and down that gets me.

We went to the beach at around four thirty and stayed for three hours or so. At the snack bar I practiced my Italian. "Two bottles of water," I said, learning as the man got them that it comes in a box. We'd worked fairly hard on our language lessons before arriving, but now it seems futile. I got to say *la domicilia* and *la firma* this morning while renting my bicycle. It's a ten-speed with normal handlebars and I like it a lot. After paying, Hugh, Dario, and I went to buy a few things at the market. It was noticed that my bike light didn't work and Hugh told me no less than fifteen times that I had to take it back and have the guy fix it.

When he started in for the sixteenth time I said, "OK, you can stop talking now." This doesn't mean "shut up," exactly—well, yes, I guess it does. I went back to the bike shop and used the word *torcia*. The kid was very nice and fixed it so that now the light cannot be turned off. I wanted to say something while he was working, ask a question, make a comment, but I don't know the words for that kind of thing. It made me remember when I first came to France and learned

421

to point out the objects in the room. Still, though, I guess the little bit I know is better than none at all.

August 20, 2000
Alghero

I sat in a lounge chair yesterday afternoon and got a tan on my forehead. Today I'll try to get one on my back and chest. I'm the color of a French chicken and really stand out here. The people surrounding the pool are impossibly brown. They arrive in the morning and roast until six at night, pausing every now and then to bob around in the water. I haven't seen anyone use sunscreen. Neither have I seen anyone with a burn. I guess it's their skin. What little tan I get will start to peel within a few days, so the only souvenir of my vacation will be the scrapes and bruises I sustained during last night's bike accident.

According to the *Herald Tribune,* millions of Italians returned from their vacations yesterday. Alghero seemed a little less full this afternoon, but it was by no means empty. It was my job to find a place for lunch, so after riding around for a while I settled on a restaurant called Mazzini. It wasn't fancy. In the corner a TV played dubbed American soap operas. People always complain that the French are rude, but I've found the Italians to be much colder than Parisians. The hotel desk clerks are nice, but in the stores and cafés, they've all been blustery.

Our waitress acted as though we'd singled her out for some terrible punishment, but then we noticed that she treated everyone the same way. She was maybe twenty years old, pretty. At the next table a group of three workingmen attacked huge plates of spaghetti and mussels, followed by big cuts of grilled meat. I ordered a seafood antipasto followed by what I thought was spaghetti and octopus. *Pulpa* sounds to me like it ought to be an octopus. I think the waitress made a mistake, as what I received was a plate of red-sauced spaghetti heaped with crabs. They were small—the size of a fifty-cent piece—and each one had been hacked in two. One normally doesn't eat the entire crab, and besides that, these were hard, with shells. I guessed they'd just been used to flavor the sauce.

Hugh tried picking apart some of the tiny claws, but it was too much effort for the stingy reward. Still, though, it was good. A table full of sailors came in during *The Bold and the Beautiful* and were followed by a young couple whose handholding suggested they might be on vacation. We were the only Americans except for the people on TV.

August 24, 2000
Paris

Yesterday morning Hugh and I watched an Italian man go for a swim with his dog, a yellow Lab with bruised-looking teats. He'd just come out of the water and was standing on the rocks when a second man confronted him and said, I imagine, that animals were forbidden on the beach. The two men argued back and forth, and then the second guy stomped off and returned ten minutes later with a scroll. I'm guessing it was the town charter. He unrolled it, but the first man was unimpressed and the subsequent argument lasted for half an hour. What amazed me was the second guy's tenacity. I'm not sure what reaction he was hoping for, but he seemed determined to get it.

August 29, 2000
La Bagotière

In search of a bicycle, Hugh and I went to Super Sport in

Flers. The store is situated in an ugly industrial park on the outskirts of town. The lighting was harsh and fell on rack after rack of cheap sweatshirts and ugly nylon tracksuits. They didn't have much in the way of bikes and had I been more patient we would have left and visited one of the shops in town. It was Monday, though, and everything else was closed. I wanted something right away, so after trying out a Raleigh five-speed (merchandise is not allowed to leave the store, so I was reduced to tooling up and down the aisles like a bear in the circus), I settled on a Gitane seven-speed with normal handlebars. It wasn't expensive, $300, but leaving the store I felt I'd betrayed the bike I already own. If I'd gotten new tires and brake pads for it, I would have been fine. What are called modernizations on the more recent models seem nothing more than an attempt by the manufacturers to save money. The current fenders and foot pedals are made out of plastic, as are the gear wheels and air pumps. In a fire my new bike would melt into a puddle. It came with a front and rear light, but I don't imagine they'll last long. The seats and handlebars are so easily adjustable that they loosen at the slightest provocation, and I worry I'll have to carry a tool set at all times. The chain came off before I left Flers, and I think it's going to take me a while to master the gears. I don't mean to sound so down on it. I guess I just feel guilty.

The lines at Super Sport were long and slow. Families were buying back-to-school clothes and every few minutes the cashier had to leave her post and answer the ringing telephone behind another register. I had to go to the bathroom, so while Hugh headed home in the car, I rode to a McDonald's located at the far end of the industrial park. I'd occasionally eat at one in Paris, but the second time I was laughed at by the counter help, I stopped going. I guess I'd been saying something wrong, but to my mind, Big Mac is an American term and should be pronounced as such. At the Flers McDonald's, I ordered a filter coffee, which is hard to find in France. It was five o'clock, the place was practically empty, and the girl behind the counter was exceedingly pleasant. They were offering the McDonald's Maxi Best Special: a Royal Cheese, large fries, and the soda of your choice for 37 francs—a little over $5—which would be expensive for the States. Inside the Flers McDonald's, there were local newspapers mounted on bamboo canes.

There were display cases offering a clear view of the latest toys, but there were no ashtrays. In order to smoke, one had to step out onto the playground. A family sat on the far end of the slide, both the parents and the teenagers puffing away. I'd been there for a few minutes when the counter girl ran out with their orders. In America you'd have to stand by the register and wait, but I guess in Flers they're willing to come to you. The family received their Maxi Best Specials and regarded them while they finished their cigarettes. The industrial park emptied and, beyond the fence, cars passed on the way home from work.

This being France, I know I'm supposed to sit in cafés with thimble-size cups of espresso. I'm supposed to return day after day until the owner finally consents to shake my hand and ask how it's going. But I couldn't have been happier than I was at my ugly little McDonald's. It was the coffee I wanted, with no fear that the waiter would ignore me. I paid immediately and didn't have to beg for my check. Plus I got to watch a toddler whiz down a slide onto a carpet of cigarette butts. I'm thinking that I might make that McDonald's my place.

October 8, 2000
Paris
Steven Barclay told me that the building our new apartment is in was the original site of Sylvia Beach's Shakespeare and Company bookstore. Hugh looked it up on his computer and found pictures of her and various literary celebrities standing before what is now the ground-floor hair salon. I've never been terribly interested in that crowd, but still it's impressive that James Joyce stood drunk and probably peed in our stairway. Hugh is thinking we can exploit our location and make money renting out our apartment under the name Finnegans Sleep.

October 12, 2000
New York
The general agreement is that I've lost too much weight. For me, the process has been gradual, but for those I haven't seen in a while, the change is drastic. People who hadn't been told about my diet probably imagine that I have either AIDS or cancer—which is a pretty good definition of bad weight loss. Andy couldn't bring himself to look me in the eye. It's as if I've had a disfiguring accident and everyone's trying to pretend they don't notice it. It's not the reaction I'd expected at all.

I went to Little, Brown and talked to H., who filled me in on the new Kevyn Aucoin book. The other night, just before his appearance at Barnes and Noble, he called saying he'd need a bodyguard. He's not snippy but says these things in all sincerity. He needed the bodyguard in case the NRA decided to retaliate for a remark he'd made in a *Time Out* interview. To him it made perfect sense that the National Rifle Association might send a hit man to kill Cher's makeup artist;

his political views are too extreme and sooner or later the Republicans will have to silence him. H. denied the request for a bodyguard, so Kevyn hired his own. He's going next week to his hometown in Louisiana and called to demand that Little, Brown arrange to award him the keys to the city. The keys to the city don't really count if you have to ask for them yourself, but H. went ahead and wrote to the mayor. Last night Kevyn was supposed to be at Bendel's from five to nine and decided to show up at around eight. I love hearing about this guy.

October 16, 2000
Philadelphia

There's a scale in the hotel bathroom and I found out that I weigh 131 pounds. The last time I weighed in, I was 157, but that was before moving to France; 131 is too low. It's a weakling's weight. I'd like to get up to 140 but still have a flat stomach and a thirty-inch waist. Is that possible?

October 20, 2000
Springfield, Missouri

Springfield has got to be the most depressing city in the United States. The trip from the airport to the hotel was hideous, and things didn't improve much between here and Hammons Hall. The land is flat and covered with failed strip malls and chain stores surrounded by empty parking lots. From my window I can see a Big Kmart (aren't they all big?), a Walmart, an ALDI, an AutoZone, a Donut Connection, a Master Wang's Chinese restaurant, a Western Sizzlin', and a Git 'n' Go. Most towns have such a strip, but here even the McDonald's is failing to thrive. You get the idea people would leave if they could only sell their houses and summon up the energy to pack.

Branson, Missouri, is forty-five miles to the south, and the fact is heavily advertised. It's aspiring to be the new country-music capital, and the Springfield roads are hugged by billboards for the Osmond Family Theater, the Grand Mansion, the Grand Palace, Bonniebrook Park, Shepherd of the Hills Outdoor Christian Theater, the Dixie Stampede, and the Dewey Short Visitors Center. I've chosen to take my few days off in Chicago but actually wouldn't have minded going to Branson to see one of the two musicals based on the life of Jesus. I could then see Andy Williams and Jeff Foxworthy at the Grand Palace and eat dinner at Buckingham's Restaurant and Oasis. Then again...

On Wednesday my watch broke, so yesterday I went across the street to the saddest mall in America. Half the stores were shuttered up and the fountain had been drained. The food court was gone except for a place called Granny's Fudgery, a wooden cart surrounded by card tables. I imagine the mall started going downhill when it accepted Walmart as a tenant. Anything you could find at Bill's Card Shop and the Record Bin could also be found there, where a customer could pay less and buy everything in one shot. I'd been to only one Walmart in my life before this and I was shocked at how ugly it was, even by American standards. It was a mammoth jumble of absolute shit made more chaotic by brightly colored signs and promotional displays. Yesterday's Walmart was even worse than the first, but the employees were incredibly friendly. Maybe that's normal, but I think my two years in Europe made it seem even stranger. You'd never get that kind of treatment at Leclerc or any of the other French superstores.

The woman at the jewelry counter replaced my battery and seemed genuinely concerned when the watch still failed to work. "What can we do?" she said. "Did you buy this here or at another Walmart? Maybe we can get you a refund."

It seemed strange of her to suppose I'd bought my watch at a Walmart, but I imagine her assumptions are most often correct. It's a hideous place, but the people are really nice, even the customers. I also bought a folder, some eucalyptus throat drops, and a cold medication called Zicam that had been recommended by Megan's father. I sprayed it into my nose and it unclogged within seconds.

For one reason or another I was flown first class from Cleveland to St. Louis and then on to Springfield. I'd never really cared about first class, but yesterday, because I was sick, I really enjoyed it. It was nice to be in a big comfortable seat and have the row all to myself. The stewardess started serving me as soon as I boarded and I received tea in a real cup. Passengers on the way to coach looked me up and down and made little comments such as "I guess I ought to continue on to the poor people's section."

On the first leg, there were five of us in first class. On the second flight, there were four, including a tall man wearing a brown suit and cowboy boots. The plane took off and shortly afterward I turned to find him clipping his toenails. It wasn't a quick effort but a virtual pedicure, followed by fifteen minutes with an emery board and a vigorous buffing session. He spent the entire flight this way, and by the time we landed, the carpet at his feet was littered with fine dust and nail trimmings.

Because of my cold, my ears stopped up upon landing. It was an odd sensation and I spent my hour and a half layover straining to hear the boarding announcements. It was as if I had a pillow over my head. The St. Louis airport has those glass smoking tanks and the ashtrays are regularly emptied.

October 30, 2000
San Francisco

I couldn't smoke in Bob and Lisa's house, so we set up a sewing table on the deck where I could sit and work. Yesterday morning I got up early and had just finished my first cup of coffee when I realized the door had locked behind me. It was seven thirty and I felt certain that if I waited a few minutes, Bob would come down to let the dog out. Chessie, their border collie, made an appearance at around eight and we regarded one another through the glass door. I hoped that envy might drive her to start barking, but aside from one quick yip, she kept her mouth shut. It was cold but not freezing, and I'd dressed in a sweatshirt and a black jacket Lisa's mother-in-law had sent her the day before.

Operating on the insane hope that maybe the door was set on some kind of timer, I got up from the sewing table and tried to reopen it every few minutes. To the neighbors it must have looked as though I were trying to break in and write about it at the same time, and I worried that one of them might call the police. I waited until around eight thirty and then I jumped off the side of the deck, walked around the house, and rang the front bell. Bob answered in his bathrobe and I was grateful I'd come to stay with him and Lisa. Were it anyone else in my family, they would have ignored the bell, hoping that whoever it was would eventually give up and go away.

November 9, 2000
Greencastle, Indiana

I called Dad last night after dinner. He asked about my visit with Tiffany and I tried to be positive. She was pretty wound up yesterday, but other than that she seemed to be on a fairly even keel. It just troubles me that she can live in such filth.

On several occasions during my visit, she referred to herself as poor, and that depressed me. Most people would say they're broke. That word suggests a temporary setback. *Poor,* on the other hand, conveys a permanence. She sees poverty as romantic and claims to be perfectly happy. Last week she found a frozen turkey in somebody's garbage can. I can see taking it home and using it for target practice, but she took it home and ate it. I hate thinking that someone in my family would eat a turkey found in the garbage.

Tiffany uses overhead lights, not caring how harsh they are. She wakes up and the first thing she does is turn on the TV. Joints are smoked early in the day, and then she gets on the phone and hustles little jobs. On Tuesday she stripped some boards for an odious antiques dealer.

There was talk about getting something full-time, maybe with benefits, but I'm guessing she'll find an excuse to reject it. She's not lazy, Tiffany, but she has a hard time dealing with expectations. Robert came by in the evenings and the two of them sat on the sofa switching from one station to another and talking through everything. I liked Robert. He seems to genuinely care about her and is a good listener.

On Tuesday afternoon she cried while telling me a story she'd recounted a year before. She cries a lot and the episodes generally end with a list of things she's doing for herself. "I get out of bed in the mornings. Do you understand? I get up." The accomplishments are tiny, but I guess they're all she's got.

November 10, 2000
Chicago
Televisions at the Indianapolis airport showed that Bush was ahead by 210 votes, with one district left to recount. Who ever thought the presidential election would come down to

the number of people you'd find in a movie theater? It might be resolved tonight, but I doubt it.

I liked the Star Market in Somerville and was surprised that Tiffany goes instead to the corner store in her neighborhood, which is much more expensive. Even a coffeepot would save her money, but instead she makes it by the cup. I always thought that Dad would be good at teaching low-income people how to grocery shop. He's smart with coupons and bulk-buying, but when you have no money and are miserable, I guess you can't get too worked up over a ten-pound bag of pinto beans. When I was broke I shopped very carefully, but then again I was never clinically depressed. I keep reflecting on my conversations with Tiffany, and it's frustrating. The slightest hint of criticism sends her over the edge, so I would wind up saying nothing. It's probably for the best, as most people don't really want advice.

November 19, 2000
New York
After landing in Denver, I ran to the smoking lounge, where I saw a woman hotboxing a cigarette while pushing a baby confined to a wheelchair. Bringing ordinary children into the smoking lounge is enough to earn you glares, but a baby in a wheelchair could possibly lead to a lynching. Boy, that took nerve.

December 14, 2000
Paris
Apparently I don't have AIDS. The French bank received my blood test and approved my mortgage, so, though I haven't yet read it on a piece of paper, I'm guessing I'm negative. This is sort of major, as, for the past fifteen years, I've just nat-

urally assumed I was infected. Every time I sweat at night, every time I get a sore or run a fever, I think that it's finally kicked in. It wasn't always at the front of my mind, but it was always there. It sounds goofy, but it's going to take a while for the news to sink in. I'm not disappointed; I just need to figure out what to do between now and the time I develop cancer.

Sophie and Philippe picked me up in a taxi and we went to a TV station in an ugly suburb. This was for a cable program called *Paris Première* hosted by a handsome anchorman who stood at a desk and read from slips of paper rather than a monitor. I'd been offered the option of speaking in English, but I just went ahead and did it in French.

The segment lasted maybe five minutes and it passed quickly. I then had my makeup removed and watched on the monitors as the host had a fit and yelled at the cameramen. There was something wrong with the placement of an object, and when it happened a second time he got even uglier. It was fun. My seven o'clock interview was canceled, so after the TV appearance Sophie and I went to the office, where I signed thirty books and then walked home.

Apparently the Supreme Court ruled in Bush's favor, so last night Al Gore conceded. I had to call Dad for some information and the conversation got scary when he started talking about the election. He's always been a Republican, but it saddened me when he started quoting Rush Limbaugh and trashing what he called "the liberal mainstream media." It's always the papers' fault. Conservatives tell the truth. Everyone else lies. Dad was foaming at the mouth over how Gore tried to steal the election. "I've been so upset I haven't been able to sleep," he said.

*　　*　　*

Last night Hugh went to dinner with Leslie and paid $130 for a baked potato wrapped in aluminum foil. It came accompanied by a teaspoon of caviar. There was a bowl of borscht and a tiny dessert, but still, the centerpiece was a 35-cent potato. He was shocked by the price and tried to justify it by saying that in the past Leslie had often paid for his dinner. He'd saved money over the years, and now he was spending a little. Yes, but for a potato? "And I got to sit next to Yves Saint Laurent," he said. This still didn't justify $130, and he knew it. Besides, ten minutes after taking his seat, Yves Saint Laurent signaled the waiter and asked to be moved. For the past week, Hugh has been painting for Diane Johnson, and the potato amounted to two days' worth of work.

2001

January 13, 2001
Paris

Yesterday at Shoppi I noticed a black man wearing a crocheted jester's hat and bell-bottom jeans trimmed in lace. The first time I saw him, he was looking at fish and pushing a baby carriage. I dismissed him as a nut, but then I decided he was just a father, maybe a musician. At the fruit and vegetable scales I stepped over to look at the child and saw that it was a doll—white, maybe two feet tall, and dressed in a hooded down jacket. It wasn't a baby but a little girl with matted blond hair that had obviously been washed with soap. Amy and I stood behind the man in line and listened as he held a conversation with her. "Hello," he said, and then, in a higher voice, "I need gloves."

It was, he explained, his daughter talking. "She is cold tonight, but so is everyone."

The man said that he and Michael Jackson were both fathers, and that it was a lot harder than it looked. He kissed the doll on the head and told me that portable phones had improved the world's mood. In the '60s everyone was very serious, but now, due to technology, people were lightening up. The doll complained about the long wait and he comforted her, saying they'd be home soon. The man was buying two whole trout and four cartons of orange juice. He was very nice to the cashier and she was nice back, each of them wishing the other a happy New Year.

I told the story to Manuela last night, and she accused me of making it up. Then I told the story of Chantal's father beating his dog to death with a stick. Hugh was there to back me up, which ultimately made my doll story more credible. Plus I had Amy as an eyewitness.

January 22, 2001
Paris

We had dinner at Peggy's with Armistead and an American painter named Richard. Steven had told me about him, but it didn't register until he mentioned he'd inherited the estate of the surrealist painter Leonor Fini. At one point, the conversation turned to a San Francisco cellist named Dorothy. "Oh, I'd love to go to her house," Peggy said. "She's bald."

I love the way her mind works. Later she told a story about her and her best friend, Flicka, dating a pair of Samoan cousins when they were in their twenties. The guy she went out with was named Ziki Fuapopo, and the story she told involved his mother, a pile of cocaine, and a group of men dressed in lavalavas.

March 21, 2001
New York

It's been two years since I've had a drink. Amy gave me a bathroom scale for an anniversary present, and, without my shoes, I weigh 132. The other day in Greencastle I weighed 144, so I'm figuring one of the scales must be wrong. Hugh will give me a present tonight when he gets home, and maybe this evening I'll have a piece of cake. It's almost best not to mention it, as any celebration of sobriety seems so painfully childlike. "I know, I'll have a tea party and invite all my invisible friends!"

April 10, 2001
San Francisco
After last night's reading, Ronnie, Blair, and I went to dinner with a critical care nurse who's in the process of writing two novels and told me that in 80 percent of all burglaries, the intruder defecates on the bed. If not the bed, he'll shit on the carpet or the dining-room table. It's done as a final *fuck you* to the homeowner but seems like an awful lot of trouble. It's hard enough to use a strange toilet, let alone a mattress or carpet, so why bother? Do the burglars save up or can they just defecate on command? Is this a trick they learned in prison?

April 30, 2001
Paris
On the front door of a restaurant I saw a sign reading DINNERS, LUNCHS, RECEPTIONS.

It's hard to say the word *lunches* with the missing *e: lunchs*.

The city of Paris is continuing last year's ad campaign. The goal is to get people to clean up after their dogs, and the billboards read YOU HAVE GOOD REASON NOT TO PICK UP. HE DOES IT VERY WELL IN YOUR PLACE. One ad pictures a child sitting on the grass and using a cookie cutter on a Great Dane–size pile of shit. Another, my favorite, shows a blind man with six good-size stools speared on his cane. Shit isn't terribly photogenic and the stools come off looking like the grilled sausages served at one of the many Greek restaurants off Saint-Michel.

May 3, 2001
Paris

I had an interview with a German man who writes for the equivalent of the *Ladies' Home Journal*. He was a portly fellow with white teeth and glasses who wore a button-down shirt and a new pair of Levi's. He told me that his sister is clinically depressed and read *Naked* during a month-long visit to a psychiatric hospital. According to him, once she'd finished, she loaned it to a fellow patient, who, in turn, loaned it to someone else. The book seemed to lift people's spirits, and as a result, the hospital has made it recommended reading. I'm not sure whether I believe this, but it's extremely flattering to think my book is being passed around a German asylum.

May 5, 2001
La Bagotière

Until last night we slept on a bed that came with the house and felt as though it had been stuffed with marshmallows. We'd lie down and roll to the middle, where we'd sink to the bottom and wake up feeling like someone had taken to us with a stick. I've been offering to buy a new bed and finally Hugh accepted. We went to Lepage in Flers, an ugly aluminum-sided building filled with equally ugly furniture. Our salesman was a small man with blond hair who invited us upstairs and pointed out the various features of the display models. *"Allez-y,"* he said.

The beds had plastic pads at the feet so that you could test them out without soiling the mattresses. Hugh went from one to another and lay down, looking as though he'd been sent to his room. He eventually chose the hardest, and as we went downstairs to pay, the salesman sussed us out, asking if the two of us looked forward to our good night's sleep.

This was surprising, as it fell under the category of a personal question.

"The two of you" implied that we might be sleeping together, and he said it sneakily. I don't mind a personal question, but Hugh does, and rather than answer, he walked away to inspect a fake-leather footrest that resembled a half-deflated medicine ball. "Yes, well," the salesman said.

The mattress and box spring were on sale and came to $800. A delivery was arranged and as I handed over my credit card, I noticed the salesman's startling BO. It always shocks me when someone smells like that and wears a suit. A deliveryman brought the mattress at five thirty and the two of us spent the evening looking forward to bedtime. Hugh turned in at midnight and had a great night's sleep. I went to bed at one and lay awake for hours, feeling as though I were stretched out on a length of pavement. The mattress is too hard for my taste and I woke up with a sore jaw, having dreamed I'd been hit by a car.

May 12, 2001
Atlantic Beach

When at Dad's house, one drinks coffee from a Rush Limbaugh mug. Walking to the kitchen for a refill involves passing a thank-you card from George Bush and Dick Cheney, who stand embracing each other. Dad wanted me to ride to the beach with him, but I just couldn't. "Why the hell not?" he asked. I looked at his Honda Civic, the seats matted with dog hair and the bumper sticker reading AL GORE IS A RISKY PROPOSITION.

I rode with him as far as Paul's and ducked down low in the seat. He's started driving like an old person, and I worried it might take days to reach the motel. On the ride from his house to Paul's, he never exceeded twenty-five miles per hour.

May 17, 2001
Paris

I received a long, confusing letter from a German woman that begins, "Dear Mr. Sedaris, To be forced expressing myself in English makes me become a daisy! A fatal starting point for me. By the way—I cannot find anything which I could present you as an equal output—I am a petitioner, that's the fact."

I'm not sure what she wants, but she mentions *SantaLand* and *Season's Greetings,* referring to the latter as "a cutting, ambiguous, controversial, subtle text giving us laughing the creeps."

May 27, 2001
La Bagotière

I biked to Flers and was inching past a red light when I heard someone blow their horn behind me. They honked a second and third time, and I turned to find a police car carrying three officers, two up front and one in the back. You see that a lot here, and it always seems strange to me. The driver yelled, "Hey, that light is red," and I got off my bike and moved it onto the sidewalk, pretending he'd said, "Here's that butcher shop you were looking for." I could physically feel the common, stupid expression on my face and I stood there looking in the window at meat until they had passed.

May 30, 2001
Paris

One of yesterday's interviewers brought me a Swiss army knife. She was a small blond woman from Zurich who arrived complaining about the heat. *Complaining* is too strong a word. She commented on it, as did the earlier Swiss interviewer.

Both journalists found Paris to be boring and asked me what I thought of Zurich. I told the second woman that I liked the grocery store at the airport and she said, "Yes, we all go to the airport on Sunday."

And *Paris* is boring?

I'd thought the store was for travelers who wanted to pick up a few things on the way home, but it's actually a way around the Swiss blue laws demanding that shops close from Saturday afternoon until Monday morning. The laws apply everywhere but the airport, so they built a massive supermarket in the Swiss Air terminal. "It's the place to be on a Sunday," the woman said.

I received a letter from an American woman living in Paris who wrote to say she'd read my interview in the *Minneapolis Star Tribune*. "I fully intend to read your book," she said, "as I, too, have hoped to 'Talk Pretty Someday.'" It's always queer when people work a book title into a headline or sentence, especially this book title. She wrote about her two-year-old daughter and their upcoming move and finally got to the point. "My reason for this note is because of your comments on smoking. Because of you and others with similar opinions, people like me cannot eat in Paris restaurants (except McDonald's). I hope you are never the victim of a smoking-related illness or have to care for someone who is—believe me—then 'talking pretty' will not be an option."

There's no return address so she won't be hearing back from me.

June 5, 2001
Cleveland, Ohio

I was met at the airport by Marilyn, a widow who looks to be in her early seventies. It was chilly and she wore a handsome felt coat along with no fewer than fourteen bracelets. Marilyn has a great heap of wild gray hair and wears the sort of heavy-rimmed round-framed glasses favored by architects. When I told her I wanted to arrive at the bookstore an hour early, she shook her head and said she didn't see the need. "I'll get you there fifteen minutes beforehand. That'll give you more than enough time."

I've never appeared in a Cleveland bookstore and had no idea what to expect, so I said fine. We arrived at Joseph-Beth at six forty-five. Pulling into the crowded parking lot, Marilyn suggested that someone in the surrounding neighborhood must be having a party. "They do that sometimes and park here illegally."

We walked into the store and she put her hand to her face, saying, "Goodness, they must be having a sale." Susan, the manager, counted four hundred people in the audience. I signed for twenty minutes beforehand and three hours afterward, and when I was done the managers gave me a T-shirt. On the way back to the hotel, Marilyn said it was nice that so many people just happened to be in the store.

June 10, 2001
Chicago

I'm still not sold on the bow tie and have been asking people for their opinions on it. "What do you say, yes or no?"

I'd worried it suggested a wacky uncle and felt comforted when a woman at Borders said it made me look like a shy scholar. This carried me through to Barbara's, where a young man defined it as "the pierced eyebrow of the Re-

442

publican Party." This should probably put an end to it once and for all.

June 12, 2001
Iowa City

The best thing to be said about the Iowa City Sheraton is that it's connected to a fast-food concern called T. J. Cinnamons. In my room, there are hairs and flecks of shit clinging to the inside of the toilet bowl, the tub still hasn't drained from last night's bath, and even the complimentary pen is broken. The room-service coffee is served with nondairy creamer, the furniture is stained, and the closet has only one coat hanger in it. Yesterday afternoon the outside temperature reached one hundred degrees. I'm guessing it was also one hundred in the lobby and hotel restaurant, which were both without air-conditioning. All in all, it's the most depressing hotel since the Holiday Inn in Portland, Maine.

June 13, 2001
San Francisco

On the way to the bookstore I asked Frank, the escort, what he thought of my bow tie. He hesitated for a moment and then said, "A bow tie tells the world that the person wearing it can no longer get an erection."

June 25, 2001
Paris

While I was gone Hugh, Manuela, and Dario attended Franck's surprise fortieth-birthday party. One of the guests was a sophisticated mother of three who announced that she hated the zoo at the Jardin des Plantes because it was cruel to keep the animals in such small cages. She went on and on and then, at the end of the evening, she unlocked her car and released her golden retriever, who'd spent the last six hours in the trunk.

July 13, 2001
Tübingen, Germany

This is my new favorite German city, and it's nice because I really didn't expect it. It's a college town, but the old center is remarkable, crammed with steep-roofed buildings and intersected by a network of streams. Living here would undoubtedly get dull, but it's beautiful to look at. We arrived yesterday afternoon. It was a three-hour ride involving two separate trains and a change in Stuttgart. On our first train we sat in a smoking compartment and reviewed our evening in Nuremberg. "That couple last night were really trampling on my nerves," Tini said. I just love her English. It's not as grammatically correct as Gert's, but I find it infinitely more charming.

On the way to Tübingen we passed a smokestack with the word *dick* written on it.

July 16, 2001
Paris

While eating, Tini discussed her friends' upcoming move to New York. They're a pair of reporters going from Hamburg to West 68th Street. Hugh said the move will be difficult, especially if they smoke, and Tini said, "No, they have finished their smoking." She said it as though when born, they'd been allotted a certain number of cigarettes. They'd depleted their supply and now it's all behind them. Later she made a reference to the restaurant's delicious smashed potatoes.

I called Lisa last night. She's been getting a lot of compliments on her garden and when she mentioned this to Dad, he said that Gretchen too had been spending a lot of time in the yard. Lisa said that Gretchen's garden was mainly wildflowers and Dad said, "Yes, well, you're you, and Gretchen is extremely creative." She told him that I was number one on the *New York Times* list and he said, "Well, he sure isn't number one in the *Wall Street Journal*."

July 21, 2001
La Bagotière

We rode first class from Paris to Briouze, and while it was nothing special, I worry there's no turning back. On the bigger trains it makes a difference, but on the tiny locals an upgraded ticket doesn't get you much of anything. The car's a little less crowded, but that's about it. I sat on the aisle and looked across the way at one of the ugliest men I've seen in a long time. He was a short guy, bearded, and his acne-scarred face was crosshatched with deep creases. It was the sort of face you might find in a Western. He got off in Dreux and was replaced by an elderly gentleman in a three-piece suit.

In first class, you count on your fellow passengers to make you feel good about yourself. You're supposed to look around with pride, telling yourself that these are your kind of people. The gentleman made me feel good about being in first class, while the prospector had depressed me. Then I got depressed thinking that I was probably depressing the gentleman in the suit. Then I stepped out of the first-class car and got dirty looks from the people standing in coach.

July 22, 2001
La Bagotière

Hugh is proudly cooking with things from his garden, so last night, along with our steaks, we had oddly shaped potatoes and deep-fried zucchini fingers. He also made a 1-2-3-4 cake, which calls for one cup of butter, two cups of sugar, three cups of flour, and four eggs. I ate half of it, which amounts to one entire stick of butter.

We brought some CDs out to the country, and just as we sat down to dinner, I put on Joni Mitchell's *Hejira*. It came out twenty-five years ago, when I was living in Mom and Dad's basement. Back in Raleigh I listened to it at least a thousand times, fantasizing that I, too, was some shell-shocked traveler running either to or from another doomed relationship. The problem then was that, at the age of nineteen, I'd never had a relationship. Normally I'd play the same song over and over, but this was the rare record you could listen to from start to finish, constructing a different imaginary love interest for each song.

Hejira was the wrong CD to play at dinner, as Hugh had also grown up on it. We sat at the table, neither of us saying anything until the record had ended. For me it's ironic that, on a certain level, all my nineteen-year-old fantasies have come true. All I do is travel from one place to the next, staring out my hotel windows.

What's missing, what made the idea so incredibly romantic, was the instability, the series of boyfriends bound to run off with someone else the moment your back is turned. That's the sort of thing you write songs about, not zucchini fingers and a perfect 1-2-3-4 cake sitting in the refrigerator. In that regard, I'm an equal disappointment to the nineteen-year-old Hugh, who twenty-five years later sits across from me at the dinner table, kindly allowing me to hit replay after "Song for Sharon."

July 31, 2001
Paris
Our next-door neighbor returned yesterday afternoon to

complain about the noise. Hugh was chipping out the wall behind the bookcase and I was in the bedroom, waxing the floors. I missed the whole thing, which is good, as hopefully she'll forget what I look like. The woman works at home and wanted to know when the noise would end. She wanted a definite cutoff point, so Hugh told her he'd be finished by four o'clock. She said that contractors should put up signs stating that the noise would start on one date and end on another—which would be great but is never going to happen. We'd been told the work on our apartment would end in April and here it is, almost August.

The woman then started in on the building across the street, and Hugh cut her off, saying that she was bothering him just as the noise was bothering her. He won't own up to it, but I'm assuming he shut the door in her face. A few months back, while they were installing the bathtub, we were visited by our neighbor on the other side, a man in his forties. He complained about the noise, saying that he didn't get off work until after midnight and couldn't show up at his job with circles under his eyes.

Hugh asked what he did for a living, and, with great importance, the guy said he sold tickets at a movie theater. He wanted the plumber to do quiet work—dusting or whatever—until the early afternoon and start with the loud stuff at around three. Everyone has a plan except for the workmen, who show up whenever they want to.

I turned on the TV last night and was delighted to find *Cops*, which translates to *It's Worth the Detour*. It was dubbed in French, but you could still hear faint bits of English in the background: "He claims"; "The suspect"; "Knucklehead."

The first segment involved a long, high-speed chase along a California freeway. The driver was shirtless and you could tell he took great pride in his feather-cut, shoulder-length blond hair. When he was dragged from the car, his first impulse was to comb it out with his fingers and then gently fluff it up. He was the kind of guy you'd see hanging out at Atlantic Beach, and I wondered what the French would make of him. Who do they think our criminals are? Mexicans were behind the wheel in the next high-speed chase, and because they were juveniles, their faces were covered with diamond patterns.

My favorite segment involved a truck driver wearing a leopard-print one-piece woman's bathing suit. Someone had apparently taken his wallet, but I couldn't understand the details. I'm hoping that *Cops* comes on every night and that the French will eventually develop their own version. Who are the criminals here? I have absolutely no idea.

August 1, 2001
Paris
Last night on Arte I watched part of a documentary about a gang of adolescents living on the streets of some African city. The boys slept in a little room made of cardboard and spent most of the time huffing glue and looking for things to steal. At one point they offered protection to a prostitute, and when she rejected their offer, they threatened to kill her. They were just kids, but there were a lot of them, and that gave some weight to their threat. Hugh and I had plans to go to a ten o'clock movie and while we were walking down the rue des Écoles, I imagined that I could take the gang of boys to a restaurant. "Anywhere you want to go," I'd say.

I imagined them eating until they were full and then I pictured them stealing the silverware and the salt- and pepper shakers. The theater was hot, and after the movie started I realized I'd seen it two years ago. It was Ernst Lubitsch's *To Be or Not to Be,* starring Jack Benny and Carole Lombard as a couple of Polish actors. Fifteen minutes into the movie, Warsaw gets bombed, and again I felt sissyish and spoiled. I'm supposed to be enjoying this new apartment, but I can't help but feel guilty for the fancy oven and brand-new washer and dryer. We sit around like people in a magazine, but it's not the sort of magazine I'd ever subscribe to.

August 7, 2001
Paris
On the train to Florent's, a man entered the subway car and said he was unemployed and needed money. He was tall and out of shape, with greasy hair cut like Sir Lancelot's. On the train back, a different man, slighter and more desperate, crawled down the aisle on his hands and knees, stopping every few feet to hold up his hands in prayer, saying, "Please? Oh, please won't you help me?"

It's pretty rare for French Métro beggars to single you out personally. Generally they enter the train, make a speech, and then move through the car with their hands held out. The crawling man pleaded with a woman and when she turned away, he popped out the upper plate of his dentures, proving that he was even more pathetic than he looked. He crawled over to me and when I gave him 10 francs, he asked if he could also have my pen. It's the small aluminum Muji ballpoint I keep inside my police notebook. He said he needed it in order to write a letter to his wife, and when I said no, he gave me a hateful look.

August 9, 2001
Paris
The other night I went to the Action Écoles to see *Stardust Memories*. It was raining and just as I stepped beneath the narrow awning, an attractive young woman asked if she

449

could use my umbrella. She said she needed to get something from her car and that she'd be right back. It seemed ungentlemanly to say no, so I handed it over, figuring I'd never see it again. The line was short and after buying my ticket, I waited out front. People walked up and down the street and I realized I'd completely forgotten what this young woman looked like. I could pass her tomorrow and never know that this was the person who'd stolen my $70 umbrella.

I waited for five minutes and was just about to give up when she ran into the theater with a bag in her hand, saying, "Thank you so much," and "You were so nice." In the theater I took a seat against the wall. There were people in the middle of the aisle, three Americans who did nothing as I tried to pass. I mean, they didn't even pull in their legs. It was like I was invisible. I always stand when someone passes and naturally expect others to do the same. Just before the movie started, a tall guy took a seat in front of me. I had to lean to the left in order to see the screen and during the two hours, I seem to have pulled a muscle in my back. It feels like I've been shot and the exit wound is right below my left shoulder blade. I'm blaming the three Americans who refused to stand as I took my seat. Had they been more cooperative, I would have moved and spared myself this pain. I mean, it really hurts.

August 12, 2001
Edinburgh, Scotland
The RER crawled to de Gaulle and stopped for twenty minutes at Aerogare 1, so we missed our afternoon flight to Edinburgh. I don't remember the last time I missed a plane, and it took me a while to get beyond the shock of it. For the rest of the afternoon I thought, *If only we'd left sooner. If only we'd hailed a cab.* It always helps that Hugh takes these things a lot harder than I do. He decided that fine, he'd just

stay home, and it took a while for me to change his mind. There was another flight at nine and the woman at the desk gave me the last ticket.

Hugh was put on standby and promised that if he made it on board, he'd never complain again. Those were his words: *never again*. I drew up a little contract and he signed it. I now have it in writing. "If I, Hugh Hamrick, get a seat on tonight's flight I will never complain again." He got his seat, and every five minutes I pulled out the contract and gloated.

It was a small plane. Our flight attendant was named Daisy and she served us a frozen dinner featuring a slab of meat and some sort of jelled-rice concoction. When I say *frozen*, I don't mean "thawed" or "reheated," I mean *frozen*. Hugh's rice concoction was impenetrable and my meat was trimmed in ice. I was free to complain all I wanted, but, having signed the contract, he could do nothing but smile and chip away at his rock-hard brownie.

August 13, 2001
Perth, Scotland

On the BBC's recommendation we visited a coastal town called North Berwick. It was a small place with a wide beach offering a view of several craggy islands set a half mile out to sea. I call it the sea, but according to Hugh it was actually the Firth of Forth, a cove. North Berwick was noted in our guidebook for its handsome public toilets, which were decorated with flowers and little signs asking you to keep the place clean. Lunch was taken at the Butter Cup Café.

At the table next to ours sat two white-haired women, one of whom was blind and carried a folding cane. The blind woman talked a lot, and as she spoke, her bored friend looked out onto the street, saying they'd better get going before the rain started. "Oh, I'm used to the rain," the blind woman said. "If I let the weather stop me, I'd never get any-where." She buttoned her coat and then settled back in her seat to finish her tea.

Our meals arrived and just as we started eating, the blind woman decided it was time to go. She rose from her chair, collected her purse, and farted in Hugh's face. It was a small trumpeting sound that was talked about for the rest of the day.

August 17, 2001
Paris
Yesterday outside the movie theater I saw a Japanese albino. He was a young man in his late twenties with hair and skin the color of cotton balls. Maybe it was due to his pale skin, but his teeth looked really yellow. They were crooked, too, and crammed into his mouth. He had a rash covering his jaw and a half dozen tattooed stars burned into his arm. The poor guy was just a mess. It was four thirty in the afternoon and I was at the Saint-Germain-des-Prés to see *Love Streams,* which was playing as part of their Essential Cassavetes series.

His movies are often too long and sometimes dull. When Gena Rowlands is on-screen I'm in heaven, and when she goes away I sit in the dark and think about other things—the Japanese albino, for instance.

I've been here for three years but still won't stop a stranger to ask for a match. People ask me all the time, but I just can't seem to do it myself. Neither can I walk into Fnac and ask where I might find a certain CD. Instead, I just roam around, not even knowing which genre it's under. In French record stores, the CDs are grouped under strange headings, many of which include the word *black*. I believe they have a sec-tion called Black Rage. After looking at Fnac I walked to

Montparnasse to catch the 96 bus. I could have just as easily walked home, but I thought it might be fun to visit the train station with no luggage.

August 18, 2001
Paris
I walked into the kitchen this morning to find a pigeon sitting on top of the cabinet above the sink. There are always dozens of them roosting on the ledges of the surrounding buildings, and I was surprised one hadn't come in sooner. I don't know how long the pigeon had been here or what she'd done with her time alone. I spilled some couscous on the counter last night and found it was still there, so I'm guessing she didn't have the opportunity to eat. I'm no expert, but it seems that pigeons would like couscous.

Yesterday I had my picture taken by an American named Anthony. He's been in Paris for seventeen years and his girlfriend just had a baby, which has changed his life. "It's different now," he said. "When you're single you maybe have an affair and your girlfriend decides to break up with you. So it's painful, but you just go out and find someone else."

It seems to me that if you're having an affair, the person being cheated on has dibs on the word *painful*, but I didn't say anything. Anthony has done a lot of work in Russia and used to keep an apartment in Moscow. "Those Russian women will destroy you," he said. He's trying to be a family man, but I don't have much faith that it will work out.

September 12, 2001
Paris
Last night on TV I watched people jump from the windows of the World Trade Center. I watched the towers fall in on them-

selves, I watched the burning Pentagon, and then I watched people jump from the windows of the World Trade Center. From my kitchen, office, and living-room windows, I saw my neighbors watching the same thing, each with a remote in one hand and a telephone in the other. It felt like everyone in the world was in front of the TV. Now it's the next day and I still haven't gotten it through my head. The thing that gets me the most are the hijacked planes. I can't imagine what it must have been like to realize you're actually *aiming* for something. You're not going to land in Afghanistan or be held hostage on some tarmac; you're going to die in three seconds. What's frightening is that it was so ingenious and perfectly orchestrated. Who did this?

Patsy and I met at six o'clock at the café on Saint-Sulpice. She'd been watching CNN and told me that, as Americans abroad, we're supposed to keep a low profile and avoid speaking English on the street. It's a standard warning the State Department issues whenever there's trouble. French police have blocked off areas of the Marais and are stopping pedestrians to ask for their papers. Flights en route to New York returned to de Gaulle and I'm not sure when they'll resume. All American airports are closed, as are the bridges and tunnels leading into Manhattan. I tried calling Amy, but all the lines were clogged. She doesn't get out of bed before noon, so I'm assuming she's OK. Steven called me at midnight to tell me that Rakoff and Sarah are fine, as is Art Spiegelman. On the television Giuliani is saying that as many as ten thousand people might have died. On the radio the event's being compared to D-day. Bush called it "an attack on freedom itself," while Jacques Chirac, much more eloquently, called it an attack on civilization.

September 14, 2001
Paris

Last night, we attended the memorial service held at the American Church over by the Musée d'Orsay. Unlike Wednesday's service at the American Cathedral, this was a full-fledged media event, with appearances by President Chirac, Prime Minister Jospin, and the mayor of Paris. I'd never been in a room with a president and thought it was nice the way he paused every so often and made eye contact with the audience. The church isn't very big, and half the pews were reserved with signs reading PARLIAMENT, HIGH DIGNITARIES, and DIPLOMATIC CORPS. This being the American Church, I'd assumed the service would be in English, but, aside from a few opening remarks, everything was said in French.

Brief, five-minute sermons were delivered by a Protestant minister, the grand rabbi of Paris, and a Muslim cleric with a strange gray comb-over. The choir sang, the service ended, and just as the dignitaries were filing out the door, someone in the back of the room started singing "God Bless America." The man started and his countrymen joined in, including Jessye Norman, who placed her hand over her heart and sang as if she were an average devastated woman rather than an opera star. The thing about "God Bless America" is that, after a certain point, nobody really knows the words.

There's always a weird mumbling that follows "Stand beside her and guide her," and lasts until "From the mountains to the prairies." Then there's that bit about the oceans white with foam, which is just a strange thing to mention in a patriotic song. What killed me, what killed many of us, was the very end: "My home sweet home." Because, whatever else Paris might be, this *is not* our home, it's just the place where we have our jobs or apartments. How could we have forgotten that?

September 24, 2001
Amsterdam

The day before yesterday a chemical plant exploded in Toulouse. Patsy called to tell me about it, and, as we'd done a week earlier, we both turned on our TVs and continued to talk while flipping between channels. Twenty-nine people were reported dead and hundreds were injured. Windows were smashed for miles around. A woman lay on the sidewalk crying. Men mopped their bloody faces with the sleeves of their sport coats. The first assumption was that it had been a bomb, but after an hour or so, they attributed it to human error, which was a huge relief. The thing is that we'd been expecting something. Everyone's just sort of waiting for the next big event. Yesterday morning the phone rang and I heard Hugh say, "Oh, my God. You're kidding. When?"

I was sitting at my desk, imagining the worst, when he covered the receiver and said that Leslie had chipped a tooth.

September 28, 2001
Paris

Don called last night to talk. I'm thinking that before he dials he makes a list of topics, adding little notes pertaining to this or that subject. *Haffmans. Sent faxes. No response.* Anything unexpected seems to throw him off balance and it's painful to listen as he tries to right himself.

"Amsterdam, right. That reminds me of, oh, it was that movie with what's her name, when she and the guy get thrown into the water and so forth. It was...no, maybe that was Venice, or rather they made it in Amsterdam because of course everything's so hard when it comes to the Italians. But

Amsterdam, that reminds me of, oh, he was this great old guy who was up near...I think it was Greenland and he got lost somehow and, well, what with the weather and so forth he got...the thing with, the disease and he had to cut off his own feet, which is what's happening right now to Bradbury with the diabetes. They didn't remove the entire foot, but they took a part of it and, oh, it's just been a rough couple of weeks here."

October 2, 2001
New York

I called Amy at four a.m. Paris time and finally got through to her. She told me that, a few days after the World Trade Center collapsed, she went to a play rehearsal on the Upper East Side. The trains were moving faster than she'd anticipated, and she wound up arriving early, with half an hour to kill. There's a Gucci boutique up on Madison Avenue, and, although the brand has never appealed to her, she went inside and looked around. The saleswoman was pushy, and within ten minutes, Amy was strapped into a pair of shoes with very high heels. They were uncomfortable, and when she removed them, she noticed that the insides were stained with blood. Wet blood. Her blood.

The shoes had caused her to pop a blister, but rather than writing it off as an accident, the saleswoman told Amy that now she pretty much *had* to pay for them, to the tune of $500.

I can't fault Amy for giving in, as I would have done the same thing. She bought the shoes she'd never liked in the first place and was leaving the store when she was approached by what she described as two hippies. She meant the new, anti-globalization hippies, who are even more self-righteous than the old ones. The pair moved up the street, and as they passed her one of them spat, "The world is falling apart, so let's all go shopping, right."

Feeling now both shallow *and* taken advantage of, Amy went to a deli and asked for a brown paper sack. She transferred the shoes into it, threw the box and the Gucci bag into the trash, and continued on to her rehearsal. Eventually she got the bloodstains out with an ice cube, but she couldn't return the high heels, as she'd thrown the receipt into the trash can. The world is falling apart and now she's stuck with this pair of shoes.

October 6, 2001
Paris

A stranger called and left a message saying that he too knew someone who'd attempted to "talk pretty." "My friend tried to say he was hungry, but instead he said, 'I am a woman'! Ha! Anyway, keep writing!"

I'd never anticipated that people would want to work the book title into a sentence, though I guess I should have expected as much. They did the same with *Naked:* "I told a friend to get *Naked*. Ha!" or "I was reading *Naked*—but, hey, not literally!" Yesterday's stranger phoned from the airport and apologized for not having called me sooner.

October 7, 2001
Paris

The French meteorologists have gone on strike, meaning that no one knows what the forecast will be from one day to the next. The TV weathermen are still there, but they have no reports to deliver. Instead of predicting what might happen tomorrow, they discuss what already happened today, saying things like "Well, as you can see, we had some rain." It's a news report designed for shut-ins.

458

October 8, 2001
Paris

When hauled before the new world court of folly and decadence, I will have to admit that when the war broke out, I was standing in the Paris branch of the Jil Sander boutique talking to a woman in a calf-length Prada vest trimmed with the fur of aborted fetal lamb. An American press had just published the collected snapshots of Dennis Hopper and we'd been invited by Leslie to the launch party. The first bombs fell on Iraq as the guest of honor made his way to the second floor, and the news was delivered by Lauren Bacall, who wore a fist-size jeweled hair clip, the tiny stones arranged into the message *I love Paris*.

October 10, 2001
Paris

The news gets more distressing every day. I'm lucky, then, to have Hugh, who's taken the calm and logical approach. Last night before going to bed he said, "What are you so worried about? The guy's finished. He can't even come out of his cave." I thought of how strange that might have sounded a year ago. "He can't even come out of his cave." Who would I have thought he was talking about? What kind of a person lives in a cave?

What initially set me off was bin Laden's television appearance. It wasn't live, of course. It was just a speech recorded in, well, his cave. The language was very baroque and I would have laughed were he not calling for the complete annihilation of my country. It was both horrible and horribly overwritten. "America is scared," he said. "From the north to the south. From the east to the west."

Why not just say that America is scared all over?

His call for a holy war was backed up last night by a taped

message from his al Qaeda network; a spokesman said that more planes would be hijacked. I don't necessarily believe they'll be able to do it again, but with every broadcast, they inflame more of their followers.

It's really disheartening to see those narrow streets choked with people, raising their fists and calling for our death. I was uncomfortable but felt better after talking to Paul. "Listen," he said, "those folks running from the World Trade Center, they eat with knives and forks. They wear shoes, understand? See, we've moved on. We've progressed while they're sitting around in the dirt just toiling with that shit. OK, they fucked us up a little. We let our guard down and they got us. This shit happens, but it won't happen again." That Paul. They should put him on TV.

This afternoon we went to look at sofa beds at a store on the boulevard Raspail. I was just wondering if a certain model came in a smaller size when the saleswoman interrupted me and asked if I was English. I said that I was American and for the next twenty minutes she talked nonstop, the words gushing from her mouth like water from a fire hose. "You have to stop this bombing," she said, "because the people, they'll get mad and we don't know what they're going to do next. They could corrupt our drinking water and then what? You open the tap and you die, or maybe they'll blow up our nuclear power plants, and then what? It's over, all of this, the whole world is over and, yes, what they did was terrible, but you're only going to get them stirred up. They're crazy, the Israelis are crazy, and when they're done fighting, whoever wins is going to come after us. They'll poison the earth and the water and there'll be chaos and rioting and we'll all die!"

I understood her fear, but is that really the way to sell a sofa bed?

October 17, 2001
New York

There certainly are a lot of flags here. The first was the size of a place mat and waved from the taxi I took from JFK. The driver was Polish and said that "the thing" had made it hard for all foreigners. "I call it a thing," he said, "because I don't want to say the word for what it is. I won't say his name neither because, to me, he has no name, he's just a chickenshit motherfucker." He said that at least Hitler had been a gentleman about things. He'd said he would start a war, and he did. "But the chickenshit, he didn't give any warning at all. The motherfucker."

I saw flags glued to bumpers and waving from car antennas, and then, when we arrived in the city, I saw them everywhere, mainly in the windows of businesses. Many of the flags are on posters saying either UNITED WE STAND or WE WON'T LET THEM BREAK OUR SPIRIT. Had I known nothing about the events of September 11, I probably would have thought it was some sort of holiday. On my own, though, I wouldn't have noticed the missing World Trade Center. I walked south a few times but looked at the spot where it used to be only because it was no longer there. On my way downtown I walked through Union Square, but, except for a few signs and posters, the memorial shrines are gone. Mainly it just seems a lot quieter than usual. When someone is loud or overly joyful people stare for a moment, pursing their lips, and then they turn away.

October 18, 2001
New York

Yesterday's cabdriver told me that anthrax had been piped through the air ducts at the White House and infected three hundred people. He said it with great authority, claiming to have heard it on the radio, but it turns out not to be true. The volume control is broken on my hotel television. I turned on CNN as soon as I got into the room and heard, along with everyone else on my floor, the newscaster screaming that thirty Washingtonians had been infected. She mentioned Tom Daschle's office but said nothing about the White House. I'm finding it hard to get upset over anthrax. Yes, it's bad, but I can't help thinking it's the work of an American nut. It's not efficient enough to be a terrorist plot, unless, of course, the goal is simply to spread panic. I thought of watching the news before going to bed, but it was just too loud.

I've gotten spoiled so it put me in a very bad mood when Air France told me I would not be upgraded to business class on yesterday's flight. Steven had arranged a transfer using my frequent-flyer miles, but according to the woman at the counter, the airline was "not making that today." The plane was half full and I was on the aisle of an empty, four-seat middle section. Before takeoff, a French couple left their assigned places and took two of the ones on my row, leaving an empty space between us. Moments later, the true owner of the far aisle seat arrived, so the couple moved down, making ours the only full row on the entire plane. I was seething. Then the man in front of me reclined his seat and I was reduced to six inches of lap room. I couldn't even read a magazine. The movie was *Cats and Dogs,* but I couldn't bend forward to get my headphones, so I just sat there, hating the French.

Ronnie called last night to tell me I'd been a question on *Jeopardy!,* the answer being "He wrote the *SantaLand Diaries.*" I don't know what the category was. She told me that a week after the bombing, members of her local chamber of commerce approached the businesses on her street, asking them to display a picture of the flag with the caption WE MOURN OUR VICTIMS. Ronnie agreed, and a few days later she was approached by the same people, who wanted her to display a sign reading HATE-FREE ZONE.

She said she'd rather not and they got angry at her, thus betraying the spirit of the sign they were asking her to hang in her window. "Everyone else is doing it," they said. "You've got the flag in the window, so what's your problem?"

The problem, she explained, was that it was just stupid. "Like, what," she said, "some vengeful person is going to see the sign and say, 'Whoops, I can't buy shoes here. This is a hate-free zone'?"

If things truly worked that way, she'd hang up a sign reading SHOPLIFTING-FREE ZONE or IMPULSE-BUYING ZONE. The businesses on either side of her agreed to display the new signs and now regard Ronnie's shoe store as a haven for the disgruntled.

October 19, 2001
New York
The flags are much larger uptown. On 5th Avenue they're big enough to cover football fields. Walk down the street and you hear someone playing "The Star-Spangled Banner" on a trumpet, competing with the guy across the street who's pounding out "America the Beautiful" on one of those Caribbean oil drums. What's missing are the tourists who would normally stop to listen. It's not exactly dead, but most of the people who are out and about seem to have business here. Shops are hurting, and when you enter a store the salesclerks fall all over you. Buying things you don't want or need has become a patriotic duty, so I went to Barneys and got a tie.

October 20, 2001
Wilkes-Barre, Pennsylvania
Where do I start with Wilkes-Barre? My hotel is located on

the town square, which is bedecked with hanging electric flags, these interspersed with regular cloth versions the size of beach towels. They hang from wires, lampposts, and a huge metal armature built to support the dozens of speakers used to broadcast a looped tape of patriotic songs and marches. I arrived to "The Battle Hymn of the Republic," which was followed by "God Bless America," "America the Beautiful," and, strangely enough, "Dixie." After these came a number of marches, including the song played when the president enters the room and something I recall hearing once on a coffee commercial. When finished, the tape returned to "The Battle Hymn of the Republic" and started all over again. The hotel feels like an indoctrination center.

"Our mayor is crazy," everyone says. "He's completely lost his mind." Wilkes-Barre is shut tight by six o'clock, but still the music blares, playing for an audience of no one.

October 23, 2001
Allentown, Pennsylvania
As part of yesterday's program I met with students at the local college. Normally I try to get out of things like that, but I wound up having a good time, mainly, I think, because of the teacher, a bearded forty-eight-year-old named Alec. He met me at the airport and after the reading we joined a few of his colleagues for dinner. One of them was a papal scholar who told us that in the eighteenth century, the Catholic Church canonized a dog. Alec asked if that would be Saint Bernard and, though it was corny, I can't remember the last time I laughed that hard.

October 31, 2001
Cincinnati, Ohio
On CNN I watched a discussion about post-9/11 America.

One of the panelists was the editor of *Good Housekeeping,* who reflected our new seriousness by placing the Stars and Stripes atop the traditional gingerbread house gracing the December cover. This is the sort of bullshit CNN is becoming famous for. I looked at this woman, thinking, *Just...get the fuck off my TV.*

All Things Considered featured a report on a Kentucky man who was recently recognized as a hermit by the Catholic Church. The segment made it sound as if being a hermit were an occupation, like being an accountant or an engineer. "Tell me," Linda Wertheimer said to a woman connected with the Kentucky archdiocese, "do you have any guidelines for hermits? Do your hermits live in proximity to other hermits?" The woman said that many of her hermits held part-time jobs as weavers, which, again, sounds so ancient. "Do you think this is on the rise?" Linda Wertheimer asked. "Being a hermit?"

"Oh, definitely," the woman said. "Especially now."

November 1, 2001
Dearborn, Michigan
I had the night off so went to the multiplex across the road from the hotel to see *Joy Ride.* The only people in the theater were me and an obese woman dressed like a witch. I'd seen her earlier in the lobby, noticed the tall black hat, and thought, *That person is going to sit in front of me.* And so she did, *directly* in front of me, though there were hundreds of empty seats for her to choose from. "Fucking...witch," I whispered.

November 2, 2001
Dearborn
I talked to Amy yesterday. She'd just gotten off the phone

with Tiffany, who's having a fight with her boyfriend. He can't stand it when she pees in front of him so a few days ago, after sitting on the john and groaning, she dropped a bar of soap into the toilet. He thought she was defecating and what was supposed to be a joke soon escalated into a fight. Tiffany argues that because he never takes her out to dinner, this is the sort of girlfriend he deserves. It's part of her new identity as a poor person, and it illustrates how she's making things up as she goes along. Tiffany's poverty is noble, but I guess this nobility doesn't extend to her boyfriend. Somewhere along the line she's decided that money has a direct correlation to manners, meaning that a minimum-wage girlfriend shits in view of her company while a salaried woman can afford to close the door. As a poor person, she's decided to identify with Osama bin Laden, whom she sees as a Middle Eastern Robin Hood.

She and Paul had a huge fight when he wore a turban and a fake beard to visit a neighbor. She told him he was being disrespectful and he called her a whore.

November 20, 2001
New York

At Provence on Prince Street, our waiter led us to the kitchen, where we saw the restaurant's prizewinning entry in the recent New York Restaurant Show. The theme was Tragedy, so the chef constructed a replica of the remnants of the World Trade Center surrounded by a trio of firemen. Made from animal fat and sugar, the sculpture literally embodied the term *bad taste*. "It was nicer last week," the waiter reflected. "A few days ago it started to melt, and some of the walls have fallen in."

November 22, 2001
New York

The other day the president pardoned a turkey named Liberty. The two of them were pictured on the front page of the *Times,* the president joyous, the turkey indifferent. Something tells me she would have been eaten had her name been Chris or Becky. Instead of being served for Thanksgiving, she'll be sent to a petting zoo.

Late last night Hugh and I walked up Central Park West to watch them blowing up the balloons for the Thanksgiving Day Parade. In the 1930s Macy's would cut them free and pay a reward for their return. It sounded like a nice idea, but by the second year they were being brought back with bullet holes in them, shot down by people desperate for reward money. In the past, you could step up close and watch the inflation, but now they block off the streets, either for security or the fear of lawsuits. We got as close as we could, but it wasn't very satisfying.

November 23, 2001
New York

Dad called last night to say, "You looked terrible." He'd seen my *Letterman* appearance and was angry that I hadn't worn a bow tie. "I told you a hundred times. Hell, I even *gave* you the ties and still you didn't listen to me." My shoes were a disappointment as well. "Jesus, what were you doing up there? You had no personality at all." It's Dad's opinion that a bow tie enhances everything you say, elevates it into a language of elegance. With my brown shoes and knit English tie, I looked common, unspecial, boring. "God, I just...want to shake you."

November 25, 2001
Paris

On WNYC I listened to a report informing us that New York's paranoid schizophrenics were having a difficult time coming to terms with the events of September 11. It was another example of something we probably could have figured out for ourselves. The reporter interviewed the tenants of a halfway house, people convinced that the hijacked planes had been aiming for them personally. The solution, as with everything else, is counseling, counseling, counseling.

December 13, 2001
Paris

On Friday we're supposed to receive our first euros, which will come in little 100-franc packets distributed by the post office and the Bank of France. I say "supposed to" because both the post office and the Bank of France are threatening to strike starting Friday morning. Apparently this euro business is making them work too hard, and before the program's even started, they've decided they need a raise. Elections are coming up so this year the strikes are even heavier than before. All of them want to get their licks in before the new administration.

December 17, 2001
Budapest, Hungary

The *Eyewitness Travel Guide* describes Budapest as a glittering jewel—"the Paris of the East." On closer inspection, the book is full of errors. It reports, for example, that in winter the city gets only two and a half hours of sunlight a day and cranks the figure up to eight for the months of June, July, and August. I'd expected it to get dark at around ten a.m., but it turned out we had light until four in the afternoon. What they probably meant to say was that each evening, the city endures two and a half weeks of darkness. The nights feel impossibly long here, partly because it's cold, but mainly because things are so poorly lit. Everything not pictured in our guidebook fades away once the sun sets.

It's as if the country has run out of both paint and lightbulbs. When people leave their apartment buildings—most of which are missing great patches of their facades—we peek into the grim, peeling foyers. They burn brown coal in Budapest, and everything is coated with soot. You just want to put the entire city in a bathtub and take to it with a wire brush.

I thought our hotel rating was another typo until I realized it had been judged by a different standard. I think in Hungary they give a star for electricity, a star for heat, a star for running water, and so on. The fourth star signifies that the Astoria has cable TV. They boast forty channels, not mentioning that twenty-three of them broadcast the exact same programs. Our hotel is fronted in scaffolding, and our rooms offer a view of a mangy, narrow side street. The one thing they excel at here is stoking the furnace. It's below zero outdoors, while inside our rooms we could roast chickens by leaving them on the nightstand. There's a large group of French people at the hotel and I heard one of the women saying she's so heat-swollen that her rings no longer fit.

December 21, 2001
Paris

Gretchen's plane was an hour late and landed at de Gaulle alongside three other flights from the United States. It took a while for her to get through passport control, and while waiting, I watched other travelers reunite with their people.

Beside me was a family of Americans who'd talk in English and then launch into perfect French, the kids' phrases ending with slangy *quoi*s. I got the idea they'd lived here for quite a while and were waiting for family members who'd gone home to the States for college.

When the young people appeared, their parents would rush forward—crying, most often. The hugging and kissing that ensued was normal, but I think the tears were for September 11.

"I'm just...I'm just so glad you're OK," one woman said.

Her son had arrived from Houston. "Well, I'm glad you're...glad," he said, embarrassed by the attention.

Don called last night, and during the course of the conversation, he forgot my name. "So Pietsch said, 'I don't know that we can give...can give...can give...Sedaris both the audio rights *and* the ten percent.'"

I was thinking he could have solved the problem by using the word *you*, figuring the discussion probably pertained to the person he was calling. When he forgets other people's names, I normally help him out, but it seemed more awkward when the name was my own. "Oh, Lord," he said, "this is going to be a tough day."

December 29, 2001
Paris

Hugh made me a belated-birthday cake, decorated with the candles Patsy gave us for Christmas. When told to make a wish, I settled back in my chair, realizing I should have given it some prior thought. One option was an apartment in London, but in the end I wished for the opposite: the absence of things. Over the past few years I've fallen deeper into the luxury pit. I used to get pleasure from sitting at the pancake house with a new library book, but now I mainly buy things and work crossword puzzles. In my twenties and early thirties I was able to disguise my shallowness, but now it's written all over my shopping bags. On my forty-fifth birthday I looked across the table at the director Mary Zimmerman and thought, *That's what I want, to be like her.* I wanted the change to be immediate. Oh, but first there were perfumed soaps to be opened.

Gretchen went to the National Museum of Natural History with her friend Patty, and I walked alone to the zoo, the little one at the Jardin des Plantes. I hadn't been in years and it was a good day for it. In the reptile house I saw two small children confined to wheelchairs. Both wore glasses and were pushed by their fathers. Crocodiles dozed on the concrete shores of their pen, and I noticed a number of dead cockroaches floating in the water. I saw a lot of unintentional animals yesterday, mainly birds and insects taking advantage of the free food. The keepers had just fed the vultures, and the floor of their cage was littered with what looked like a medium-size dog chopped in half with a hatchet. I thought vultures were always hungry, but rather than eat, they stared toward the big cats, where a man in a hat chipped away at a block of marble. You often see people drawing and painting at the zoo, but I'd never seen anyone with a chisel, sculpting.

2002

I'd always imagined Susan Sontag as delicate, almost brittle, but seated beside her at the dinner table, I noticed that her wrists were easily as thick as her ankles. She was tall and bulky, her trademark skunked hair now dyed a solid black. Steven had done the seating arrangements and it was his joke to place me beside her. We talked privately for a minute or two, but most of the conversation was central, with topics ranging from Henry James to a ninety-five-year-old Polish poet I'd never heard of. I was prepared for the worst, but aside from a few displays of obvious boredom, Susan Sontag was, if not warm, then at least well behaved. She said she couldn't possibly eat cheese off her dinner plate, but that was her only show of fussiness. Outright hostility was reserved for an Englishwoman named Hillary who looked like Candice Bergen. "I've just been to Libya," she said, "and have noticed that we're really much better off than the rest of the world."

Susan Sontag said she'd been "noticing" this every day of her life, but the jab went unchallenged.

"I mean, really," Hillary continued, "there are places where one can't find so much as an aspirin!"

Susan Sontag said that, yes, we all need aspirin.

Seated around the table were Diane Johnson and her husband, John; Paolo, Susan Sontag's Italian translator; Steven; Hugh; James Ivory; and Ismail Merchant. James and Ismail are making a movie of *Le Divorce* and they start shooting in early March. Ismail was seated on my right and was just as gracious as he could be. After dessert he took us up the street and gave us a tour of his grand apartment. He made everyone feel special and interesting, while James Ivory was a bit more businesslike. Diane and her husband are lively and engaging, but for the most part, it was an uncomfortable evening. *Uncomfortable* meaning that I tried my best to keep my mouth shut.

January 4, 2002
Paris

Don called with a business question but lost his way while wishing me a happy New Year. One moment he was discussing the new book contract and the next thing I knew, he was in a cab with Ray Bradbury and Zero Mostel. "He had an apartment on Seventy-Second and wanted to show me this...cloth he'd put things on...painted things on. These...paintings he'd done."

January 7, 2002
Paris

It snowed twelve inches in Raleigh, and my brother's street was blocked off. He lives at the bottom of a hill, and people came from all over with their seldom-used sleds and toboggans. Dad dropped by late in the morning and warned Paul against overdoing it, saying, "You're fat now and you've got to be careful. You might hurt yourself."

He said it the way one might warn a senior "You're old now," as if Paul's condition were irreversible. To prove him wrong, Paul tried a complicated trick and dislocated his shoulder. Unable to sled, he now sits in the house eating cookies and growing fatter.

Every day feels the same, in part because every day looks the same. Again yesterday it was cold and cloudy, the sky the flat gray color of a nickel. We'd planned to go to Normandy, but it turns out the agency in Argentan has no more rental cars. Going without one means that Hugh will spend the entire week in a sour mood, threatening every fifteen minutes to sell the house and move back to New York. We'd both looked forward to getting away, but I'm definitely handling the disappointment better than he is. I just watched as he poured an entire bag of coffee into the stovetop espresso machine. Grounds spilled onto the counter, and when I asked what he was doing, he brushed them onto the floor, saying flatly, "Making coffee."

January 23, 2002
Paris

Monday night was our co-op meeting, which was held in the coiffeur's shop on the ground floor of our building. Hugh had attended one last spring, but this was my first. The apartment owners, seven of us all together, gathered up chairs and sat in a semicircle facing an architect and our efficient syndic, a thin woman in her early fifties whose job it is to manage things and who tended to interrupt whoever was speaking with *"C'est normal, c'est normal."*

What wasn't normal got her full attention for a period averaging between thirty and forty-five seconds. The main point of business was to vote on the roof repair. Two estimates had been given and the architect suggested we accept the higher bid, claiming the lower would wind up costing us more in the long run. Madame S. presented a case for fixing her retaining wall, saying it had been moistened and damaged by the leaking roof. "I'd said as much to my husband," she said.

I'm not sure exactly how long her husband's been dead, but Madame S. mentioned him at least a dozen times, most often in the context of some prediction. "I told him...," "He told me..." In the middle of the meeting, she pulled out a test tube containing a tiny lump of calcium. She'd harvested it from her drain and waved it in the air, hoping to make a point.

"*C'est normal, madame,*" the syndic said. "*C'est normal.*"

Though everyone was civil, I sensed that our neighbors had long ago grown tired of Madame S. Smiles faded as soon as she opened her mouth. The syndic examined her notes. The architect doodled in the margins of his floor plan. At one point she complained that the third-floor tenants of number 98 boulevard Saint-Germain had held a party. "And the noise! The music!"

"*C'est normal,*" the syndic said.

Of all the partners, my favorites were the couple who own the tiny apartment on the half landing between the first and second floors. They've got a leak in the roof, but their biggest problem is their tenant, who hasn't paid the rent in months. "Oh, him," everyone said. "He's crazy." The husband was honey-colored and spoke with an accent I couldn't identify. He was maybe in his late sixties, but his face was unlined and surprised-looking. "Well, we *know* he's crazy," he said. "I just wish we'd known it sooner."

The meeting proceeded, and just as it was winding up, the syndic laid down her papers. "Who's been building fires?" she asked. The informer, of course, had been Madame S., who conveniently reexamined her test tube of calcium. According to the syndic, fires are essentially illegal in Paris. People build them all the time, but apparently not *her* people. If it simply came down to asphyxiating Madame S., she'd be all for it, but legally any death would be the syndic's responsibility. Our options are to "entube" the chimney, which would allow us to build charcoal fires, or tear down the building and reconstruct it from scratch. I left the meeting, my face burning. I'd chosen this apartment specifically because of the fireplaces and if we can't use them, I'd just as soon move.

At the Odeon Métro stop I saw a baby lying alone in her basket next to an ashtray and a little sign reading AIDEZ MOI SVP. The mother was hanging out at the top of the stairs and would look down every few minutes, checking to see if she'd earned any money.

January 26, 2002
Florence, Italy

   Me: What do you want as your main birthday gift?
   Hugh: I want to attend Madame S.'s funeral.

January 28, 2002
Florence
Florence often smells like toast.

January 30, 2002
Paris
It took over twelve hours to get from our Florence hotel room to our apartment in Paris. Hugh and I awoke at four thirty a.m. and walked through our door, finally, at ten to five in the afternoon. The first problem was the fog. We'd boarded our plane at seven fifteen and spent an hour and a half parked on the runway, listening as the guy behind us crabbed at his wife.

Actually, *crabbed* is too gentle a word. He screamed at her: "For God's sake, will you just shut up!"

He was an American in his seventies, tall and bearded, who'd topped his greasy hair with a black beret. "I'm sick of hearing about it, so just shut up. Can you do that? Shut. Up." Boarding the plane had put him in a foul mood, and his mood worsened when they sent out a bus and returned us to the airport.

Like most of our fellow passengers, the American couple had a connecting flight in Paris. At ten a.m. they still had a chance of making it, but by noon all hope was gone. While Hugh and I talked with a Canadian schoolteacher, the bearded man roamed the waiting room, loudly complaining to whoever would listen. His wife sat alone, huddled in her mink, and after a while I stopped feeling sorry for her. You don't just suddenly *become* an award-winning asshole. It takes years of practice, years she'd doubtlessly spent mortified in other, larger waiting rooms with pay phones and magazine racks. They had us reboard at around one, and again her husband started yelling. He screamed when a man with glasses accidentally took the window seat, "You'd think he'd never been on a goddamn plane." He screamed when his wife tried wedging her purse beneath the seat, and he screamed when a fat man arranged his coat in the overhead compartment. "Hey," he said, "you want to back off?"

"Excuse me?"

"You're invading our space, goddamn it."

"I was just trying to—"

"Bullshit, you're knocking against my wife. Back off."

The fat man was also from the United States, clean-shaven with gold-rimmed glasses. "You, sir," he said, "are being an ugly American."

"Piss off," the bearded man said.

"An ugly, ugly American."

The fat man laid his self-help book on his seat and called for the flight attendant. "Excuse me, miss," he said, "but you might want to keep an eye on this gentleman."

"Oh, kiss my ass," the bearded man spat.

He was quiet for a few minutes but started up again when the pilot announced a baggage-identification check. A few of our fellow passengers had gone missing and we couldn't proceed until their luggage had been removed from the plane. This involved unloading the cargo hold and spreading its contents out on the runway. In groups of twenty we were instructed to disembark, identify our suitcases, and reboard. The process took over an hour, and we didn't take off until two fifteen, by which point the whole thing had become a terrible comedy. The bearded man brightened with his third glass of champagne and fell asleep shortly afterward. Her crossword puzzle finished, his wife put her head on his shoulder and quietly, so as not to wake him, chewed the end of her pencil.

February 8, 2002
Paris

Yosef called yesterday afternoon, asking if I'd found the time to read his screenplay. I told him I hadn't and he said, "Well, I read your book and hated it." He translated my laugh as "Tell me more, please," and went on to offer a detailed critique of *Barrel Fever.*

It didn't bother me, as the book is almost ten years old and I hate it now too. On top of that, it's sort of exciting to know someone who's that direct. I listened to him, certain that, should I hate his screenplay, I'd never admit it. The directness will always be one-sided.

February 9, 2002
Paris

I met Yosef at the Viaduc des Arts and we took the train to his riding stables in the Bois de Boulogne. Before leaving I'd resolved to be more interesting, but by the time we reached the Métro station, I felt that I'd failed and it was too late to make up for it. He's a very nice guy, but I couldn't seem to remember what friends talk about. "What did you have for dinner last night?" I asked. "Did your dog sleep well?"

He asked me a few questions in French and then resorted to English, saying, "I forgot. It's easier for you." I wanted to say that French was fine but felt it would be burdening him even further. "What will you eat tonight?" I asked. "Will your dog stay up late?"

The stables were large and broken up into different areas. In one building, a teacher instructed a group of young women in how to apply a horseshoe. He kept telling his pupils, *"Decontractez,"* which means "relax." Yosef said it's the most used word in any sports-related conversation. He said that the French invented both laziness and the belief that rules were meant to be broken, and I wondered if he was saying that because he's Swiss.

We walked around in the mud and rain and then visited the stable café for a cup of coffee. It was a large, sad place, nearly deserted. Through a glass wall we could see teenage girls on horseback trotting around in a circle. While we sat there, Yosef told me of the time he visited Munich and stole a bicycle. It's the second episode of petty theft he's admitted to, and again he made it sound very reasonable. "All around me, people were riding bikes and enjoying themselves, so I thought, *Why not me?*" He said he'd planned to return it when he was finished, but the police stopped him before he could even leave the park. "It was," he said, "a real fiasco."

479

On the train back, Yosef asked what kind of animal I might be if I were suddenly transformed into a cartoon character. I didn't quite understand the question, so he offered an example, saying that he himself would be a bear. "Sometimes I am cuddly like a panda," he said, "but if I get in a bad mood, watch out!" I tried to imagine him as a cartoon bear dressed in a raincoat and yellow sneakers and decided that, with his red hair and penchant for stealing, he'd probably make a much better fox.

"So come on," he said. "What are you?" I'd never given it much thought but figured I'd probably be an ant. When Hugh and I moved into the new apartment, I carried everything but the furniture, making six or seven trips a day from the old place to the new one. When I pictured all our belongings, it seemed futile, so I never thought beyond the load I was transporting at the time. Books, shoes, pots and pans, the television: I was like an ant deconstructing a scrap of bread.

Yosef seemed dissatisfied with my answer and announced that I'd most likely be an oyster. "Because sometimes you look at me and I have no idea what you are thinking."

"How can you tell if an oyster is looking at you in the first place?" I asked. "They don't even have eyes, do they?"

"Well," Yosef said, "you know what I mean."

It seemed vaguely insulting to be compared to an oyster. I wanted to replead my case for the ant, but instead I just let it go. He invited me to his house for a piece of pie, but I begged off. "I'm super busy right now," I said. Then I came back to my apartment and took a bath, counting the hours until Hugh came home.

Over coffee Yosef taught me the word *beauf,* which is short for *beau-frère.* It means "brother-in-law," but the shortened version connotes an element of tedium. A *beauf branché* is a brother-in-law who mistakenly considers himself to be hip.

February 12, 2002
Paris

Sunday at three a.m., an American couple had a fight on the street in front of our building. I'm guessing they were in their late twenties, both drunk. Apparently the girl had had her jacket stolen at the bar.

> Her: Well, I told you to watch it.
> Him: That isn't the point.
> Her: Then forget about it. I can get a new fucking passport.
> Him: Well, I'm not going to forget about it. I'm *not*.
> Her: You're just mad because you gave it to me.
> Him: Hey, that is *not* the point. Yes, I gave it to you. It was expensive. It looked damned good on you, but that is *not* the point.
> Her: Oh, please.
> Him: The point is that you just stood there and let them laugh at you.
> Her: They weren't laughing.
> Him: They *were*. You said that stupid stuff and let them laugh because—(*He grabbed her by the shoulders and slammed her against the wall, a separate slam for every word.*)—you (*slam*) don't (*slam*) have (*slam*) any (*slam*) self- (*slam*) respect (*slam*).

She recovered herself, and then, as if it were a scene memorized from a play, they started again from the top.

> Her: Well, I told you to watch it...

March 2, 2002
Paris

In return for our help getting her hot-water heater installed, Peggy took us to dinner at the Hotel Bristol, where I learned about foams. According to her, it's the new trend. Stocks are reduced to a potent broth and then whipped up to resemble scum. I had a foie gras soup that looked as if it had been pissed on. Hugh had sea urchins, the shells emptied out and filled with what looked to be dirty bubble bath. The problem with foam, aside from its general ugliness, is its texture. Unlike, say, a mousse, it doesn't really take to the mouth. The flavor was there, but I missed the heft of a heavy fork. I missed chewing. Also I realized that, should the trend continue, you'd never again be able to tell if the waiter had spit in your food. At the Café Marly, some things are foamed and others are not. Hugh ordered the pig head and received a perfectly recognizable nose and ear surrounded by vegetables.

March 5, 2002
Paris

I went to see *The Honey Pot*, a 1967 movie starring Rex Harrison and a very young Maggie Smith. Even in her twenties, her face unlined, she had the eyes of a man. They're heavily lashed but somehow seem to contain masculine information. Maggie Smith's eyes know about shaving.

March 9, 2002
La Bagotière

Little, Brown forwarded an envelope of mail, and I realized after reading it over that every single letter wanted something from me. The senders included:

a college student writing an article on magazine reader-
  ship. "I'm on a deadline so email me as soon as you
  get this!"
a Cleveland man who's written a gay travel guide and
  wants my help finding an agent.
an Indianapolis human rights group wanting me to attend their rally. "Your agent says you haven't got the
  time, but I suspect you do."
a Seattle drama group asking for an essay on how theater has changed my life.
three Nashville High School students assigned to read a
  bestseller and write the author with questions such as
  "Have you written any other books? Where do you
  get your ideas?"
a German woman writing her PhD on the role of the diary in contemporary American fiction. She too is on a
  deadline and asks that I call her Tuesday, Wednesday,
  or Thursday, trying several times per night until I
  reach her.
a gay choral group asking for mementos they might
  auction off at their upcoming fund-raiser, *Life Is a
  Cabaret.*

March 13, 2002
Paris
Hugh and Manuela are wood-graining the study of a well-
known actor. Yesterday they asked him what color carpet
he'd chosen, and he answered, *"Tête-de-nègre."* This translates to "nigger's head," and he repeated it several times.
There was a black man installing baseboards in the next
room, and when Hugh suggested he maybe keep it down, the
actor said, "It's not racist—it's a color. Ask anyone."

483

March 21, 2002
Paris

Again I reported to the polyarthritis center in the 19th. I'd signed up for volunteer work, hoping it might improve my French, but yesterday afternoon I said nothing more complicated than hello and good-bye. The promised new shelves still hadn't arrived. Papers couldn't be sorted, so instead of filing, I cleaned and carried out trash. I mopped the floor and washed the windows and after a while I started feeling like a foreign maid, the type people smile at as they say, "Let me just get out of your way." I didn't necessarily mind. It just wasn't what I'd expected.

March 30, 2002
New York

On Wednesday, Milton Berle, Billy Wilder, and Dudley Moore died. The papers have been running nice, long obituaries, the fondest for Billy Wilder. I read his notice in yesterday's *Times* while on the way to Amy's. I read Milton Berle's in the *Tribune* while waiting in the Delta check-in line. On yesterday's flight, I was surprised by the number of families flying first class, parents with children. The couple in front of me had two adolescents who complained about the wait. "This is like the line for coach or something," the girl said. "Just like in Barcelona."

April 6, 2002
Raleigh

At the Austin airport, the magazines *Swank, Busty, Stud, Playboy,* and *High Society* are grouped under the heading "Sophisticates." *The New Yorker,* on the other hand, is placed under "General Interest." A few hours later, at the Dallas airport, I saw a sign reading PATRIOTIC T-SHIRTS 50% OFF. That pretty much represents the national mood. Tax time is here and people are realizing that pride costs money.

I was on the second leg of my trip to Raleigh, standing in the bathroom, when I noticed how old I looked. The lights were fairly harsh, and I studied myself as I simultaneously peed all over the floor. It looked to be a good sixteen ounces, and when the plane pitched, a small lake flowed toward the door. It was panic time, and after trying to mop it up with toilet tissue, I switched to paper towels. They couldn't be flushed, so I had to throw them in the trash bin, which was already full. So there I was, a pee-soaked paper towel in each hand, looking really, really old.

April 18, 2002
Houston, Texas

The Lancaster is described as an "older, luxury hotel located in the heart of the thriving theater district." I arrived yesterday afternoon and was greeted by a bellman, who reached for my suitcase. "Oh, I've got it," I said. "Really, it's no problem at all."

He was a black man in his sixties with gray hair and a bushy beard. "Are you sure?" he asked. "There's no obligation."

At the desk I checked in. The manager and concierge introduced themselves, then handed the key to the bellman, who said he needed to take me to the room. "I have to show you a few things," he said, "otherwise you might not be able to figure them out." He pointed out the first-floor restaurant, which was marked by a large sign reading RESTAURANT. "There's the restaurant," he said, "and one flight up we've got what we call the mezzanine." By this time he'd wrangled away my suitcase, which he rolled into the elevator. "You're on nine," he said. "So we'll just push this button right here."

I imagined that my room was protected by some incredibly technical security system, but it was just the standard lock and key. The bellman opened the door and pointed to the armoire. "Now that's your TV, in there," he said, "and it operates by remote. You've got an alarm clock, a fax machine, and a bathroom." Had I lived my entire life in a dark forest, his little speech might have been helpful. "*My* bathroom? For *me?* To *use?* What's a TV?"

As it was, his little tour amounted to a shakedown. You can't not tip a bellman, so I gave him $5, feeling all the while that I'd been taken advantage of.

April 19, 2002
Los Angeles

While packing to leave Houston I felt a mounting anxiety about the bellman, whom I'd grown to hate. He'd be waiting downstairs, and while finishing my exercises, I imagined the many things I'd say when he inevitably tried to wrestle away my bag. "Sir, no," I'd say. "I said *no.*" If he took it anyway, I'd simply leave him without a tip and say, "Look, I told you not to help."

Fifteen minutes before checkout I carried the typewriter down to the lobby. They'd gotten me a Selectric rather than a Wheelwriter, and it weighed a ton. "Oh, you didn't have to do that," the man at the front desk said. "We would have sent Larry to fetch it."

The bellman, who I guess was named Larry, swooped in to scold me. "Now, that's not right," he said. "Mr. Sedaris, whenever you're ready, I'll go get that suitcase. Goodness, carrying that heavy typewriter all by yourself."

I said I wouldn't be needing any help, and he skulked off

to bide his time. A car was coming at eleven, and as I waited out front, he moved in to brag about his city. "Houston's a beautiful place, but best of all is our people," he said. "The friendliest folks on earth." He said he'd once gone to New York and tried to engage a stranger in conversation. "The guy said, 'Look, I don't know you and I don't want to know you, so just buzz off.'" Larry shook his head. "That ain't no way to be 'cause, see, I'm from Texas. I like to see a smile."

The car pulled up and he pried my suitcase out of my hands. "Really," I insisted, "I can do it myself." The driver opened the door to the backseat, and Larry ran around and opened the opposite one, saying, "This is the side a person should get in on." I wish I could say I'd given him nothing, but of course I caved in, hating him all the while.

April 20, 2002
Escondido, California
According to my complimentary postcard, the Rancho Bernardo Inn boasts an eighteen-hole championship golf course, two award-winning restaurants, twelve tennis courts, a full-service spa, and a fitness center. "Lovely outdoor pool and courtyard areas are accentuated by the numerous antique fountains imported from Italy and Spain. Rancho Bernardo Inn guests enjoy the warmth, taste, and style of a fine country home." My room is very pleasant and features a private deck overlooking one of the many wishing wells mentioned whenever someone is giving you directions. "Turn left at the wishing well," the concierge says, or "Walk past the wishing well."

I looked into my wishing well yesterday afternoon, expecting sparkling coins, and found a Bic pen floating beside a golf tee.

April 22, 2002
Eugene, Oregon
Yesterday's highlight was washing my clothes. There's a combination Laundromat, tanning booth, and espresso bar over near the university, and while walking to it I passed a large antiques mall, empty in the way such places usually are. I went in, and an elderly saleswoman followed behind as I wandered from room to room, pretending to admire the beer steins and World's Fair mementos. My favorite object was a lamp with a base made of stacked books. They're common enough, but usually the books are classics: leather-bound editions of Plato and Mark Twain. Here they amounted to *American Drug Index, Bugles and a Tiger, Management Policy and Strategy,* and *Slimnastics.* I copied the titles as the saleswoman walked back to the register and told her associate, "Well, at least he's writing something down. That's always a good sign."

April 26, 2002
Portland
I went into the bathroom after my walk with Lisa yesterday afternoon, and when I came out there was a hostage situation on TV. "I've always been straight with you," a man said. "Take me, not her." The killer pointed a gun at a woman's neck. "Back off or she's dead!" he shouted. "I'm serious."

Lisa had made it for all of ten minutes before turning on the television in our hotel room. It was five o'clock in the afternoon and she was lying in bed in her pajamas. "I love Portland," she said when I asked what she was doing. "Have you seen this show?"

Having watched so many similar programs in her lifetime, Lisa is able to divine the future. The killer's wife tries to talk him down and confesses that she's pregnant. "That's true, all right," Lisa said. "But it's not his baby." Moments later I learned that she was right. The real father was the killer's brother.

"They're going to shoot him the moment he turns that gun over," Lisa predicted. I was thinking, *No way, the guy's too good-looking to die.* But the moment he handed in his weapon, a bullet came through the car window and caught him in the neck.

"That always happens," Lisa said. I thought she might treat the commercials the same way, saying, "Those stains are going to come right out," but the ads are too predictable, so she ignores them.

Earlier yesterday morning, after the plane had been sitting on the Minneapolis runway for forty-five minutes, the pilot announced it would take three and a half hours to fly to Portland. For the first time since beginning the tour, I honestly didn't think I could live that long. What made the flight unbearable was my excitement over seeing Lisa. We landed at two thirty and I found her by the baggage claim, sitting patiently with her rolling suitcase.

In the afternoon we took a walk through downtown. "Can I ask you something?" Lisa said. "How often do you and Hugh have sex?" A man on the curb stopped to watch the passing traffic, and I waited until we were safely across the street to tell her, wondering if this was what other middle-aged brothers and sisters talked about. I answered her, of course, as it would never have occurred to me not to. We talked about it again later that night while lying in bed.

April 27, 2002
Seattle
I normally try to keep my hotel rooms just so, but within

minutes of arriving Lisa had the lamps blazing and the television on. Things were piled on the coffee table and she was sitting on the sofa watching a made-for-TV movie while looking over a sheet of algebra problems. She's taking a math class at Forsyth Tech and currently holds a 102.7 average. When asked how it could be over 100, she tapped her pencil against her forehead and said, "Extra credit."

Lisa's able to do anything while watching TV. Yesterday morning while I packed to leave, she caught the last half hour of *Matlock*. "Isn't it true," Andy Griffith asked the defendant, "isn't it true that *you* bought the briefcase and planted it on Coach Williams?"

"Don't you just love him?" Lisa asked.

May 1, 2002
San Francisco

Ronnie, Rakoff, and I spent the afternoon wandering around before his reading at Books Inc. on Market Street. We went for coffee and then walked over to the Castro Theater to use the bathroom. The doors weren't open yet, but the guy at the box office was nice and said we could go inside. Ronnie had worked at the Castro in the late seventies and was showing us around when we were approached by an usher who asked if we needed any help. The man was maybe in his fifties and wore a suit and tie. Around his neck was a strand of fat fake pearls. His ear was pierced and his gentleness suggested a slight learning disability. We used the bathrooms and he caught up with us in the lobby on our way out.

"It's so bootiful, isn't it?" he said. "I just love this place. It's like a big ol' home to me." Ronnie asked about his accent and we learned that he was from Asheboro, North Carolina. "But I went to NC State and I love Broughton High School. Sanderson too. I got both their yearbooks." He held up two fingers. "There was this Broughton girl, Barbara Mooney— I'll never forget it—and when she didn't make head cheerleader she said, 'Then I'll just transfer to another school,' and so she went to Sanderson and they made her the head. I'll never forget it. She worked at a dress shop."

The Asheboro accent is lazier than that of Raleigh. "I'll just transfer to another schoo-ul." This man seemed familiar with every movie theater in the state of North Carolina and reported their closings and renovations as if he were filling us in on old friends. "The Piedmont in Hendersonville is gone, but they did a bootiful job fixing up the Carolina in Waynesboro. And do you remember the State Theater in Charlotte? I hate that town but used to work there when old Jeanette Tucker was in charge. Then she got married and, I'll never forget, she told me, 'My husband got transferred and there's no way I'm moving to old hicky Hickory.' I'll never forget it. But she did move there, yes, she did, Jeanette Tucker."

We talked about this man for the rest of the day. Rakoff had turned on his mental tape recorder and every few minutes he'd stop and say, "She worked at a dress shop," or "I moved here in 1988 and I was scared to death." We wondered where the usher lived and if his parents were still alive. It must have been horrible living as a homosexual in Asheboro and we tried to imagine his wonder at moving to a city that allowed him to wear pearls.

May 3, 2002
New York
The dumbest words ever spoken in New York are "I think I'll wear my new shoes." I left the hotel yesterday at ten, and when I returned seven hours later, it looked as if I'd jumped into a wood chipper. My socks were stained with blood and I had just enough time to change and iron a shirt before I went

to the BEA party, where I spent three and a half hours on my feet. Now they're red and swollen, resembling strip steaks.

May 22, 2002
Barcelona, Spain

We went for dinner at a tapas restaurant halfway between here and the city center. The food kept coming and went from the sublime to the ridiculous: octopus and beets followed by goose-liver ice cream and wild strawberries topped with rosemary foam. I sat across from Heidi and next to a young woman named Amanda, a New Yorker traveling with the Cirque du Soleil. At the age of seventeen she had a play produced off-Broadway. She's sold a few stories to the *New York Times Magazine* and seems like the kind of person who could do anything well and effortlessly. On top of that, she looks all of fourteen years old. Amanda's brother runs a private yoga studio in SoHo. "Oh, my God," Heidi said. "Your brother is *Eddie? The* Eddie?"

It was a real New York conversation. The subject turned to celebrities, and then restaurants. Heidi used to work at the MercBar, where the rule was "No suits after ten p.m." When the time came, the staff had to push out all the Wall Street guys who weren't considered cool enough. One night there was an altercation, and the bouncer had his nose bitten off. "They found it in the gutter and were able to sew it back on, thank God," Heidi said.

June 2, 2002
Dublin, Ireland

While on the bus, waiting to board our flight, we saw our plane defecate onto the tarmac. They were emptying the sewage hold and accidentally opened the valve before the hose was in place. "Look," someone said. The man was Irish and sounded like the leprechaun from the Lucky Charms commercial. "Look, over there."

We turned to watch human feces and used toilet paper drop from the plane and onto the runway. Moments later we watched as the luggage handlers set our bags into the flowing river of waste. "Mother of God," the Irishman said. A maintenance worker shouted something to our bus driver, who moved us to the other side of the plane, effectively blocking our view.

If this was the worst that had happened I might have laughed it off. "So there's some shit on my suitcase, who cares." Sadly, however, there was more. After boarding, we waited on the runway for an hour, arriving in Dublin at just after ten. It took another hour to get our luggage, which finally arrived soaking wet with Irish rain. On a positive note, the rain helped rinse away some of the shit so, again, I shouldn't complain.

June 5, 2002
Ballycotton, Ireland

It was my idea to go to Cork, which, according to our guidebook, is the second-largest city in Ireland. I'm not sure what part of town we wound up in, but it was full of teenage mothers leaving fast-food restaurants. At Hillbilly's Fried Chicken a lot of the moms had nose rings. They looked to be around sixteen, all of them chubby and most of them accompanied by their mothers. It was the same story at Wimpy's and Supermac's, where three generations stood on the sidewalks sharing sacks of fried food. In this particular part of town, all the shops were practical, offering outfits for 22 euros, handbags for 6, electric woks for 9.99. We had lunch at a sandwich shop, walked around for a little while, and then drove on to Midleton, home of the Jameson Distillery. I'd just wanted to visit the gift shop and was disappointed when Hugh bought tickets for a tour, which began with a fifteen-minute filmstrip titled "Water of Life, River of Time." The narrator described Ireland as being "bejeweled by beauty" and then outlined the distilling process, first learned by perfume manufacturers in the Orient.

He covered the tragedy of Prohibition and put down Scotch whisky at every opportunity. Unlike Irish whiskey, Scotch is distilled only twice. It's de-crudded long before it reaches the still, but they made it sound as if the average Scotch bottle includes a few used Band-Aids and at least one cigarette butt.

Following the filmstrip we were given a tour by a young woman in her twenties. There were maybe thirty of us—Danes, English people, three motorcycling Germans in leather pants, dragging rolling suitcases. The woman took us through each step of the process, then led us to the bar, where our ticket stubs were exchanged for glasses of whiskey.

Afterward we returned to the hotel for tea. As we drank it, we listened to the couple at the next table. "Well, he's a bit affected, isn't he?" the woman said. "The accent, the clothing, he's, well, affected. A lovely man, but incredibly affected." She must have said it thirty times.

June 13, 2002
London

We've gotten ourselves a mortgage broker named Marcus Paisley, a man we obviously chose for his name. Hugh spoke to him yesterday morning and we spent the rest of the day imagining future calls. "I'm starting to see a pattern here, Paisley, and I don't like it."

The solicitor is named Marco and both he and Marie Cécile have begun sending faxes and emails, long, complicated documents I can't even pretend to read. When this is all done I won't stop Hugh from referring to "his" London apartment. It may have been my idea to buy a place there, but he's done all the work.

Dad has rented an apartment to Enrique, one of Paul's employees, and Enrique's mother, who arrived from Mexico late last summer. She's in her early sixties and was recently hospitalized for depression. In many respects her life is better now, but it's hard to adjust when you have no friends and can't speak the language. Dad decided that her problem was low self-esteem. Work would make her feel needed, so he hired her to scrape paint. It was only a two-hour job, a $16 opportunity, but after ten minutes he snatched the tool from her hands. "This is how you do it!" he yelled. "Like *this*." When she failed to catch on, he screamed at her all the louder. "Oh, get off it. You know what I'm saying."

The episode left her more depressed than ever, which, Paul says, is the way it works with the Lou Sedaris Self-Esteem Program. "You're a big fat zero is what you are, so here, scrape some paint." A foreigner will learn the phrases "Can't you do anything right?," "Everything you touch turns to crap," and "Are you kidding? I'm not paying you for that."

June 20, 2002
Paris

Yesterday afternoon I opened my *Pariscope* and there it was: *Planet of the Apes* was playing at the Action Écoles. "The original," the ad read. "The one, the only." When the movie first came out, I saw it seventeen times. I've seen it since, on TV and video, but I don't really count TV and video. Watching it last night on the big screen I found myself laughing at the spaceship computers, big bulky things with dials and switches. The sleep capsules had once seemed sophisticated, but now they looked like props from an old game show. Before turning in, Charlton Heston stubs out his cigar and places it in his pocket. It's relit later, on the barren desert, and I thought to myself that, though it was stale, it must have felt good to smoke again. After a few moments, his shipmate discovers plant life, and, following a brief examination, Charlton Heston throws his unfinished cigar on the ground and crushes it with his boot.

Well, that's not right, I thought. *Why would he throw away his only cigar?* Later on, I wondered why he didn't offer his silver fillings as evidence that he had, in fact, come from another planet. You saw them, gleaming, every time he opened his mouth, yet they were never mentioned. I noticed lots of little inconsistencies, but that's to be expected when you're watching something for the eighteenth time.

June 21, 2002
Paris

Peggy Knickerbocker is in town and took me yesterday afternoon to see Paintings by Doctors, an exhibit at the École de Médecine. It was the last day of the show and several of the cardiologists had come down on their prices. "Look!" the gallery director said. "Twenty percent off!" I'd expected a high level of quality, but it looked much like an exhibit of prison art or paintings done by mental patients. The one exception was a group of still lifes, deft and moody and very accomplished. "Oh, those," the gallery director said. "Those are by a doctor's wife."

After the medical school we walked to the zoo at the Jardin des Plantes and examined the ostriches' assholes. They're very complicated and involve what looks like a retracting tongue. When together, Peggy and I always come across some type of interesting assholes. On her last visit, they belonged to prizewinning cows. Yesterday they were ostriches and, later, monkeys. "If mine looked like that I think I'd kill myself," Peggy said. "I mean it."

June 26, 2002
Paris
At some point early this week Paul stopped thinking of the *Esquire* article as a tribute and began thinking of it as a five-page advertisement for himself. Then again, maybe it's my fault. He's been working on a website and I mentioned to him last month that perhaps they could print the address alongside my bio on the contributors' page. I didn't realize he was looking for a way to sell things: T-shirts, baseball caps, and, now, barbecue sauce.

When I told him I wouldn't be on the contributors' page in this issue, he asked if the magazine could print the address of his website on the photos. Andy said it wouldn't be possible, so Paul called and asked that I work the web address into the story itself. He doesn't understand the difference between an article and an advertisement, so I had a hard time explaining the difficulty. I settled, finally, on an analogy. "It's like with the Dr. Povlitch story," I said. "Wouldn't it have been distracting to say, 'After the accident, my mother took me to see Dr. Povlitch (see www.drpovlitch.com or www.braceyourself.com), who began proceedings for a root canal'?"

Paul was silent.

"Doesn't that sound wrong?" I asked.

"No."

After we spoke, Dad called me. "Hey," he said, "why won't you put Paul's web address in your story?" By nightfall I was public enemy number one, the mean guy, the fusspot refusing to do his brother this one little favor.

July 8, 2002
La Bagotière
Hugh and Leslie left early this morning for Paris. I was supposed to go with them but decided at the last minute that it's really not a good time for me. I can't leave my spiders, for one. On Saturday I started feeding Clifton, who lives above the kitchen sink. He's big, the size of a pearl, and I'm trying to make him bigger. Yesterday he ate two flies and a moth. The flies took him about three hours each, and the moth, I have no idea. He was still working on it when I went to bed. This morning it's hollow, propped like a scarecrow on the edge of the web. "Good work, Clifton," I said.

I love the moment when he feels the prey trying to escape. Their wings vibrate the web and he comes from his little cave to size them up. The other day I threw in a bee. Clifton ran out, saw what he had, and hightailed it back to the corner as if to say, *Goddamn, I can't eat that. Don't you know anything?*

With moths and flies it's a different story. He attacks directly, paralyzing them with a bite to the back or stomach or forehead. Once they're unable to move, he drinks them alive, empties them out, and throws the bodies into the trash. I started feeding Clifton on Saturday and began feeding Coretta Scott yesterday afternoon. The flies are easy to catch, especially the old, clumsy ones. During the day they bat against the windows and at night they can be found sleeping on the ceiling. I felt a little guilty about the moth, but flies, who cares?

July 9, 2002
La Bagotière
All day yesterday Clifton stayed folded in his chamber, suffering, I guessed, from a stomachache. He'd eaten three

things larger than himself and so, figuring he'd had enough for a while, I concentrated on Coretta Scott and Jerry, a new spider nesting in the window between the stove and the bathroom. It was a slow day for flies, but I managed to catch three of them. Last night I noticed a new colony of spiders on the living-room ceiling. Their webs are complex and sprawling, resembling the new art museum in Milwaukee. There were four of them, and at around midnight they started going crazy, leaping around for no reason. There was a lamp on the table beneath them and the light cast their shadows huge upon the ceiling. I caught each of them a moth and then went to check on Clifton, who was gone. His web is empty except for carcasses, and I'm wondering if he went off to mate.

July 11, 2002
La Bagotière

Hugh returned from Paris and I was delighted to see him. It's scary here alone at night, frightening the way it was when I was a child. In the first place, the house is crawling with creatures—insects, rodents. There's probably a snake curled up here somewhere. Then there's the world outside desperately trying to get in. Lie in bed alone and you can hear animals in the yard—something's outside the bedroom door, something's overturning a trash can. Before going to bed on Tuesday night, I made the mistake of reading. It's the memoir of a forensic pathologist, so on top of everything else, I thought of skeletal remains and the way coffin lining sometimes fuses to the bone. It occurred to me that I'd maybe left the door of the milking chamber unlocked, but I was too frightened to get out of bed and check. All in all, it was a terrible night's sleep.

*   *   *

My fingertips are haunted by the feel of struggling flies. It's like holding a living, determined raisin. Coretta Scott's web has gotten ragged and fragile. Prey no longer sticks. I keep thinking she'll take up repairs or maybe spin herself a new home, but no. Jerry, the spider in the window, is suffering a similar fate. I threw in a fly and it struggled free. I threw it in again and again, eventually knocking it unconscious. Then I thought, *What am I doing?* When it revived, I threw the fly to the new, enormous spider on the living-room ceiling. He attacked immediately, no hesitation whatsoever, and I felt as though I were rooting for the Nazis in a Holocaust movie. It's easier with Hugh around, but when left alone I feel I might be losing my mind. *Let me catch just one more fly,* I think. *Just one more!*

July 14, 2002
La Bagotière
A brown bird built a nest in the flower box outside Granny G.'s bedroom. She invited me up to see the chicks, three tiny creatures resembling baby dinosaurs. They were asleep so she prodded them with a sharp stick. "Here," she said, "watch them move." I'm planning to go over this afternoon with some grubs and a set of tweezers.

Two of my newer spiders have died, but Coretta Scott just keeps on going. Her web is a mess of paint chips and mosquito parts, yet she refuses to move. I've been feeding her for a week but can't see that she's gotten any bigger. I'd kill for a good book about spiders.

July 18, 2002
La Bagotière
Yesterday afternoon Paula, the big female *Tegenaria* in my office, took down a bumblebee, which fought briefly, realized the situation was futile, and surrendered. I'd caught it earlier in the garden and afterward felt terrible. A wasp is one thing, but bumblebees don't hurt anyone. Like ladybugs, they're all about love. After Paula killed it, I looked in the mirror, expecting to see a monster staring back at me. I mean, I really felt changed, ashamed of myself for catching this thing and throwing it into her web. "This is it," I told myself. "No more feeding the spiders." Then I rode my bike to Flers, bought a magnifying glass and a book about insects, and came home to feed the spiders.

July 22, 2002
La Bagotière
This is just about the most disgusting thing I've ever seen: Yesterday afternoon I threw Paula an exceptionally large fly I'd caught in the kitchen. She took it into her cave and a few hours later I noticed her standing in the middle of her web, surrounded by maggots. I'm not sure quite how this happened, as they emerge from eggs, not live from the mother, whose dead body was now crawling with them. Maybe she'd been looking for a place to lay them and they'd hatched a little sooner than she thought? When she'd finished with the fly, Paula started in on the maggots, not eating them but carrying them to the edge of the web and tossing them onto the floor. It was a nasty job and after a while she gave up.

I took a nap and when I returned, the web was covered with ants, who carried the maggots past Paula's cave and through a crack in the door. It was as if they were servants she had hired to clean up after a party. Manuela was here, and late in the afternoon Genevieve stopped by. The Gs invited us over for aperitifs, and while the others discussed this and that, I thought of the web full of maggots. It was like a terrible secret that set me apart from normal happy people who could eat peanuts and make jokes. I thought about them some more on the way to the train station and by the time Manuela left, I was sick to my stomach.

July 24, 2002
La Bagotière

While I was at the roundabout in Flers, a child approached me and asked for a cigarette. He was maybe eight. "It's for my mother," he said. I asked where his mom was and he gestured behind himself. "At home."

Later, riding to La Lande-Saint-Siméon, I passed a swastika spray-painted onto the road.

I finished *An Obedient Father* by Akhil Sharma. The novel's main character, Ram, is a corrupt bureaucrat who raped his daughter when she was young and wouldn't mind doing the same to the granddaughter. He's odious and self-pitying, yet you can't help but like him. Here is a striking passage:

> No adult minded the small violences I perpetrated. Violence was common. Grown men used to rub kerosene on a bitch's nipples and watch it bite itself to death. For a while, the men had a hobby of lashing together the tails of two cats with a cord and hanging the cats over a branch and betting on who would scratch whom to death. When the father of a friend of mine clubbed his wife's head with a piece of wood, her speech became slurred and she started having fits, but not even the village women, friends of my friend's mother, found this

to be an unspeakable evil. Their lives were so sorrowful that they treated what had happened to her not as a crime committed by an individual but as an impersonal misfortune like a badly set bone that warps as it heals.

August 13, 2002
La Bagotière

Paul called on Sunday to say that he and Kathy are going to be parents. There were congratulations, etc., and then it was revealed that she was, by their estimation, possibly five hours pregnant. Most people wait a while before telling everyone that they're expecting a baby. Andy and his wife kept the secret for three months. Paul and Kathy started calling people the moment they got the results from the home pregnancy test. By nine a.m. Raleigh time, they'd already phoned every member of the family, both his and hers, and were working on a list of possible names.

I stayed up all night on Sunday, working in the attic and leaving my desk every hour or so to explore the milking chamber with a flashlight. At three a.m. I discovered a beetle who'd crawled in under the door and was settled beneath a web eating discarded fly heads. I mean, that's his diet. Fly heads! At four a.m. I found Gail. A member of family Dysderidae and genus *Dysdera,* she's a female *Dysdera crocota,* a bright red, putty-textured spider who normally lives beneath logs and eats woodlice. I kept her overnight and let her loose in the shed yesterday afternoon.

I've exhausted Hugh's patience as far as my spiders are concerned. Yesterday morning I found Paula's drained, desiccated body on the floor beneath her old web. There's really not much left but the legs. I invited Hugh to study the corpse with my magnifying glass, and he tossed a cigarette butt into one of my webs, threatening to clear them all out when the men arrive to begin reroofing.

August 28, 2002
Paris

Shannon called to tell me I'm at number nine. This makes fifty-two weeks—a year on the *Times* paperback list. While she was very excited and congratulatory, the news left me slightly embarrassed, the way you feel when you've stayed too long at the party and notice your hosts looking at their watches. The hosts, in this case, are all the superior writers whose books haven't sold more than a few thousand copies. On the bright side, I think I can write something much better than *Me Talk Pretty*. And if it fails and no one buys it, I can really feel good about myself.

August 31, 2002
Paris

Along with some books, Amy sent me a carton of the new Kools. For decades the packs featured simple green letters on a white box. Two years ago they changed their design, adding a picture of a waterfall, and now they've changed again. The new pack is ice blue. Beneath the logo they've written "The House of Menthol." Their way of discouraging smoking is to make the pack increasingly embarrassing. I counted yesterday and should have just enough cigarettes to last me to October.

October 5, 2002
New York

Since returning I've noticed how often the words *New York* are followed by *the greatest city in the world*. It's on billboards, on the radio, in newspaper ads. "Where else but

New York, the greatest city in the world?" An ad outside the Prince Street subway read WOULDN'T YOU RATHER BE GOING TO CHELSEA IN LONDON? and it struck me as insubordination. New York has always referred to itself as the greatest but more so after September 11. We're the greatest, *damn it.* We're the greatest, *remember.* You want to go along with it out of pity, but still, it's hard. At two p.m. it takes an hour and a half to get from Kennedy to SoHo in the greatest city in the world. Cigarettes now cost $7 a pack in the greatest city in the world.

This is definitely not the greatest apartment in the world. Our subletter now has a dog and we're thinking she must bathe it in the sink. Daily. Hugh made a snake out of a coat hanger and fished from the drain a wad of hair the size of a shrunken head. The halls are filthy. There's an air conditioner lying on the kitchen floor and no place to put anything. The hotel that's gone up next door has placed its exhaust system in what was once our backyard, and while we used to hear traffic on West Broadway, now we hear a dull, never-ending roar. They've opened an outdoor bar so in the evening the roar is accompanied by the sounds of lively drunks. It's like a party held on an airport runway.

October 9, 2002
New York
While walking from the subway to the *Letterman* studio, Hugh and I passed a man asking for money. Because of the tourist trade you get hit up a lot in that neighborhood, at least twice on every block. I shook my head no and the man went off on me, saying that I looked terrible. "You don't wear no striped shirt with a tie like that, asshole. Idiot. Fuck you with your scuffed-up raggedy-assed shoes." He was basically

505

a black version of my father, who, aside from the *asshole* and *fuck you,* will undoubtedly say the same thing.

October 10, 2002
Rochester, New York

A sniper or pair of snipers, a "marksman," a "rifleman," has shot eight people in DC, Virginia, and Maryland over the course of the past week, leading area restaurants to close their outdoor patios. The victims are random: a woman filling her car with gas, a thirteen-year-old on his way to school. A fortune-telling card was found at one of the murder sites, so I imagine that soon they'll give him a name—the Tarot Killer or some such thing. We're supposed to be outraged, but it's basically a media wet dream. Number one at the box office this week is *Red Dragon,* the umpteenth movie this year about a "brilliant" serial killer. Our novels, our TV shows, featuring FBI profilers: we love mass murderers and the people who surround them. I'm sure the screenplays for this story are already in progress and that, in nine out of ten versions, the killer is not only superintelligent but handsome.

While ironing, I listened to a local jazz program hosted by the female equivalent of Don Congdon. "That was 'I'll Cry Alone' by...oh, what was his name again? He reminds me of that other gypsy guitarist, the one with...oh, you know who I'm talking about. This is going to drive me crazy. Help me out here, folks. I know you know who I'm talking about. He's dead and I think his name started with a *J.*"

October 18, 2002
Denver, Colorado

I knew that my seatmate yesterday was going to be trouble. He was a big, shaggy man with a wild gray beard wearing an Australian bush hat. "I'm from Vancouver," he told the woman in front of me, talking, already, to anyone who would listen. "I'm Canadian, see, but I just spent a week in Bolivia."

"Oh," the woman responded, "Bolivia." She said it in a way that meant "I'm so glad I'm not sitting next to you."

"I go for work," the man continued. "I'm an engineer so I'm there once every three months or so."

The woman settled down in her seat and the man leaned forward so as to continue their conversation. "You probably think it's dangerous, but it's not. I mean, you don't want to be a gringo in Colombia—that's taking your life in your hands—but they like us in Bolivia."

"Well, that's good," the woman said.

"I suppose it helps that I speak a little *español,* but even if I didn't, I think I'd probably get along fine, at least in my field."

"Um-hmm."

"Up in Canada we learn French, but that's not going to get you anywhere in South America, I can tell you that."

"Is it just me," the woman said, "or is it really early?"

The man said that his journey had begun ten hours before. His flight from La Paz had been delayed and he'd missed his scheduled connection, which was supposed to leave at seven a.m. Now it was eight thirty and he'd just gotten his second wind.

The plane was only half full. There was an empty seat between us and the moment I sat down, the man lifted his armrest, the airplane equivalent of opening your front gate. "So where do you come from?" he asked.

No, no, no, no, no, I thought. It's one thing to ask a question as you're landing at your destination, but under no circumstances do you begin a flight with a conversation. I

507

wanted to say, *You have to move. Now.* But I'm too much of a coward. The best I could do was pretend to fall asleep, and even that didn't shut him up. "I can't sleep on planes," he said. "Don't know what it is, but I just can't."

The movie was *K-19: The Widowmaker,* starring Harrison Ford as a Soviet submarine captain. It wasn't the type of thing I would normally go for, but the headphones were my only way out. My neighbor chose not to watch, or, rather, not to listen.

His version was silent and every few minutes he'd tap me on the shoulder. "You know," he said, "I've been in a Russian submarine. They had one docked in Vancouver and there's no way on earth Harrison Ford could have stood upright, not at his size. And cramped? The thing was tiny. It's just not possible."

Back at the terminal I'd begun a crossword puzzle, working it, as I normally do, section by section, beginning in the upper-left-hand corner. On boarding I'd placed it on the empty seat beside me, and toward the end of the flight I looked over to find the man holding it. "I see it got the best of you," he said.

No Thursday puzzle will ever get the best of me, but I said, "Actually, I'm not finished with it yet."

I turned back to the movie and again he tapped me on the shoulder. "I think seventeen down is supposed to be *gigolo,*" he said.

Yes, and ten across is shut the fuck up, I wanted to say. Had I woken to find him fondling me I could have lived with it, but you don't touch another man's puzzle. I was tempted to call for the flight attendant, but instead, of course, I thanked him. "If you'll just give me back my pencil, I'll write it in," I said.

A moment later he tapped me to tell me that the movie had

ended. "You're watching an empty screen," he said. "Boy, you really must be exhausted."

"Oh, I am," I said. "You have no idea."

October 19, 2002
San Francisco
At a drugstore in Denver I bought a pack of typing paper. The woman in front of me tried to pay with a credit card and, when that didn't work, a check. Had she paid with cash I never would have noticed she was missing an ear. It wasn't gone entirely, there was still something there, but it wasn't much, a little lump of flesh.

October 21, 2002
Milwaukee, Wisconsin
At the Denver airport there's a display labeled MEXICAN SOUVENIR ALERT. In the case was a python belt, a coffee mug made from elephant hide, a leopard pelt, and two taxidermied frogs hoisting steins at a miniature bar. The mug, belt, and rug were made from endangered species, but I never understood the alcoholic frogs. What was wrong with them?

October 24, 2002
New York
We had dinner at Le Pescadou, a French restaurant on 6th Avenue. The menu was ridiculous and included such items as:
   Seared Tuna Embraced by Sesame
   Baby Pasta Ears Listening to Artichoke
   Grilled Prawns Frolicking on Polenta

October 28, 2002
New York
Driving to Greencastle we passed cars with bumper stickers

reading CHARLTON HESTON IS MY PRESIDENT and JESUS LOVES YOU. EVERYONE ELSE THINKS YOU'RE AN ASSHOLE. We passed a gun shop advertising a "Blowout Sale."

While listening to a country music station, we heard a talk/song narrated by our flag. "I flew proudly at Iwo Jima and on the blistering deserts of Kuwait, anywhere freedom is threatened, you will find me." The flag recounted being torn into strips to bandage wounded soldiers and then it explained how it hurts to be burned and trampled by the very people it works so hard to protect. When given a voice, our flag is not someone you'd choose to spend a lot of time with.

October 30, 2002
New York
After returning from New York, Dad called Lisa to tell her he was sick. "I have a flu," he said. "What should I take?" Lisa suggested he wait it out, but that wasn't good enough. "How about NyQuil?" he asked. "Doesn't Vicks make something?" Lisa said that when Bob gets sick he sometimes takes an antibiotic. "But I don't know that it really does any good," she said.

A few hours later Dad called again. The vet had put his Great Dane, Sophie, on antibiotics, and, figuring that it was all basically the same thing, he had started taking them. "I'm just not sure of the dose," he said.

Lisa then called me. "Can you believe this?" I thought she was upset that her father was taking pills meant for a dog, and then I remembered who I was talking to. "I mean, how is Sophie supposed to get any better when Dad is taking all her medicine? I just don't think that's right."

November 5, 2002
Paris
Steven sent the *New York Observer* article along with a short

mention in *Publishers Weekly*. In the first I'm described as looking "not unlike a leprechaun," my head "barely poking up over the podium." In the second I'm referred to as both "sprightly" and "diminutive," making it sound as if I could sleep in an empty matchbox.

November 16, 2002
London

Yesterday morning we awoke in our new apartment and stood, like livestock, but now we have three chairs, two of them bought very early this morning at the Bermondsey Market. It was mainly outdoors and most of the merchandise was small—the sort of stuff you pass but don't really remember. I think I saw some chandeliers, possibly a saddle.

The security office for our apartment complex is located in the basement and we went in the afternoon to introduce ourselves to Mr. Berry, the man in charge. According to our complex's newsletter, he has nine fingers and worked as a police detective, a DCI, until his retirement a few years back. "We're here twenty-four hours a day," he said. "The door is always open so feel free to drop in and have a moan at us."

I should pick a newspaper and start following it, but I can't seem to decide which one to go with. Steve suggests the *Guardian,* but I'm partial to the *Sun,* which yesterday carried a twenty-picture photo spread on Michael Jackson's evolving face. The *Sun* is like the *National Enquirer,* but every day. Hard news amounts to stories of people who almost died. Cars almost ran them down. Things almost fell on them. I listen to the BBC, but that's not enough. I need a paper.

November 23, 2002
Paris

On *Six Feet Under,* Claire and her friend took mushrooms. Most movies and TV shows get drugs wrong. Someone takes a bong hit and spends the next few hours laughing uncontrollably. Someone takes acid and steps into the *Sergeant Pepper* cover. *Six Feet Under* gets drugs right, so after taking the mushrooms, Claire and her friend hole up in the bedroom, using the sewing machine and wishing they lived in the nineteenth century. "Wouldn't it be cool if you had to make everything, and everything you did was art?" She wound up concocting a hideous pair of pants, quilted and hemmed with bells. She gave them to her mother and was mortified the next morning when she saw her actually wearing them.

December 6, 2002
London

Before *The Quiet American* we saw a funny Smirnoff commercial. It opens on a couple standing at the window, the woman softly crying and the man looking helpless and slightly guilty. We see him run down the stairs and pick something up off the street. I imagined it was a ring, but as he hands it over she smiles broadly, and we see that it's her missing front tooth. He'd knocked it out during an argument and the fact that he retrieved it causes her to fall in love all over again.

December 14, 2002
Paris

This morning two men rang the buzzer. "Yes," one said. "We're looking for English-speaking people who can answer a few questions. Is Mr. Hamrick at home?" I said he wasn't and they asked if they might speak to me.

"About what?"

"About the future. About the way you feel."

I let them in because I have no backbone. One of the men was in his thirties and the other a granddad. Both were well dressed and carried strapless briefcases. "My colleague has a problem on the stairs," the younger man said. "Sometimes his leg is not so good." It seemed I should offer them a seat, but that would have made it all the harder to get rid of them, so we stood.

"So how do you feel about the future?" the younger man asked.

It was a goofy question. A setup. I said I felt fine about it and we all stood around and looked at our feet. "I mean, yeah," I said. "It'll be different from the past, but, you know."

The younger man asked if I had a Bible in the house. I said no and he asked if he could share some scripture with me.

"I'd really rather you didn't."

"Well, can I leave you with something?" he asked.

It turned out they were a pair of Jehovah's Witnesses. This is better than being a pair of thieves, but still.

December 21, 2002
London

The BBC reports that terrorists are planning to halt the Christmas shopping season, most likely with some sort of bomb. They don't know where or when, but the public is warned to be vigilant. My reaction isn't fear so much as confusion. Don't they know the Christmas shopping season is essentially over? The time to strike was *last* weekend, not this one. Should they plant a bomb today, the only person they'd get is Maw Hamrick, who has bought nothing. "I'm thinking of getting Hugh a book or a CD," she said. "Or maybe some stationery or maybe something for the apartment. Do

513

you think he'd like that?" I almost had her talked into a pair of slippers, but Fortnum and Mason was out of his size. "This picture frame is nice," she said, "but he probably doesn't want that."

I was going to stop at Harrods on the way home from Piccadilly Circus and she asked if she could come with me. "Maybe I could find something for Hugh but, of course, I want to get him something he'll like. Otherwise there's no point."

We took the number 9 bus, and on disembarking in Knightsbridge we passed a beggar sitting on the ground with a newborn baby. "Now, that's just too depressing for words," Maw Hamrick said. "Did you see her? Did you see that *baby?*" I tried to explain that the woman was a gypsy. "That's what those people *do,*" I said, but it was too late, as the image was already burned into her mind. On entering Harrods, she was exhausted and depressed. "This is just ridiculous," she said. "I'll just get Hugh's slippers in France. Or maybe I'll get him a shirt."

We return to Paris Monday, and I'm sure she'll spend the afternoon looking at churches. She'll do the same on Tuesday and wind up giving Hugh a check for $50.

About the Author

David Sedaris is the author of the books *Let's Explore Diabetes with Owls*, *Squirrel Seeks Chipmunk*, *When You Are Engulfed in Flames*, *Dress Your Family in Corduroy and Denim*, *Me Talk Pretty One Day*, *Holidays on Ice*, *Naked*, and *Barrel Fever*. He is a regular contributor to *The New Yorker* and BBC Radio 4. He lives in England.